Boisterous Beasts & Deadly Dragons

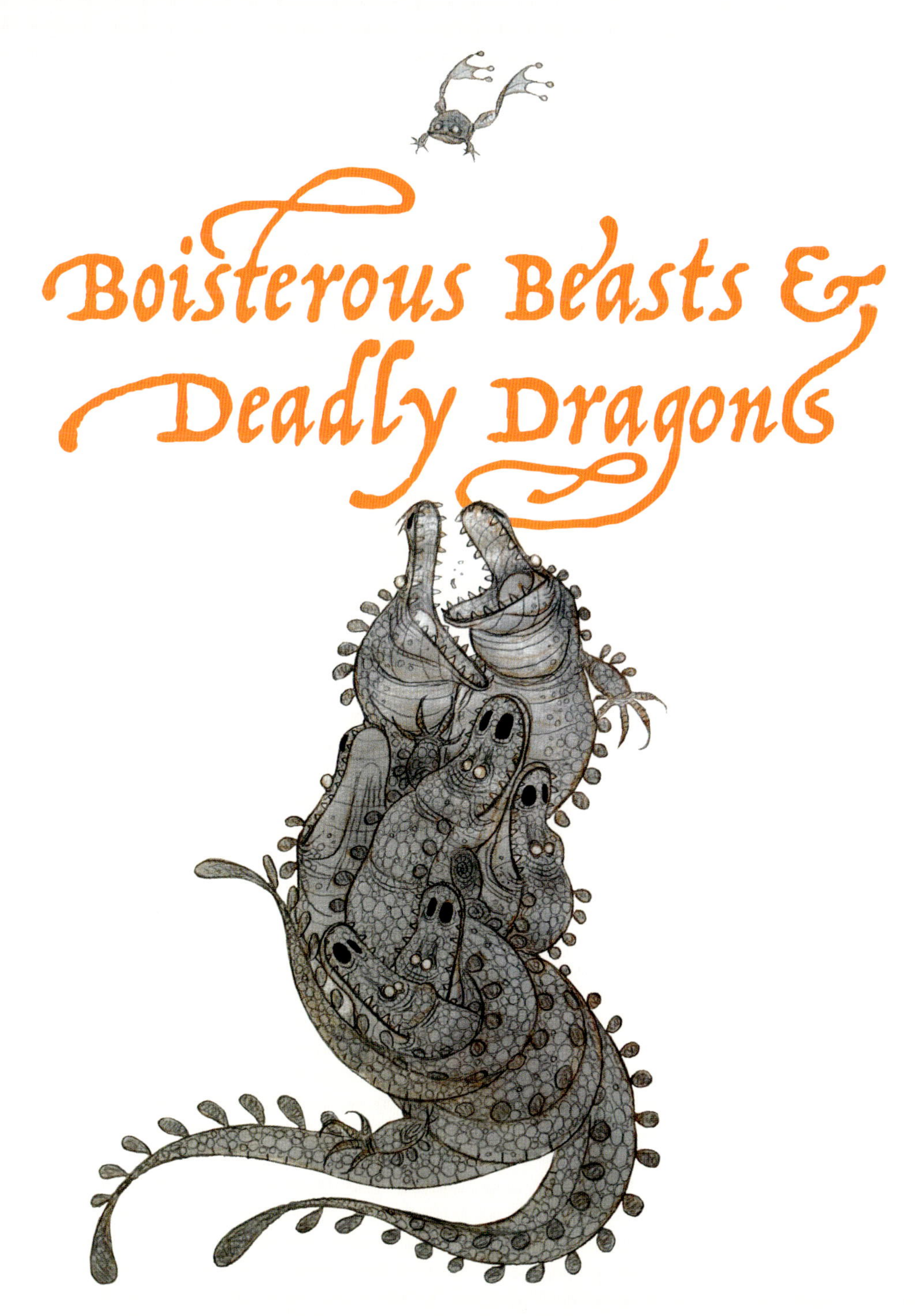

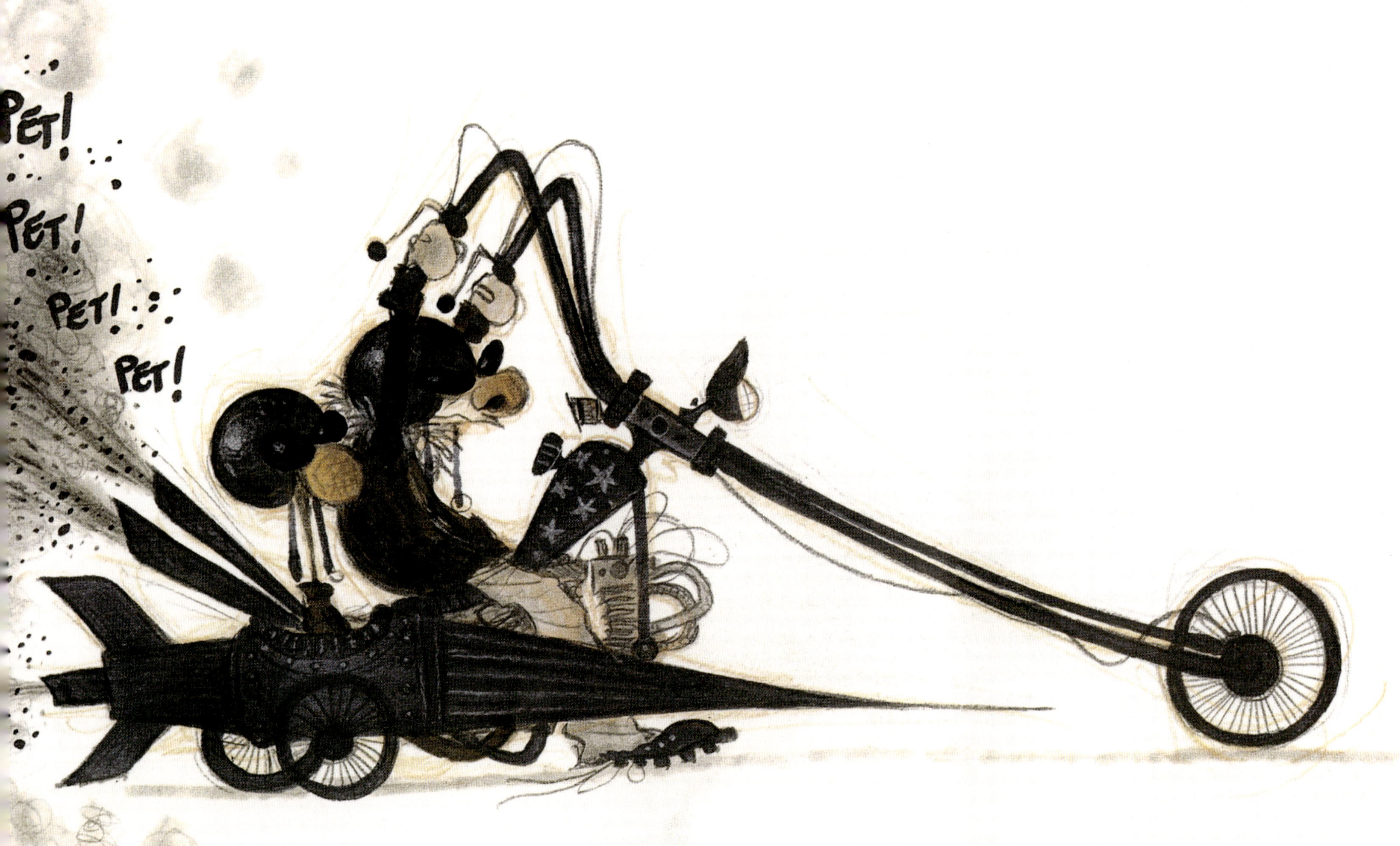
PET!
PET!
PET!
PET!

Boisterous Beasts & Deadly Dragons

The Art of Nico Marlet

†

Text by Tracey Miller-Zarneke

Foreword by Jack Black • *Preface by* Dean DeBlois

Abrams, New York

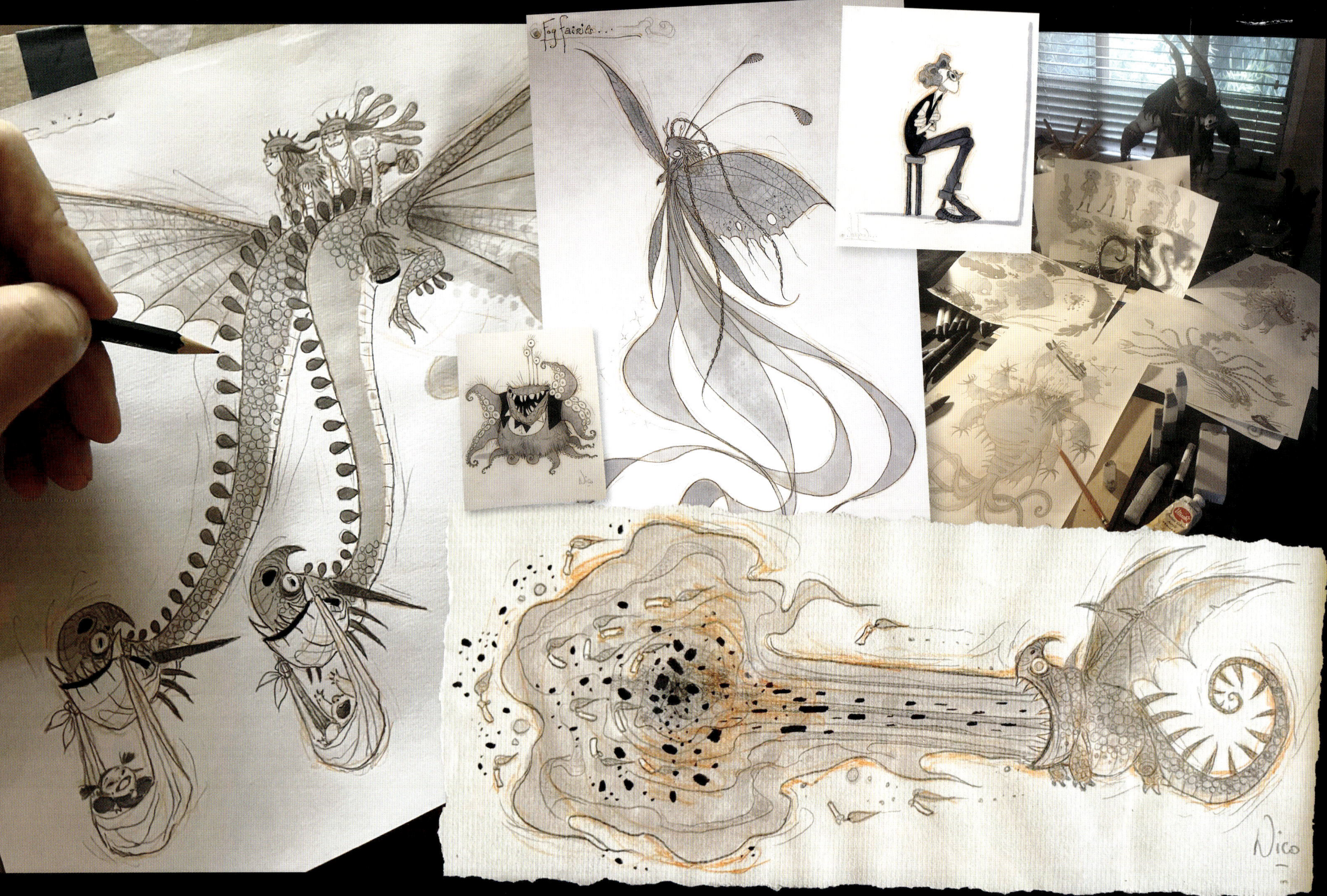
Fog fairies...
Nico

Contents

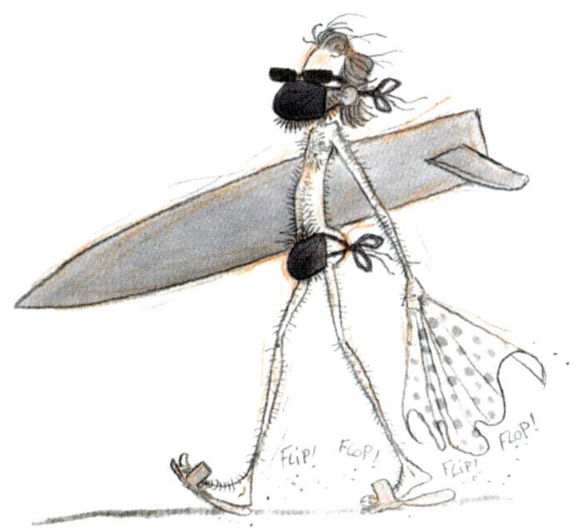

Foreword by Jack Black

When Jeffrey Katzenberg pitched me the idea of performing the lead role in a new DreamWorks animated movie about a panda who loves kung fu, I had serious reservations. I was just coming off the best movie of my career (*School of Rock*), and I wanted to pick my next project very carefully . . . but then he showed me a little test animation of a roughly sketched Po walking and talking with my voice, and the whole thing came into focus for me. This character was beautifully conceived; he looked funny and sweet and cool. I could imagine this goofball tumbling through incredible adventures. The artwork of Nico Marlet opened up the entire *Kung Fu Panda* universe before my eyes. What a genius!

And thus began an epic journey—little did I know I'd be riding that wave for twenty years! It has been the role of a lifetime and so much fun to play Po. He has so much energy and life. The creation of Po is a dance between voice, drawing, acting, and animation. It's a dance . . . a tango . . . a salsa . . . a blast.

Thank you, Nico, for Po and all your other amazing creations!

Cover, pp. 1, 2–3: Personal art • p. 4: Personal art inspired by *How to Train Your Dragon* (2010), *Monsters, Inc.* (2001), and other projects • p. 5: Personal art • Opposite: *Kung Fu Panda* (2008) character concepts

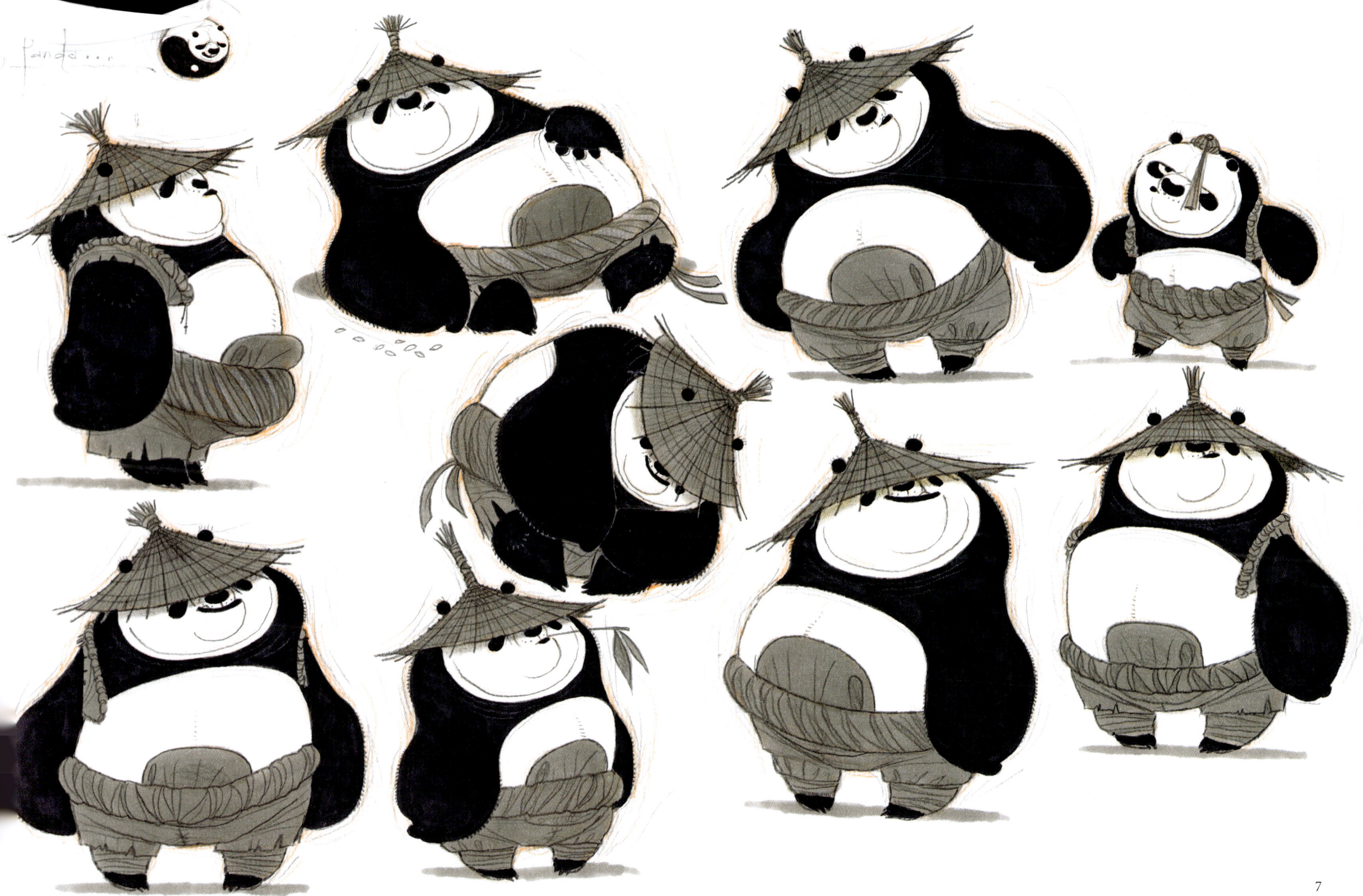
Panda...

Preface by Dean DeBlois

I have had the great privilege of working with Nico Marlet on all three installments of the *How To Train Your Dragon* animated franchise. It has been a thrill for me to facilitate his creations rising from paper to moving on-screen; these characters have been ingrained within me deeply ever since our work together on them in the early 2000s. We've seen time and again that when audiences enter their presence, they never want to leave.

Nico is a rare and incredible artist—a treasure in the world of animation and an inspiration to artists everywhere. Nico's designs are filled with such love, whimsy, and originality. He inspires the storytelling by breathing so much life and personality into his work. He not only loves to draw—he lives for it. His art seems to be his primary means of expression. The sheer abundance of his work stands as a testament to that passion. In the face of such talent, you can't help but feel a deep sense of awe.

I hope you enjoy seeing this collection of an amazing body of work, even though it is a mere fraction of the incredible characters that Nico has envisioned in the past and will continue to conjure in the future. May we all be inspired by his quiet yet exuberant talent.

Opposite: *How to Train Your Dragon* (2010) character concepts • Overleaf: *Monsters, Inc.* (2001) character concepts

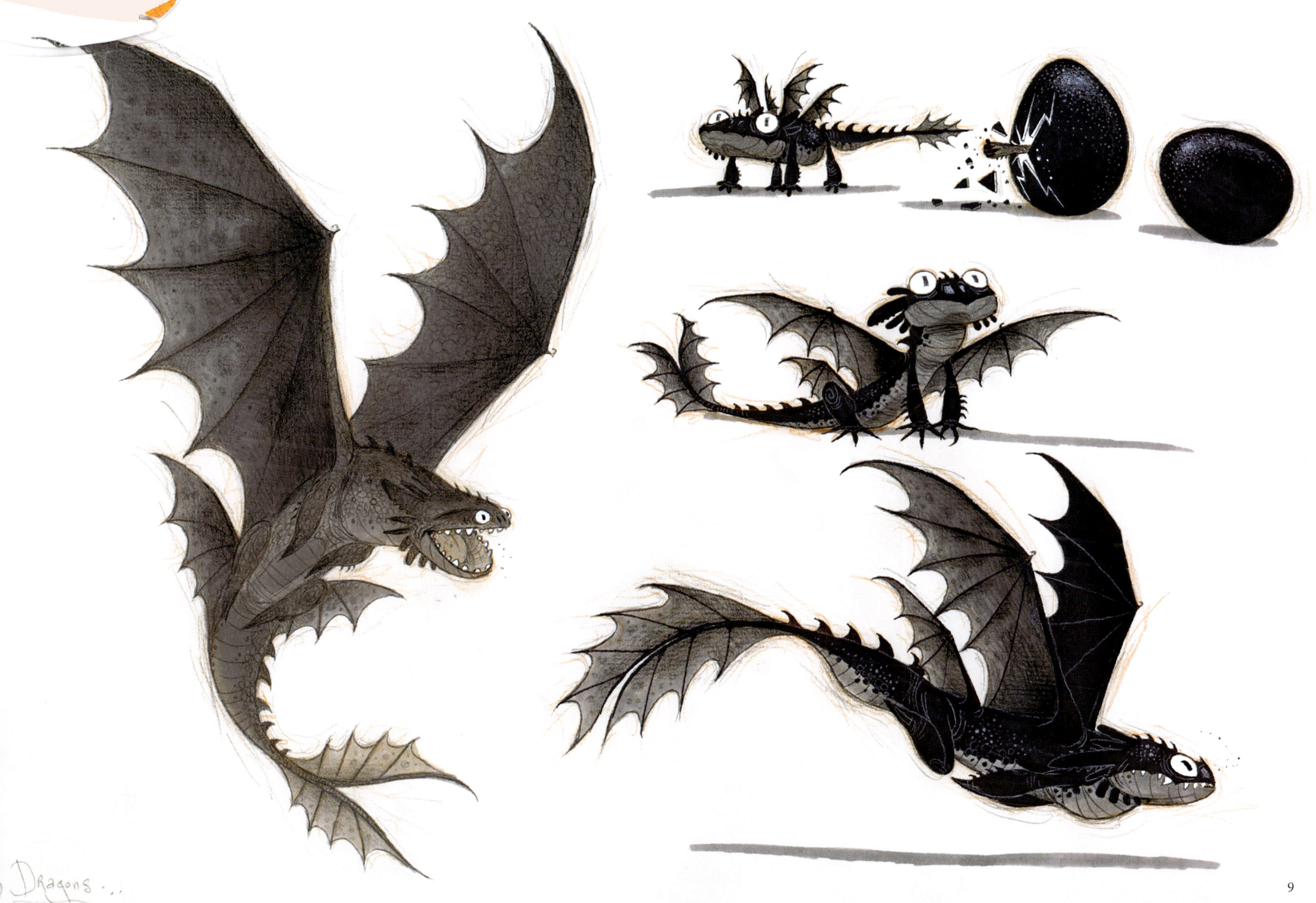
Dragons . .

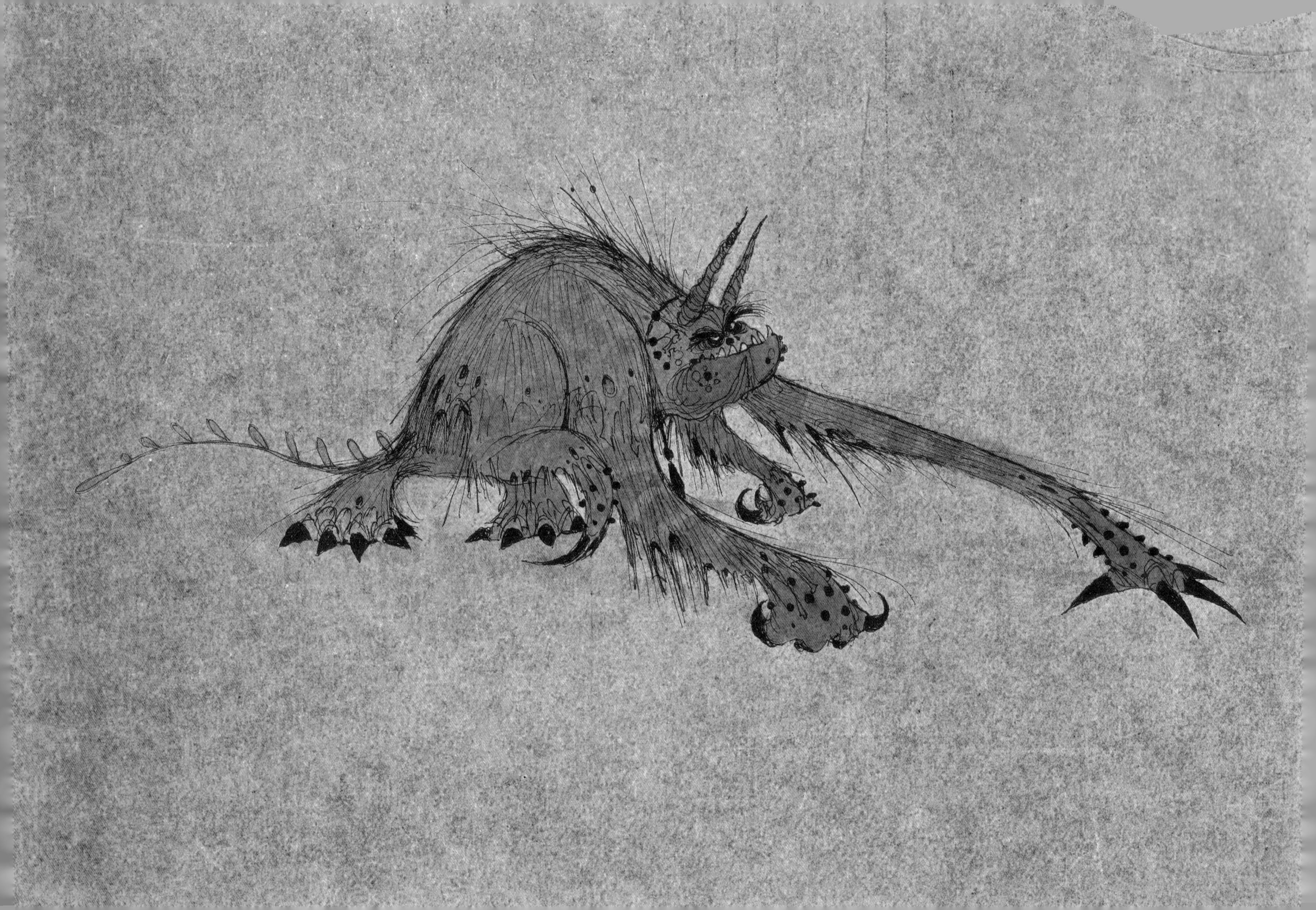

I

From Toulouse to Toontown

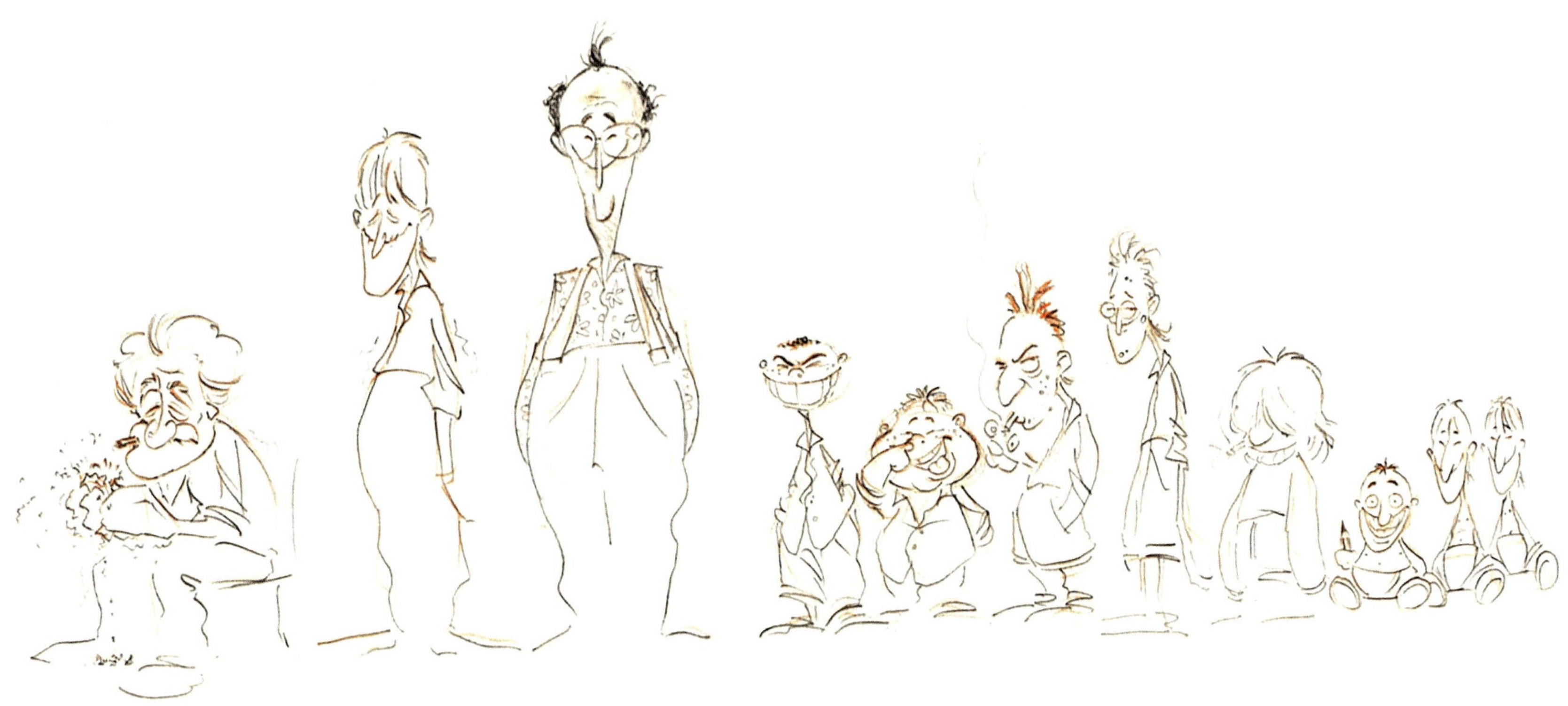

A remarkably humble artist with a heart of gold and a spirit filled with wonder, Nicolas "Nico" Marlet has been the pencil-driven well source for some of the most impactful characters of the modern animation era. Nico's creations have graced the screen in more than thirty film and television projects from six different studios, his characters first emerging into existence as richly detailed illustrations that invite deep study and reward thoughtful observers with the joy of witnessing inventive, unexpectedly playful touches. Nico has also channeled his creative energy into sculpture from time to time, but it is truly the combination of "animation paper meeting Col-Erase 20064 Orange" that conjures some of the most incredible larger-than-life creatures from Nico's imagination.

Please enjoy the creativity of Nico Marlet collected within these pages, lovingly gathered here with the hope that they instill joy and magic beyond what his work has already delivered through its expressions in animation in the past, perhaps inspiring fellow artists to help create the future.

Once upon a time in France

Born in Figeac, France, in 1969, Nicolas Marlet grew up in a family of two parents, three sisters, numerous cats and dogs, and a grandfather who might be credited with igniting Nico's artistic expression. Nico recalls, "I was very close to my maternal grandfather. From when I was maybe five years old, we used to go fishing, and while waiting for the fish, my grandpa would oil paint. He gave me pencils so that I could draw next to him."

In France, many artistically inclined young people grew up reading and replicating the work of cartoonists Guillermo Mordillo, Jean-Jacques Sempé, and André Franquin. On the topic of this inspiration, Nico says, "Simplicity is difficult. That's what they did, in fact. For me, Sempé is poetry." Nico was one of those students who drew and found that his art was a way to connect with people even though he was shy. This quiet way of attracting people has carried into his adulthood, as Nico prefers any attention to be exclusively on his drawings.

After winning first place in a contest as part of the Angoulême International Comics Festival at age seventeen and successfully crafting an animation short for TV, Nico started to ponder his future path. He chose to study animation at the world-renowned Gobelins Paris art institute, considering himself extremely lucky to be admitted. "From my first pencil tests, like the bouncing ball, it was always magical to see the drawings move," Nico reflects. "Whether it was very simple or very complicated, it was always something special. When we developed our tests on film, and even later with video, when we saw our animation unfold for the first time, it was always magical."

"'Talentedly kind'—this for me is what could sum up Nico as a person and his drawings. Behind the big, shy guy hides the freshness of a kid who, fortunately for us, still continues to draw on paper with graphite. It is this childish spontaneity that I particularly appreciate. He has a sincere naivete. His personality and constructions may appear simple but in fact conceal a well-hidden maturity he wisely puts down on paper. Let us feast our eyes and appreciate the candidly beautiful!"

—**Didier Cassegrain, illustrator**

Opposite: Personal art • Overleaf, left: Submission for Angoulême International Comics Festival (1986) • Overleaf, right: Image created for Gobelins brochure (1988)

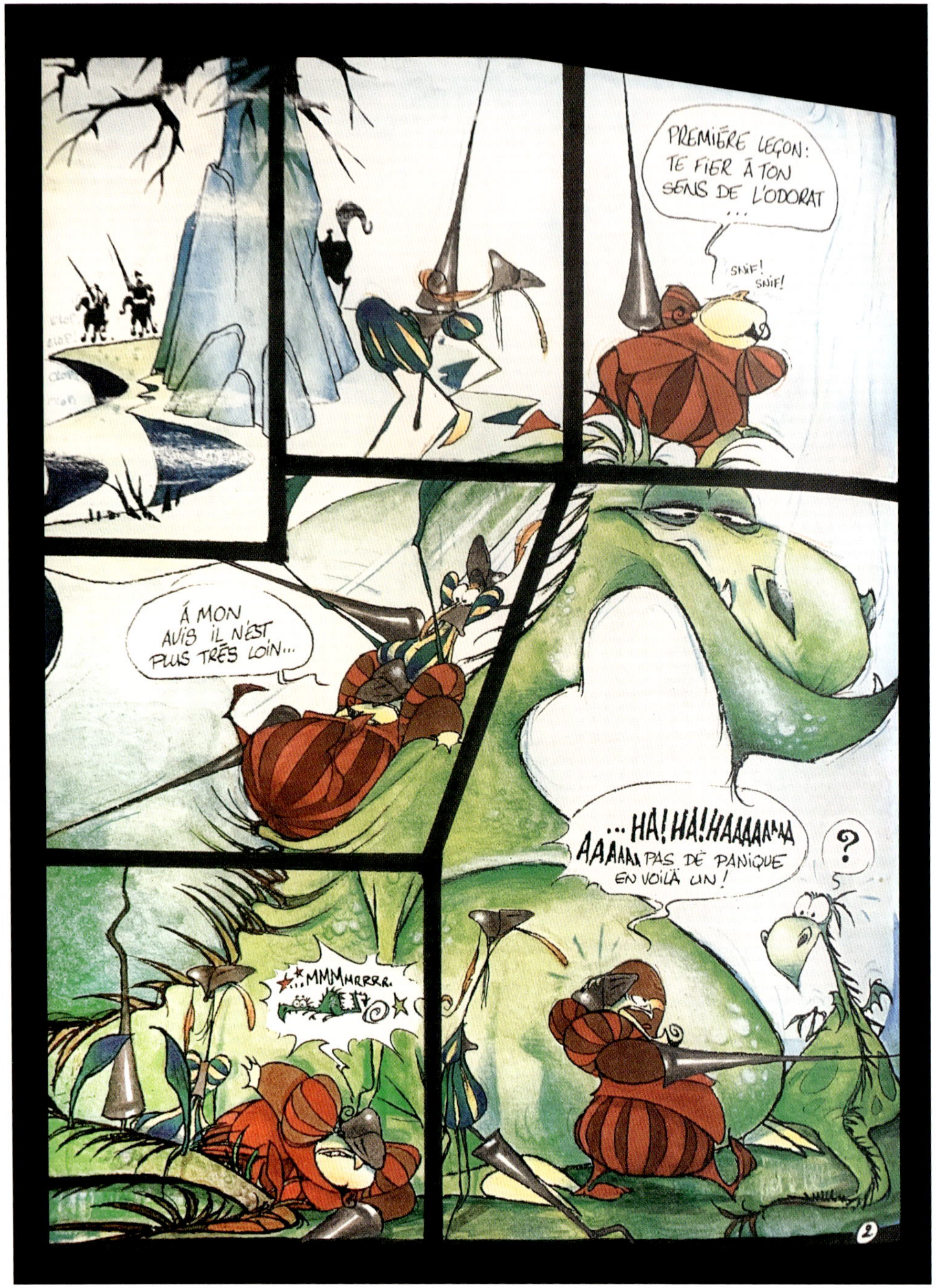

PREMIÈRE LEÇON: TE FIER À TON SENS DE L'ODORAT ...
SNIF! SNIF!
À MON AVIS IL N'EST PLUS TRÈS LOIN...
...HA! HA! HAAAAAAAA AAAAA PAS DE PANIQUE EN VOILÀ UN!
?
...MMMMRRRR.
2
REGARDE MOI BIEN FISTON! 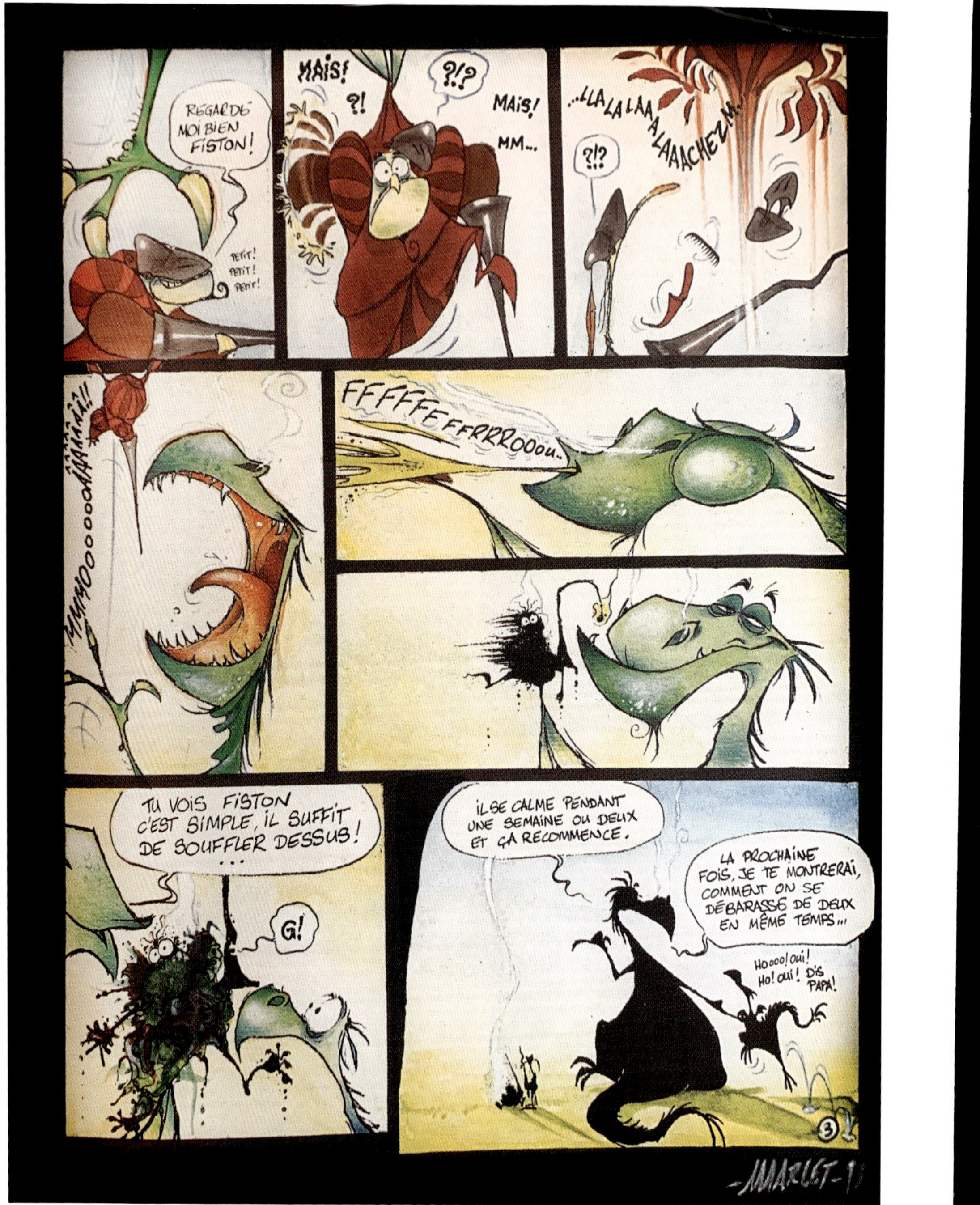
PETIT! PETIT! PETIT!
MAIS! ?! ?!? MAIS! MM...
...LLA LA LAA ALAAACHEZ M...
?!?
FFFFFFFFFRRRooou..
TU VOIS FISTON C'EST SIMPLE, IL SUFFIT DE SOUFFLER DESSUS! ...
G!
IL SE CALME PENDANT UNE SEMAINE OU DEUX ET ÇA RECOMMENCE.
LA PROCHAINE FOIS, JE TE MONTRERAI, COMMENT ON SE DÉBARASSE DE DEUX EN MÊME TEMPS...
Hoooo! oui! Ho! oui! DIS PAPA!
3

Drawn into the Industry

In 1987, Nico registered for a two-year program at Gobelins. After the first year, he failed the test to be an in-betweener. At the end of his schooling, however, Disney hired Nico directly to work as a junior animator on the *DuckTales* movie, skipping the assistant step altogether.

"I had the chance to meet Nicolas Marlet during my studies at Gobelins in 1988. He was already impressive. Despite being younger than me, he seemed to have years of experience. His standards and his understandings of drawing were already very mature. He could clearly explain and analyze the subjects he drew. We had our Franquin within reach—an artist concerned with detail and the harmony of forms. To work alongside him is a unique opportunity. His ability, his strength of caricature and burlesque vision, has certainly influenced many artists. Nicolas has become a master of his art. His creativity and humor have marked all the films he has worked on. I still remain one of his biggest fans, always on the lookout for his next creation!"

—**Patrick Delage, director**

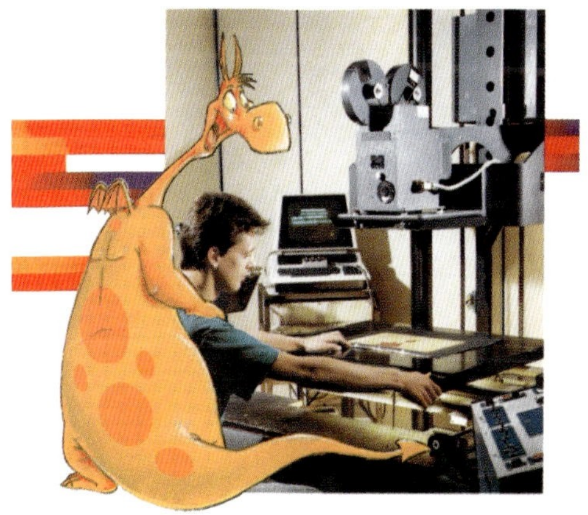

A Global shift

After wrapping his work as a junior animator on *DuckTales*, Nico went to visit friends in London one weekend, where they were working for the animation production studio Amblimation. "I came with my portfolio and showed it to Simon Wells, who was directing *We're Back! A Dinosaur's Story*, and he said, 'Yeah, if you want to start, you can start Monday.'" So Nico went back to Paris, packed his few belongings, hopped on a plane, and embarked on the next chapter in his career the following week.

"Nico was one of my students at Gobelins, but I did not remember him as particularly outstanding, probably because he was a shy person. A few years later, we hired him at Amblimation as an animator on the recommendation of his fellow students, and his first assignment was a scene with my character. I will always remember the first time he came to show me his work. The animation was not only great, the drawings were not only dead-on-model, but they were more appealing than my own! I don't remember our conversation, but I probably told him it was very good, and he probably answered, 'I don't think so, but I will try to do better next time.' He didn't stay on my team very long and went on to do character designs. From that time forward, I've always asked the studios if I could animate characters that Nico designed, and I have been very lucky to help give life to Boris, Altivo, Stoick, Burnish, and many others."

—**Kristof Serrand, directing animator**

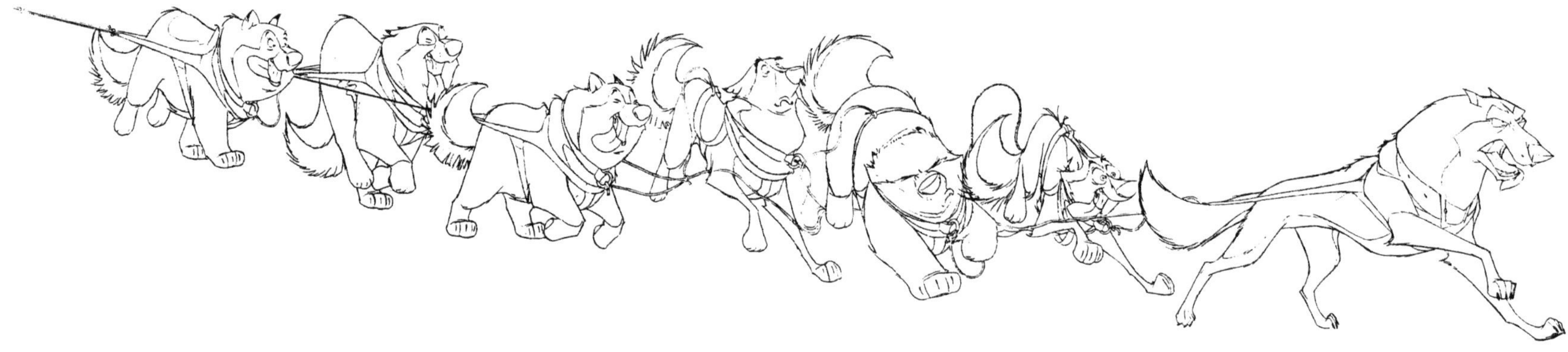

Above & pp. 18–23: *Balto* (1995) animation image • Opposite: *We're Back!* (1993) animation images • pp. 24–29: *Cats* (1998) character concepts

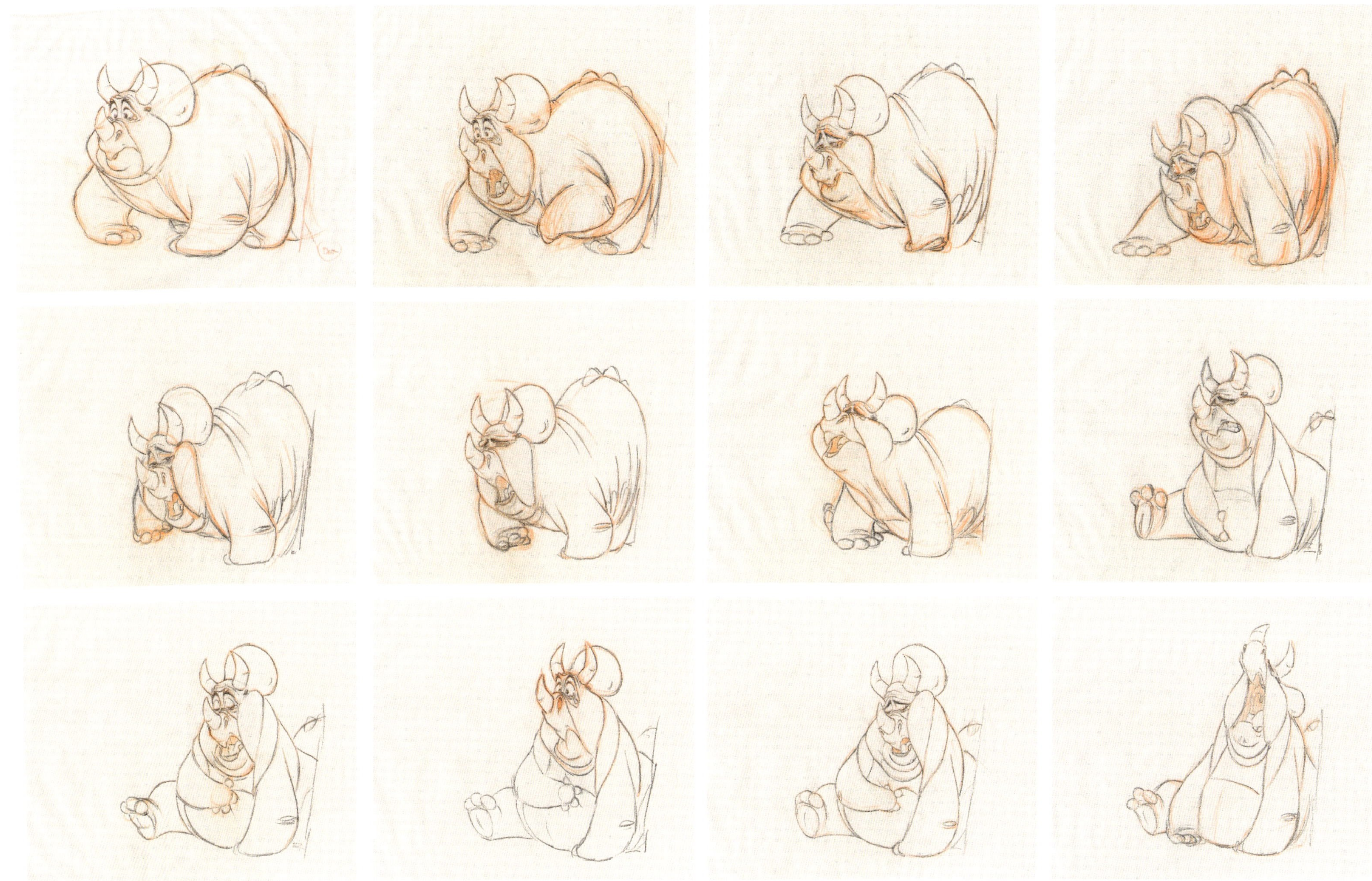

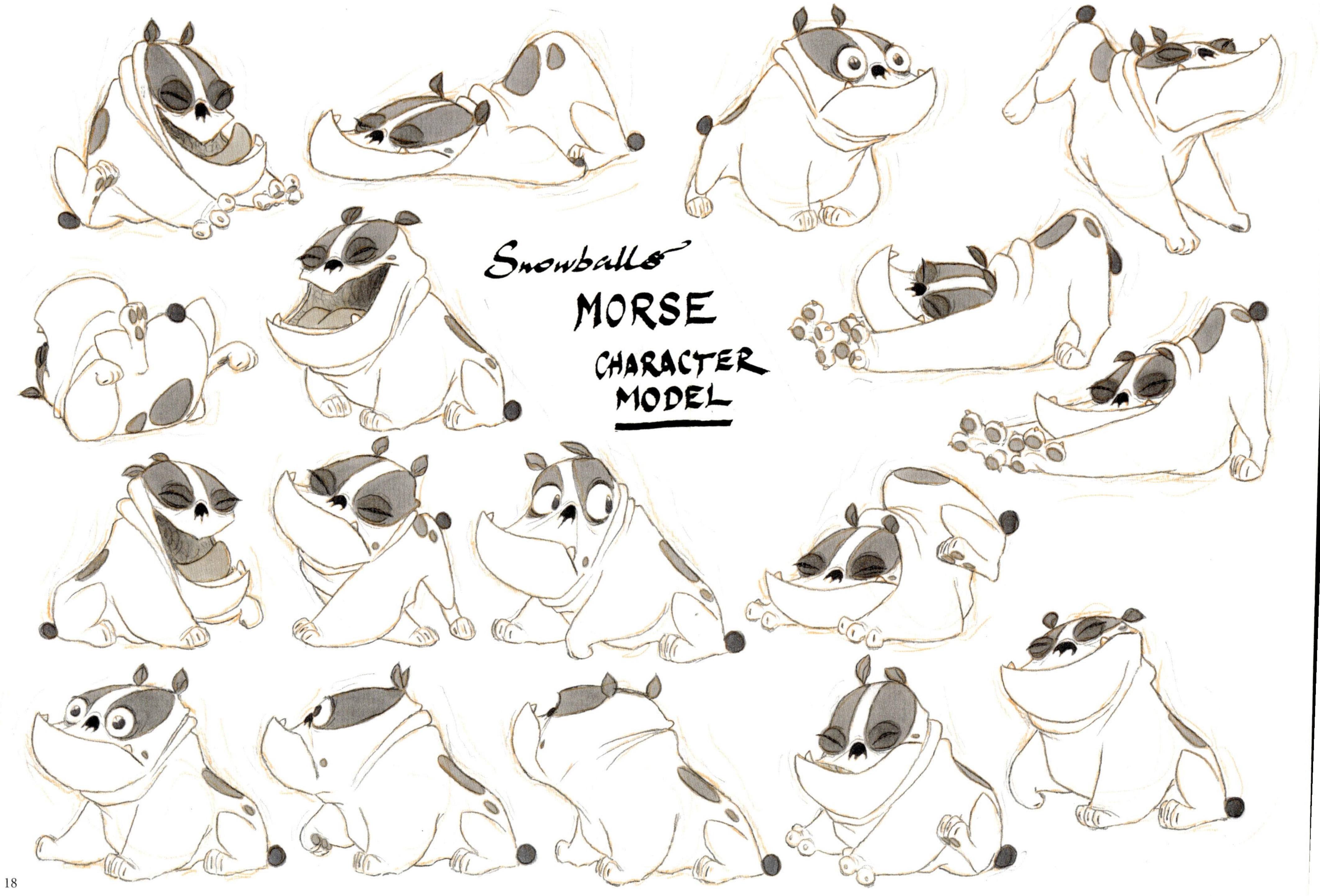
Snowballs
MORSE
CHARACTER
MODEL

Snowballs

NIKKI

BALTO

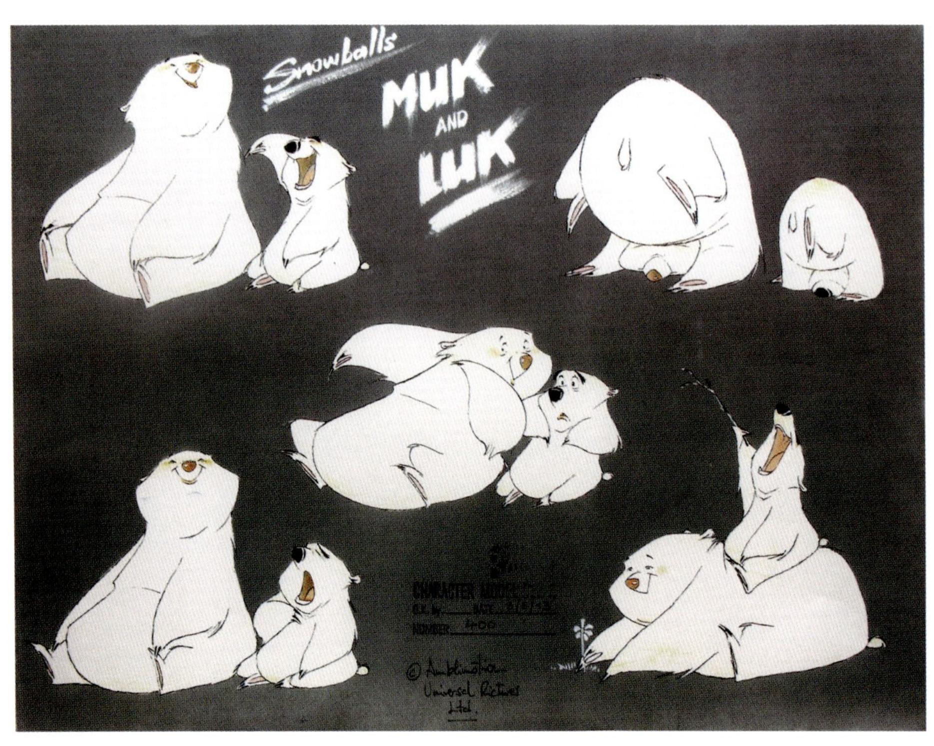
Snowballs
MUK
AND
LUK
CHARACTER MODEL
© Amblimation
Universal Pictures
Ltd.

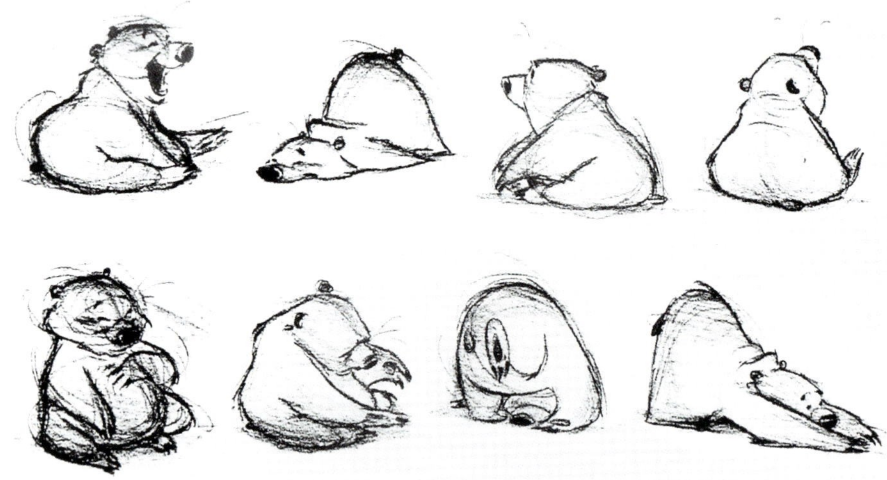

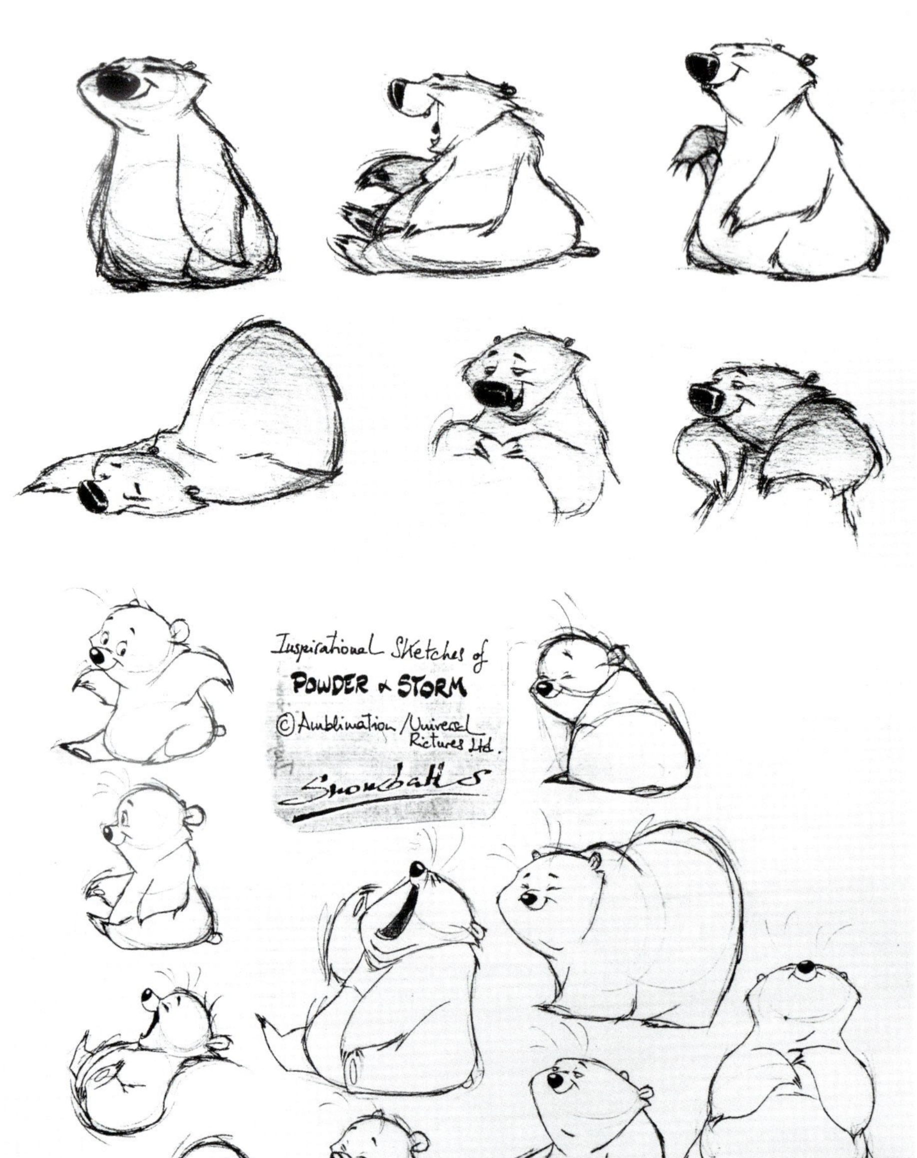
Inspirational Sketches of
POWDER & STORM
©Amblimation /Universal
Pictures Ltd.
Snowballs

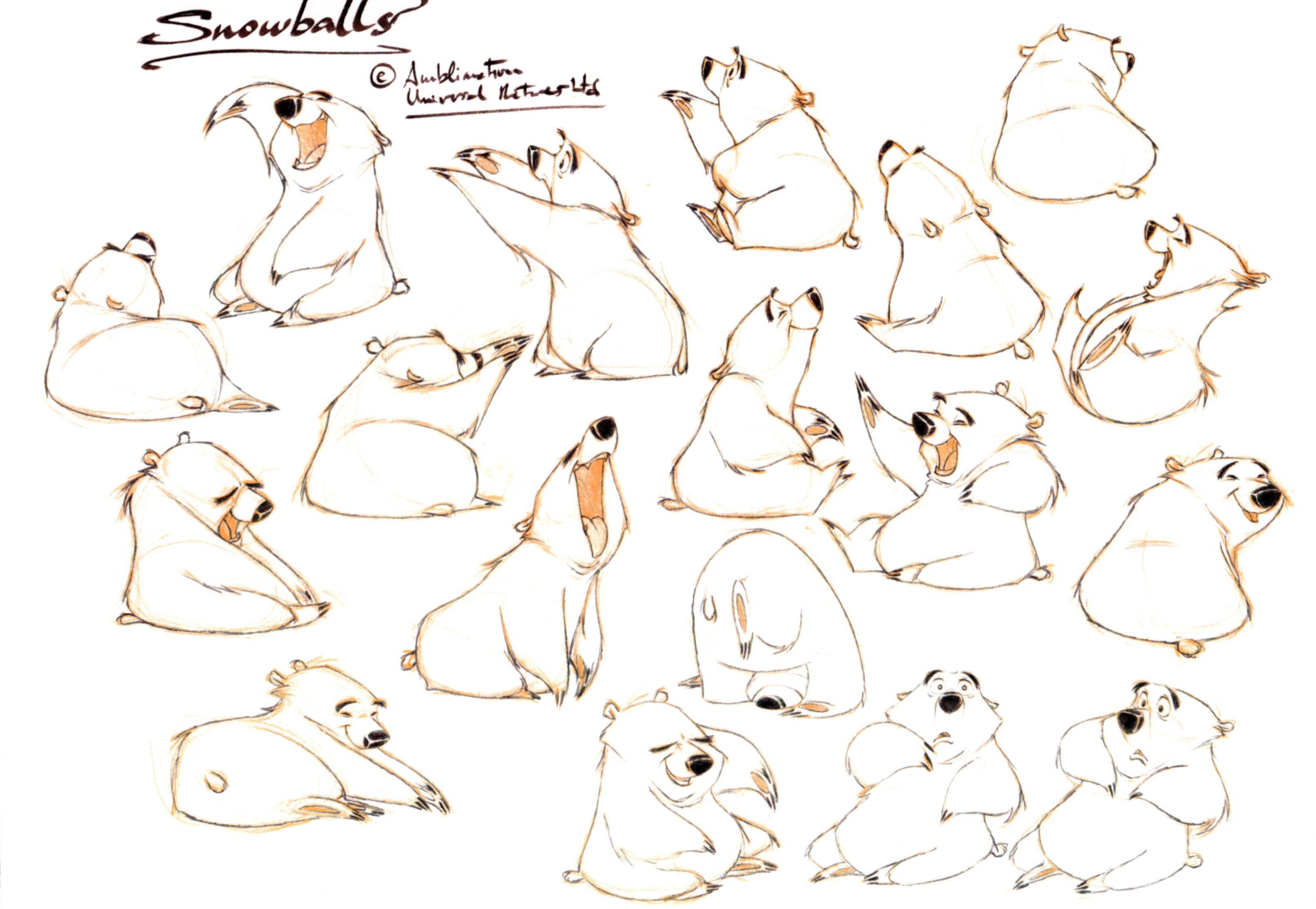
Snowballs
© Amblimation
Universal Pictures Ltd

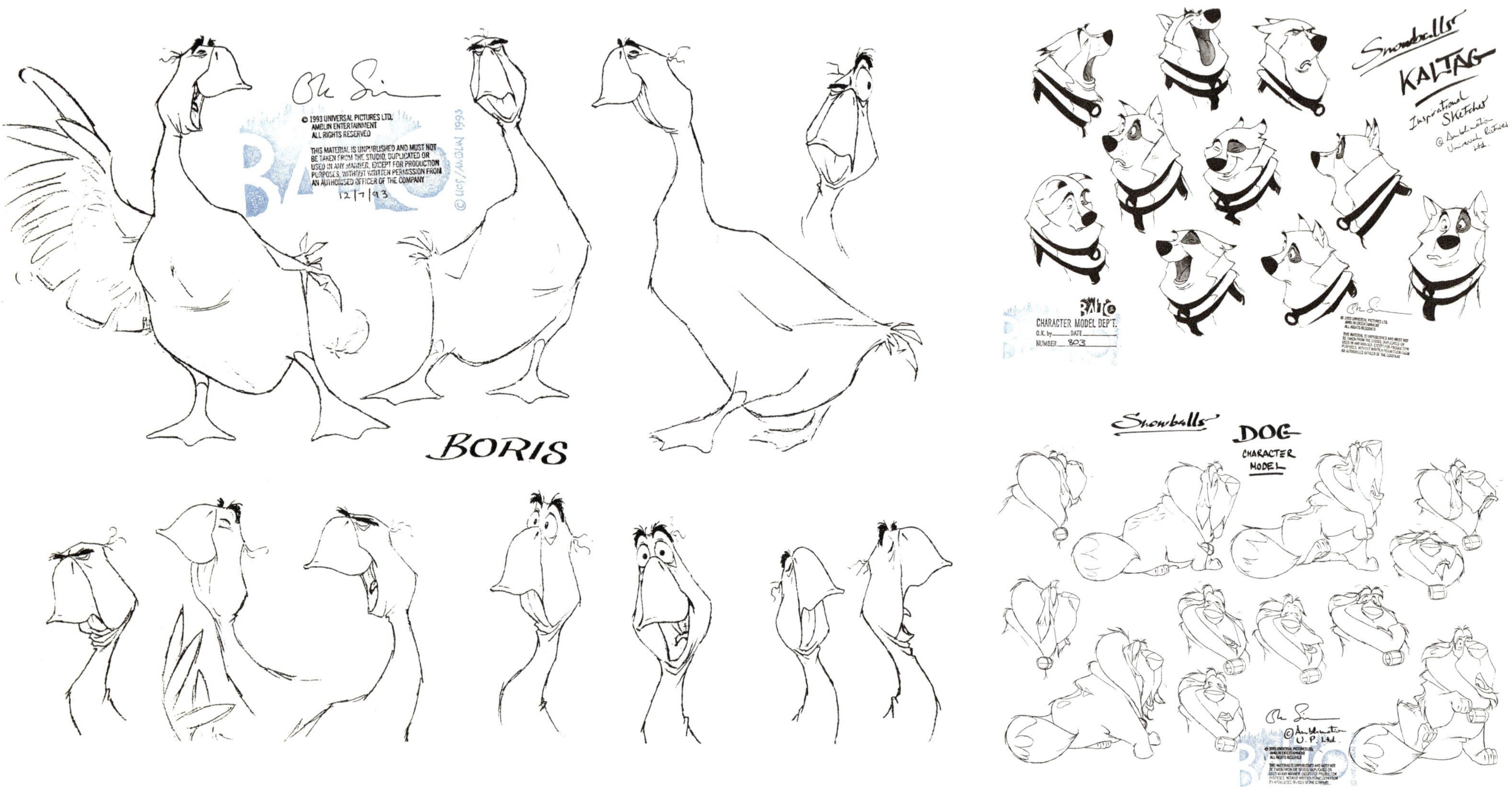
BORIS
© 1993 UNIVERSAL PICTURES LTD. AMBLIN ENTERTAINMENT ALL RIGHTS RESERVED
THIS MATERIAL IS UNPUBLISHED AND MUST NOT BE TAKEN FROM THE STUDIO, DUPLICATED OR USED IN ANY MANNER, EXCEPT FOR PRODUCTION PURPOSES, WITHOUT WRITTEN PERMISSION FROM AN AUTHORISED OFFICER OF THE COMPANY
12/7/93
© UCS/AMBLIN 1993
Snowballs
KALTAG
Inspirational Sketches
CHARACTER MODEL DEP'T.
NUMBER 803
Snowballs
DOG
CHARACTER MODEL

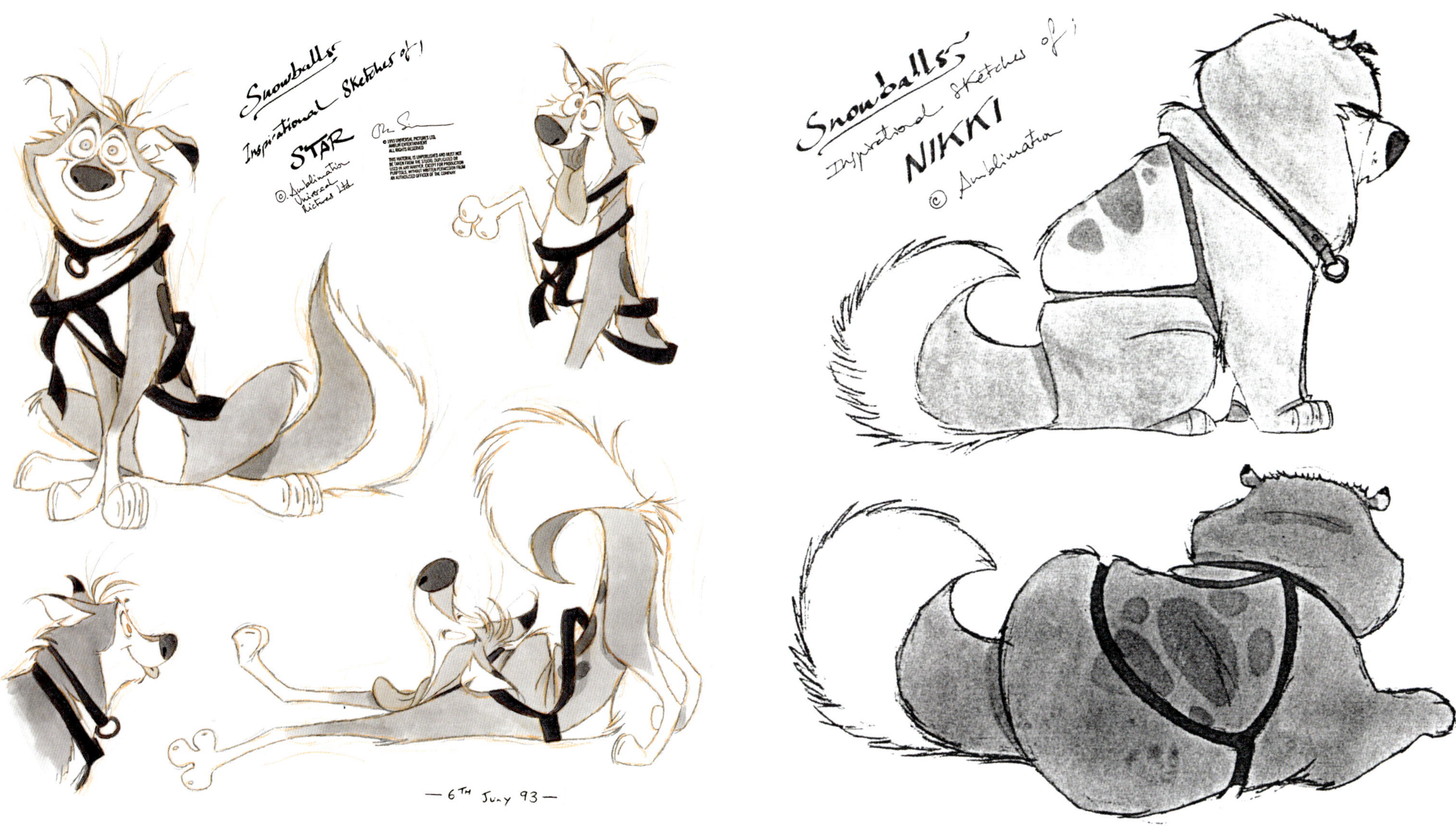
Snowballs
Inspirational Sketches of !
STAR
©. Amblimation Universal Pictures Ltd
© 1993 UNIVERSAL PICTURES LTD.
AMBLIN ENTERTAINMENT
ALL RIGHTS RESERVED
THIS MATERIAL IS UNPUBLISHED AND MUST NOT BE TAKEN FROM THE STUDIO, DUPLICATED OR USED IN ANY MANNER, EXCEPT FOR PRODUCTION PURPOSES, WITHOUT WRITTEN PERMISSION FROM AN AUTHORIZED OFFICER OF THE COMPANY
— 6TH JULY 93 —
Snowballs
Inspirational Sketches of ;
NIKKI
© Amblimation

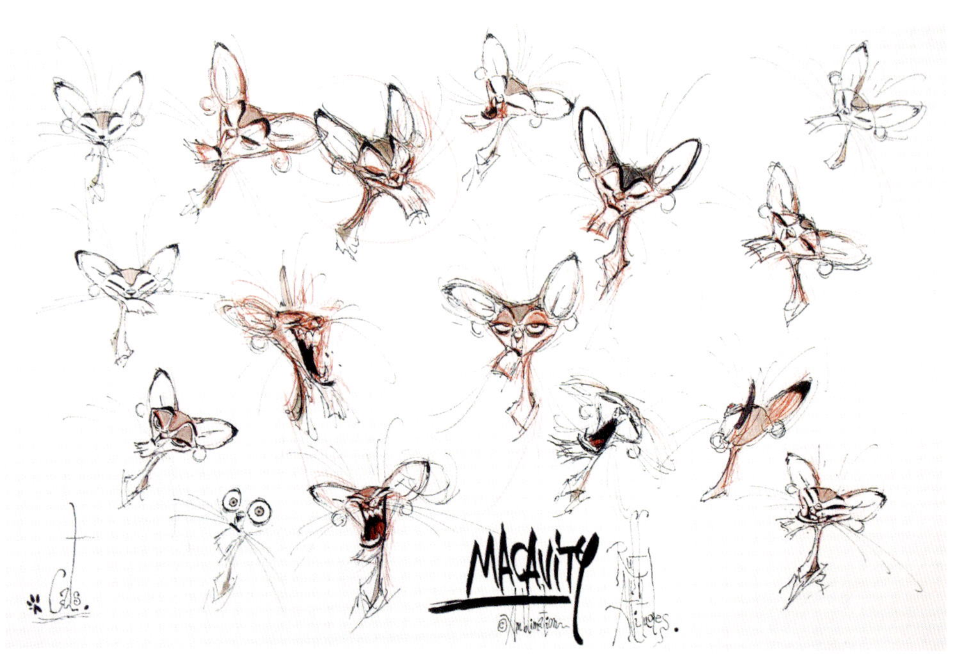
MACAVITY
Cats.

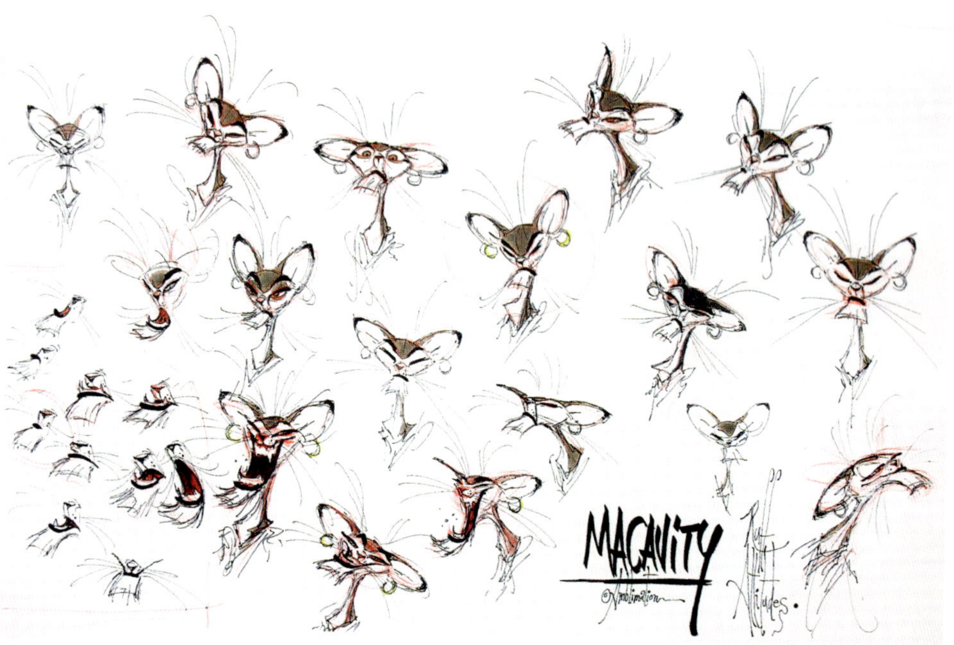
MACAVITY

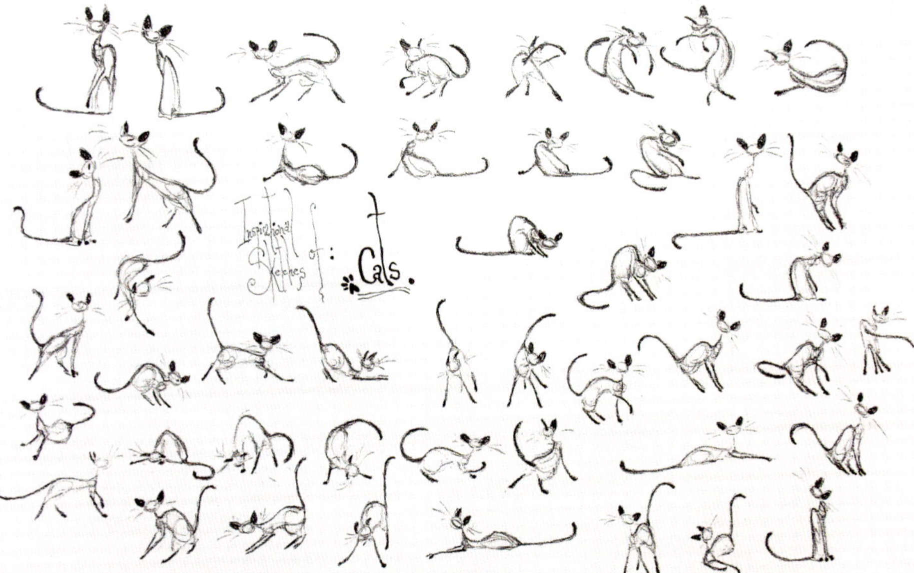
Inspirational Sketches of: Cats.

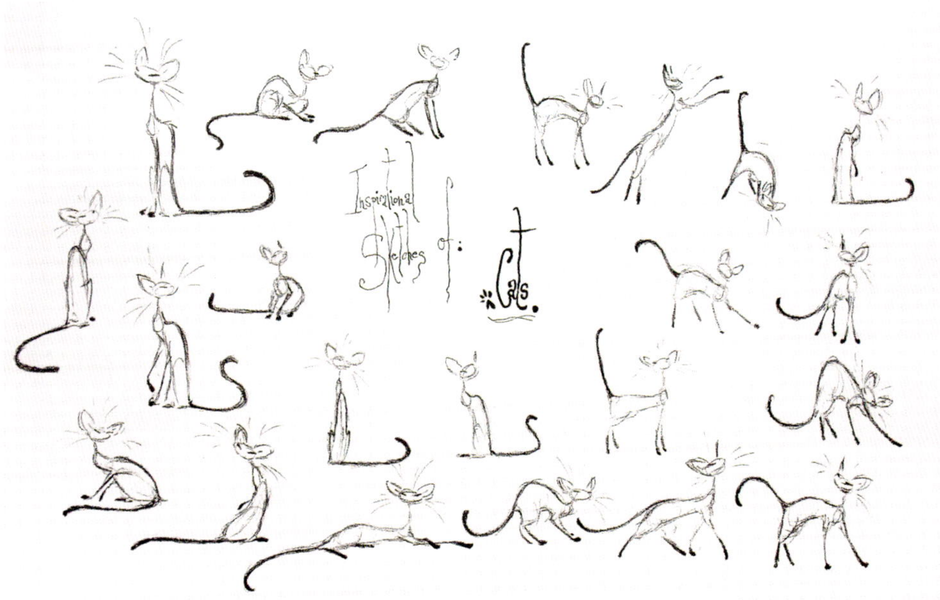
Inspirational Sketches of: Cats.

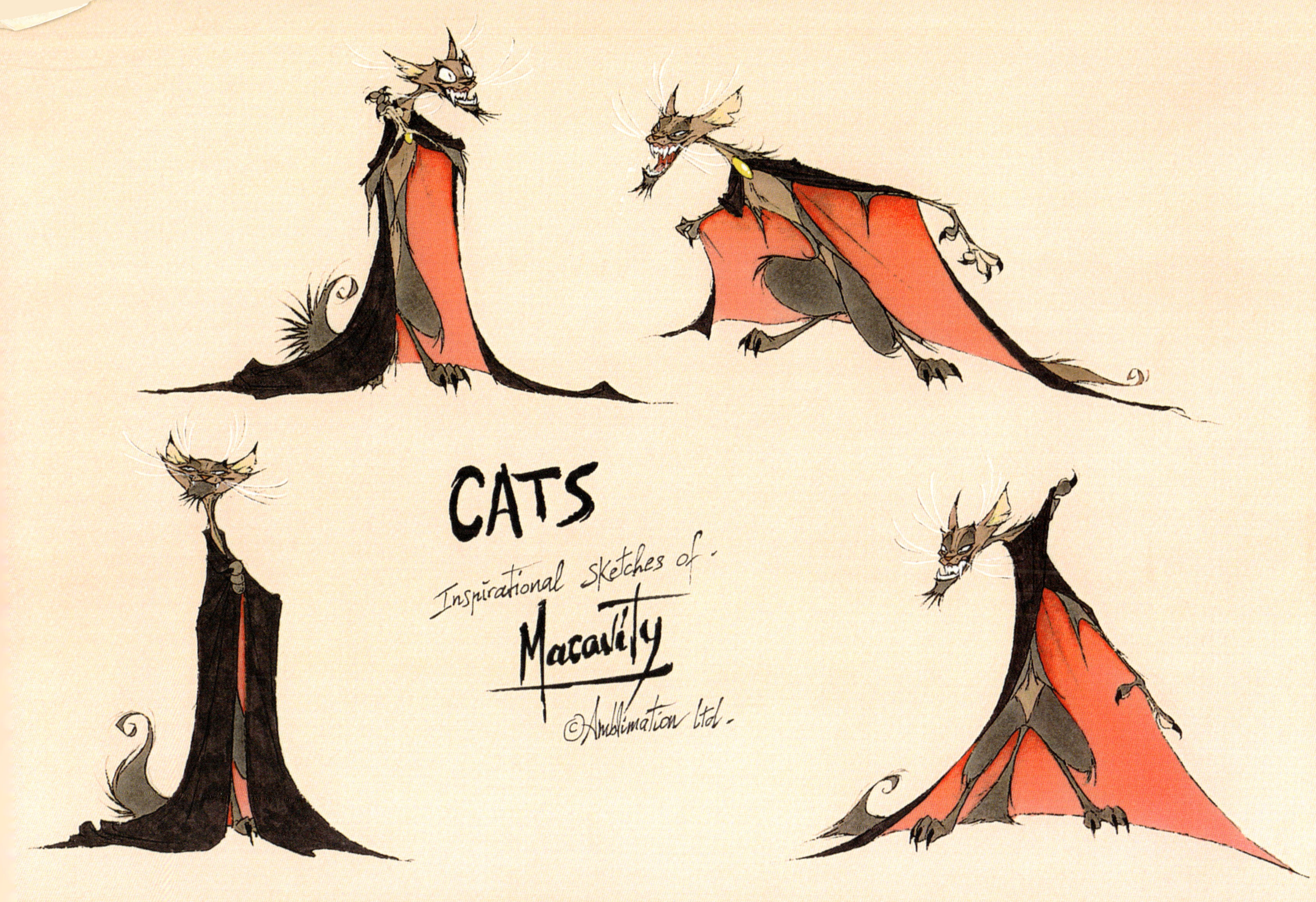
CATS
Inspirational sketches of
Macavity
©Amblimation Ltd.

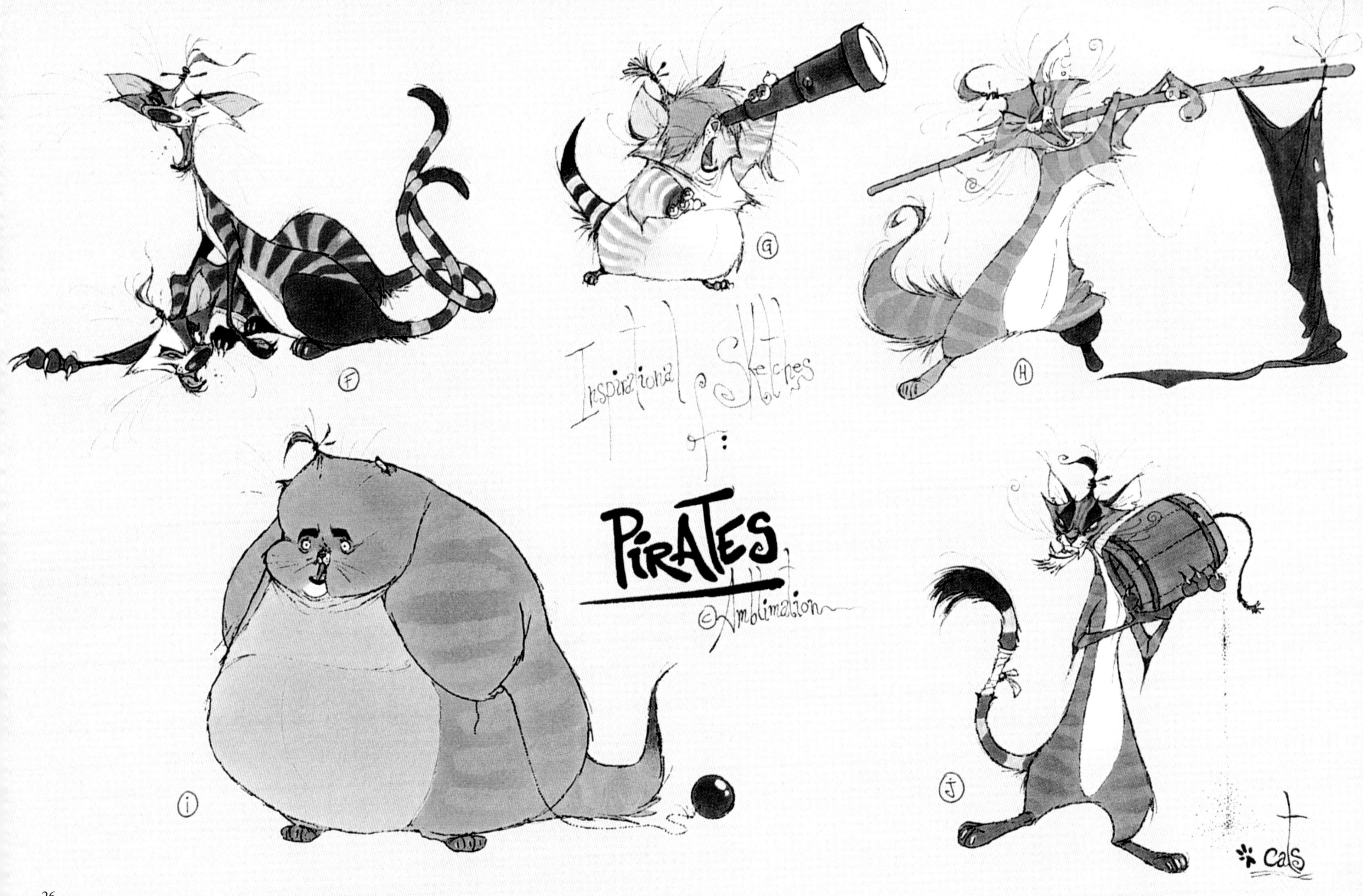
F
G
H
Inspirational Sketches of:
PIRATES
©Amblimation
i
J
cats

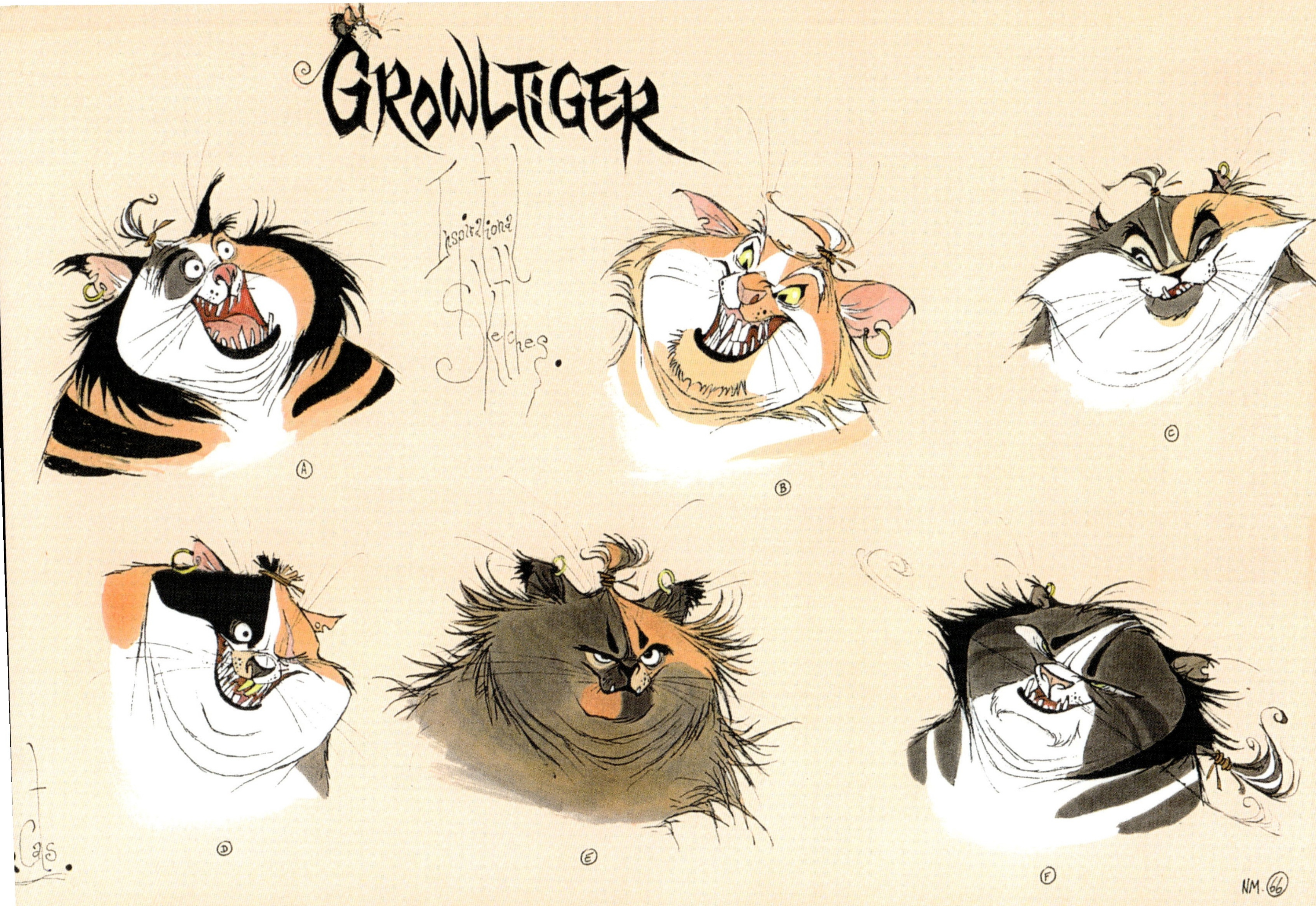
GROWLTIGER
Inspirational Sketches.
A
B
C
D
E
F
NM. 66

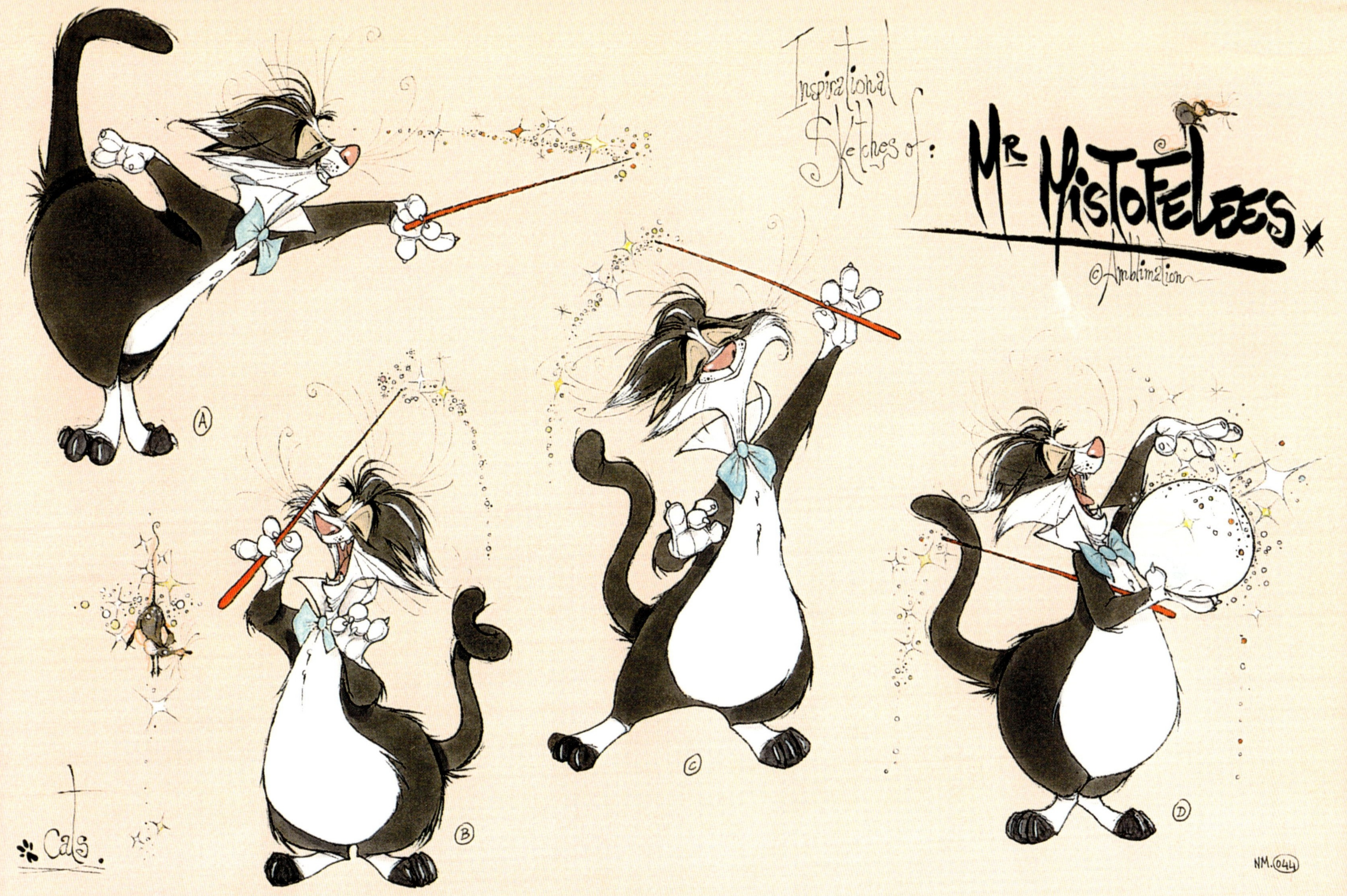
Inspirational Sketches of:
Mr Mistofelees
©Amblimation
A
B
C
D
Cats.
NM.044

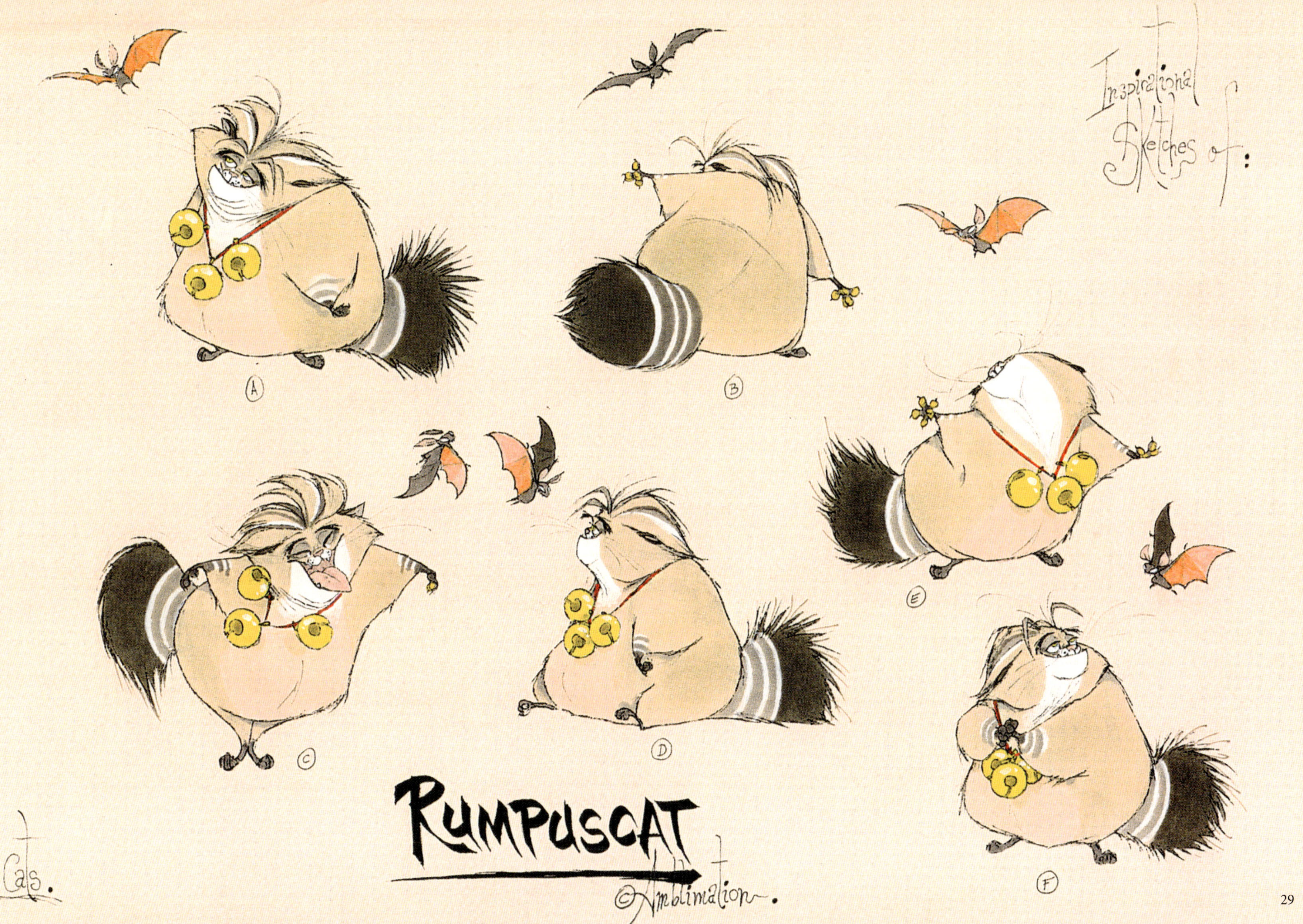
Inspirational Sketches of: Cats.
A
B
C
D
E
F
RUMPUSCAT
©Amblimation.

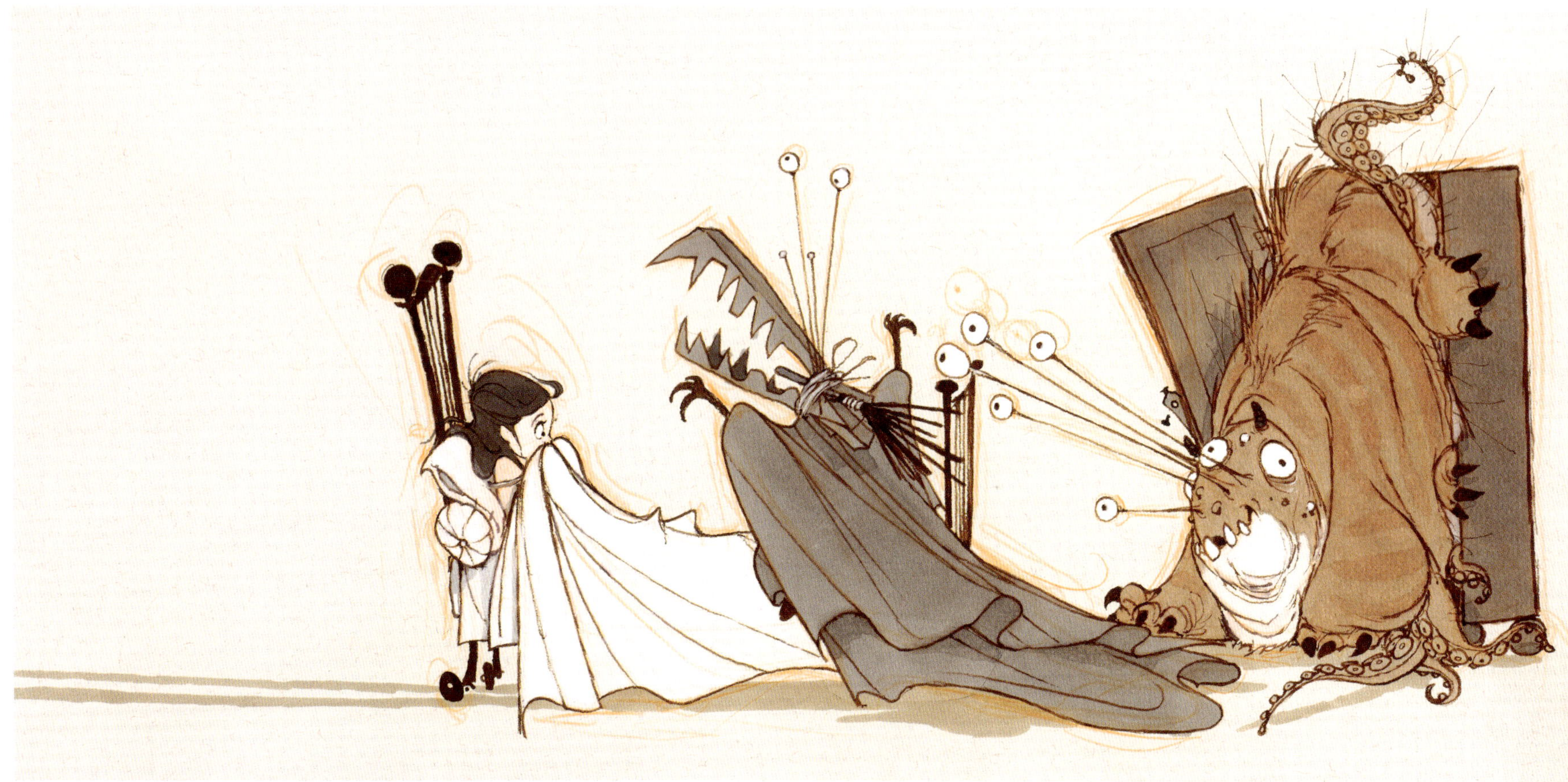

Once Amblimation announced its move from London to Los Angeles in early 1994, artists had to make the choice as to whether or not they would stay with the studio. Nico decided to pack his pencils and bags again for the next adventure, this time moving from his European base into an entirely new geographical, cultural, and professional space—in California.

Word of Nico's unique talents in character design quickly spread throughout the industry, reaching up the California coast. Nico's work was introduced to Pixar, and his imagination spawned some notable creatures for the studio that were both inspirational and aspirational, some reaching beyond the technology of the era.

"Nico's work is like that of no one else. His drawings are incredible, of course, but there are many people in this business who can draw well—and after all, it is not his drawings that appear on screen. What makes Nico so valuable are his ideas. His drawings capture the essence of a character through shape, pose, costume, and attitude. They even suggest movement!
His designs make you feel like he's drawing someone you already know."

—Pete Docter, chief creative officer/feature film director

Above, opposite & pp. 32–39: *Monsters, Inc.* (2001) character concept images

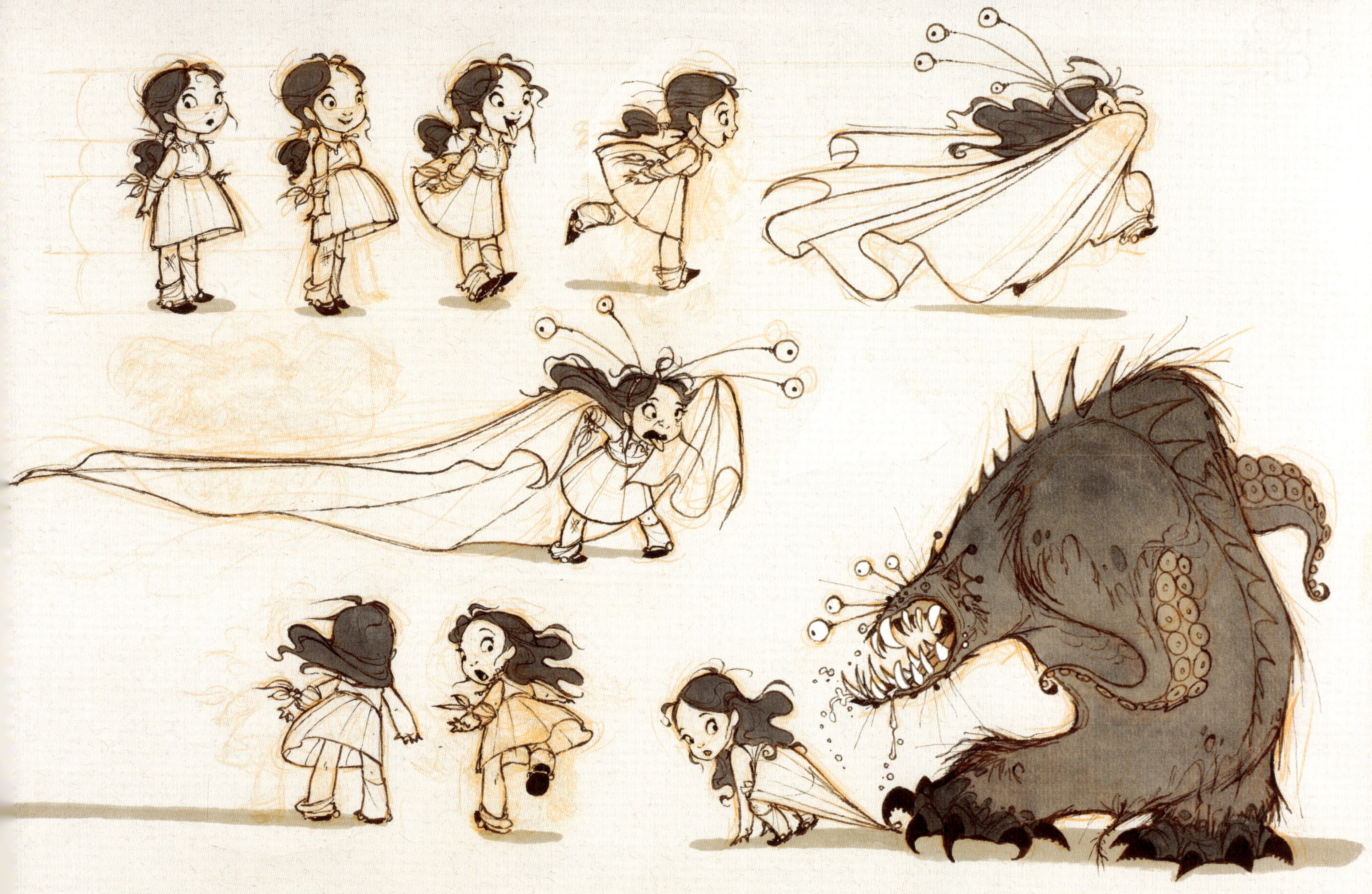

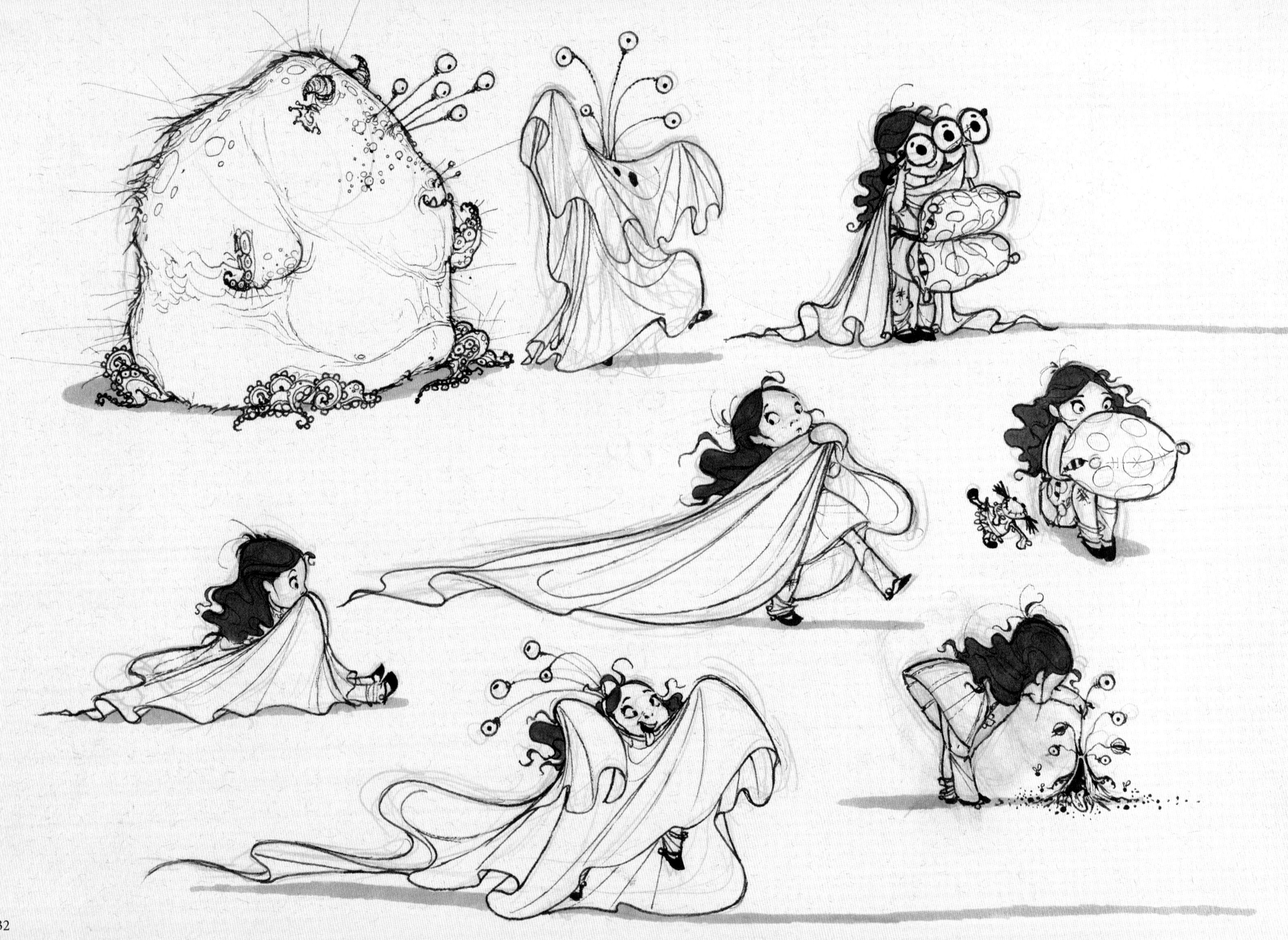

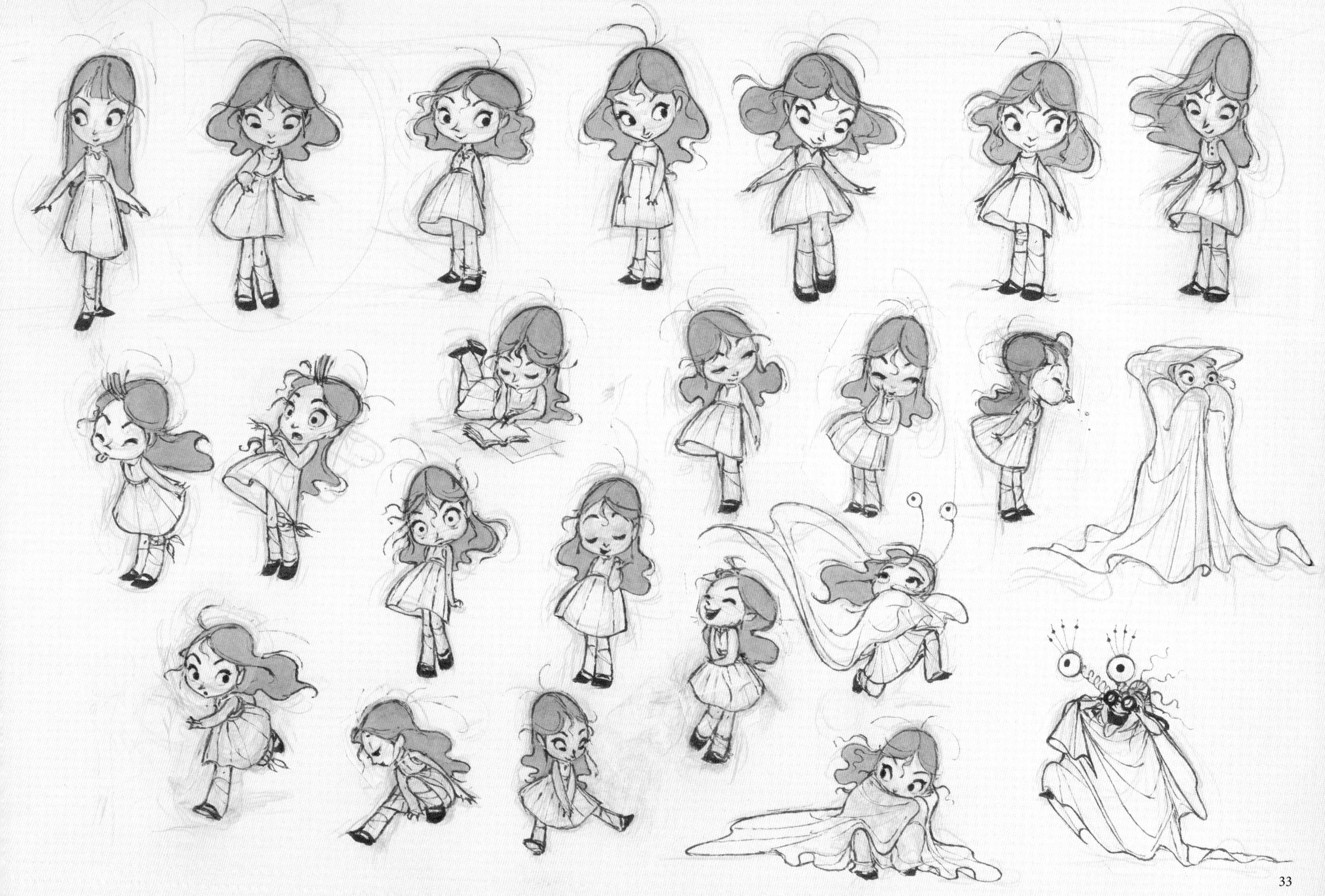

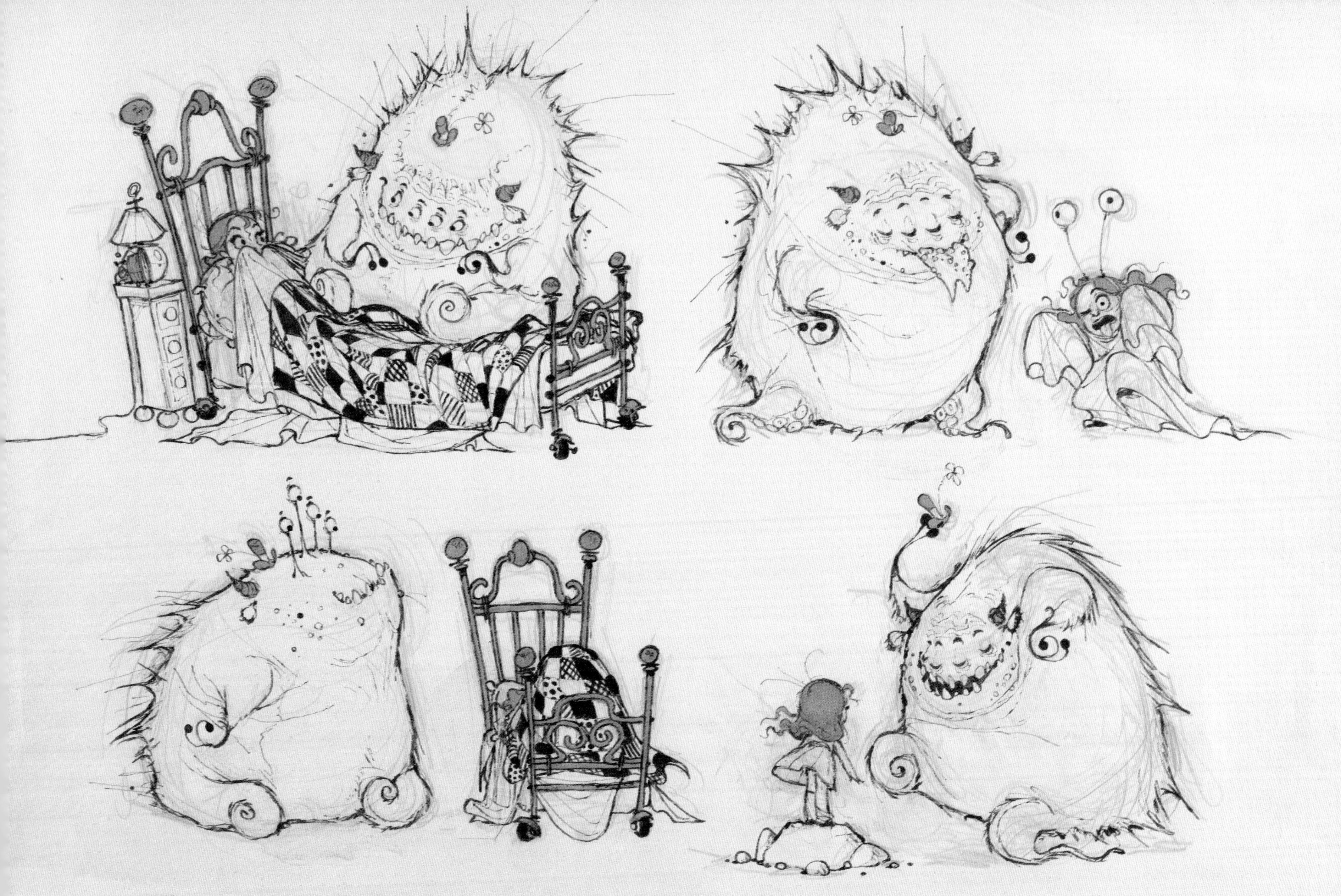

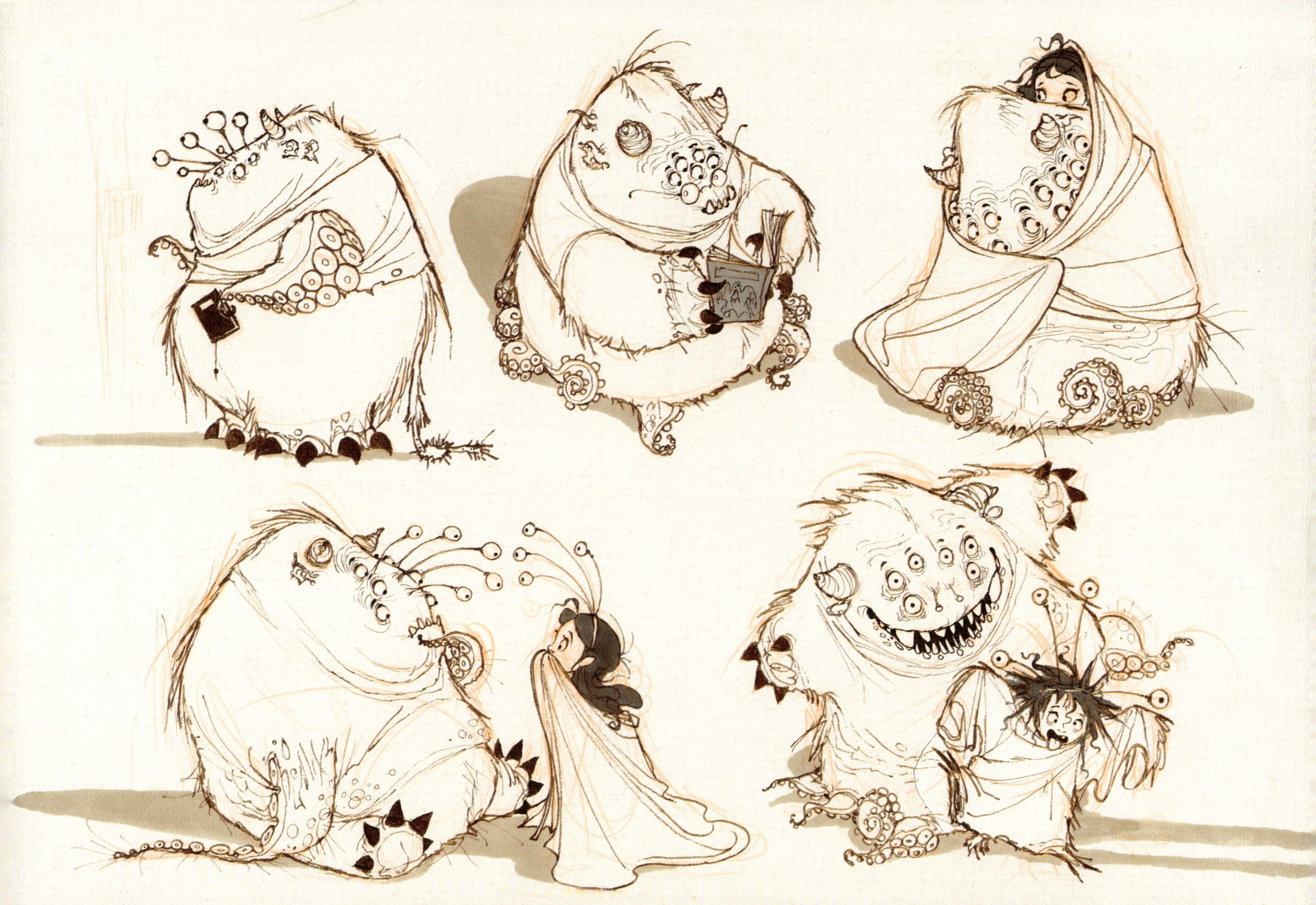

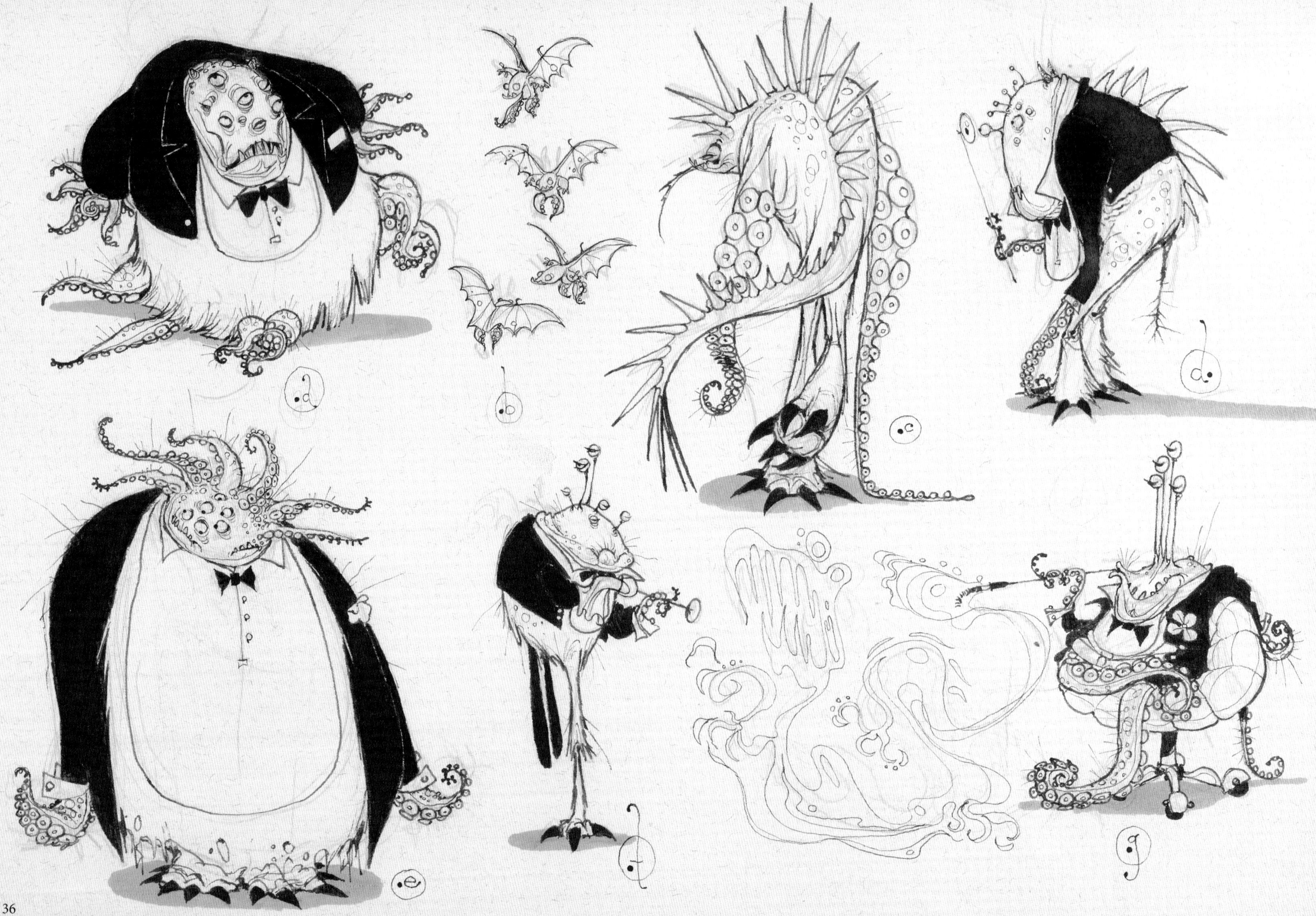
a
b
c
d
e
f
g

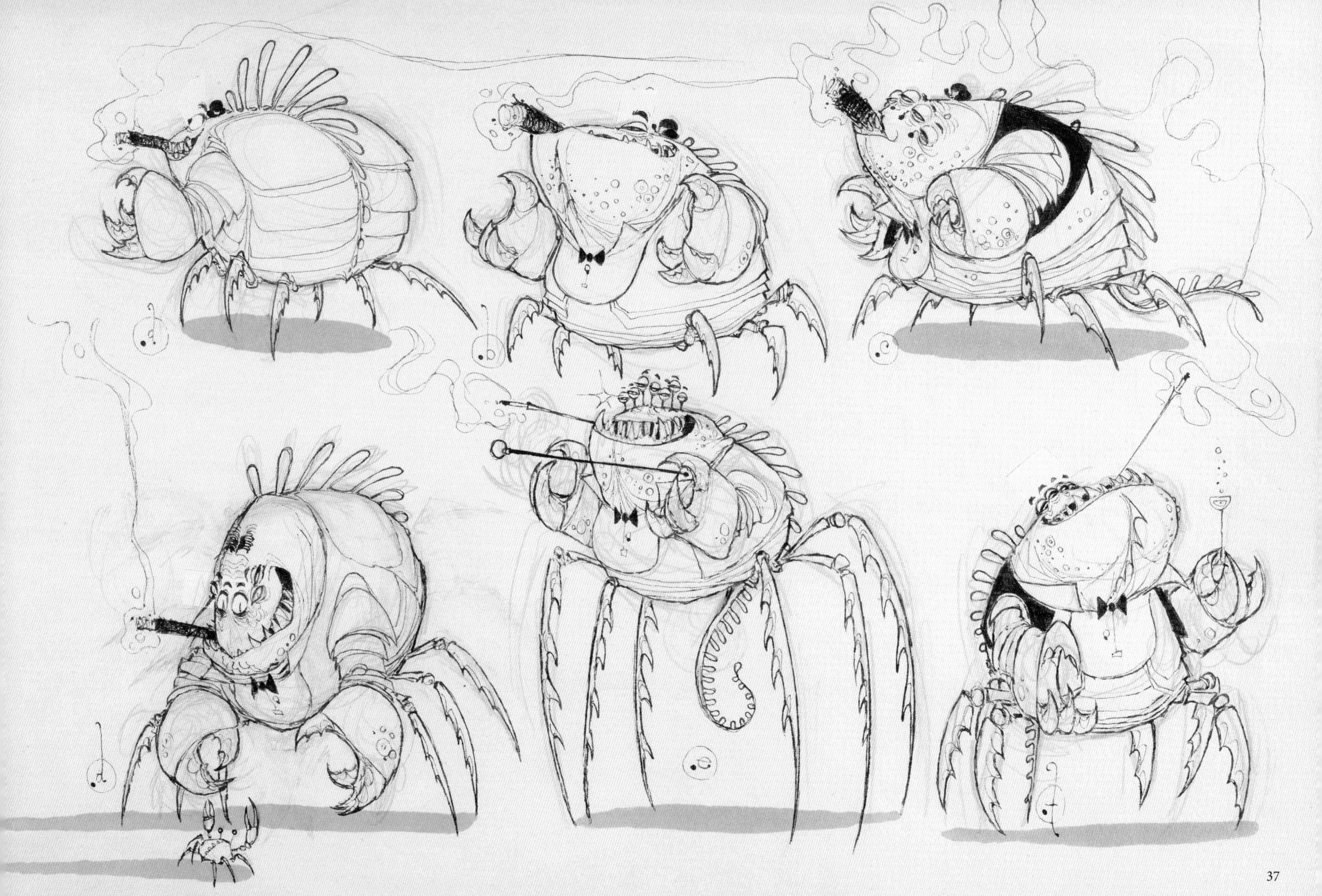

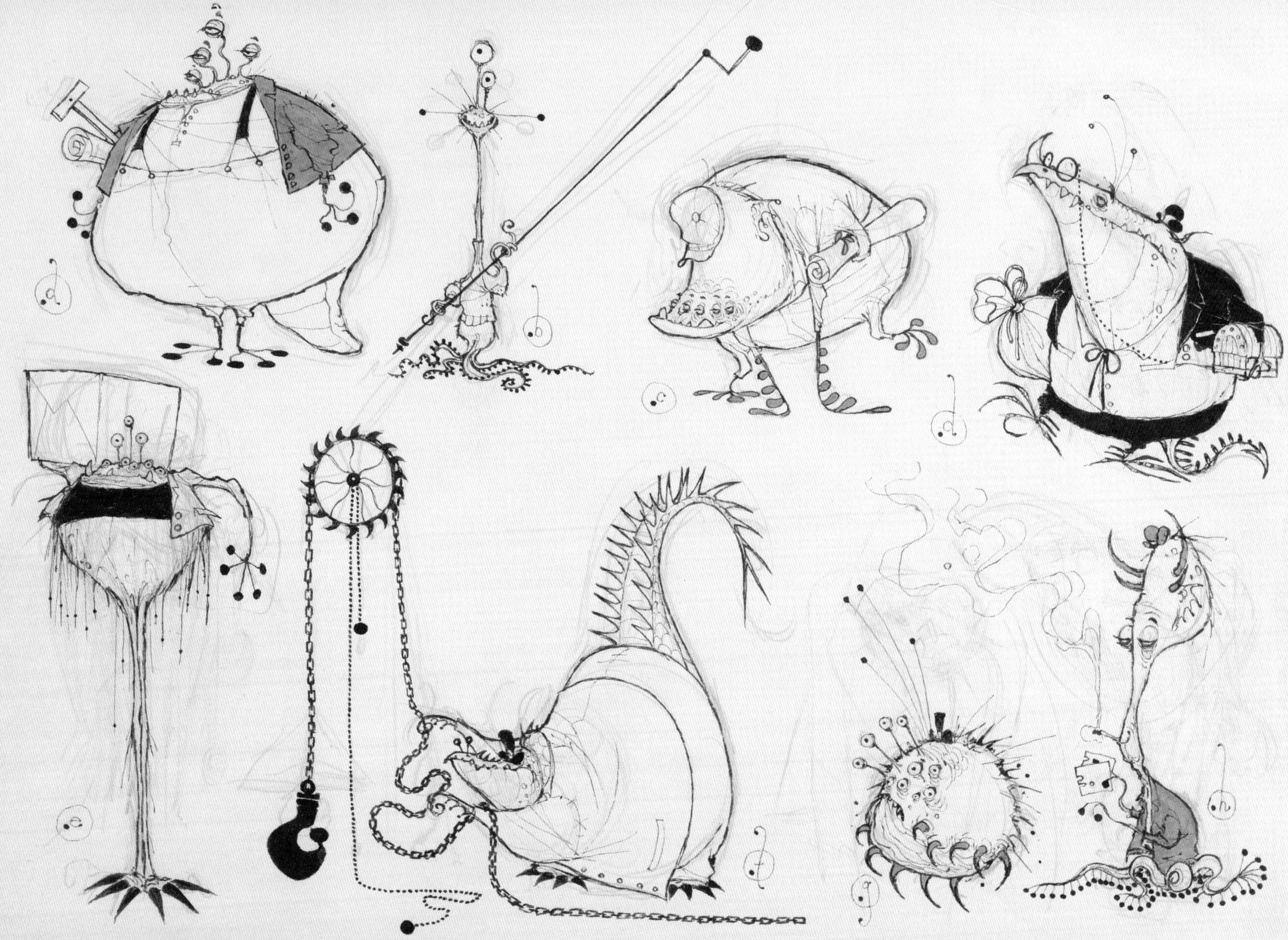

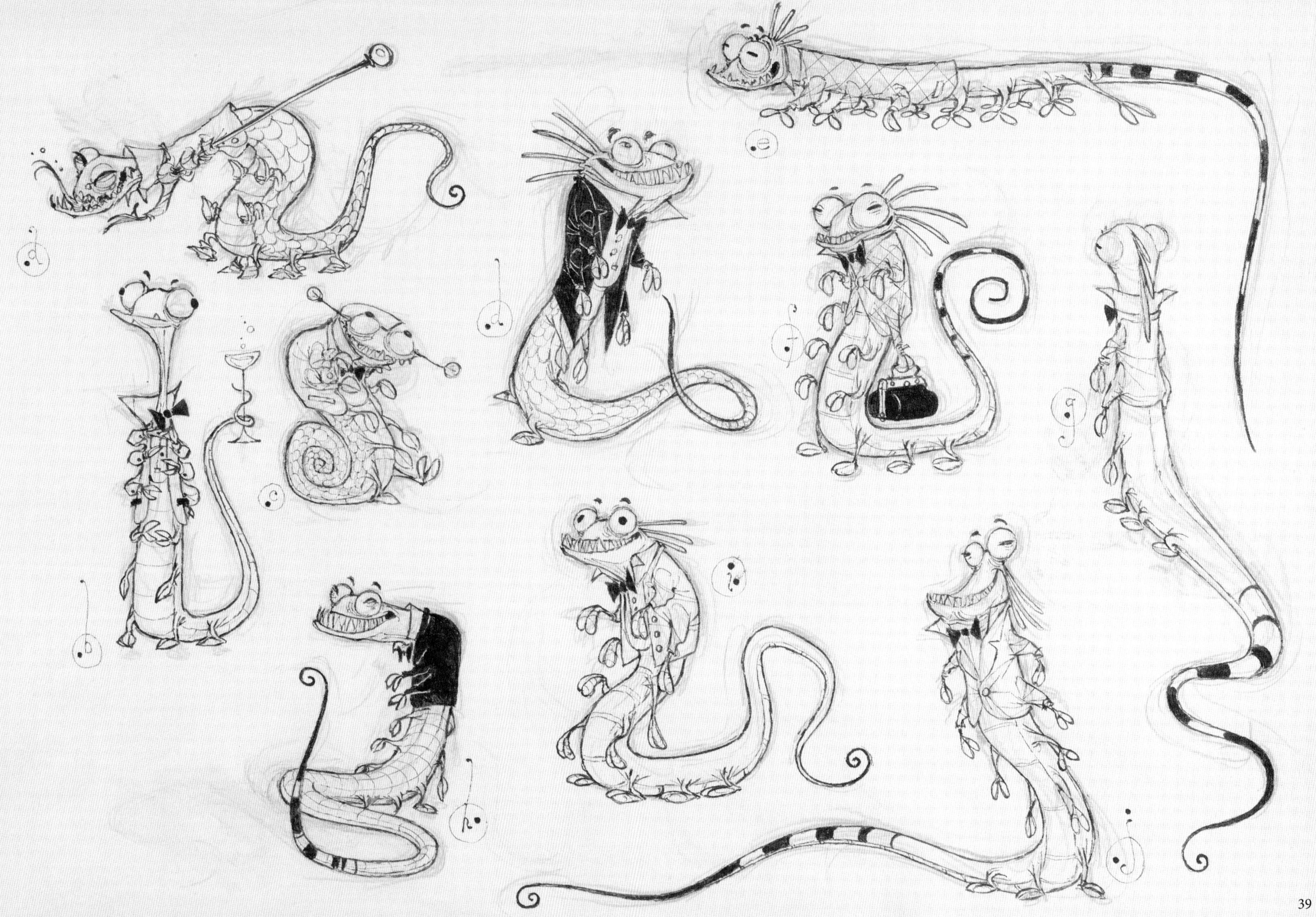

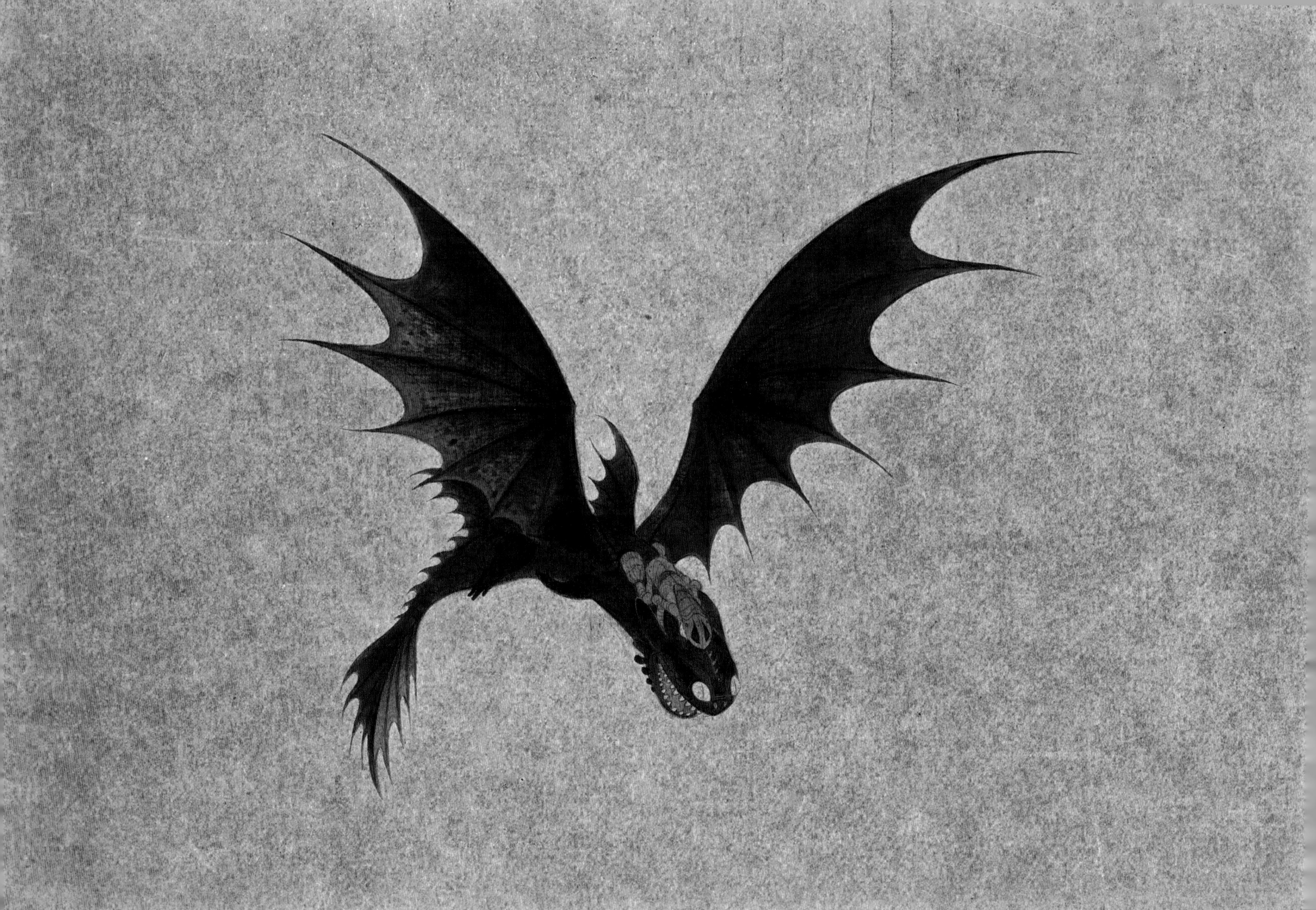

II
The Dream Awakens

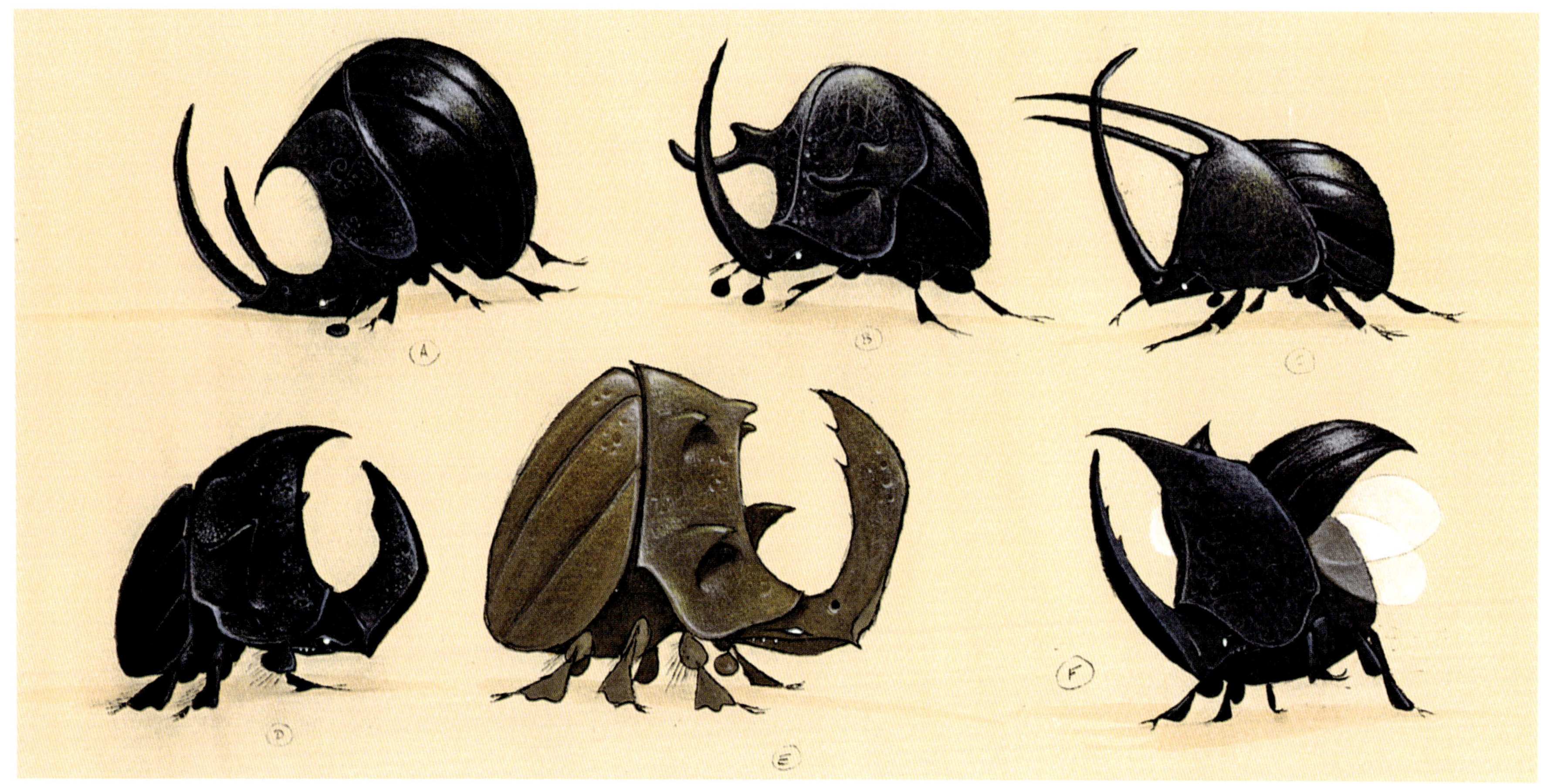

When Amblimation shuttered its doors, many of the artists were welcomed into Steven Spielberg's next endeavor, DreamWorks SKG, specifically slotting into DreamWorks Animation (DWA). The diversity and depth of characters that Nico delivered to DWA over the course of three decades is immeasurable but undoubtedly impactful.

"Anyone who sees a great animated film is inspired by the artistry of the animators who magically bring drawings to life. But who inspires the animators? At DreamWorks Animation, the answer is often Nico Marlet. He is the brilliant character designer who somehow knows what a kung fu–fighting panda should look like. Or an awkward Viking teenager who trains dragons. Or an ancient grand master turtle. Or a Night Fury. Or, or, or! The list goes on and on. Nico has created entire casts of characters who go on to become beloved icons around the world. Time and again, I've seen him start with the proverbial blank page and then hold up his sketch to have everyone in the room say, 'Yes, that's Po!' Or Hiccup. Or Oogway. Or Toothless. Or, or, or! There is truly one word for what Nico does: inspires."

—**Jeffrey Katzenberg, executive producer**

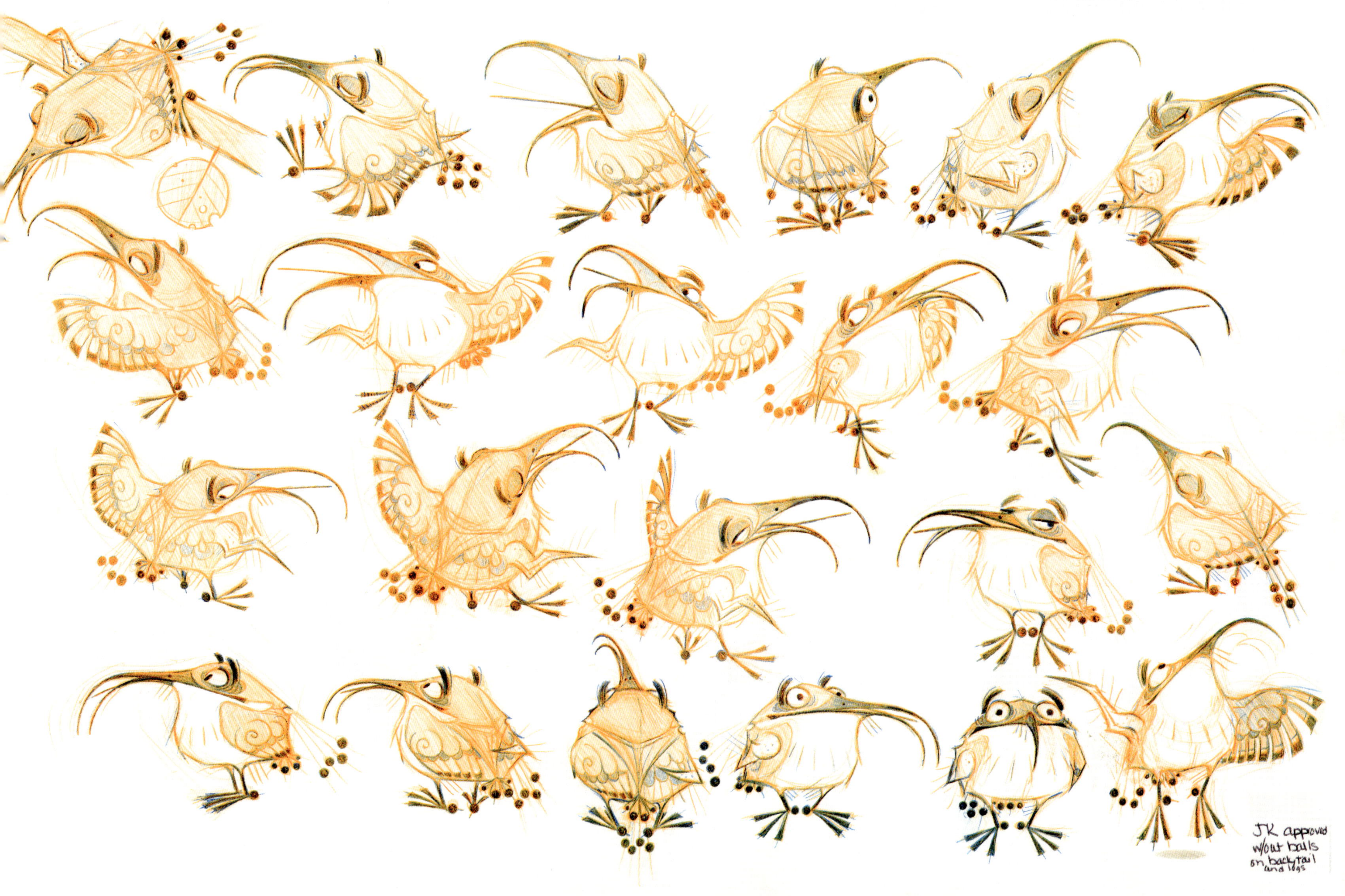
JK approved
w/out balls
on back, tail
and legs

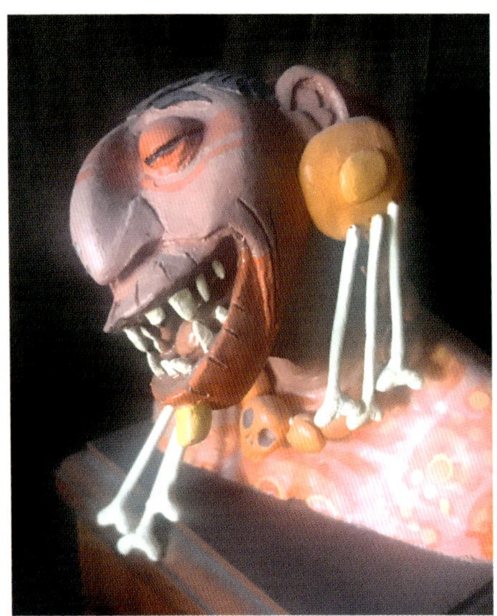

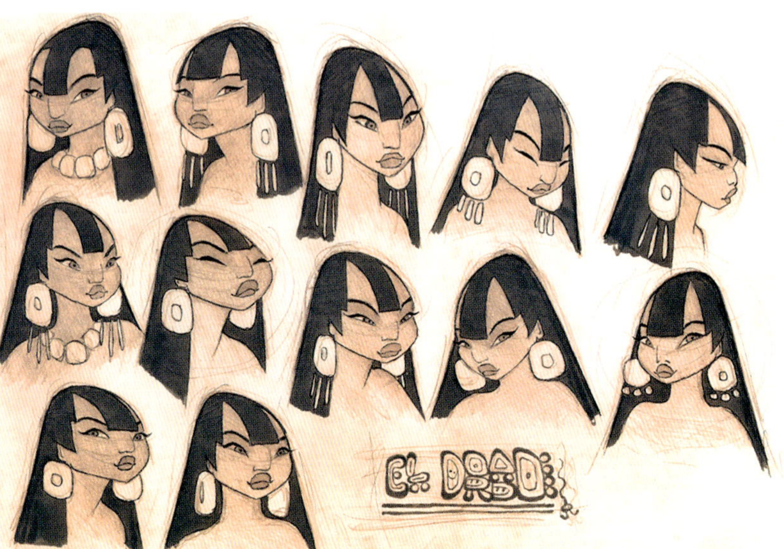

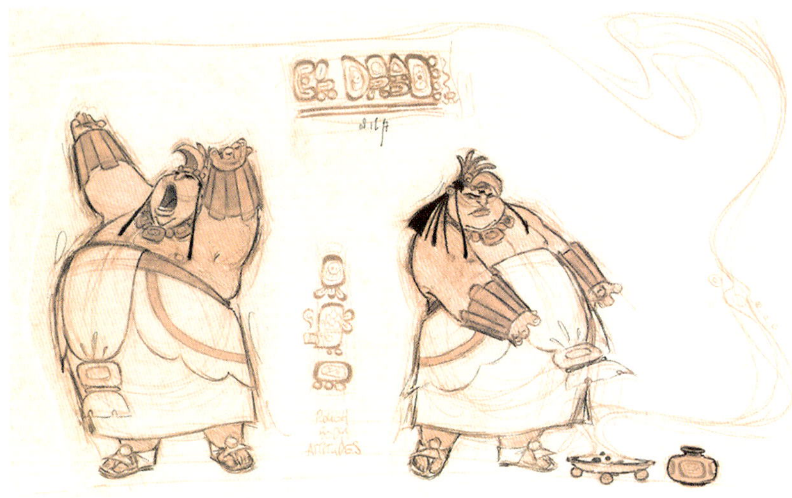

BESIDES DRAWING, Nico likes to sculpt, a form of expression that started with a charismatically complex magician for *El Dorado*. According to Nico, "I sculpted his head because nobody responded to the drawings. And sometimes if you change the medium, people start to react to it because of that. That was one of the best drawings I did—it's funny how you get different reactions."

"Nico's drawings are the essence of animation—he uses beautiful and appealing shapes to express mood and personality. Everything he does is exactly right: gesture, balance, staging of shapes, simplicity, and fluidity at its best. Nothing is unnecessary. On the professional side—unique and sublime; on the personal—loving and generous. We work together, challenge each other, and love each other."

—**CARLOS GRANGEL, character designer**

"Nico is the prince of animation, the king of character design—one of the best talents of his generation and a fan of the great André Franquin. What more to say? Nico is a gentle soul; he is discreet, kind of shy; and he loves animals. His peers love him and admire his work. His body of work will inspire future generations of artists who will have to work extra hard in the foolish hope to become better than him."

—**DIDIER CONRAD, illustrator**

P. 40: *How To Train Your Dragon* (2010) character concepts • P. 42: *Antz* (1998) character concepts • P. 43: *Madagascar* (2005) character concept images • PP. 44–47: *The Road to El Dorado* (2000) character concepts

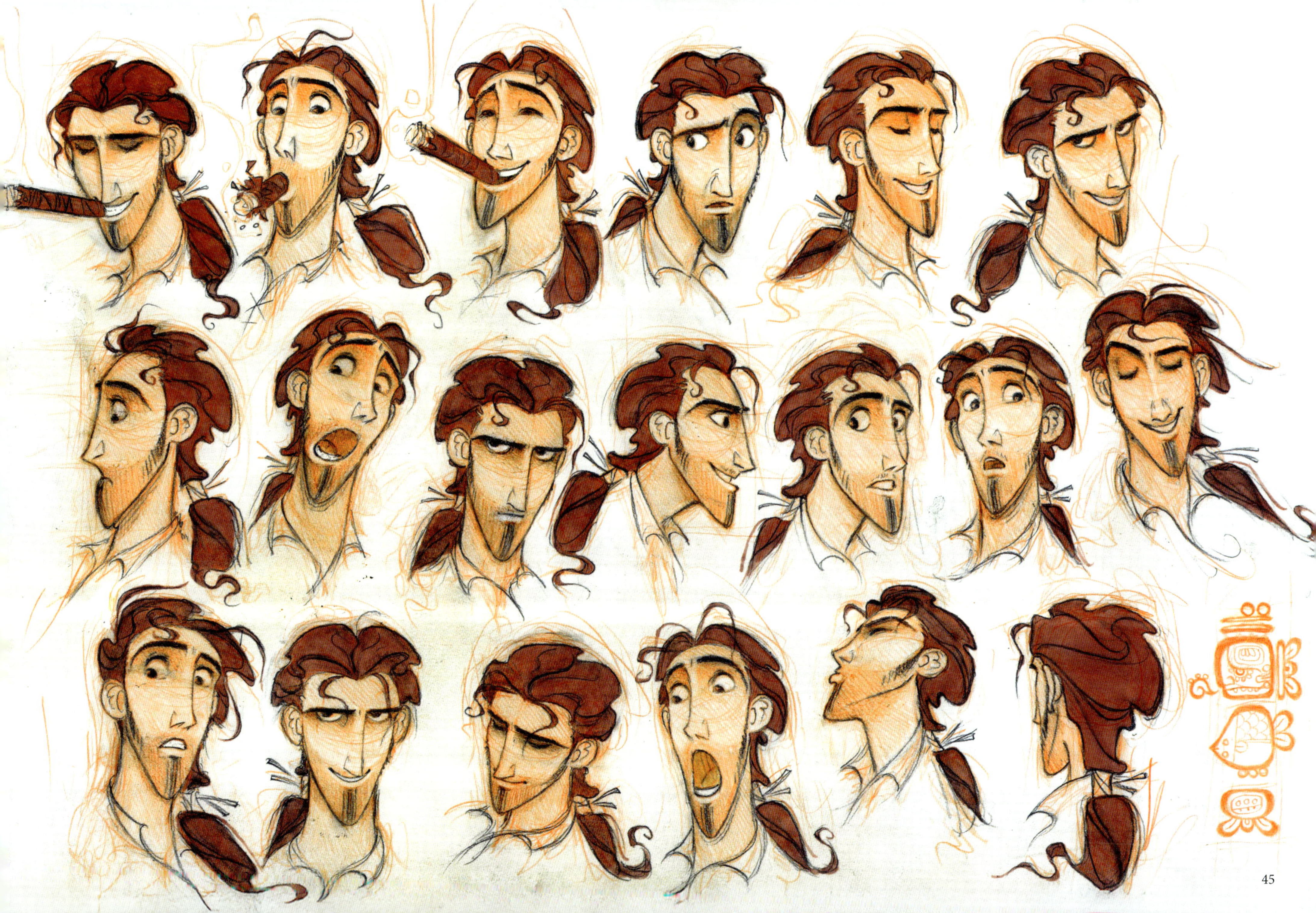

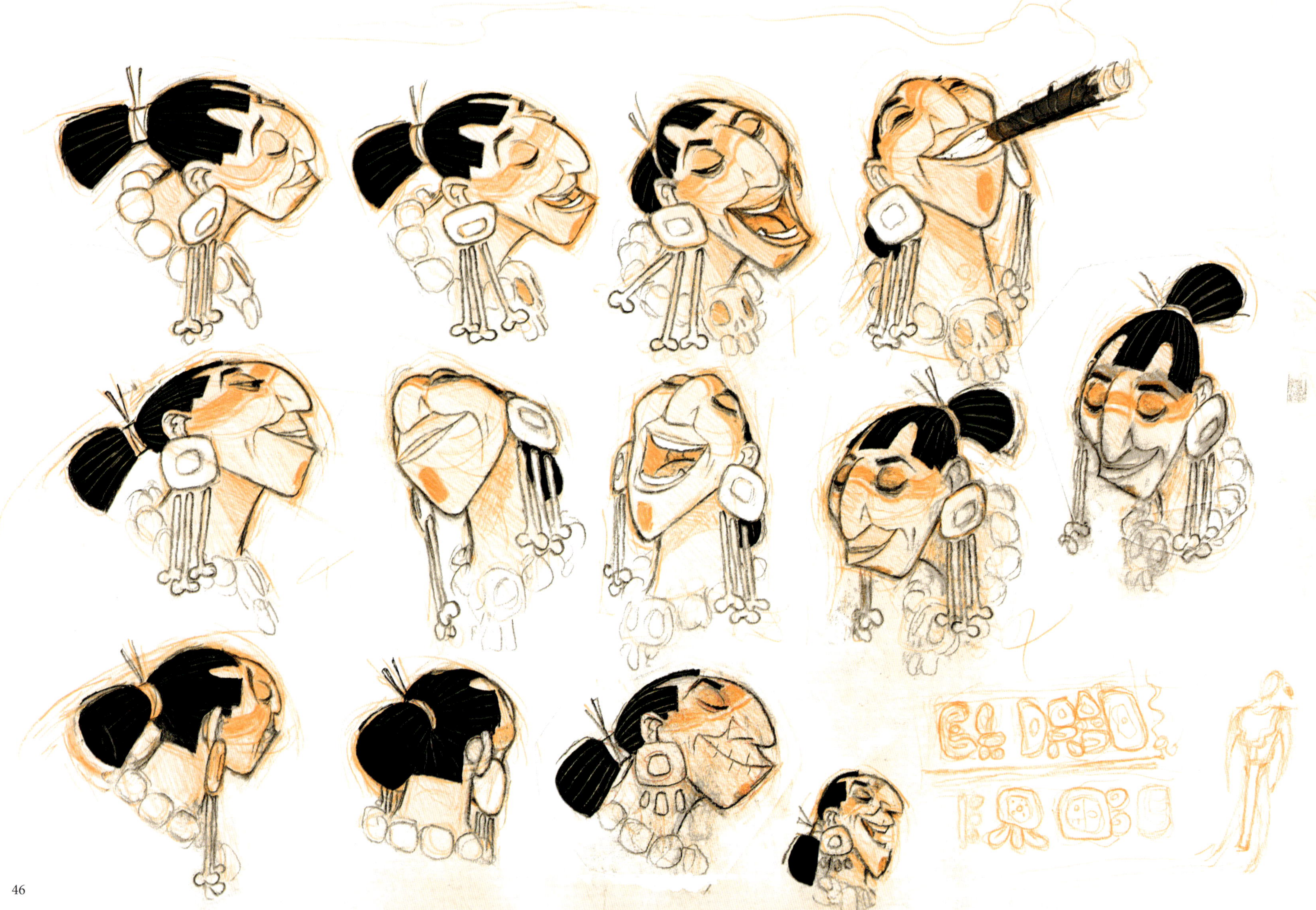

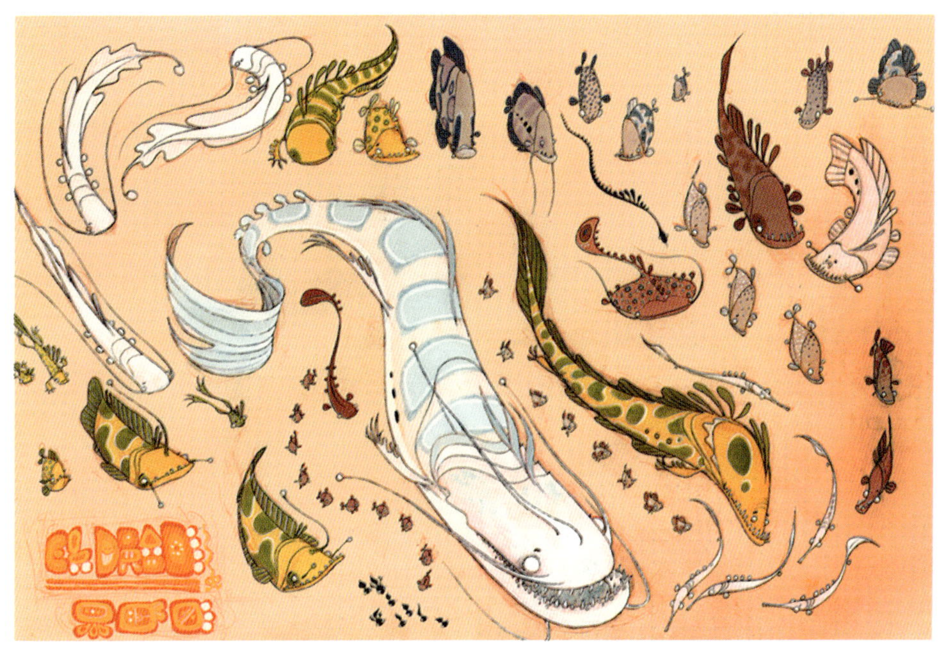

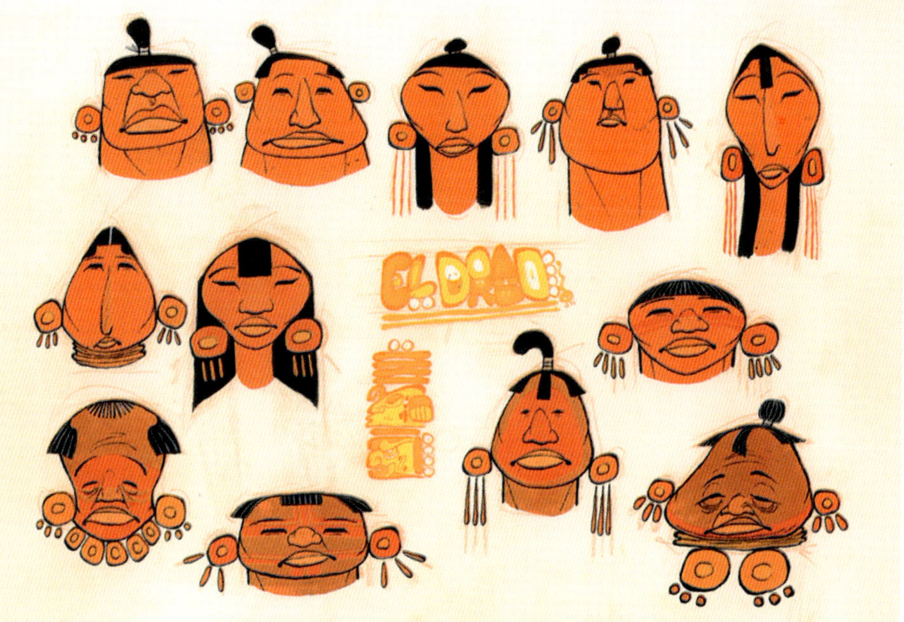

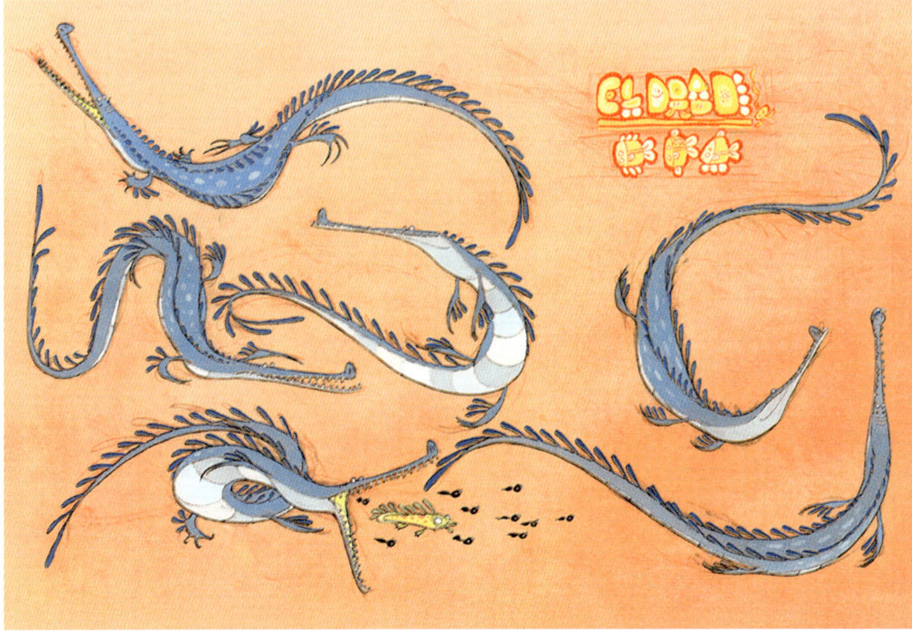

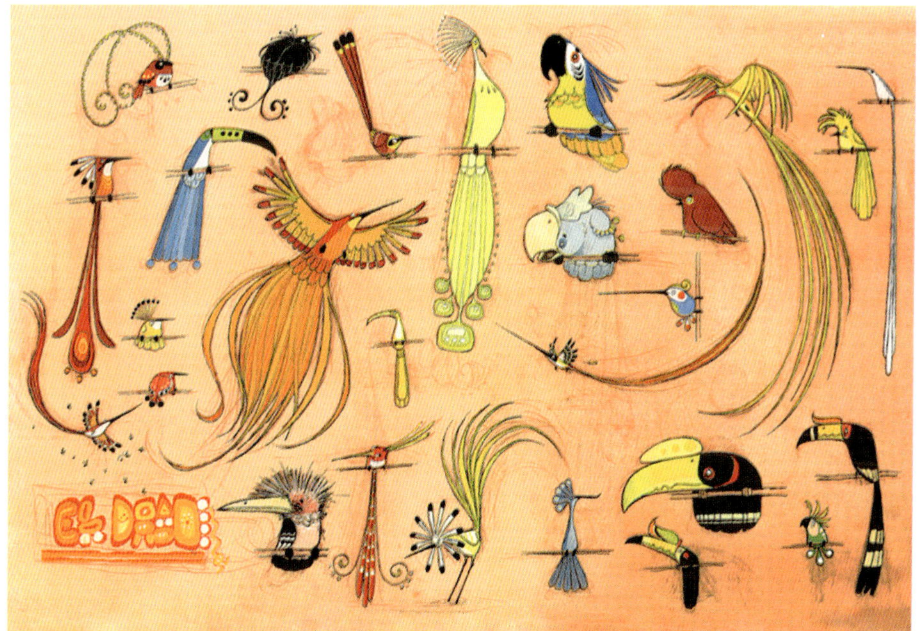

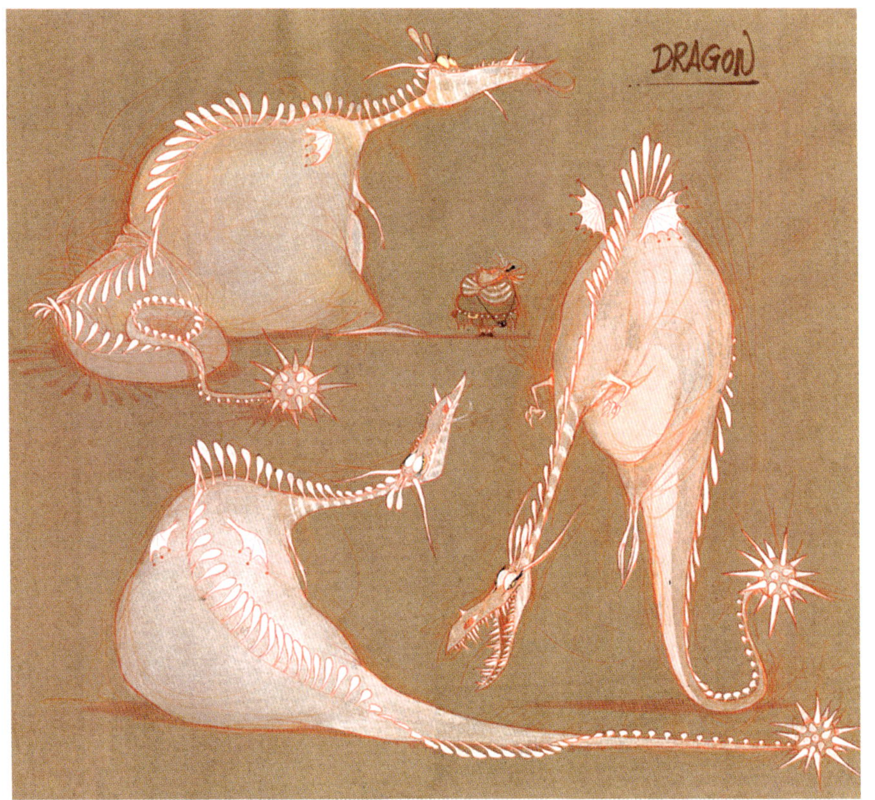

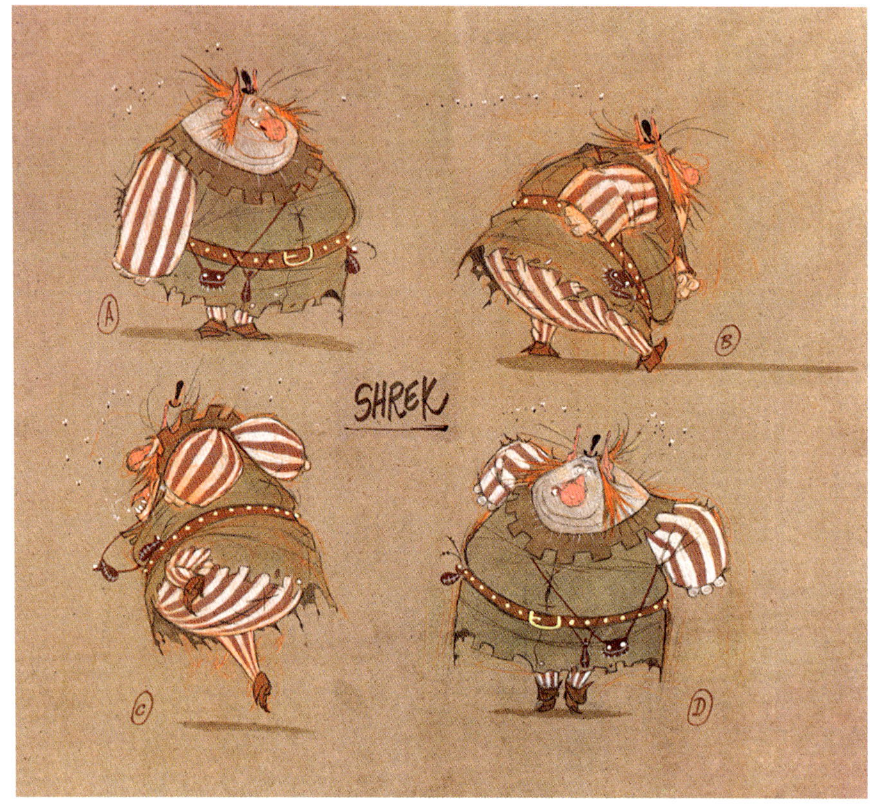

"If you're lucky, you come across a talent like Nico Marlet once in your lifetime. We met in the early days of DreamWorks, and Nico's drawings could be found pinned on every desk. Whether he fills an entire roll of paper with delightful characters in all their possible poses and expressions, or pencils a single silly sheep bounding through a tiny flip book made of one-inch Post-its—his drawings are always alive with whimsy, intricate detail, and unmatched appeal."

—Vicky Jenson, director

"What a joy to celebrate the fabulous talent of my friend Nicolas Marlet! With his accent that feels of the French sun, he speaks little and expresses himself more fully through drawing. His inimitable style is full of humor and graphic discoveries. So many unforgettable characters owe their lives to him! Like a goldsmith—from his orange pencil sketch will emerge a jewel, a drawing that is always funny, incisive, and affectionate, which he will offer to you with a sparkle in his eyes and a smile on his lips."

—Patrick Mate, character designer

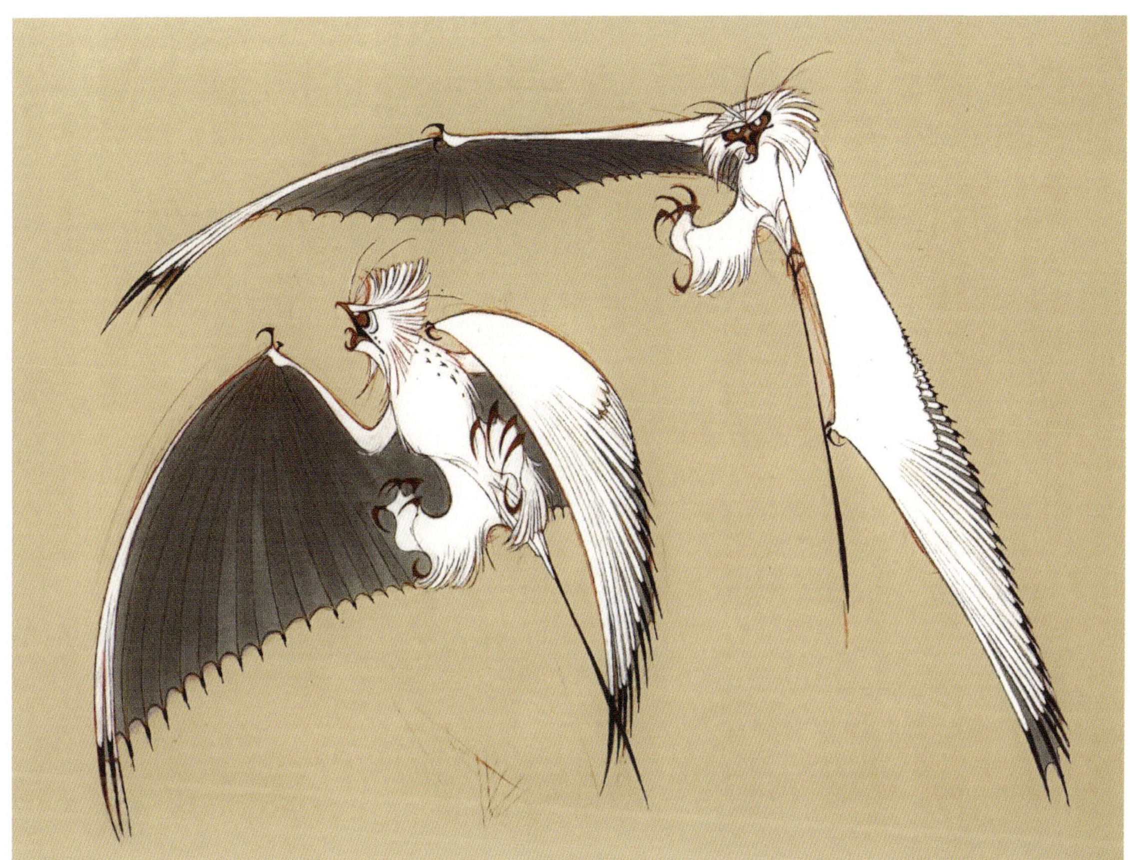

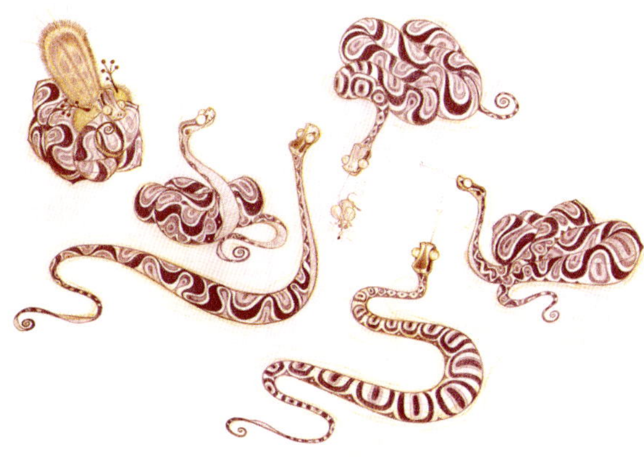

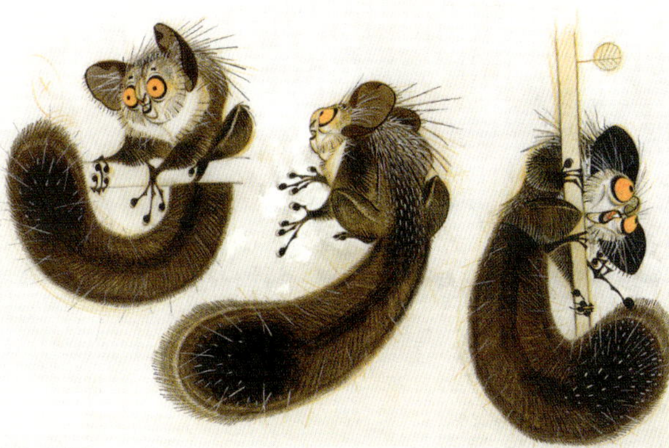

"I first met Nico Marlet when he, Carlos Grangel, and I were thrown together in a room at the studio on Barham Boulevard, where DreamWorks was starting work on its first animated project, The Prince of Egypt. *I had no clue how to be a character designer for feature animation, but I had the good fortune to be sharing a room with two of the most inspirational artists and fantastic teachers to guide me. Nico floored me with his unique lens on the world and his completely original way of seeing and drawing. To this day, I regard Nico as the best character designer in the industry. He is truly a tireless drawing machine. He never stops. Ever. I imagine his hand twitches while he's asleep, creating characters we can only imagine. And always, it's his gentle nature and huge heart that informs everything he draws and paints. I am so grateful and honored to have met, become friends with, and worked with Nico. He's a national treasure, both here and abroad."*

—**Carter Goodrich, illustrator**

Opposite, left & right: *Shrek* (2001) character concepts • Above, left: *Sinbad: Legend of the Seven Seas* (2003) character concepts • Above, right, top & bottom: *Madagascar* (2005) character concepts

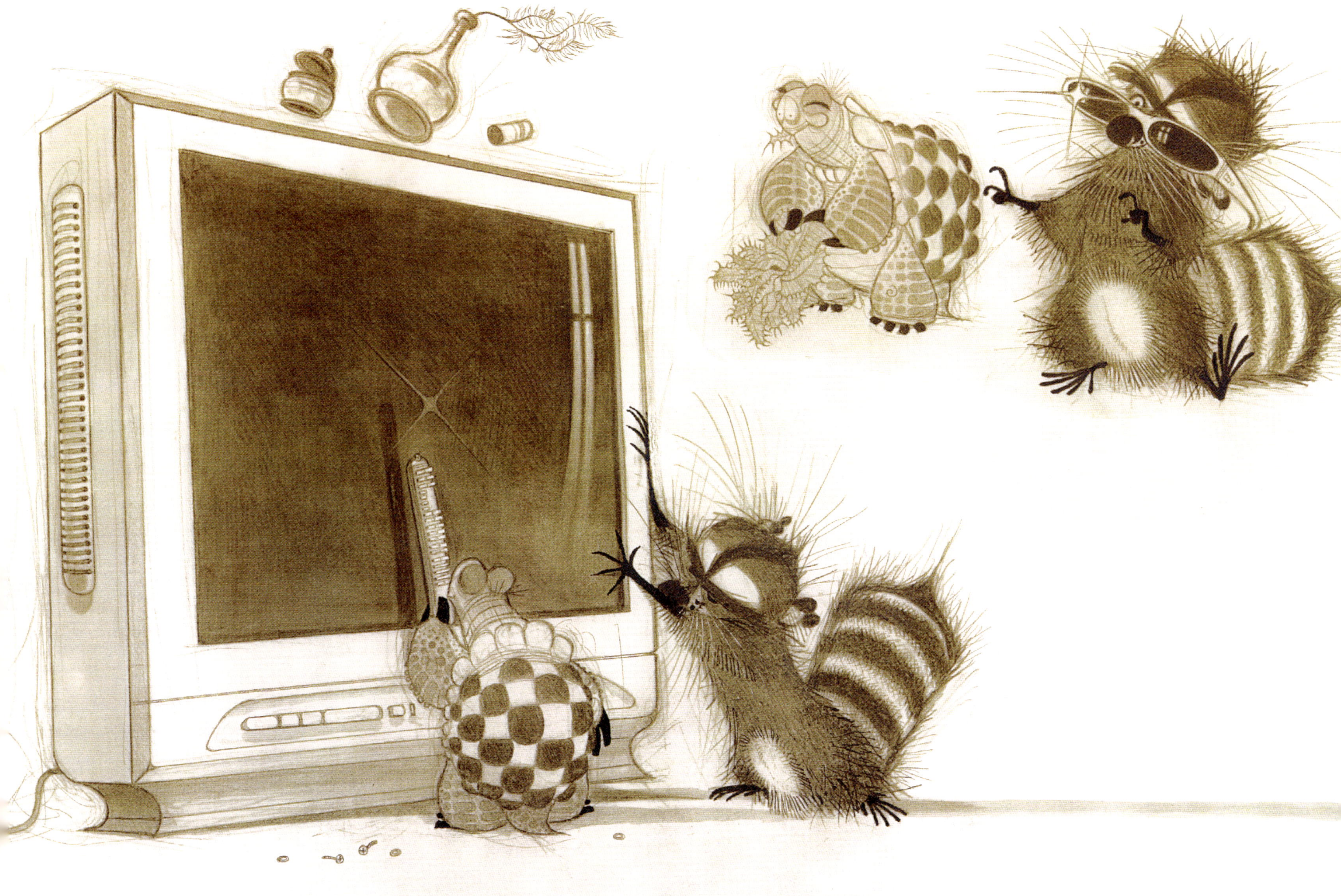

"Charm. In all the years I have known Nico and his work—and that dates back to the early nineties—I have never seen a single Nico drawing that did not radiate charm. Yes, he's got great shape language, and yes, he is a fearfully good draftsman, but the thing he can do better than ANY other artist I have ever worked with is imbue his creations with an extraordinary charisma that is incredibly hard to copy, let alone create from scratch. My admiration for his work is limitless."

—**Simon Wells, director**

"I stumbled upon Nico's artwork while I was still an animation student in Paris, and oh boy, did it inspire me! Inside of a binder was hundreds of xeroxed pages filled with the most incredible artwork I had ever seen, all drawn following the same technique: a scribbled layer of orange Col-Erase pencil to build the overall shape, a fine line of graphite pencil for clean-up and added details, and one layer of gray marker to fill in the character and give it volume. Each more perfect and inventive than the other. I was mesmerized. Energized. Revived. It totally blew my mind and gave me a standard to aspire to, a model to follow, and an inspiration to fuel my ambitions. Years later, when I started working at DreamWorks, I realized how much Nico had shaped the look of the studio's movies and was truly held as a legend by everyone there. I slowly realized that the fuel to all these incredible drawings is much more than simple talent. Nico has an outstanding ability to retain a child's view of the world, to be touched and remain in awe of everything that surrounds him, to see the beauty in all things, and to fall deeply in love with the characters that he puts down on the page. His hypersensitivity is what turns lines of graphite into visual poetry. And that is the real magic trick."

—**Pierre Perifel, director**

"Hand-drawn animators are a little different from our CGI and stop-motion cousins. We deal not only in dimensional form, but also in flat shape. Elegant, sinuous, but undeniably flat shape. Silhouettes that not only lead the eye around the body but also deceive it into thinking that this collection of lines and color is a living, breathing character. When I first encountered Nico Marlet's work when we worked together at DreamWorks, I immediately knew I had met an artist that captures this duality of form and shape more completely than any other artist I had ever seen. We went on to work on many films together. Nico calmly and humbly produced masterpiece after masterpiece of design—designs which I, as an animator, could not wait to get my hands on. He is an animator's designer, condensing caricature and personality into contours of pure charm."

—**James Baxter, directing animator**

Opposite & pp. 50–55: *Over the Hedge* (2006) character concepts

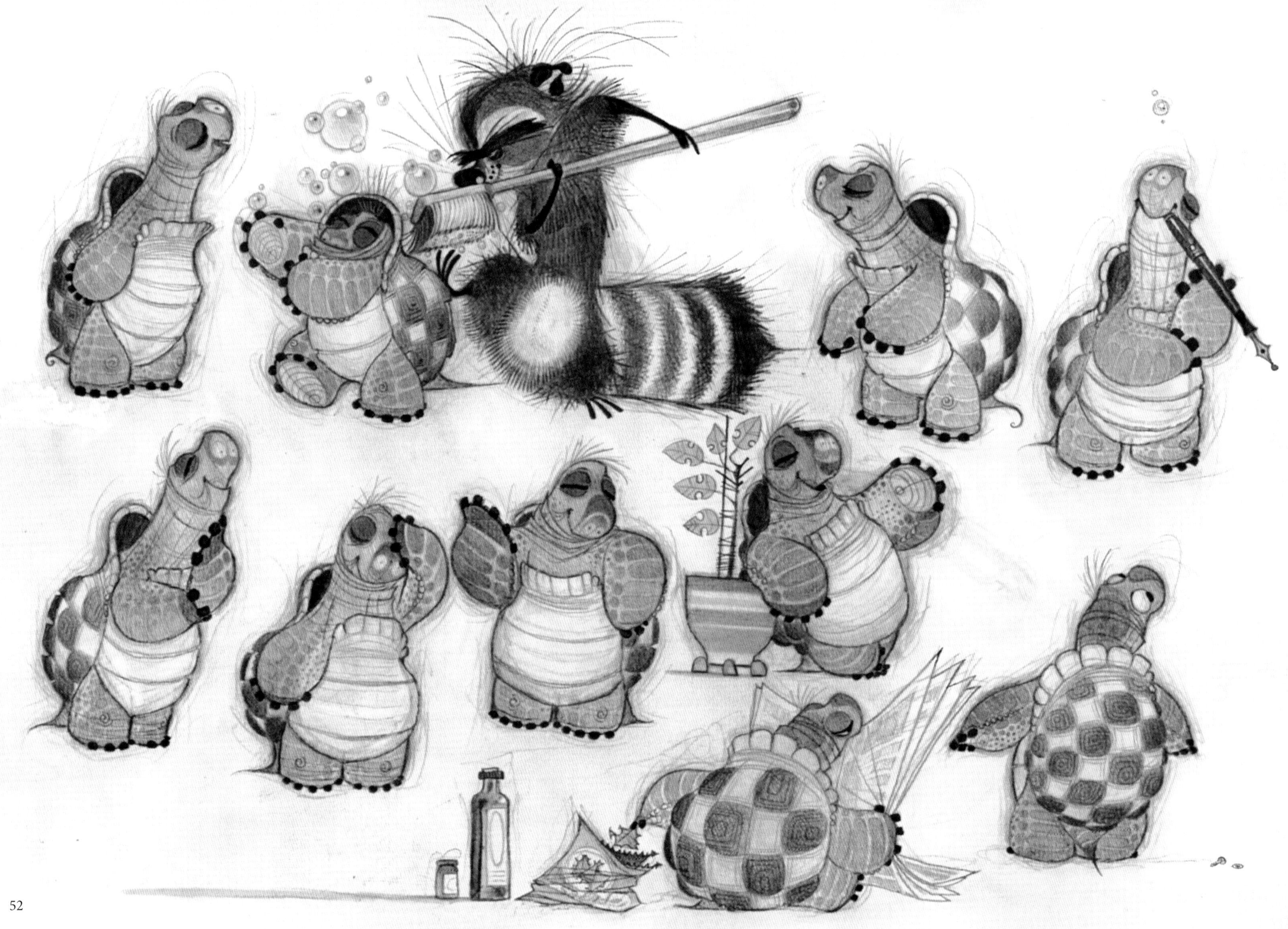

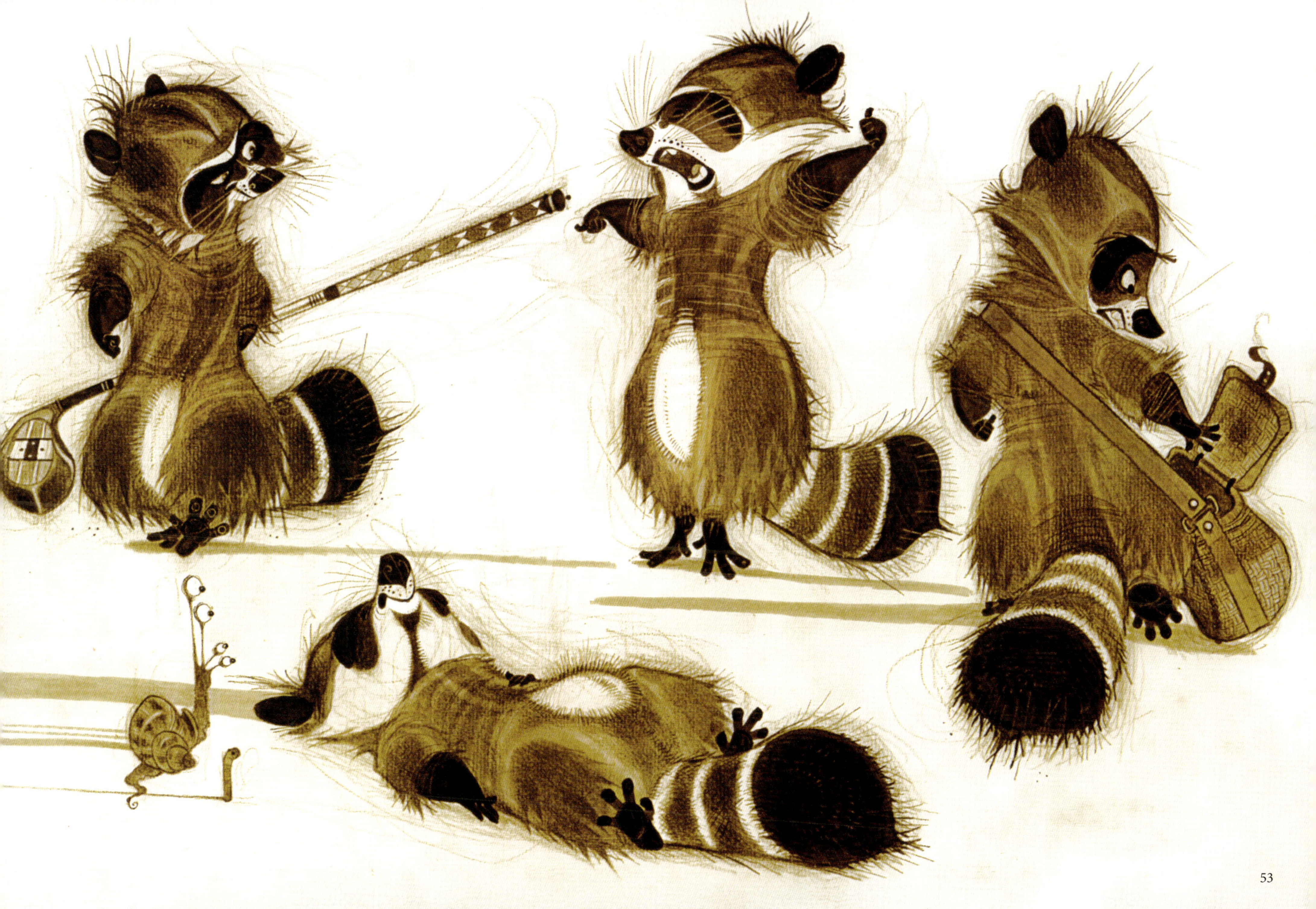

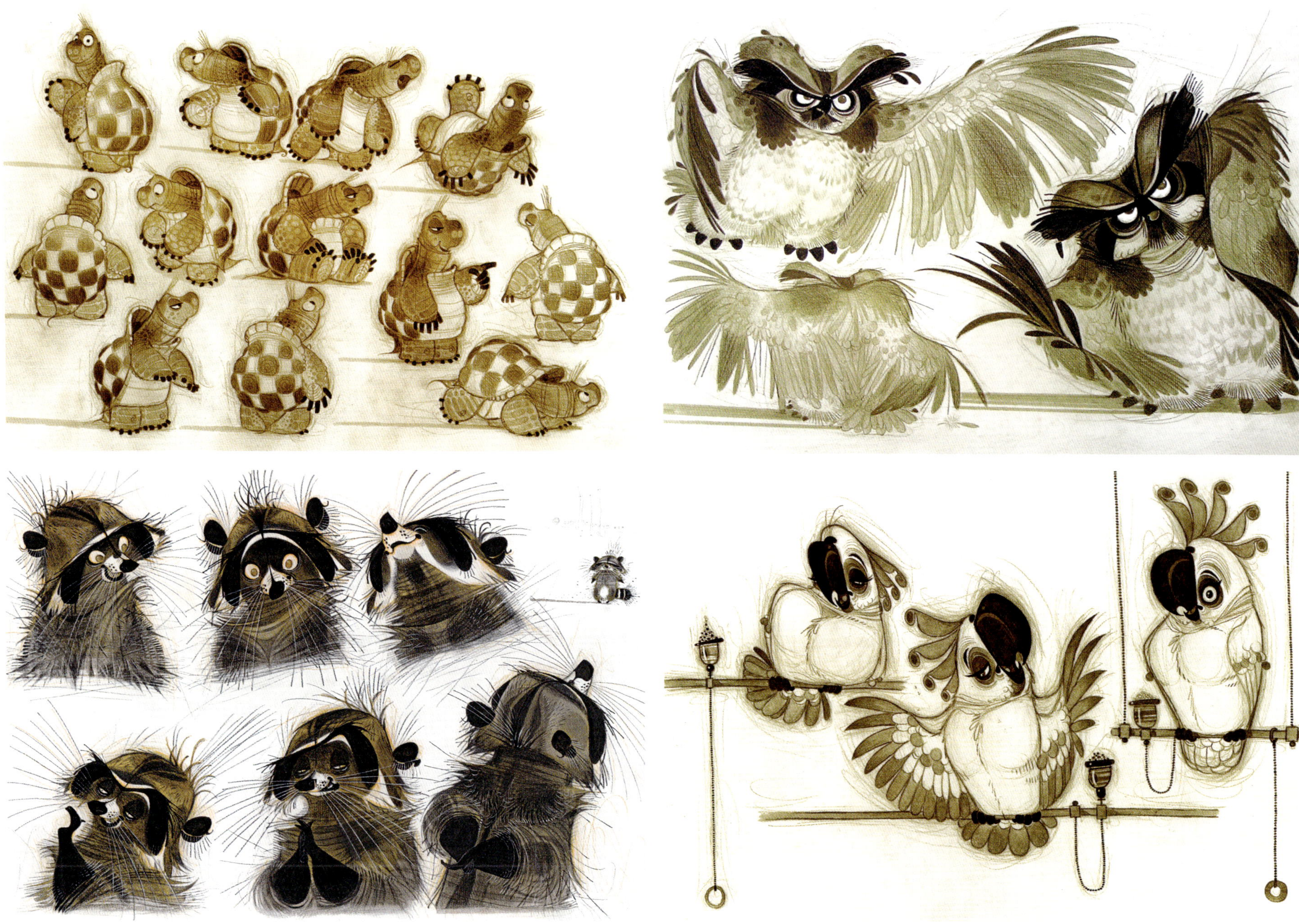

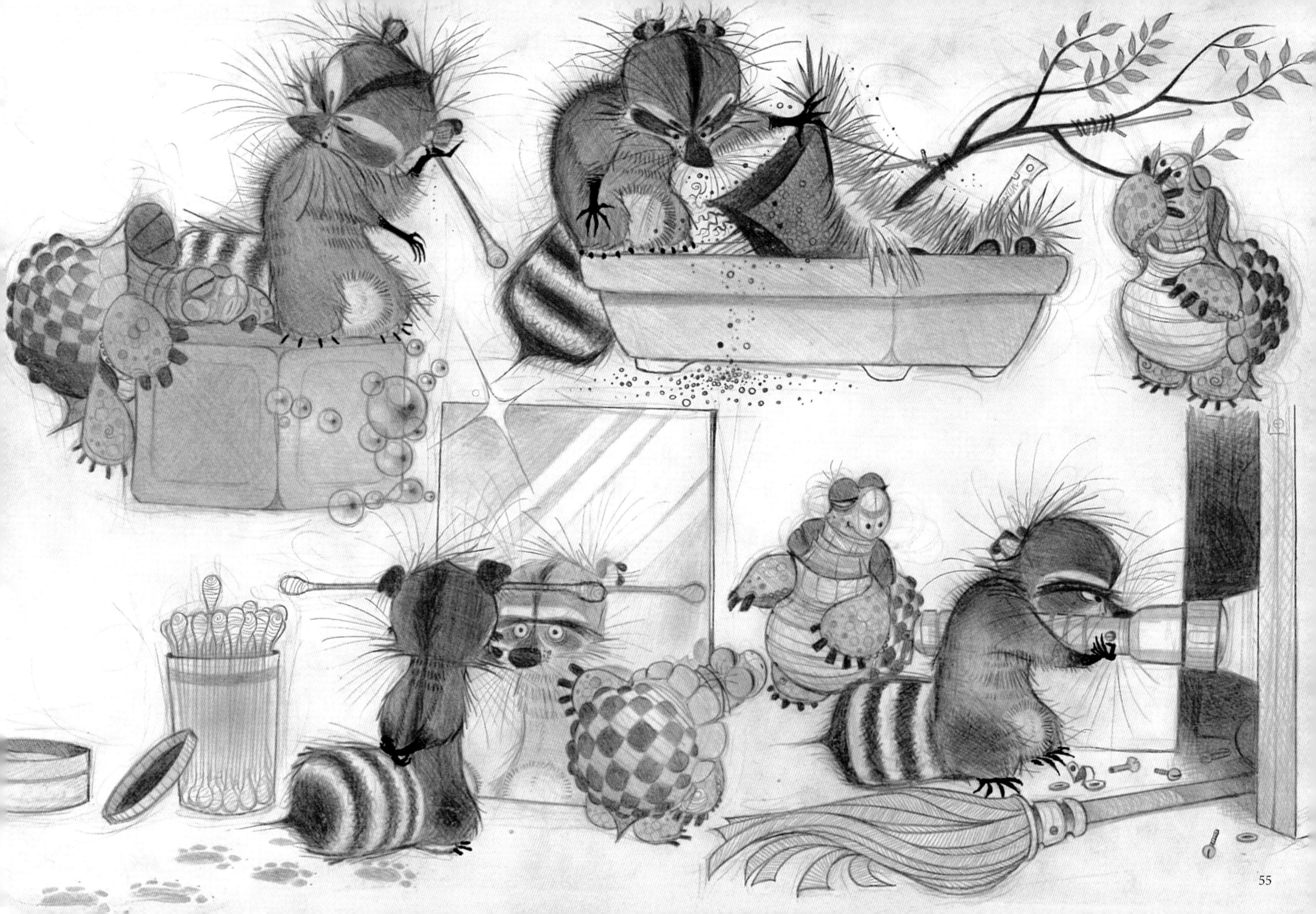

Panda Dynasty

When the concept of a panda performing martial arts arose at DreamWorks, no one knew it would become a multi-decade, multimedia legacy, but what greatly affected Nico on this project was the opportunity for him to work closely with character modelers for the first time. This brilliant collaboration brought his precise vision into technological reality. The partnership extended further down the production pipeline with riggers and animators on future projects, all hoping to include as much of Nico's design detail in each character as possible. Nico speculates: "Some might think I go into too much detail—even I think I might put too much detail into my drawings sometimes—but attention to detail is the most important thing. When you consider animation history, that's what highlights the difference between Disney and the others. It's the attention to detail."

"In animation, creativity and imagination are the lifeblood of what we do. To stand out at the very top of this medium is no small feat, and Nico's designs have done that over and over. Through his rare talent, he has helped directors discover beloved characters on so many projects. He never ceases to deliver a fresh and unique point of view. Love of nature is one of Nico's many charms. His home is filled with dogs, plants (many plants), fish, and turtles. It's a clue to how the artist in him observes life. He also collects well-designed artifacts from all parts of the globe. You can quickly tell this is someone who appreciates the world around him and that it fuels his creative nature. As a character designer, Nico is technically brilliant. His sense of shape composition versus detail always has an organic flow to it. It stuns me how he manages to get it all in there, always so beautifully balanced. He does all of this on paper with no 'undos.' It's kind of like a meditative high-wire act, pushing himself artistically the whole time. But the biggest secret is that these aren't just designs; they are well-thought-out solutions that affect the story and its viewers in profound ways. This has led to successful franchises that were built with Nico's collaboration and films with audiences who are always left wanting more."

—Raymond Zibach, production designer

"Every drawing I have seen from Nico is more than a sketch of a character; it is a handcrafted work of art that reveals a depth of understanding of what lies beneath the skin of a character. Whether it's a sketch of Santa Claus for a Christmas card or a lineup of rhino prison guards, there is a remarkable specificity and elegant line to his work that arises from a deep well of artistry that we have just begun to tap."

—Melissa Cobb, producer

Opposite & pp. 58–63: *Kung Fu Panda* franchise character concepts

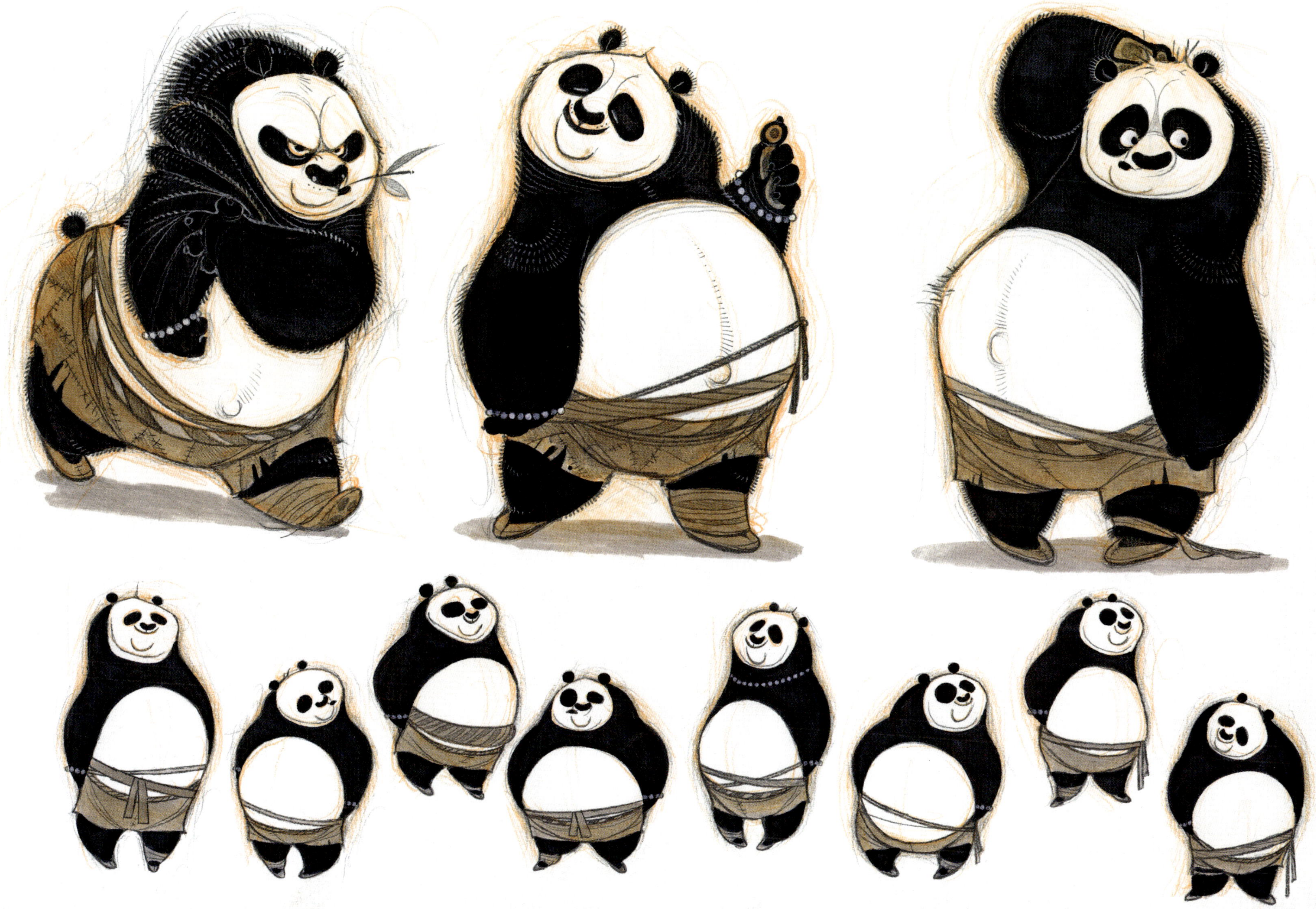

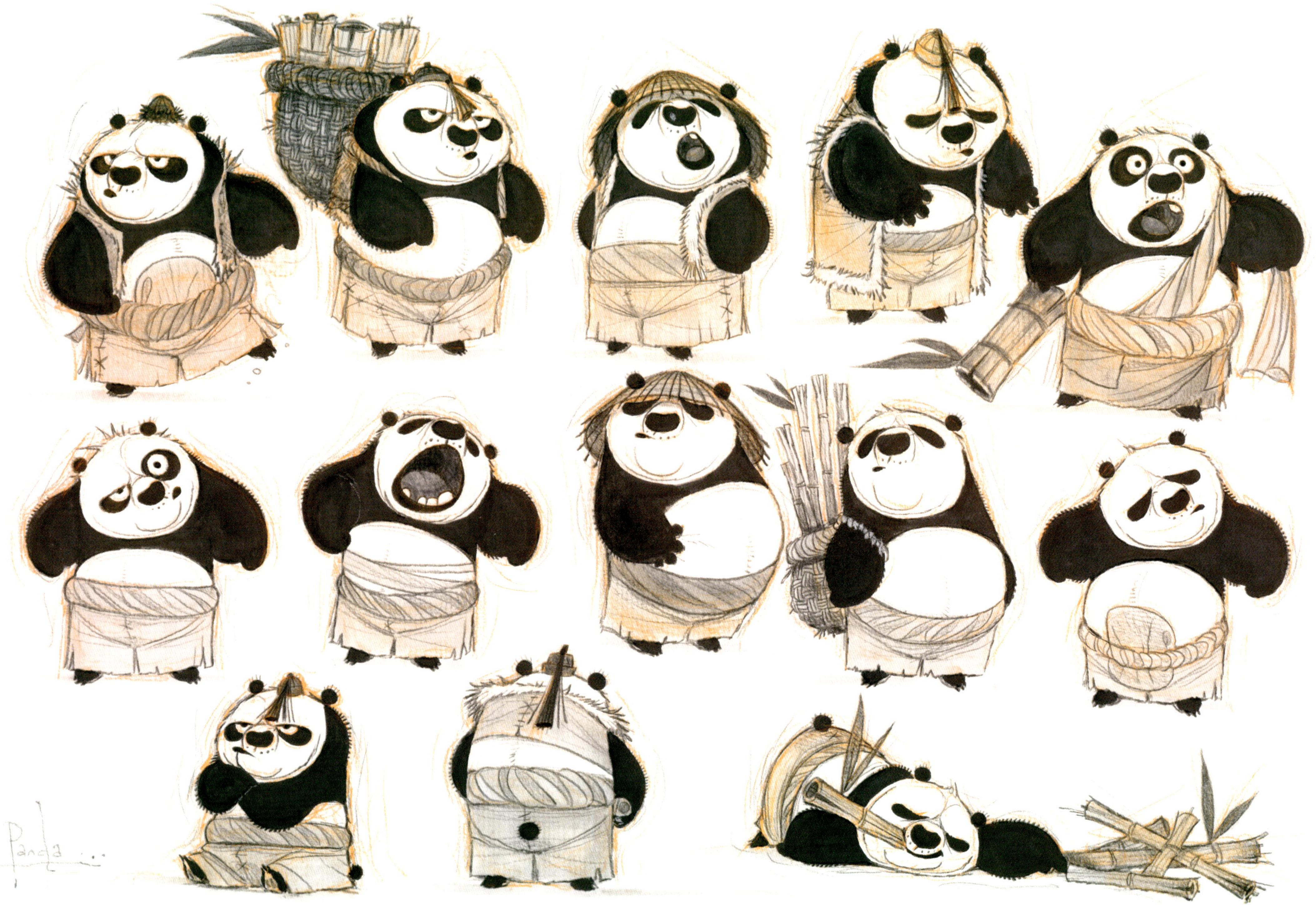
Panda

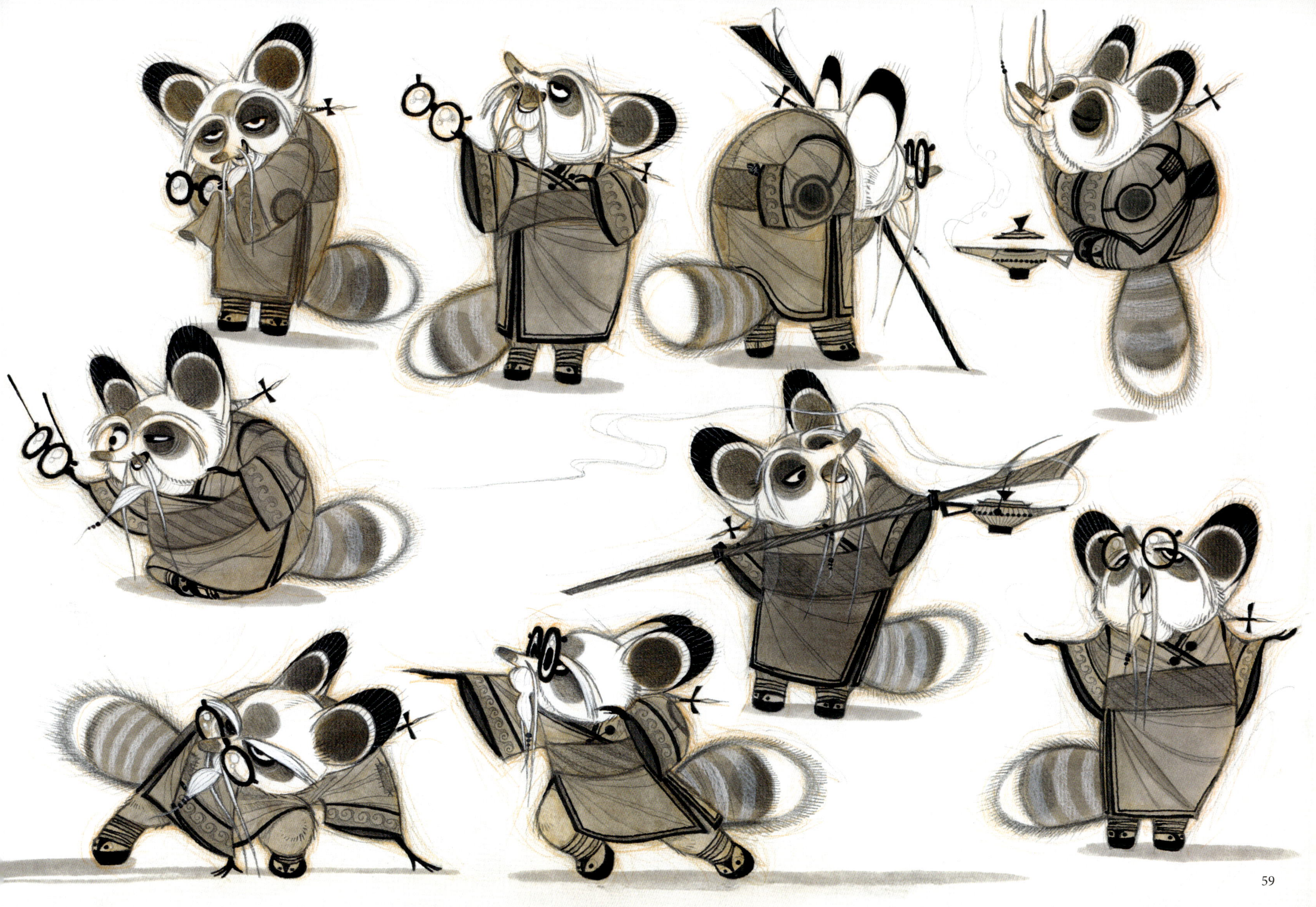

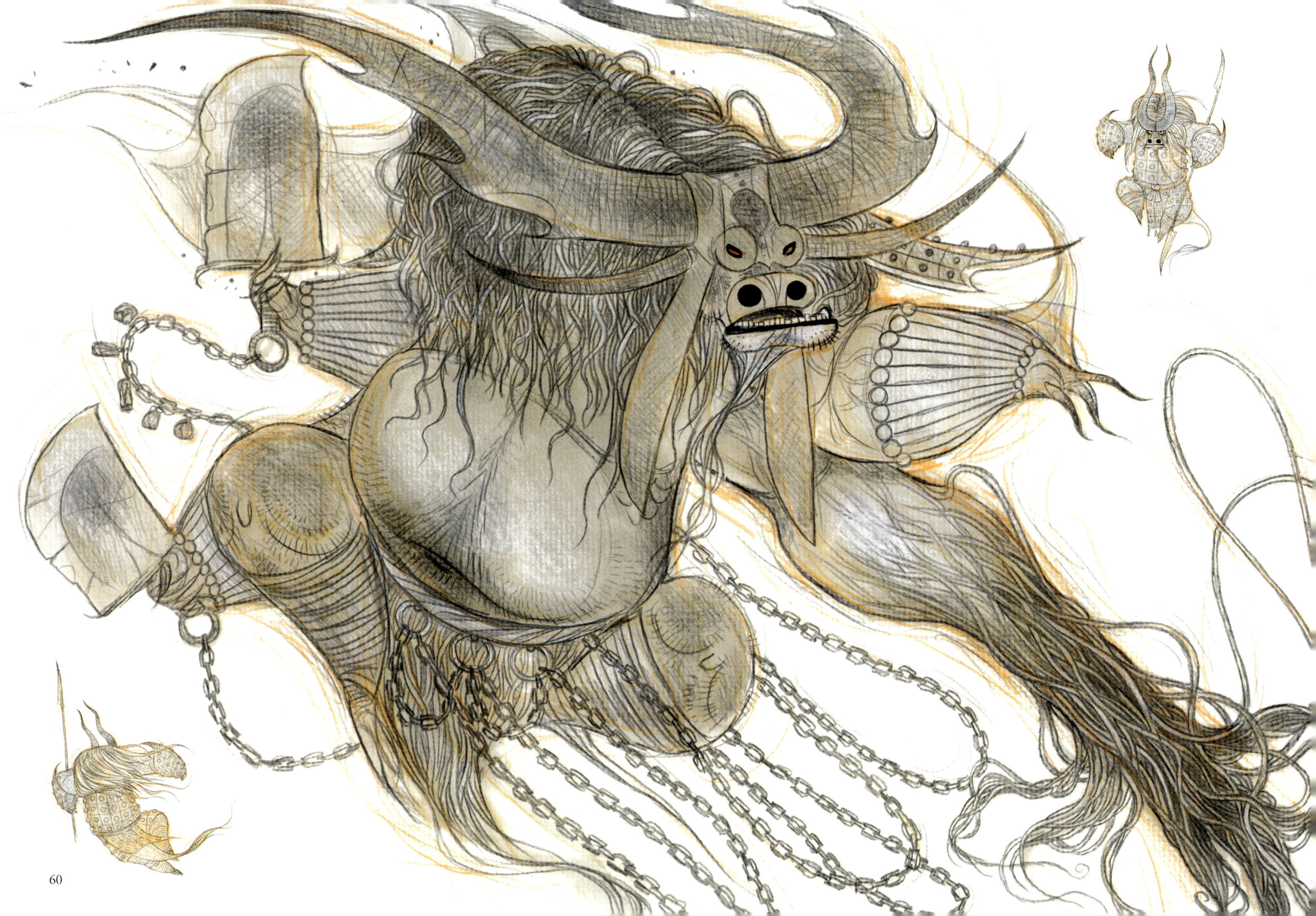

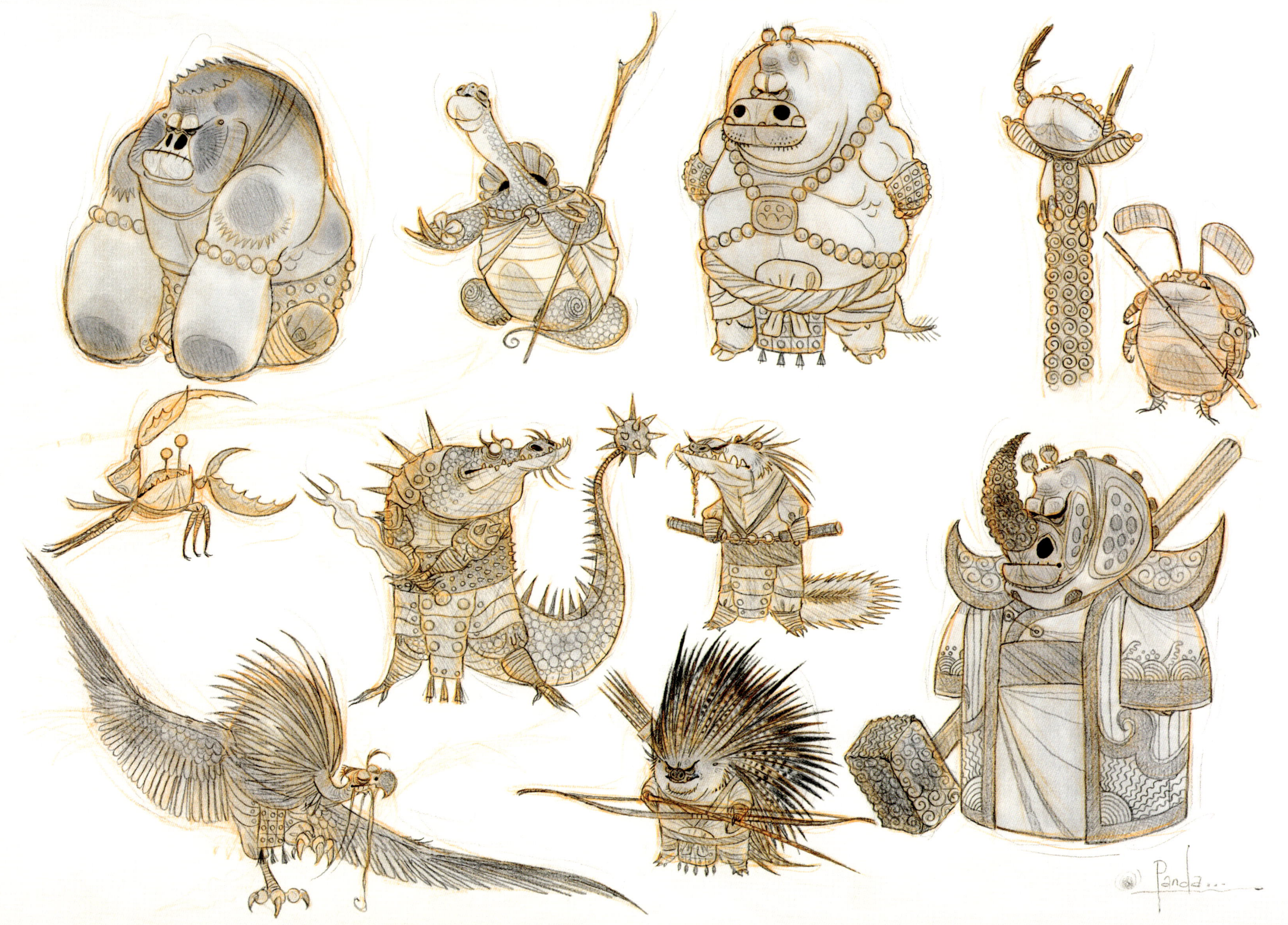
Panda...

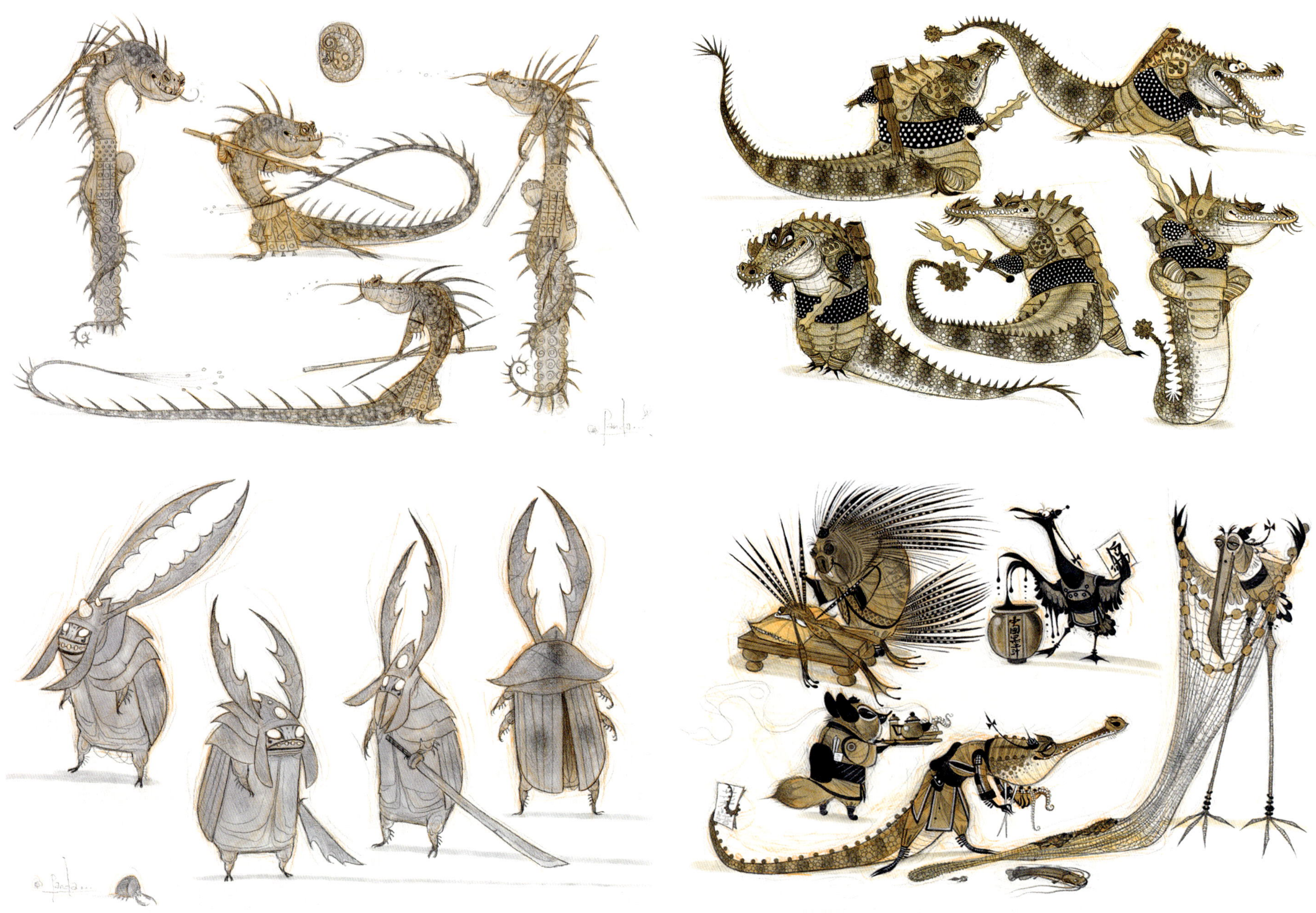

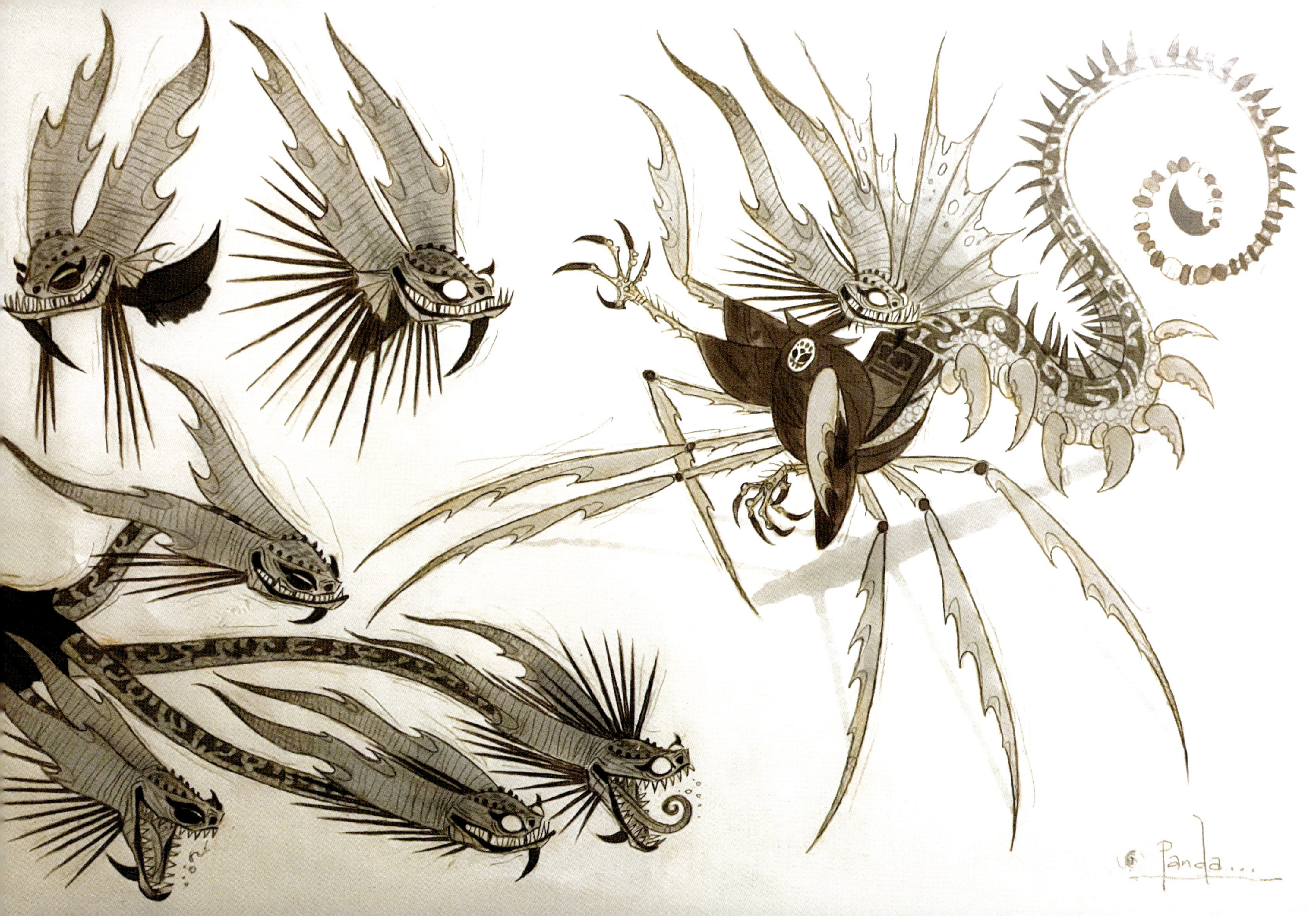
Panda...

Dragons & More

NICO'S PATH TO DRAGONS began early when he was only seven years old. "My grandfather was very cheeky with us grandchildren," Nico says. "One summer day, he gave me and my sister a shoebox with some holes in it and told us to try to capture the baby dragons out in the garden. We spent all day chasing lizards, thinking we were catching baby dragons—the way you might believe in Santa Claus. He never told us it was not true, and for years and years every summer, we would go into the garden and chase baby dragons—catching and releasing them, waiting patiently for the dragons to grow up." It seems Nico's destiny was to continue to release dragons into this world through his drawings, as manifested in the animation legacy of the *How to Train Your Dragon* films and series.

"I was incredibly lucky to have Nico Marlet draw the initial studies for the characters in How to Train Your Dragon. *They were joyous, seemingly effortless, and encapsulated the sheer range of what was going to be achieved in the eventual film. They were by turns humorous, elegant, and awe-inspiring. But what makes Nico Marlet's drawings truly remarkable is not just the beauty and the flair of his designs, but their emotional quality. He really seems to be able to explore the heart and soul of a character through his drawing. I remember his very first drawings of Hiccup, how tender and protective he made you feel toward that character. I remember visiting Nico's workspace at DreamWorks and seeing that he had pinned up a small picture of Hiccup, taken from the not-very-well-known picture book that was the first adventure of the character, written some time before I wrote* How to Train Your Dragon. *I had never told Nico that this was one of the very first paintings I had ever made of Hiccup. Nico just knew intuitively that it was important to the heart of the character, so he was using that particular picture as his inspiration. It is that intuitive sense of what is truly important that makes Nico such a great illustrator. However splendid the movie, however magnificent the special effects, what really matters is the emotional connection that the audience has with the characters. Nico can create the beginnings of that. Every stylish stroke of his pencil is filled with an affectionate understanding of the character he is drawing, be they would-be hero, fiendish but slightly incompetent villain, or breathtakingly impressive fire-breathing dragon. He has a very rare gift."*

—**CRESSIDA COWELL, author**

"Nico's imagination is limitless. His creative visual contributions to the world of How to Train Your Dragon *brought to life the human characters as well as the hundreds of fantastical dragons that populate Hiccup's home of Berk and beyond. Nico was the perfect match for author Cressida Cowell—he was inspired by her energy and enhanced and expanded her vision beyond everyone's expectations."*

—**BONNIE ARNOLD, producer**

OPPOSITE & PP. 66–85: *How to Train Your Dragon* franchise character concepts

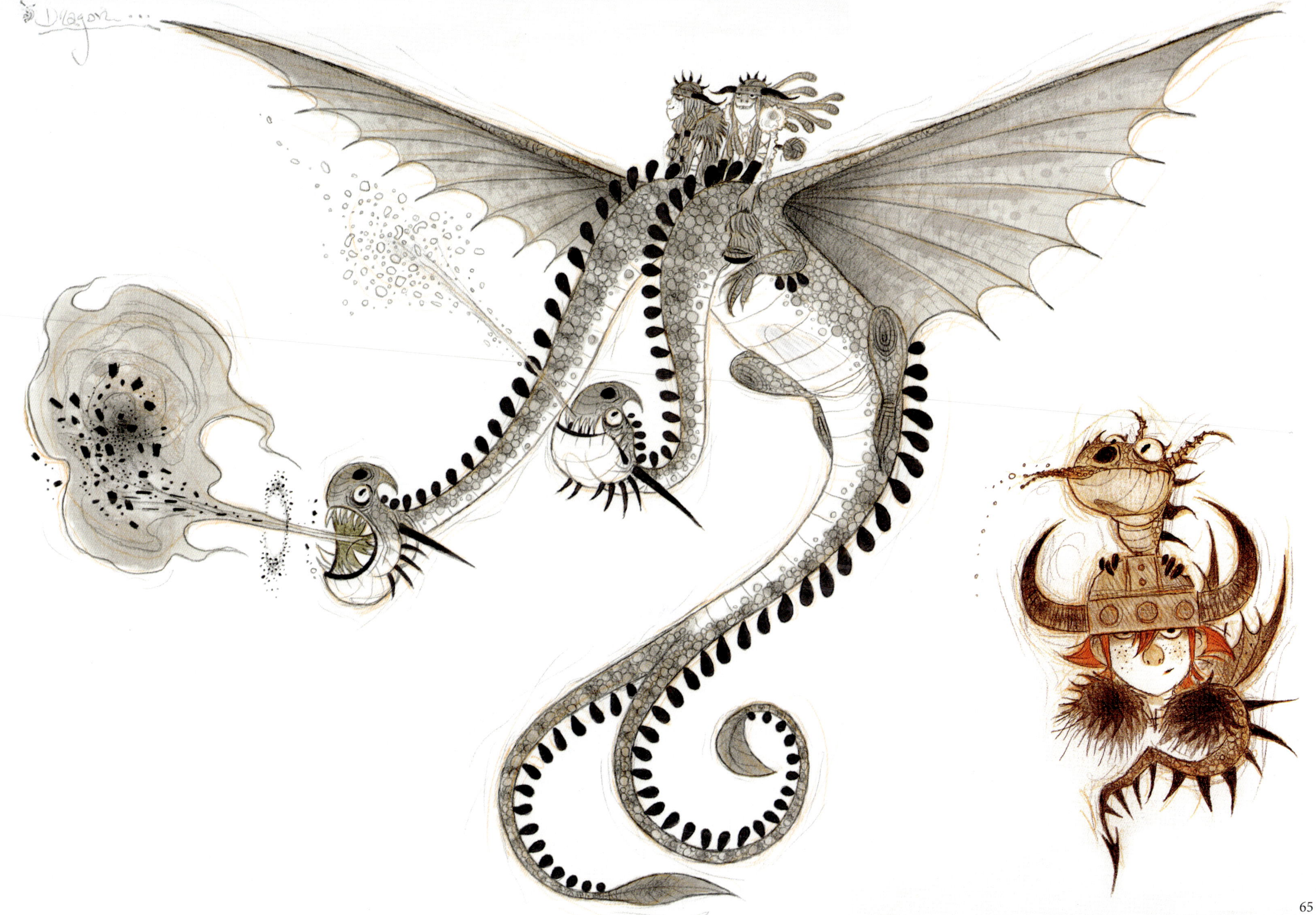
Dragon...

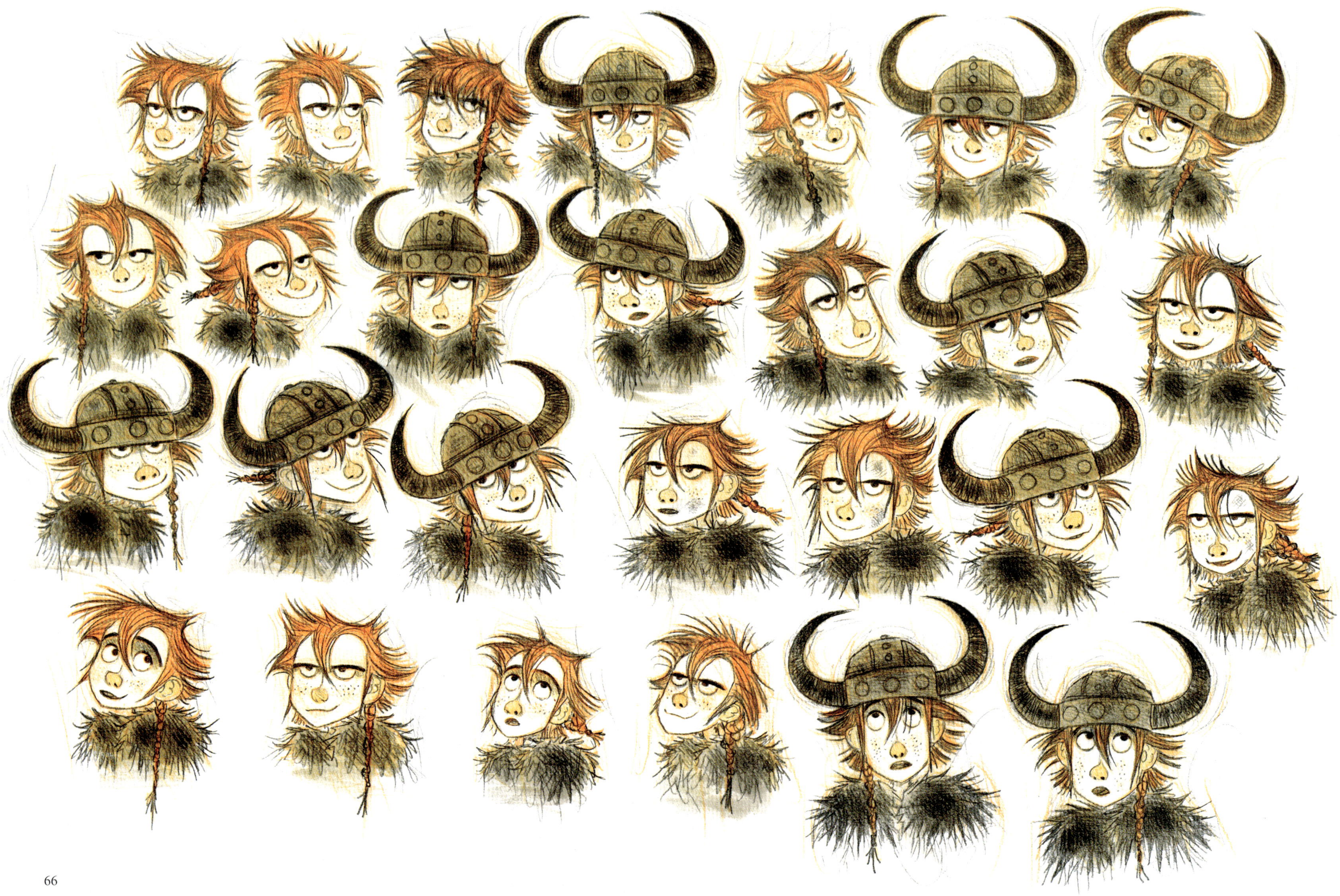

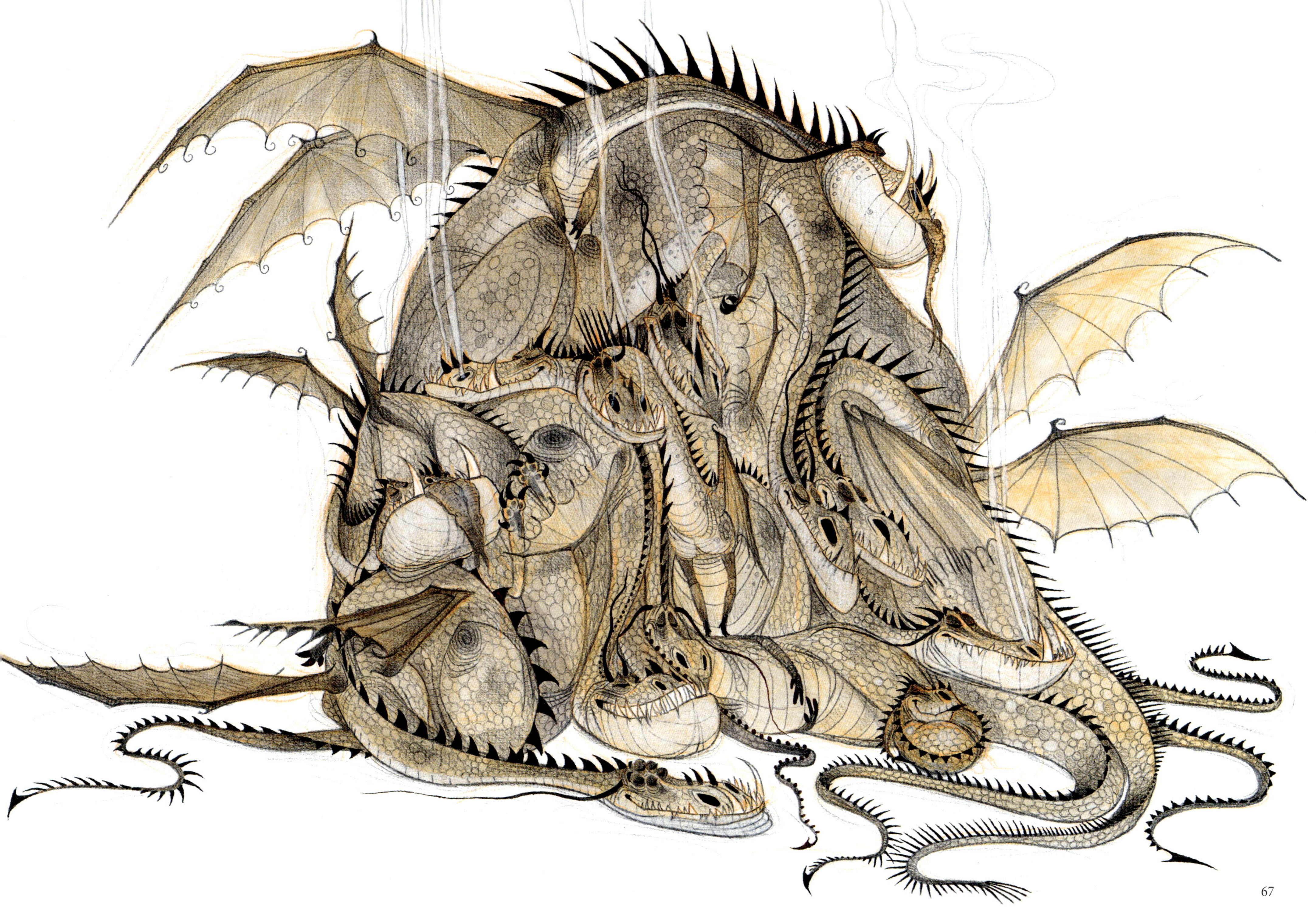

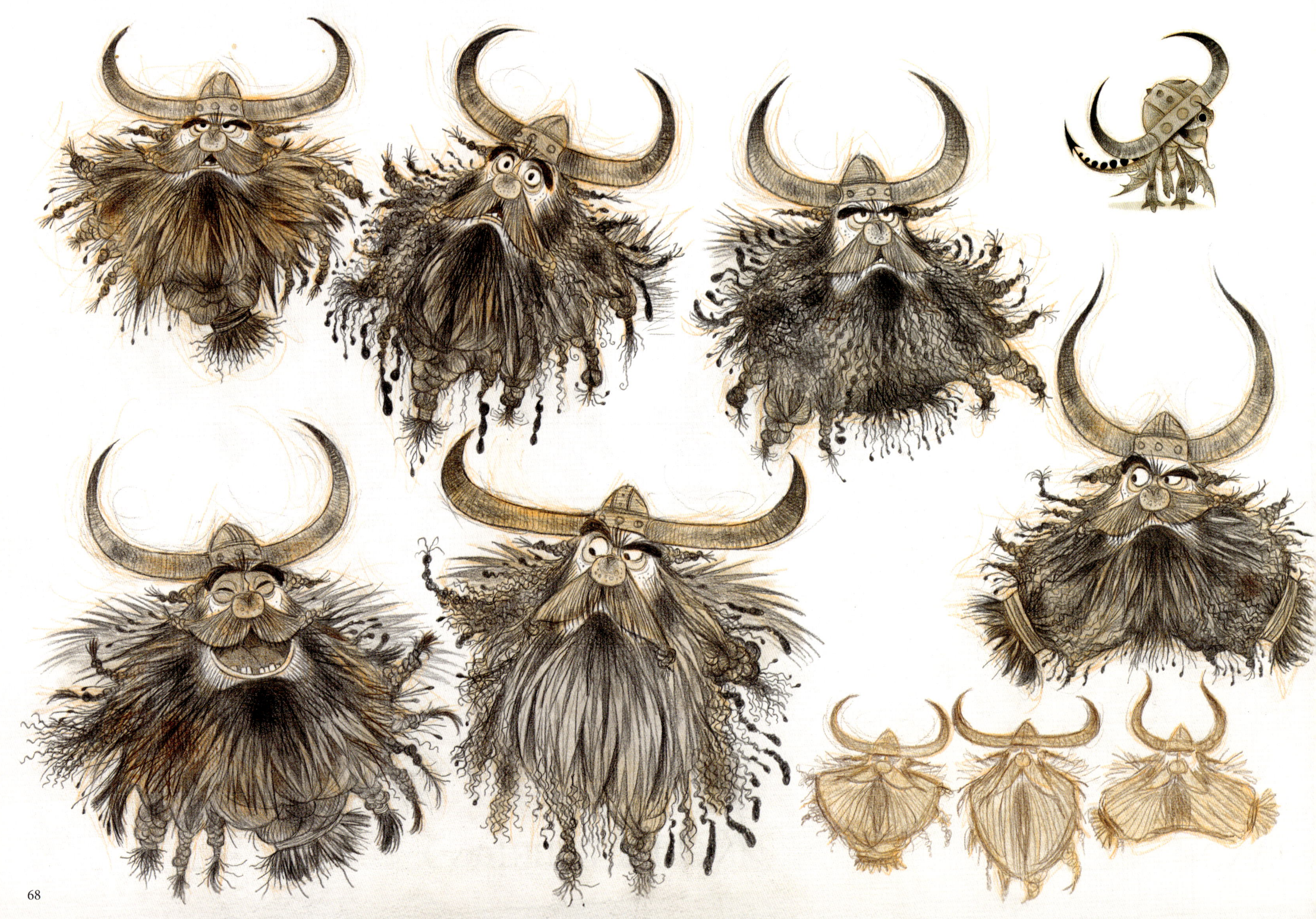

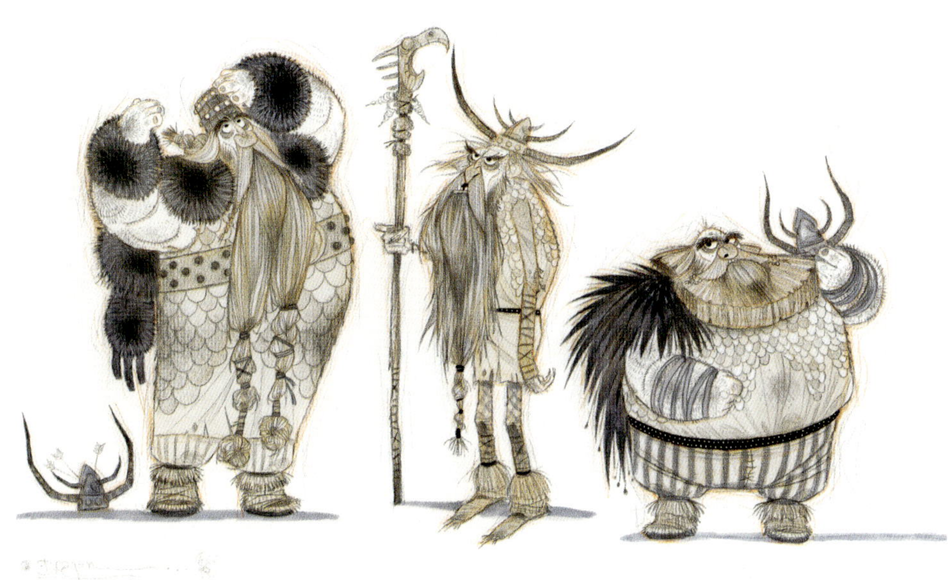

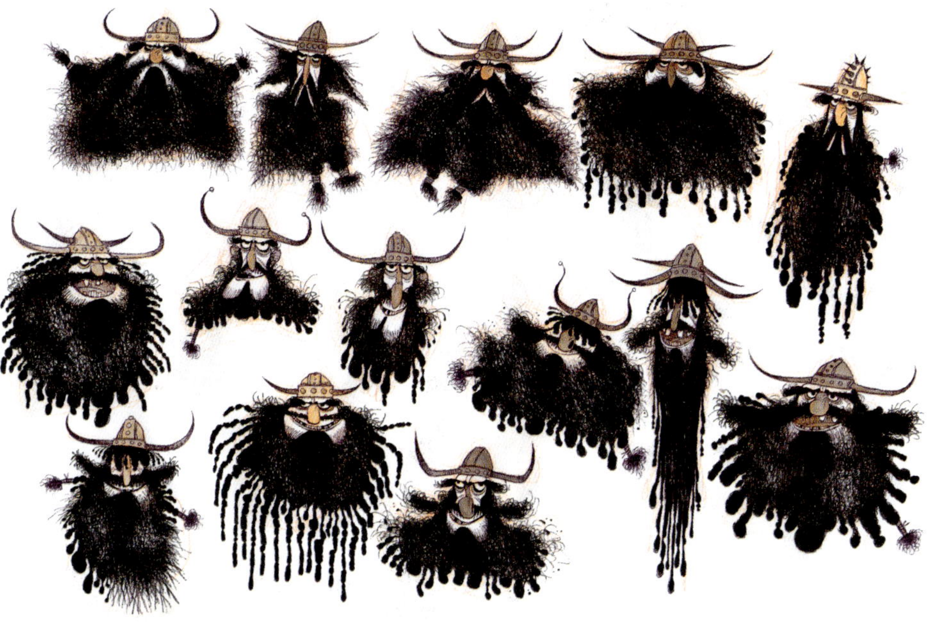

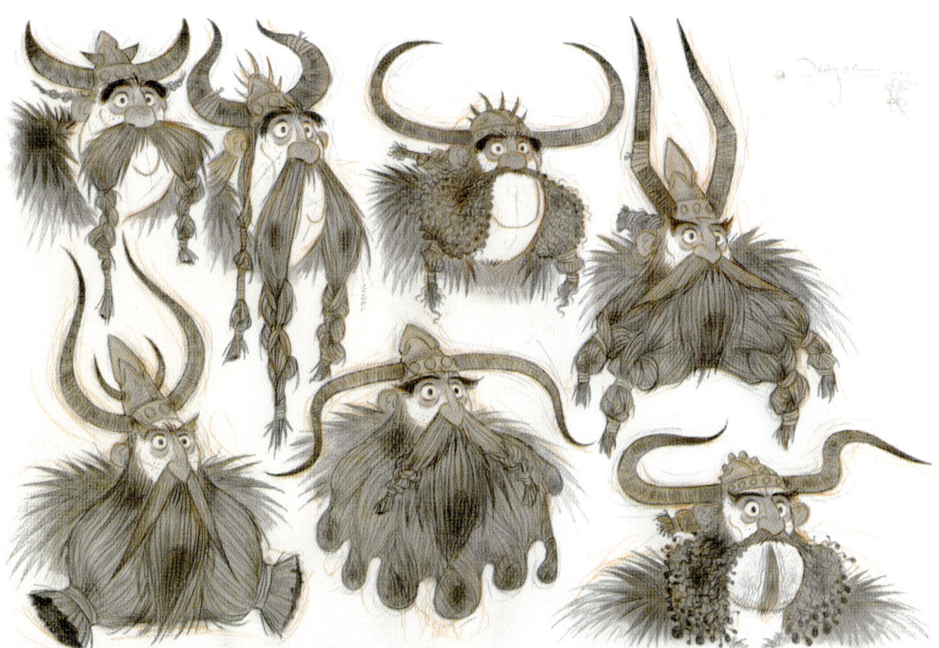

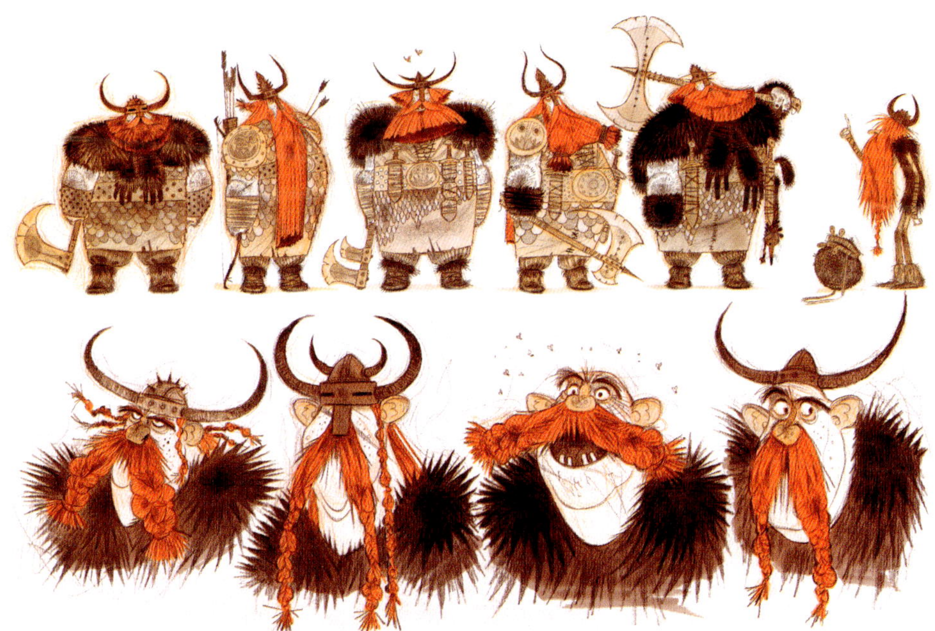

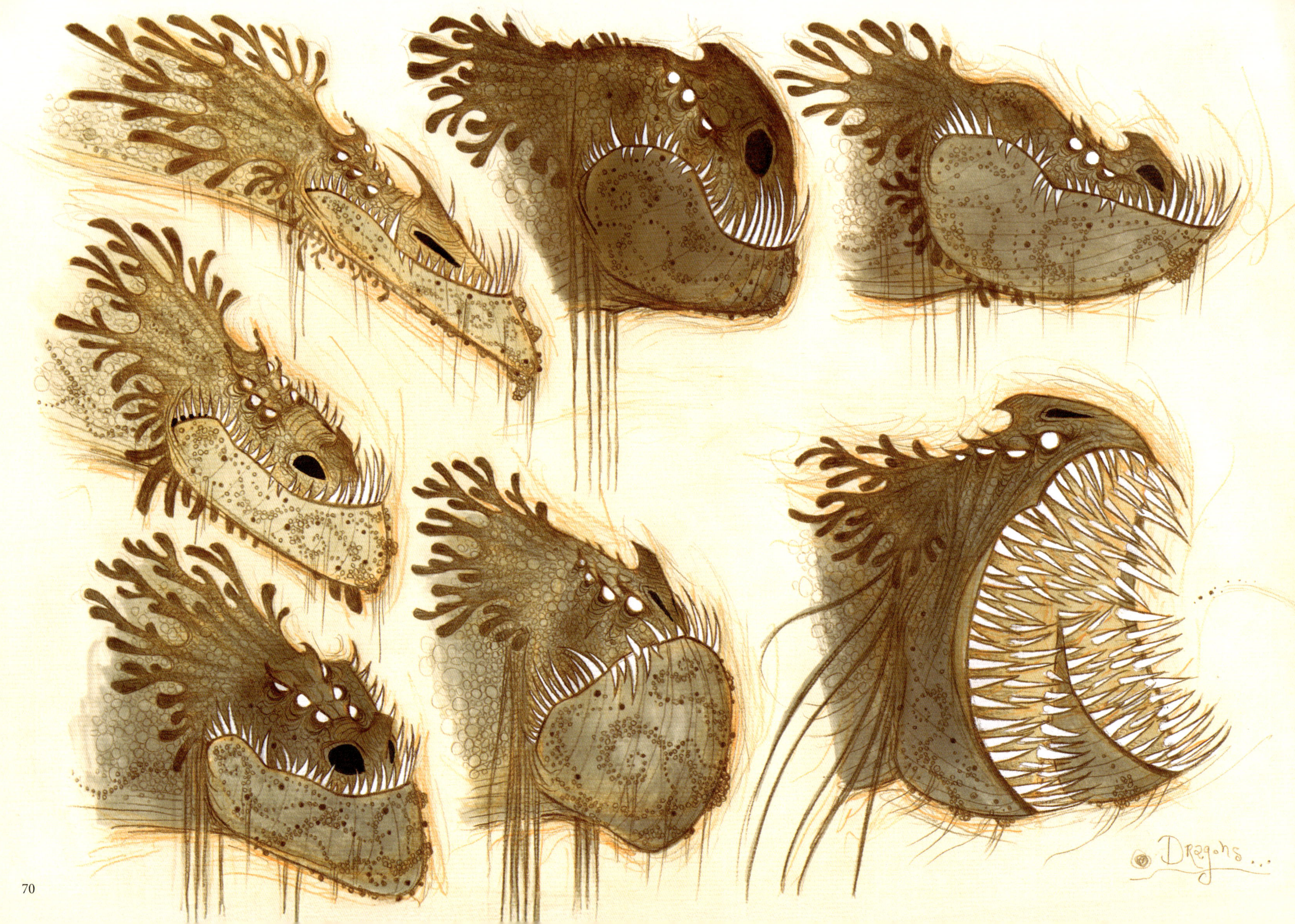
Dragons...

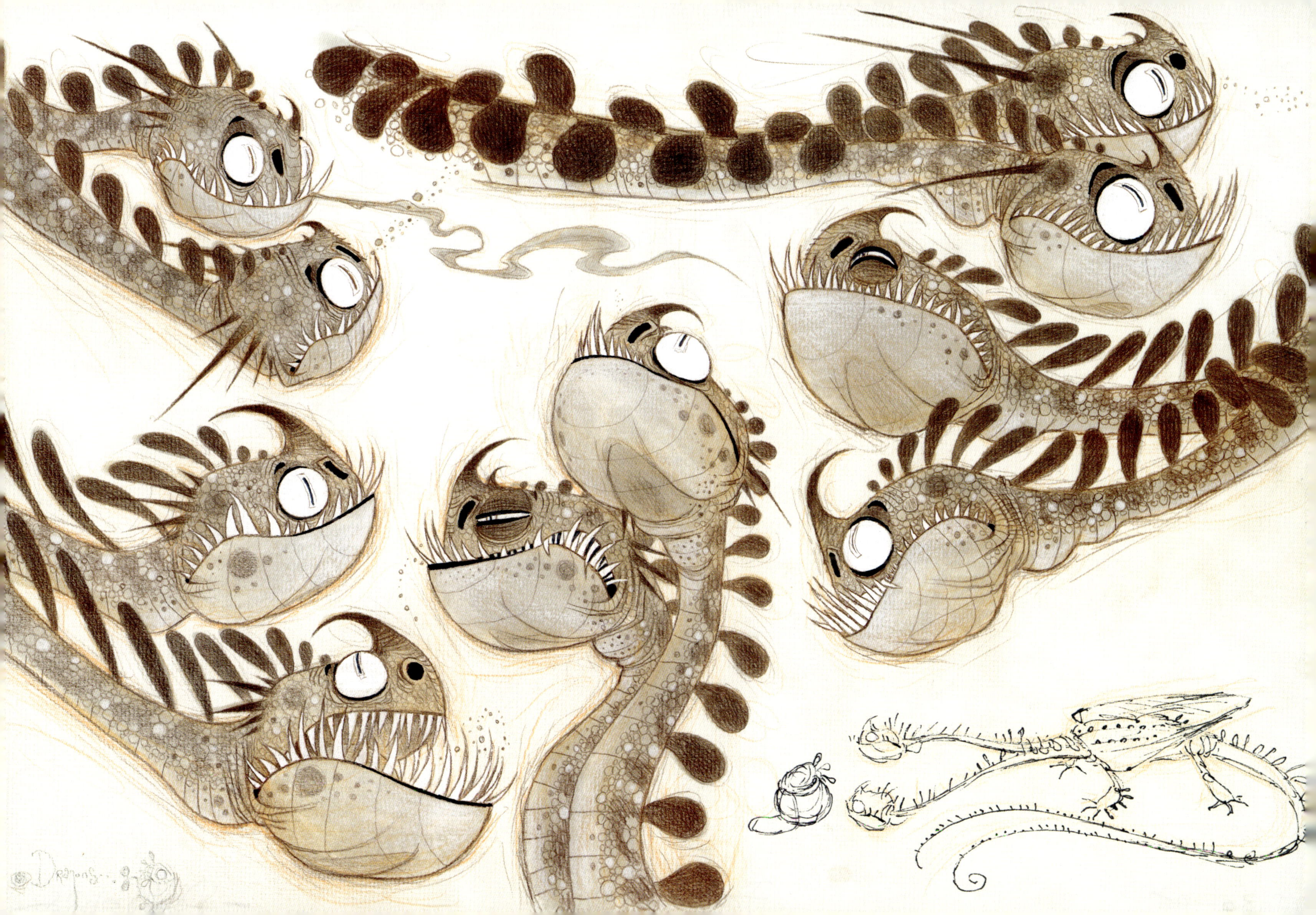

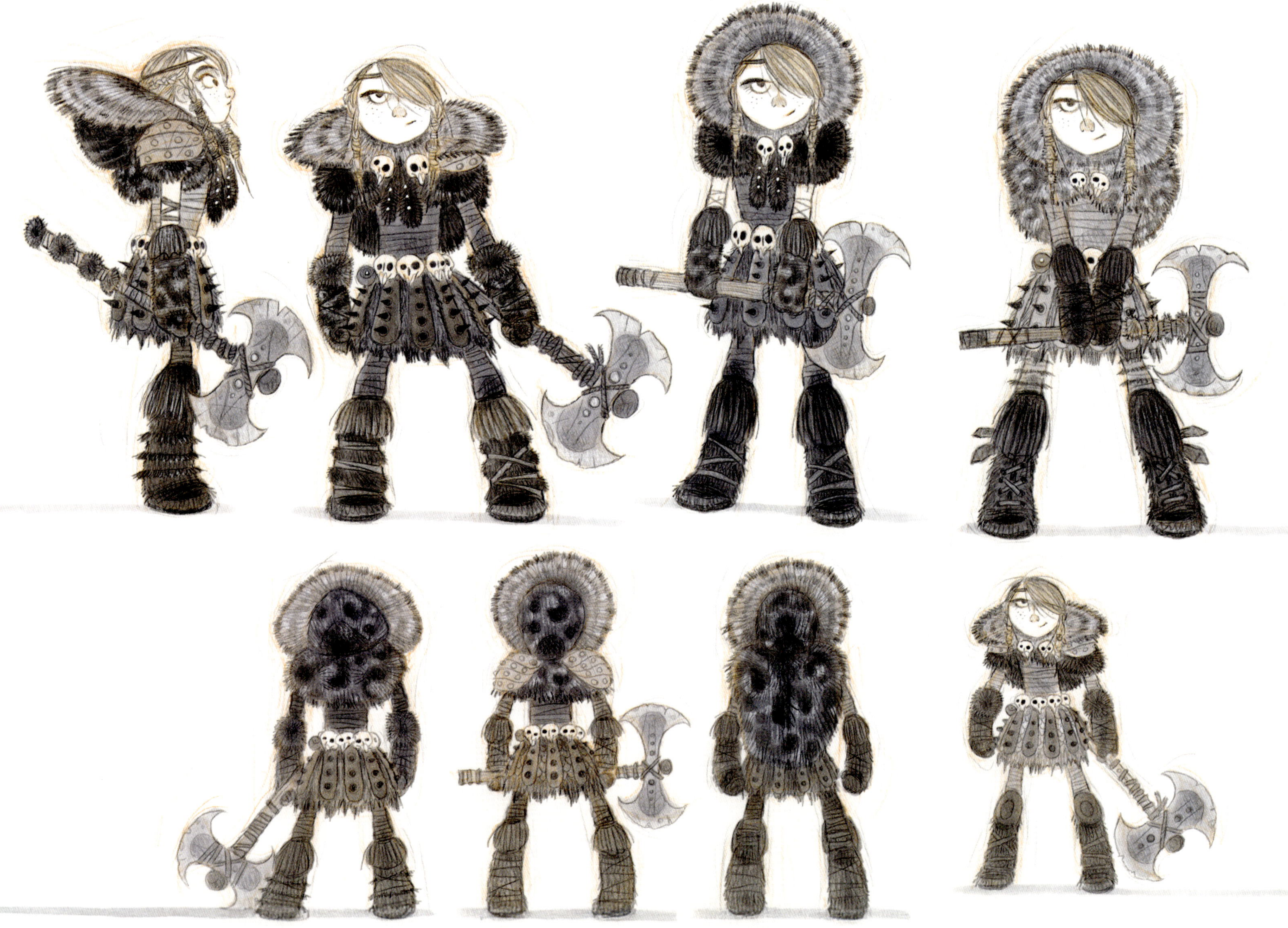

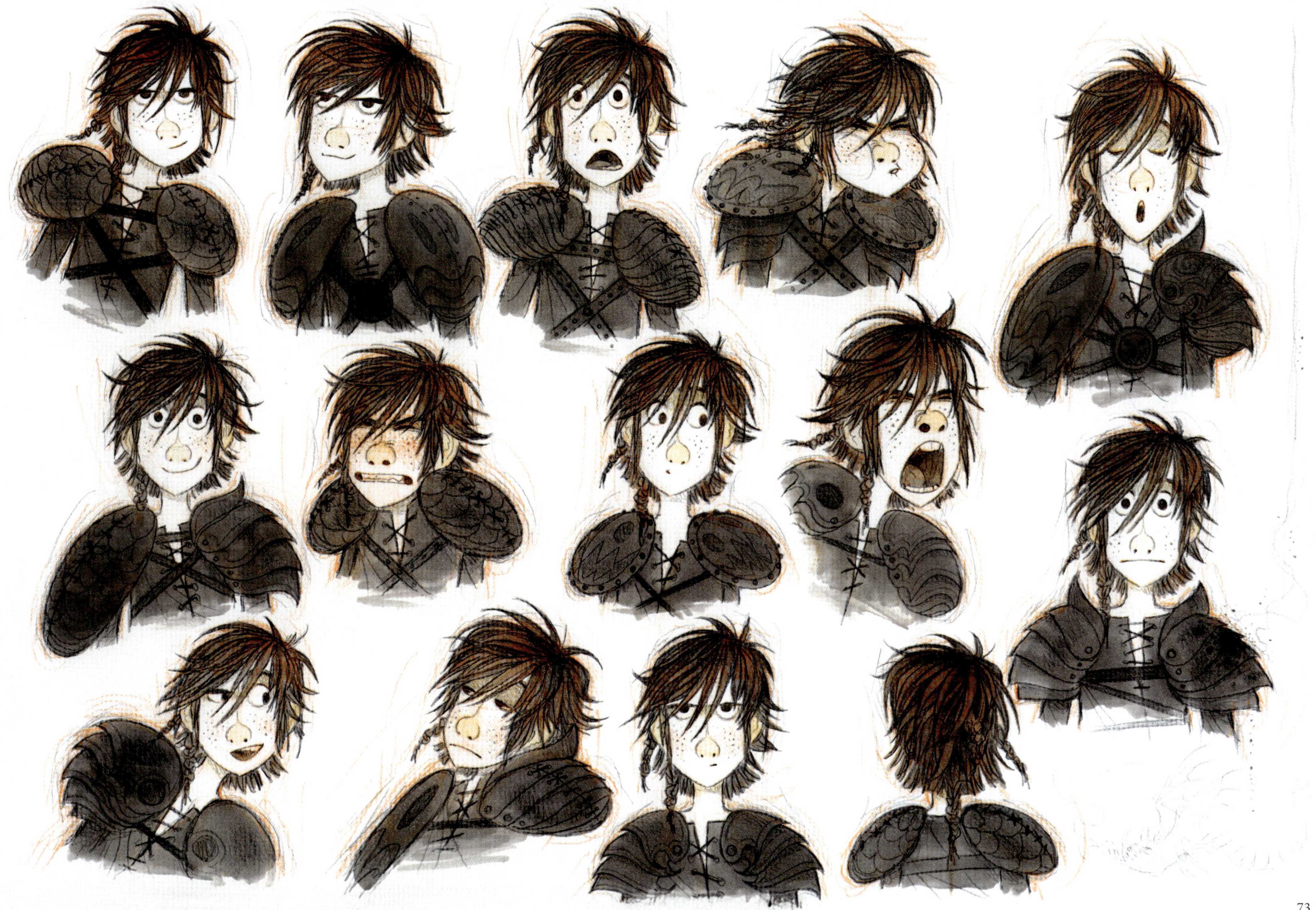

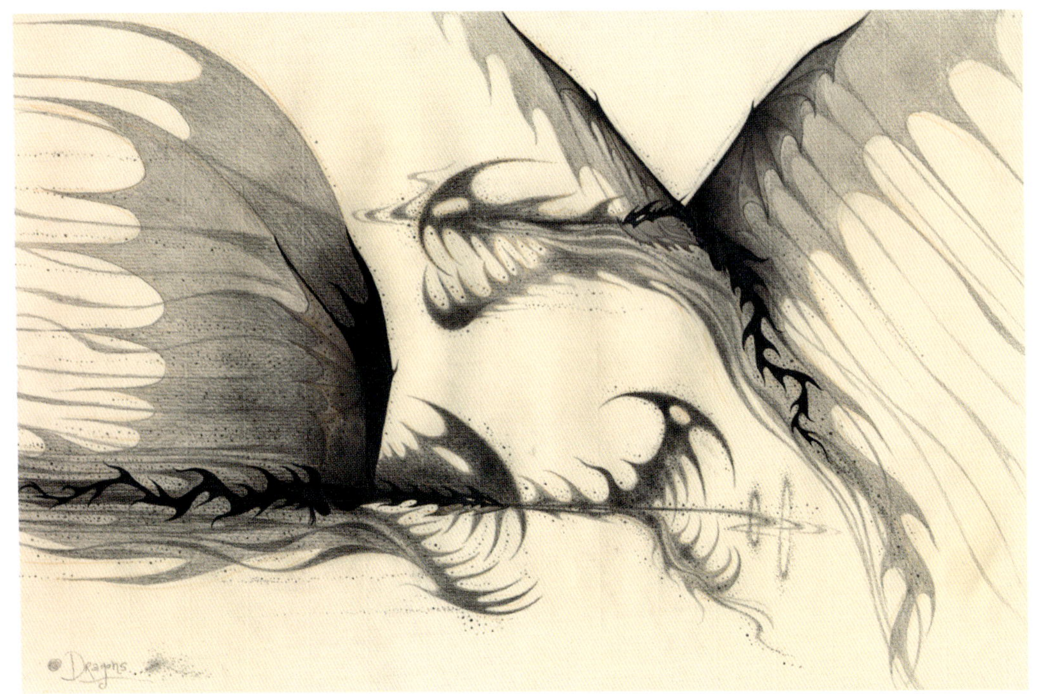

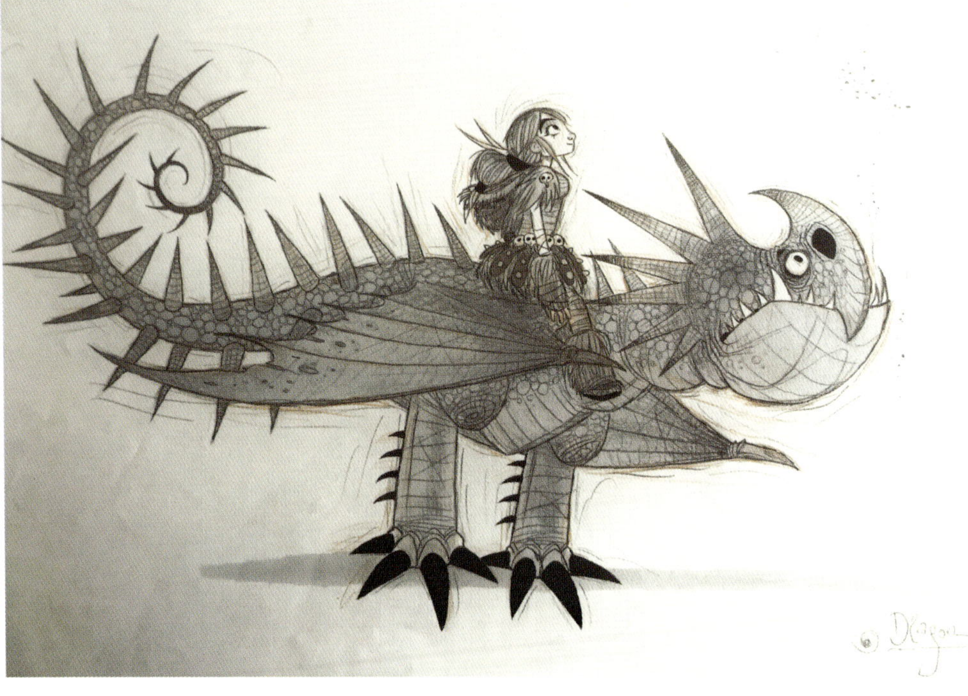

"I wouldn't be the same animator, nor draw the way I do today, without the influence of Nico Marlet's work. Copying, studying, and animating his designs has been essential to my journey as an artist. And I know I'm not alone—many animation artists would say the same. I don't believe I'm exaggerating when I say that animated films would look very different without Nico's influence. His work ranks among the most impactful character design contributions in recent [film] history. His ability to create graphically bold characters brimming with life, humor, and personality is simply stunning. Every sketch Nico produces tells a story. His work feels painted even when it's just colored pencil and paper, and each design is full of texture, movement, and meticulous detail. His characters aren't just in a dynamic pose; they tell a story, have history, quirks—and they leap off the page ready to go on an adventure. You can see his creative process in every line, how he entertains not just the viewer but first and foremost himself. As a result, his love for the characters shines through. Nico hasn't just shaped unforgettable heroes, eccentric villains, and whimsical sidekicks, but an entire generation of animators—and I feel lucky to have been able to look over his shoulders and leaf through the giant stacks of original drawings piled up around his desk."

—**Simon Otto, director**

Nico discovered that his dragon characters stir emotions unlike any previous designs, inspiring many to reach out with letters from around the world. He once gifted a friend of a friend a dragon drawing who, at "the moment she opened the package, she cried! I couldn't believe it . . . I was so happy I did that drawing; her emotion was the best compliment I ever received, actually. She wasn't expecting it, and then she cried. It's incredible."

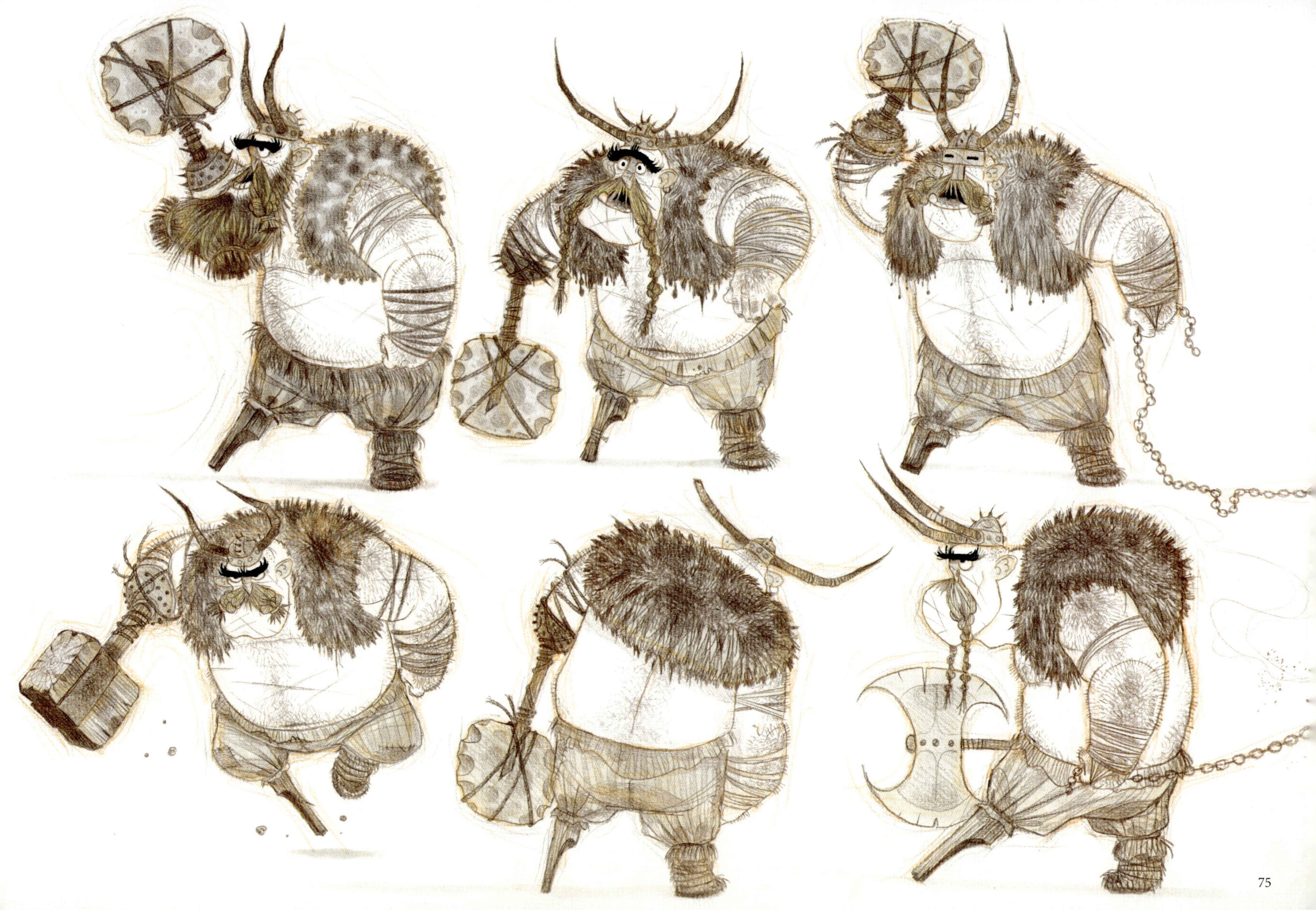

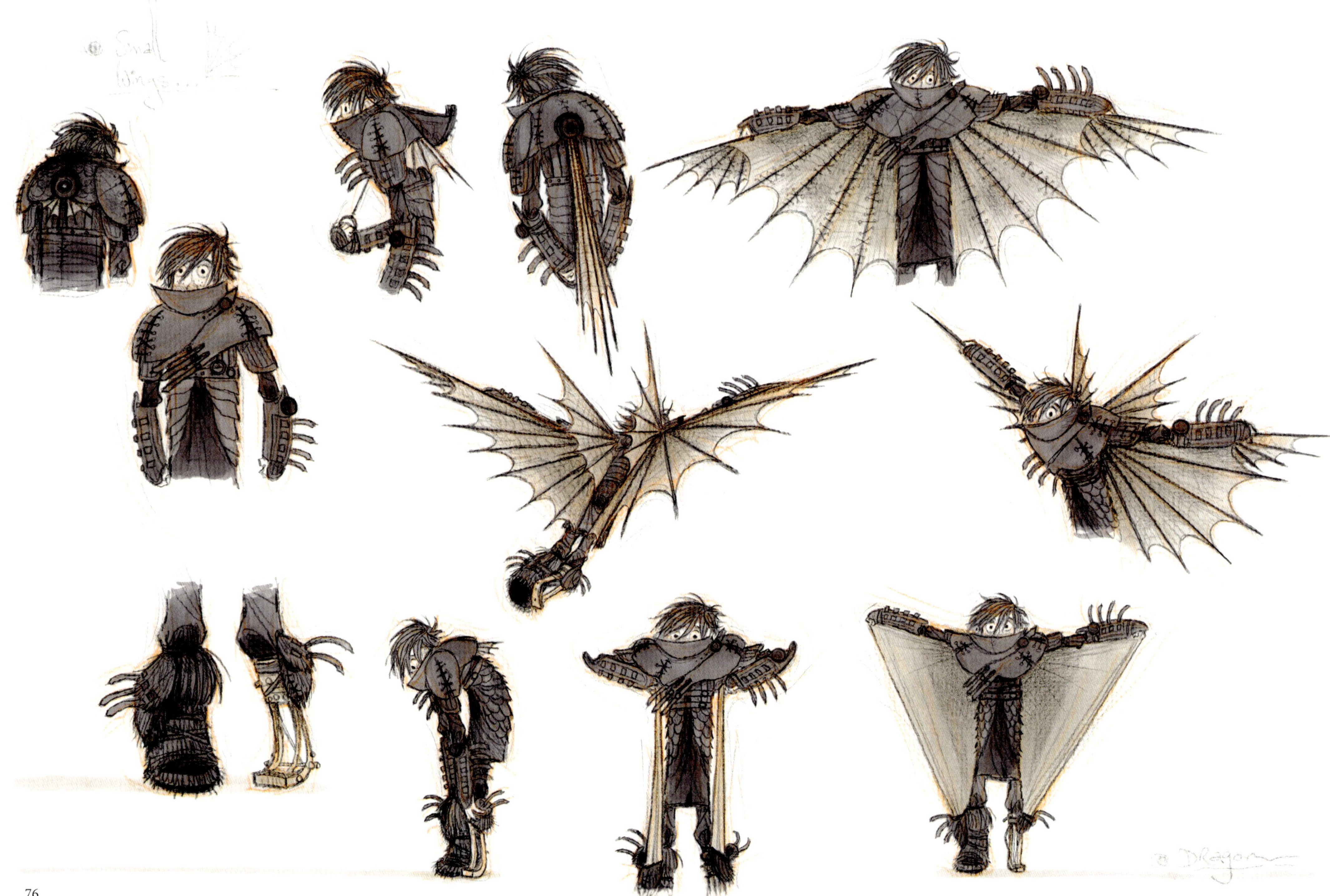
Small Wings...

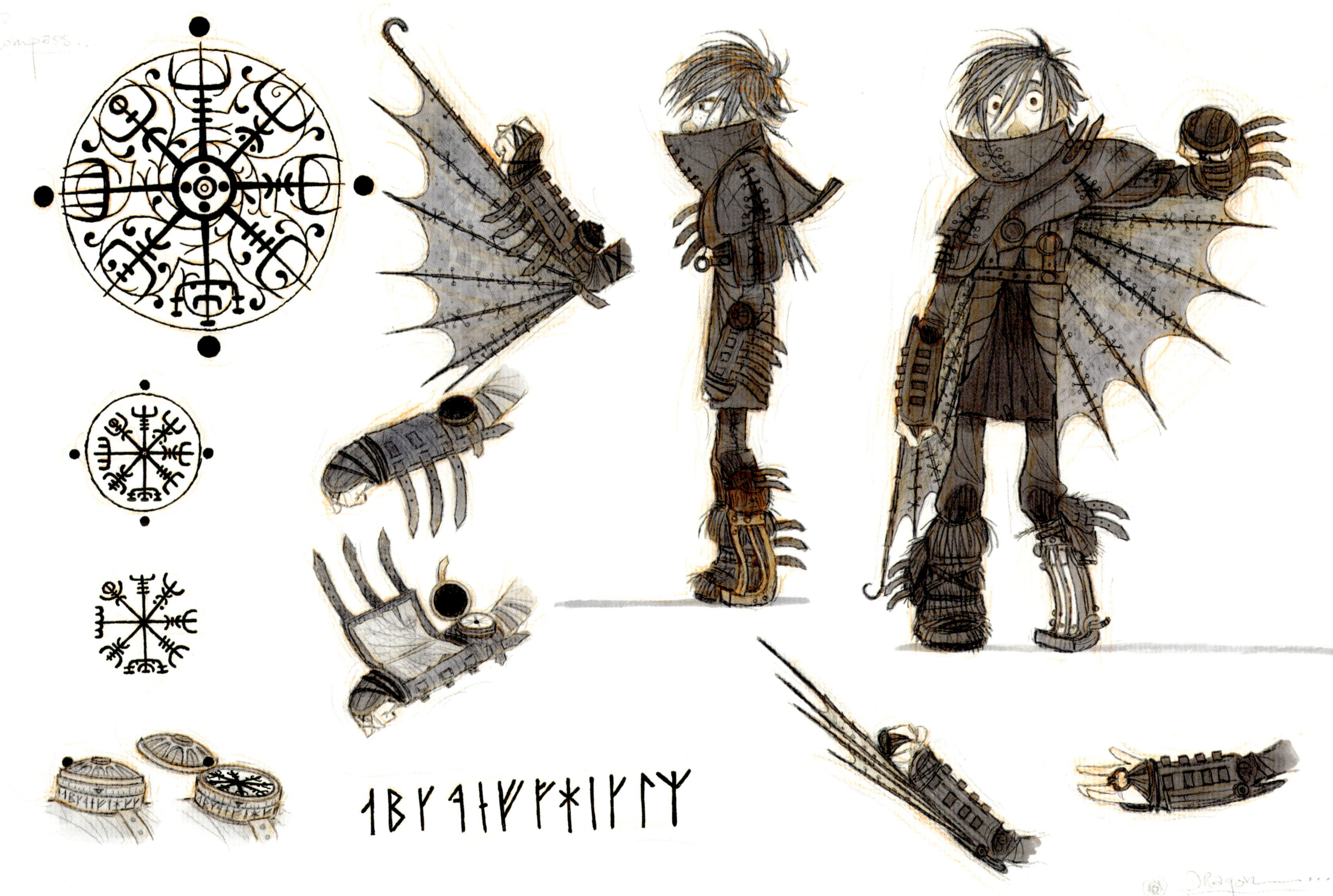
Compass...
Dragon...

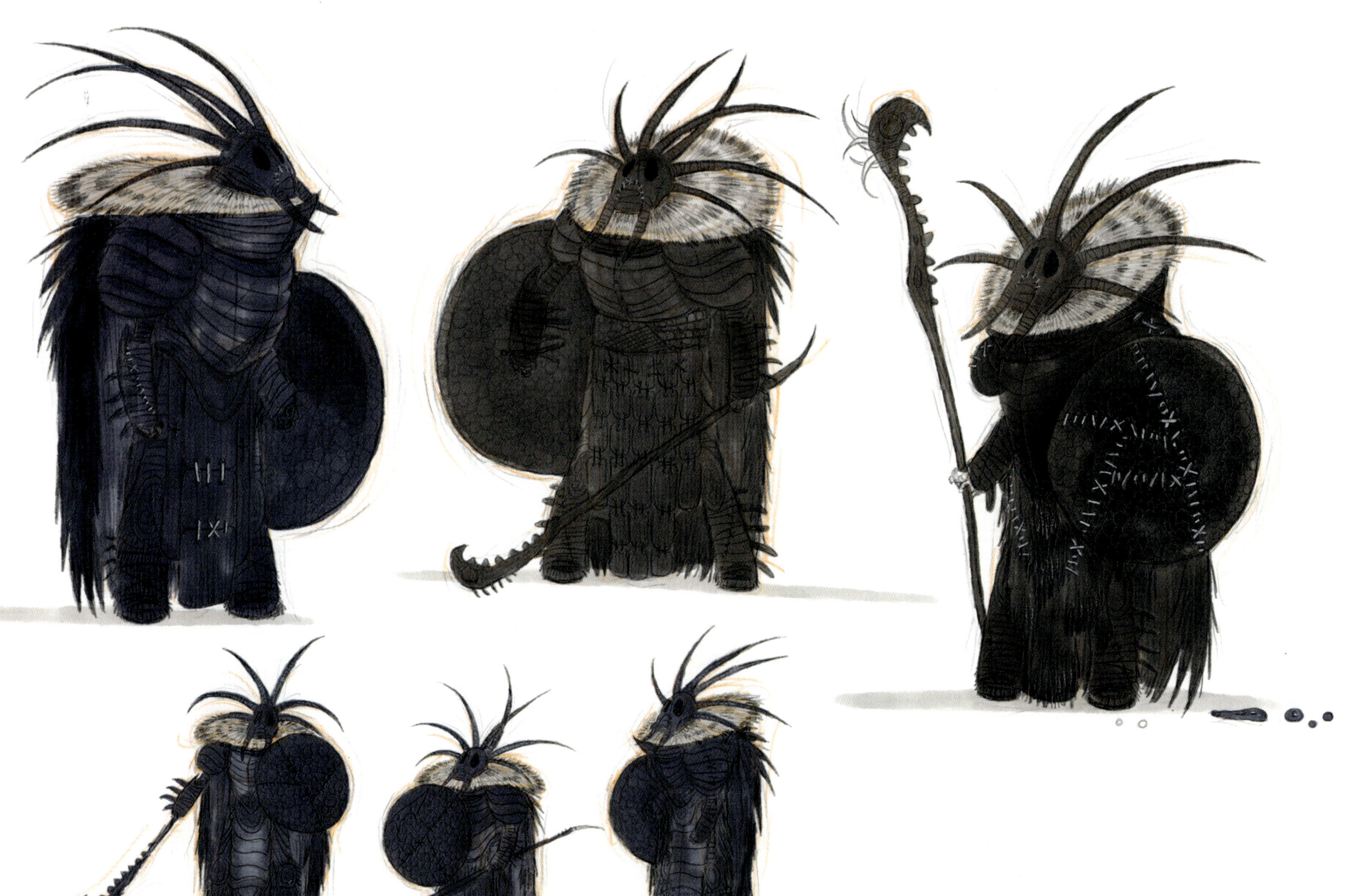
Dragon

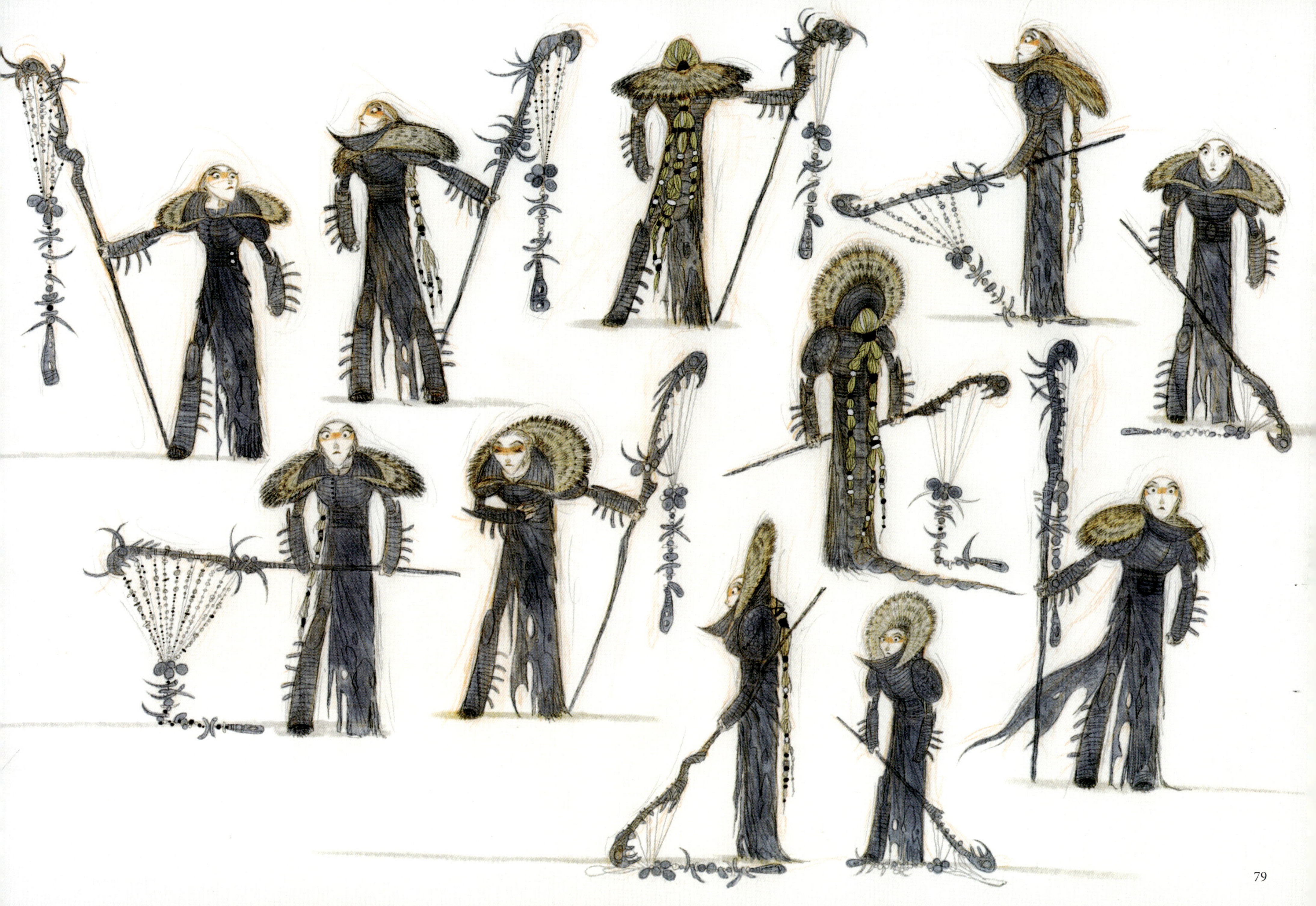

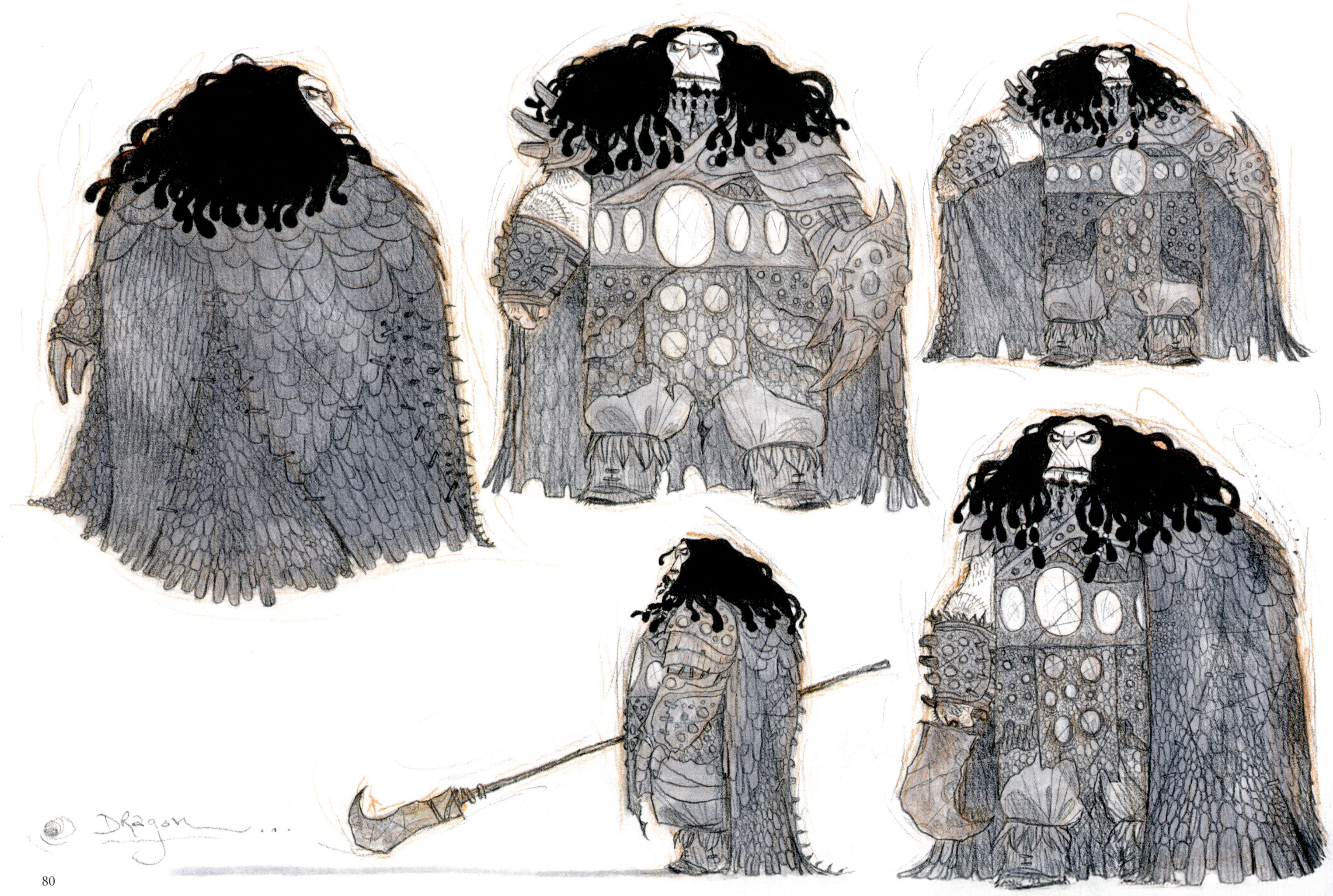
Dragon...

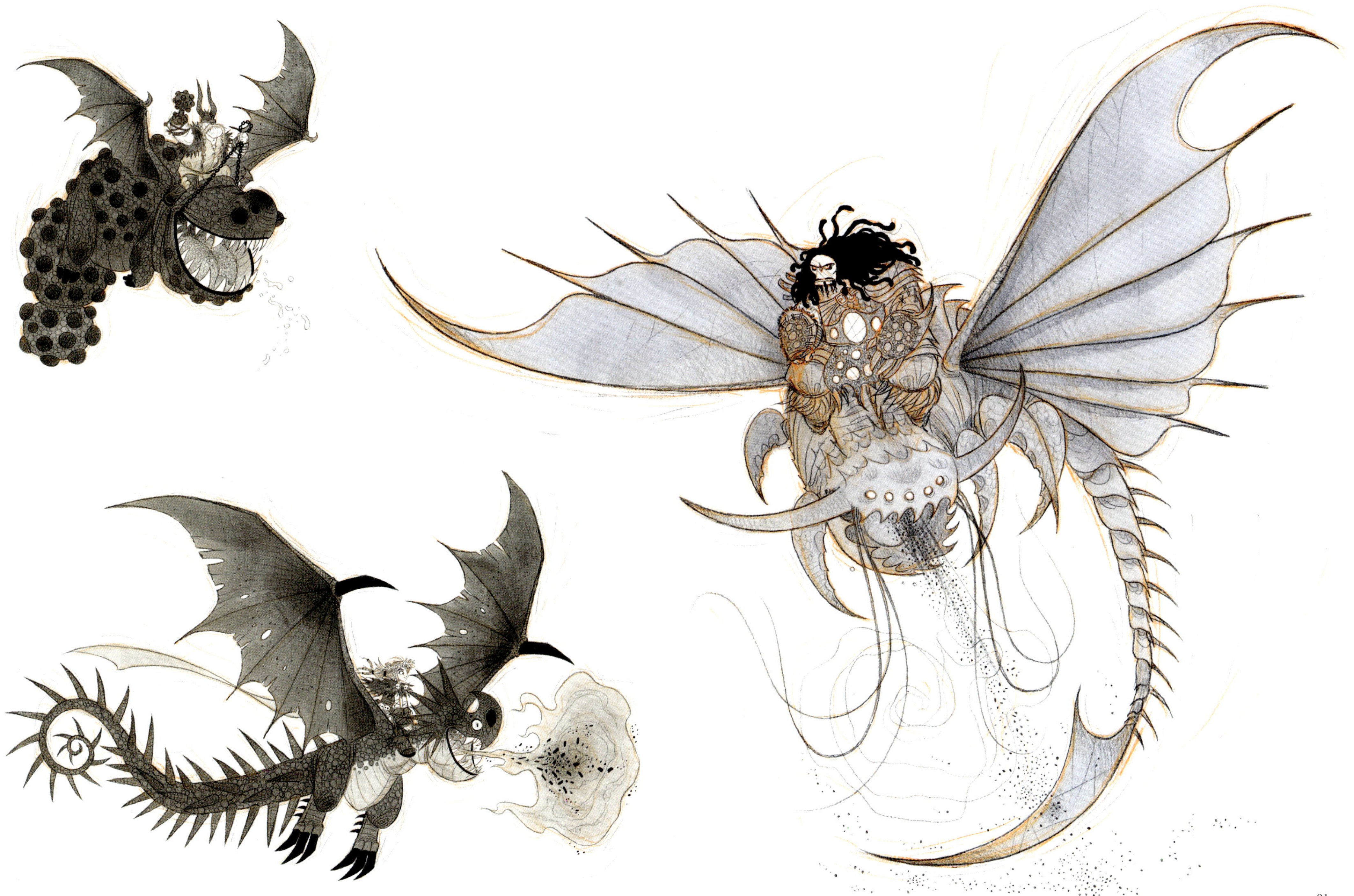

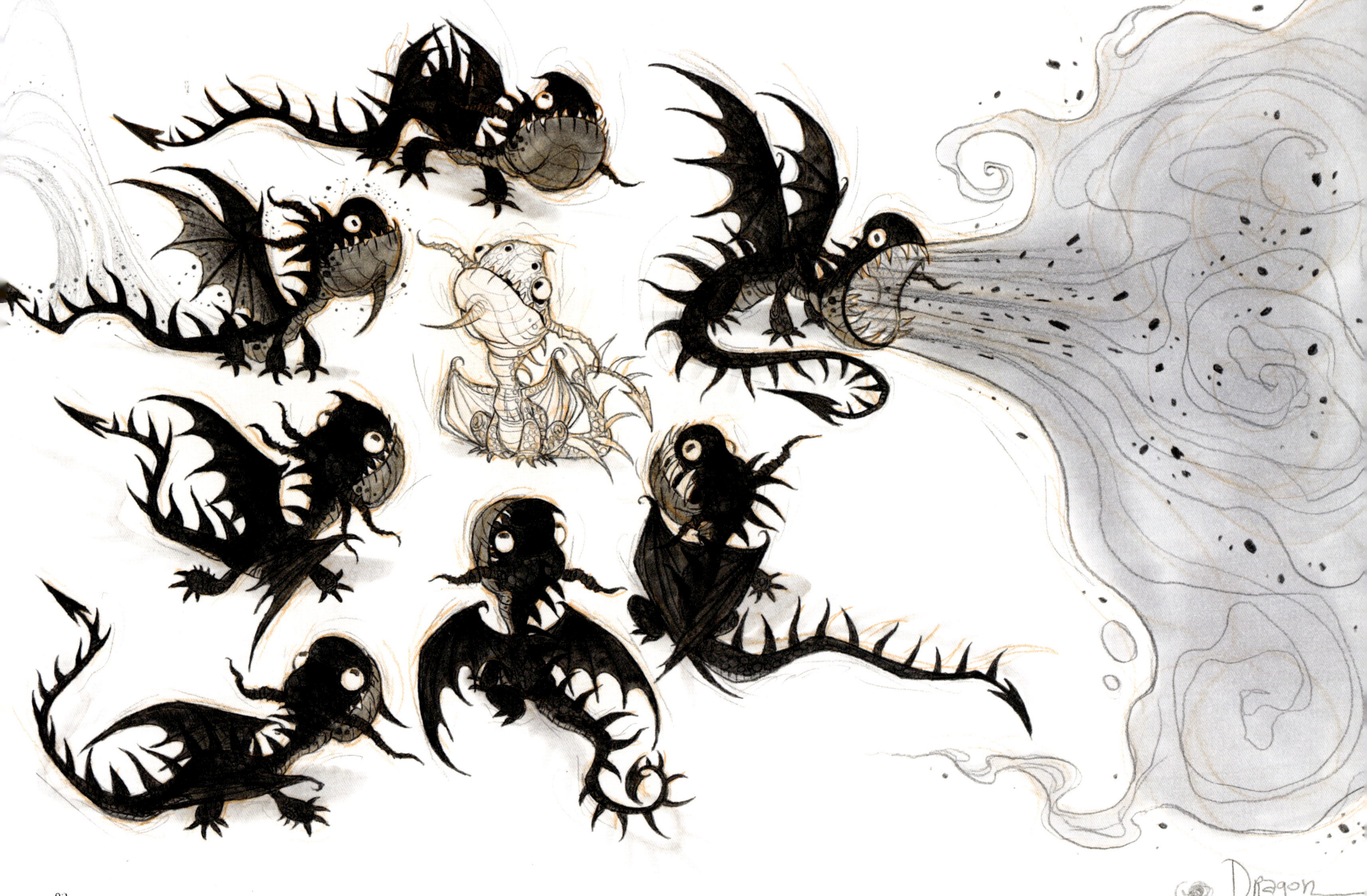
Dragon

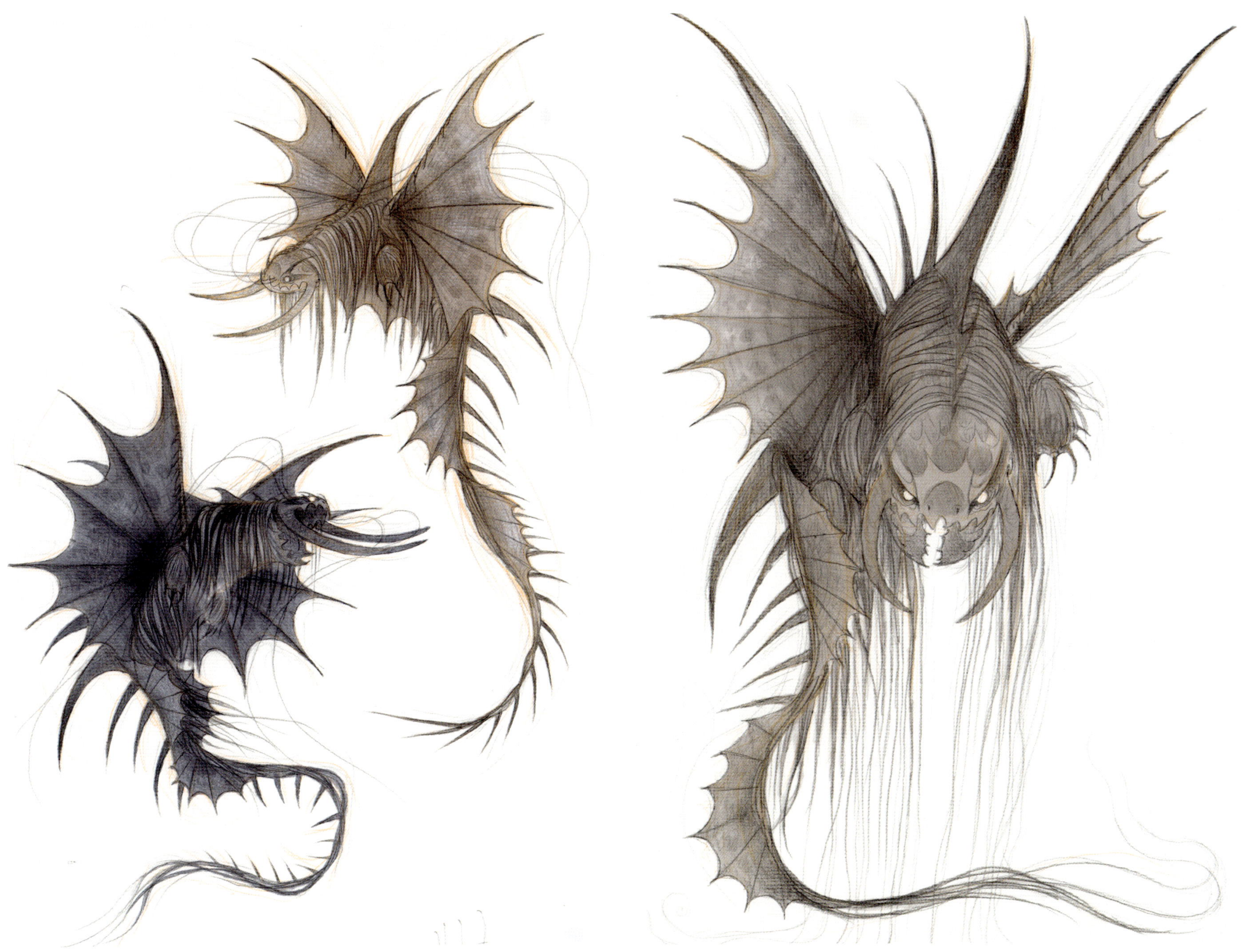

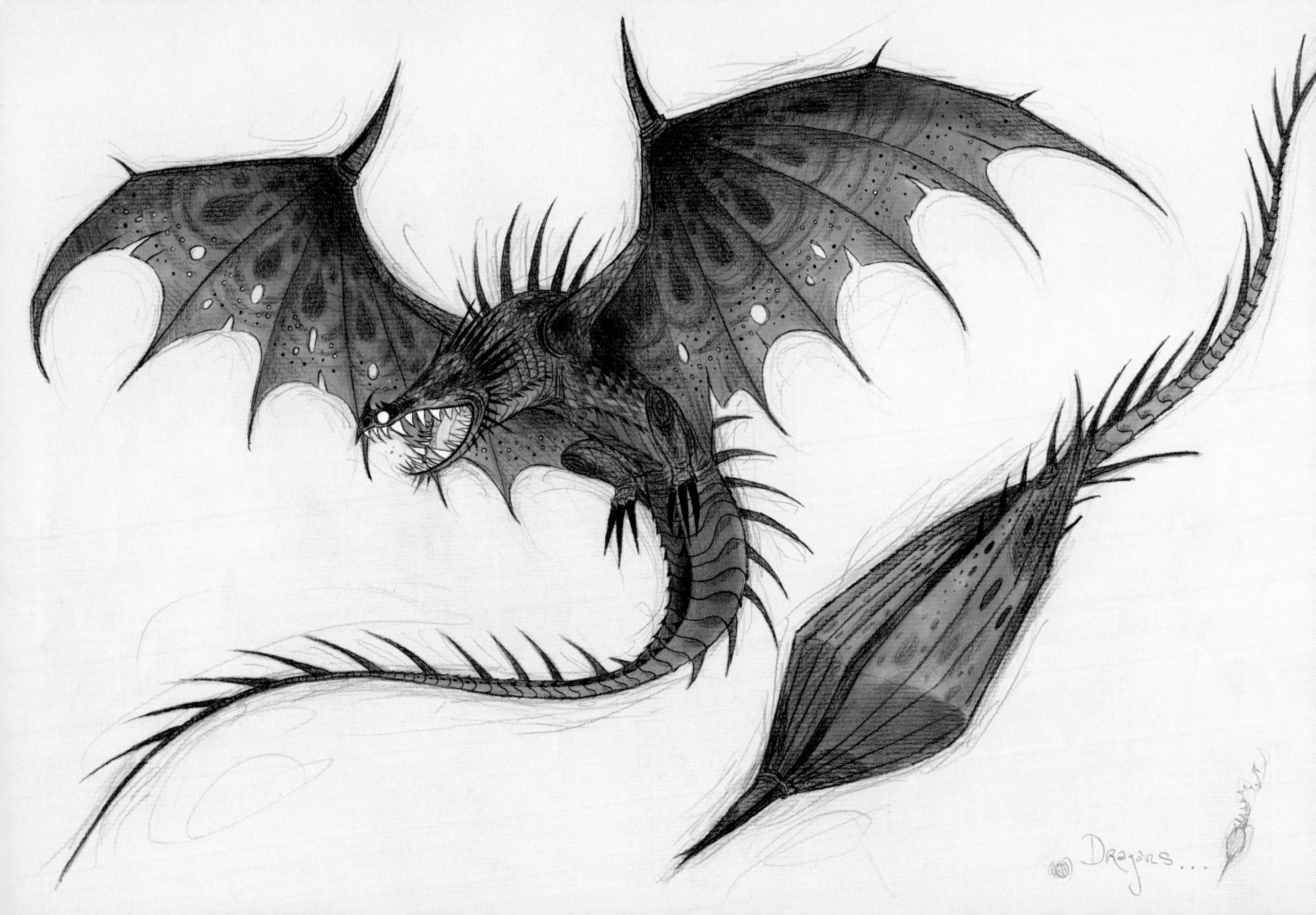
Dragons . . .

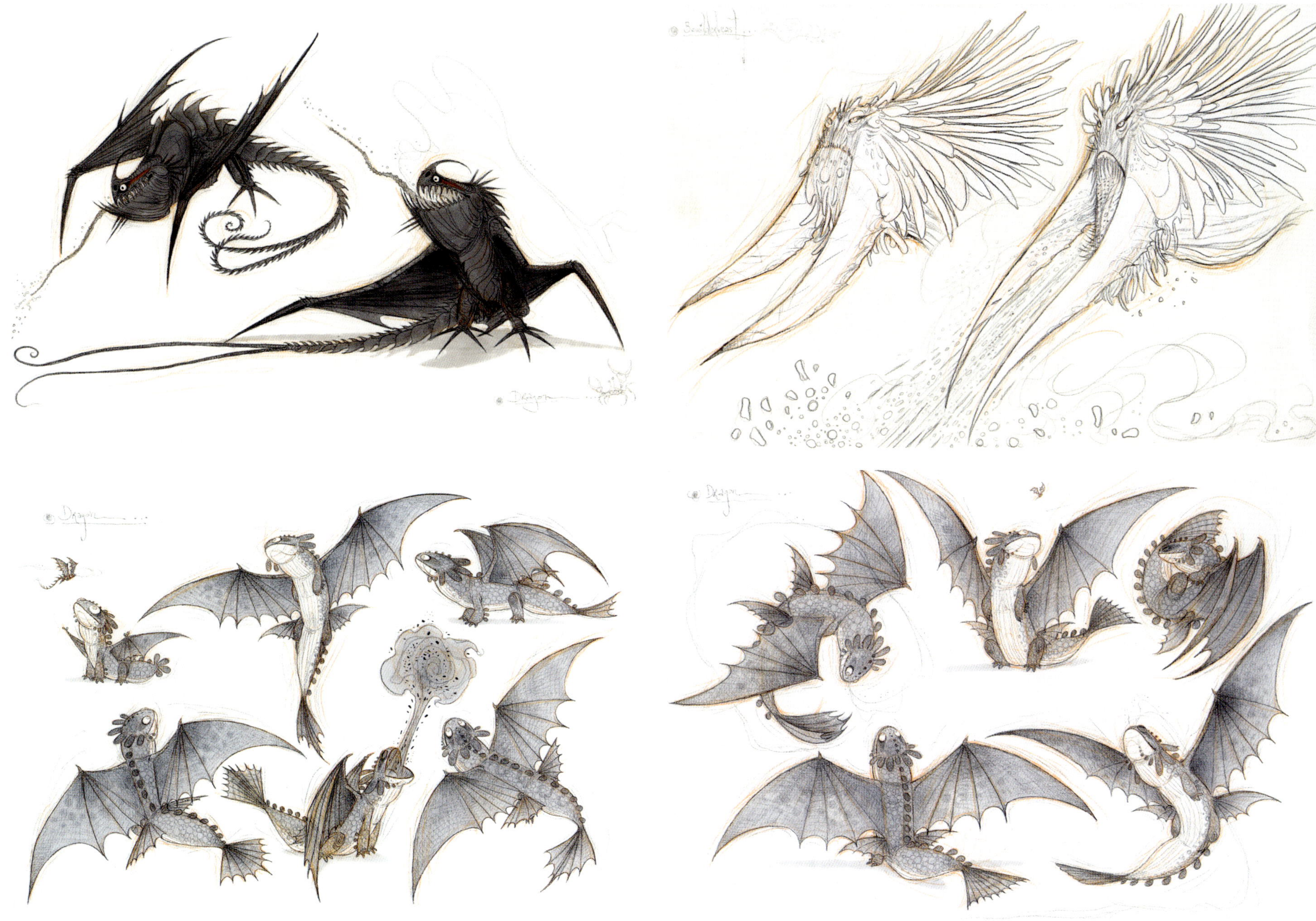

Characters Great & Small

To start drawing on a project, Nico first absorbs the director's thoughts on character personalities. For Nico, this translates into simple shapes that lay the initial visual foundation for a character lineup. "Sometimes I just draw very small shapes for all the characters. But this I keep for me, and I keep it very, very simple . . . then I try to stick with it," Nico says. Some directors respond more to what the drawing expresses in personality, others respond more to the shape and the design, and Nico watches for that knowing smile—that tiny chuckle to emanate from the director to know he's dialed in on their imagination and hope. "I know when I get a laugh that something's there. And it's the best compliment without having to say anything," Nico continues.

"This talented, soulful-eyed (and rather shy) Frenchman first landed on my radar in the 1990s when I saw his character designs for The Prince of Egypt*—princesses with flowing robes, prancing horses, and poisonous asps expertly sketched on neutral-colored paper highlighted Nico's signature style. Before my eyes, light and dark tones gave birth to characters that LEAPT off the page. His bold, graphic shapes adorned with the finest of details were precise and without mistake. The characters gestured, danced, and emoted as if they had been alive in the artist's head all along; he just needed to capture them and put them to paper! I have seen that illustrative magic again and again, having had the privilege to work with Nico on a wide variety of films at various studios. Nico is not just a designer—he is a creator of worlds, setting a style that gives way to franchises, toy lines, cosplay, and more.*

"I once asked Nico how he draws that well—what was his secret? He simply said, 'I just draw.' And he does, even in his spare time. Nico's sketchbooks are among my favorites. They are time capsules, perfect examples of everyday people just living their lives, beautifully caricatured in both look and personality. They are historically significant and capture current culture better than any photograph."

—Jill Culton, director

"Nico stands out as a rare character designer who has preserved the classic craft of drawing on paper with pencils, lending his work a timeless quality. His style is both unique and enchanting, bringing characters to life in ways that feel both grounded and magical. Many of his creatures evoke the imaginative, otherworldly feel of Hieronymus Bosch, immersing us in a universe rich with creativity and mystery."

—William Salazar, directing animator

Opposite & pp. 88–93: *Abominable* (2019) character concepts

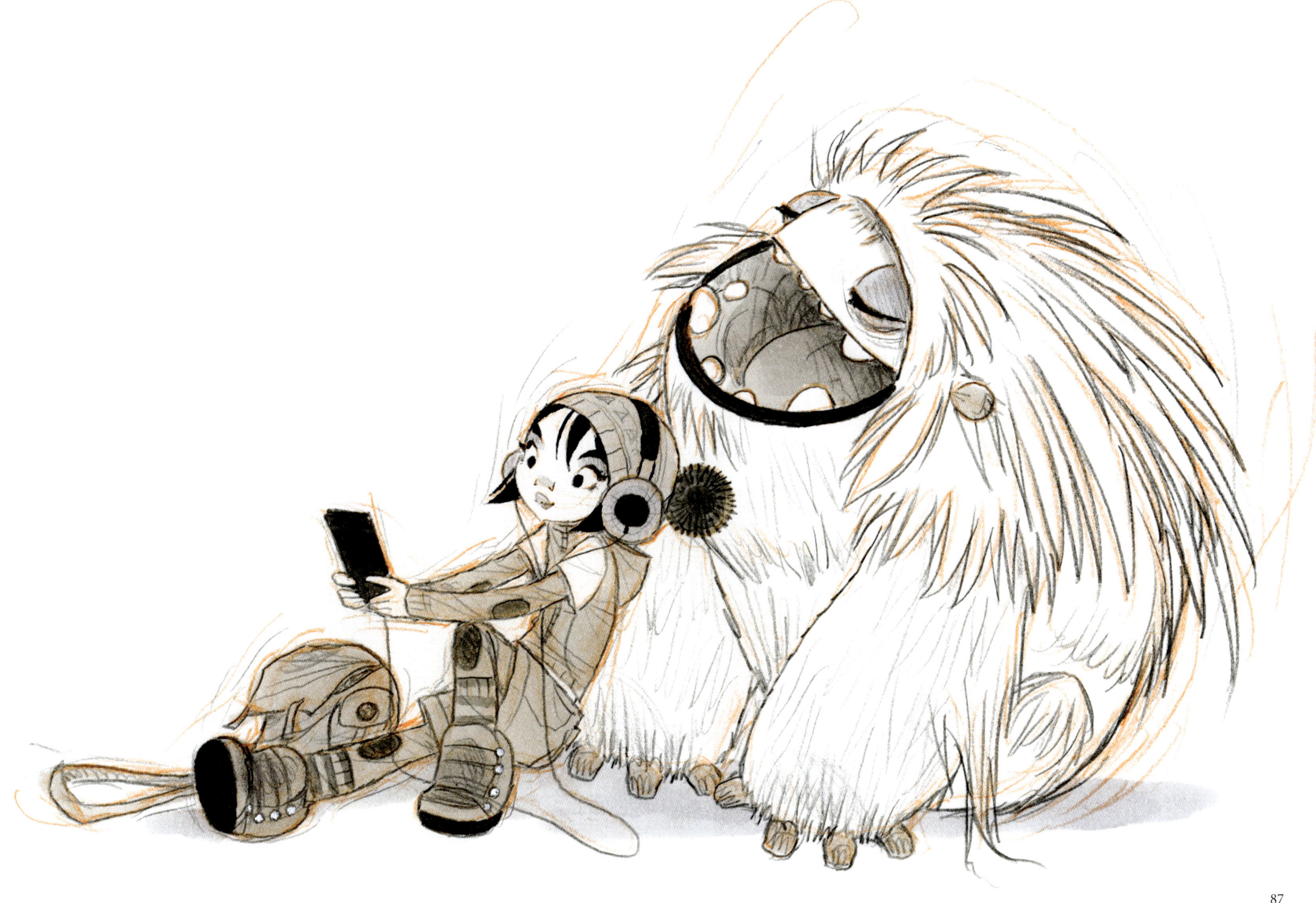

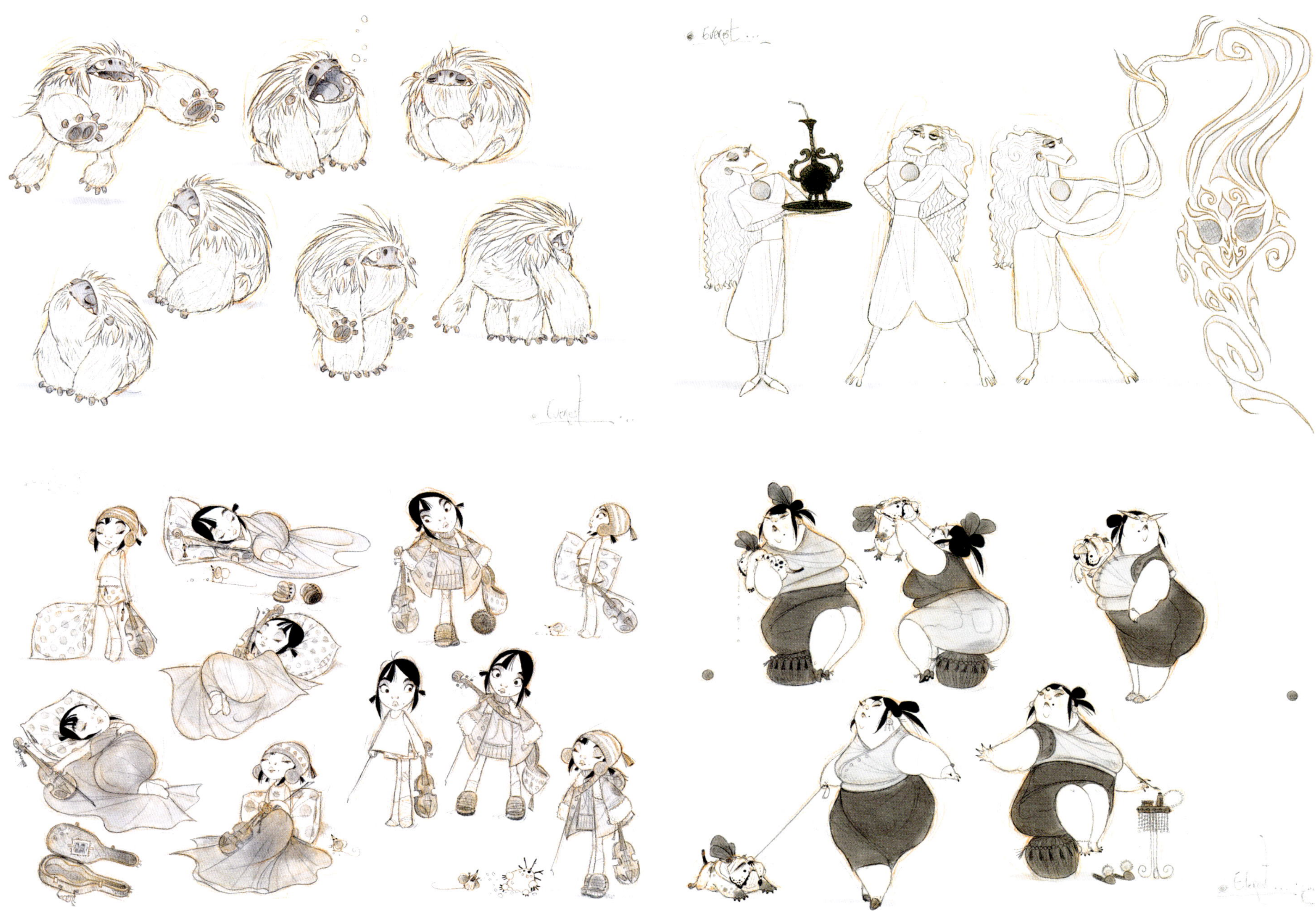
Everest...

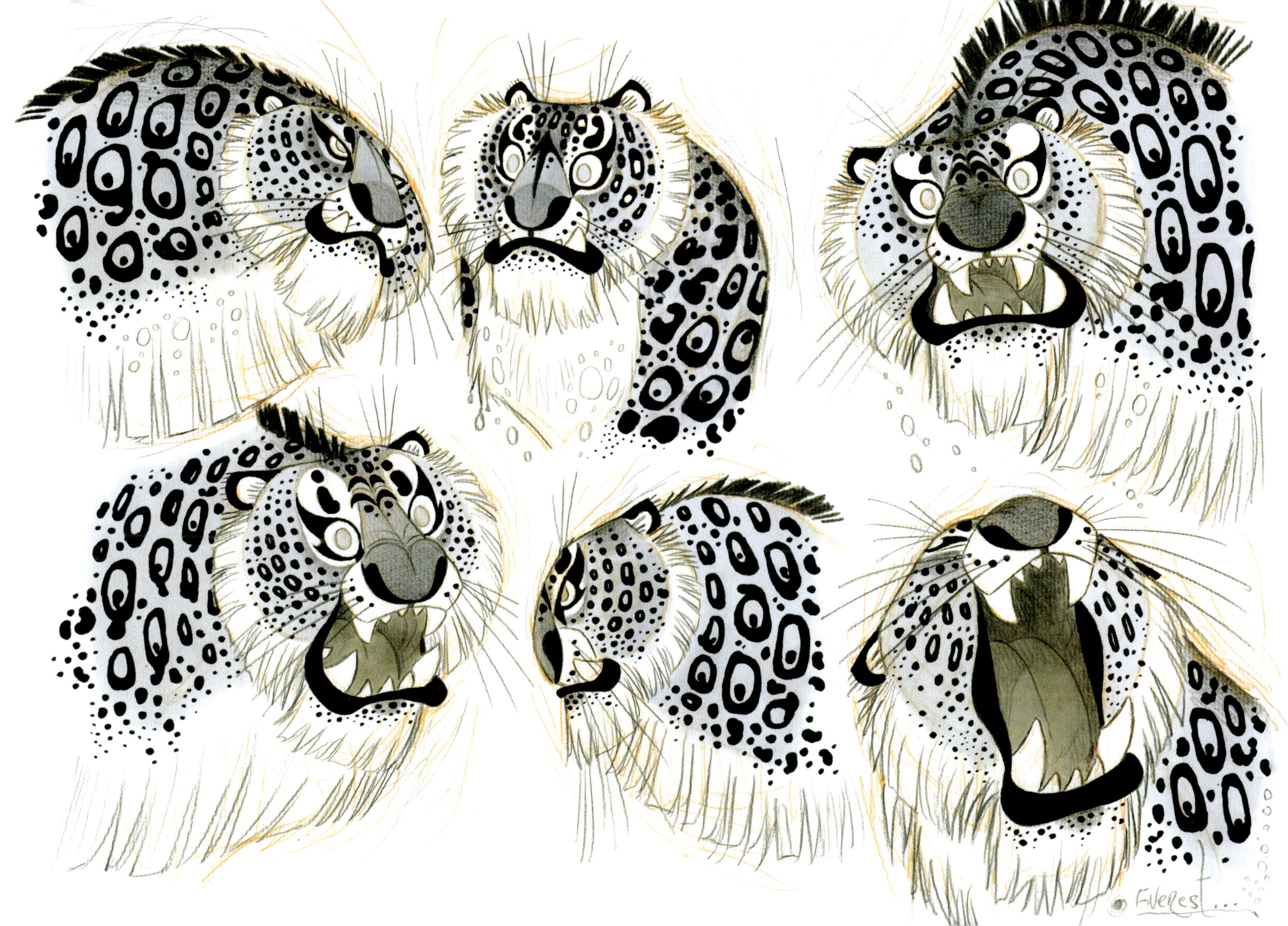

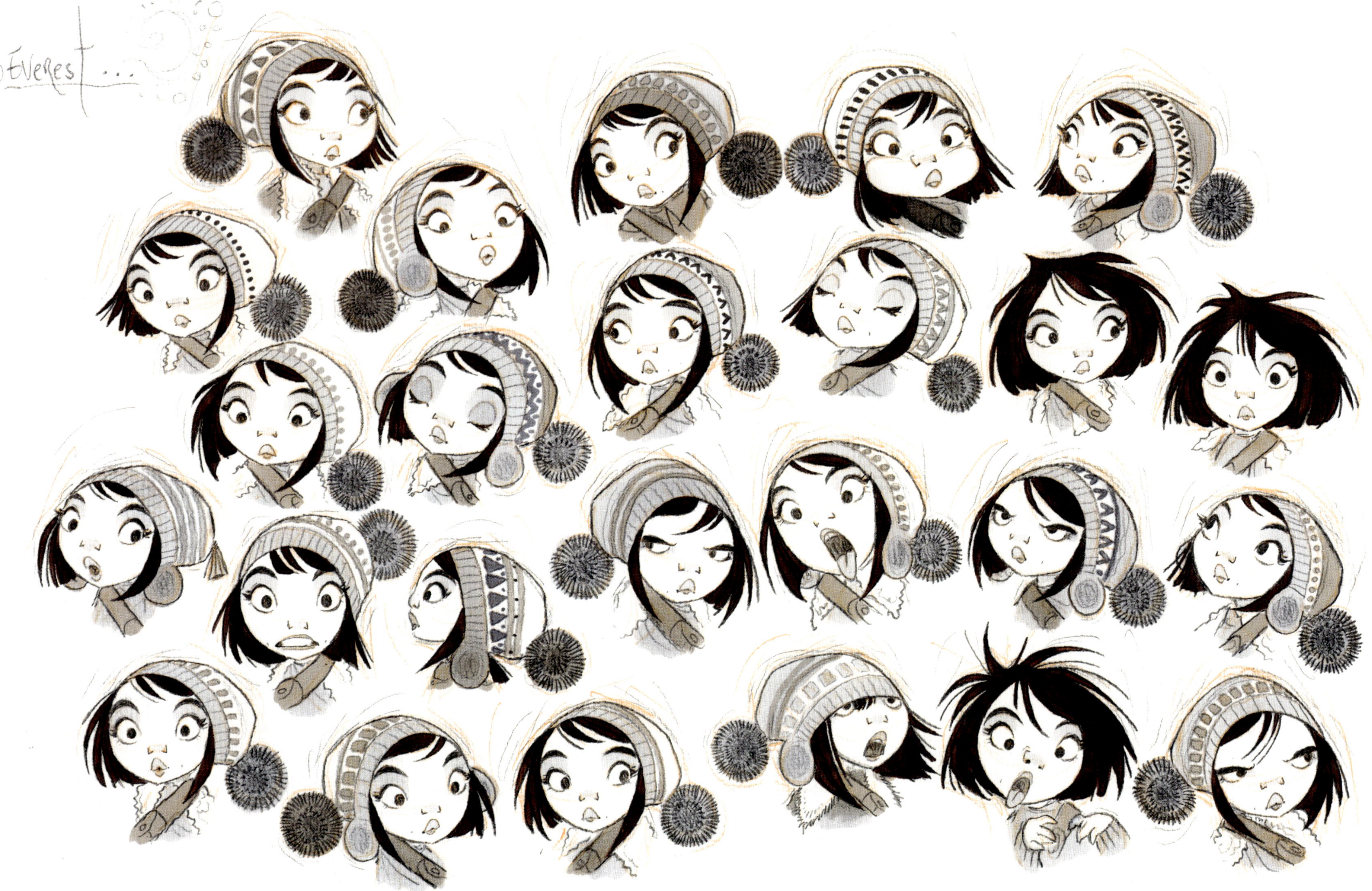
Everest . . .

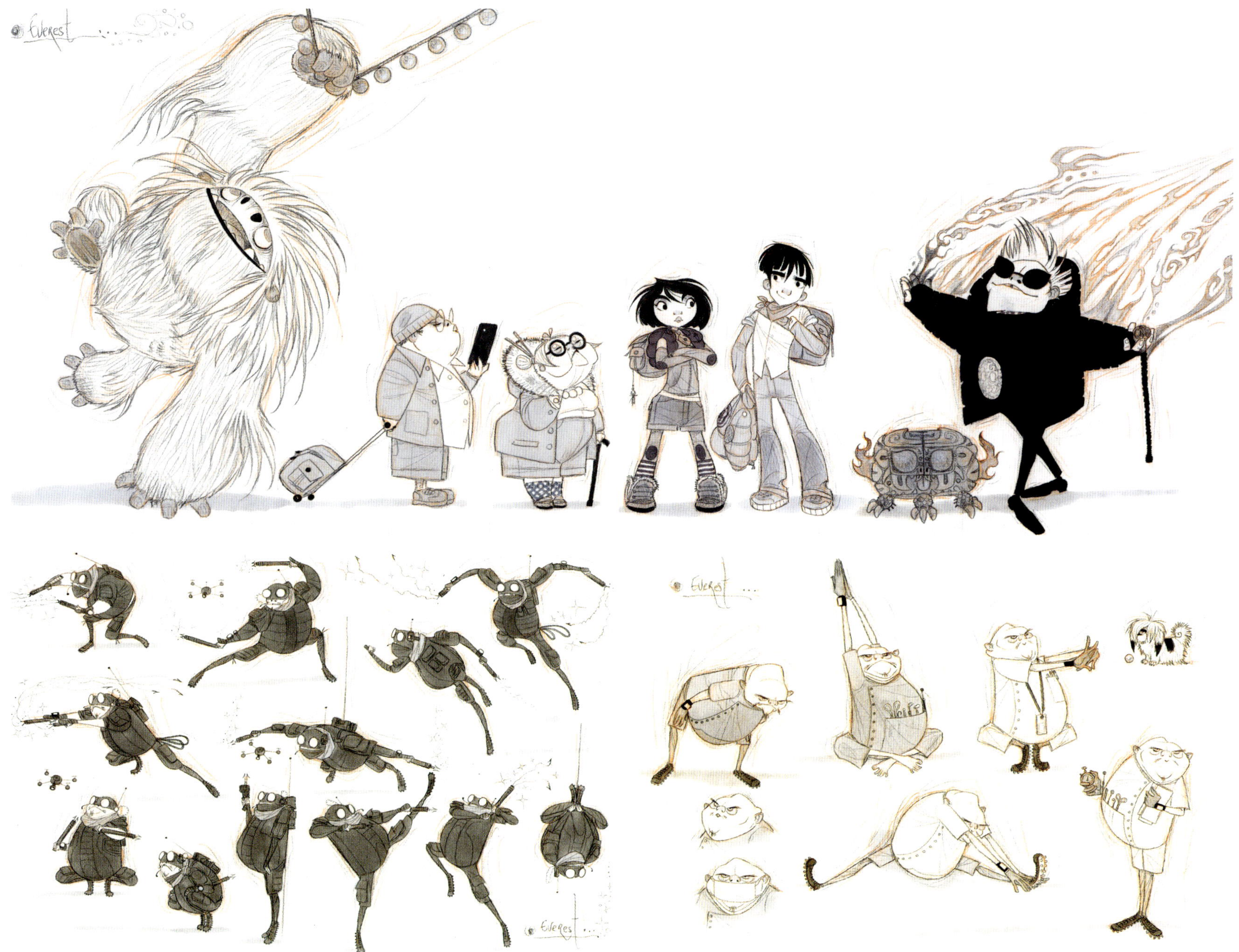
Everest
Everest
Everest

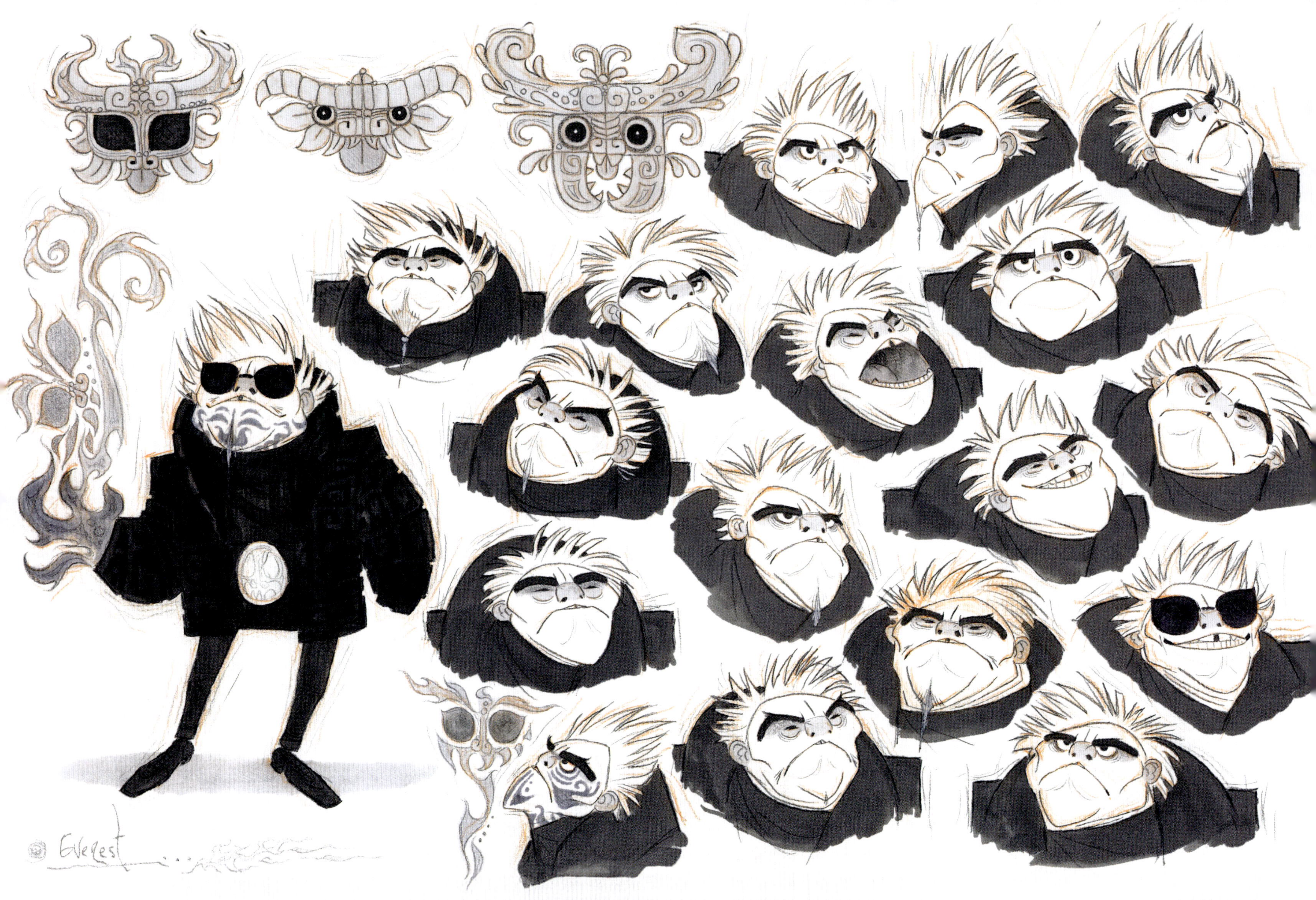
Everest

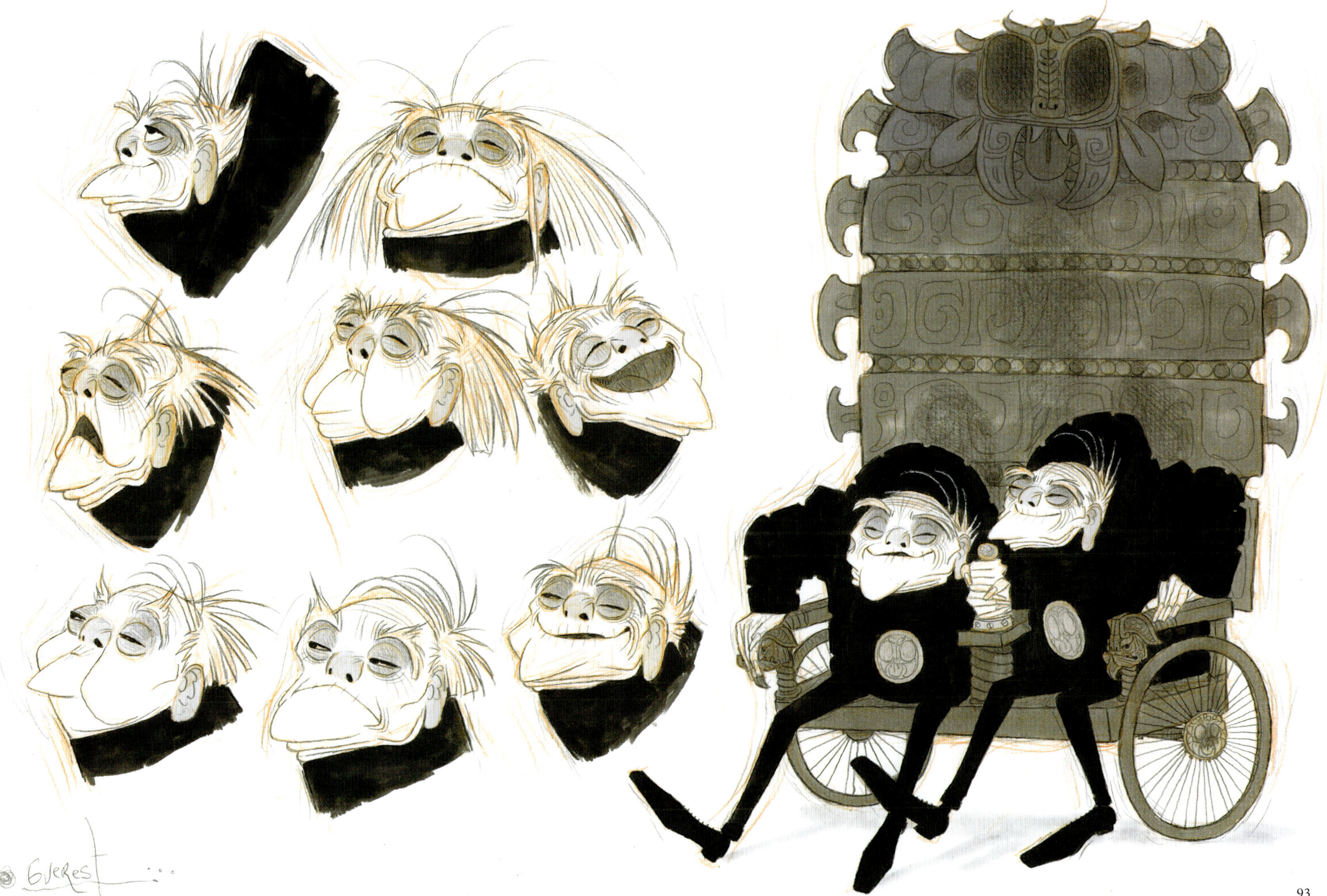

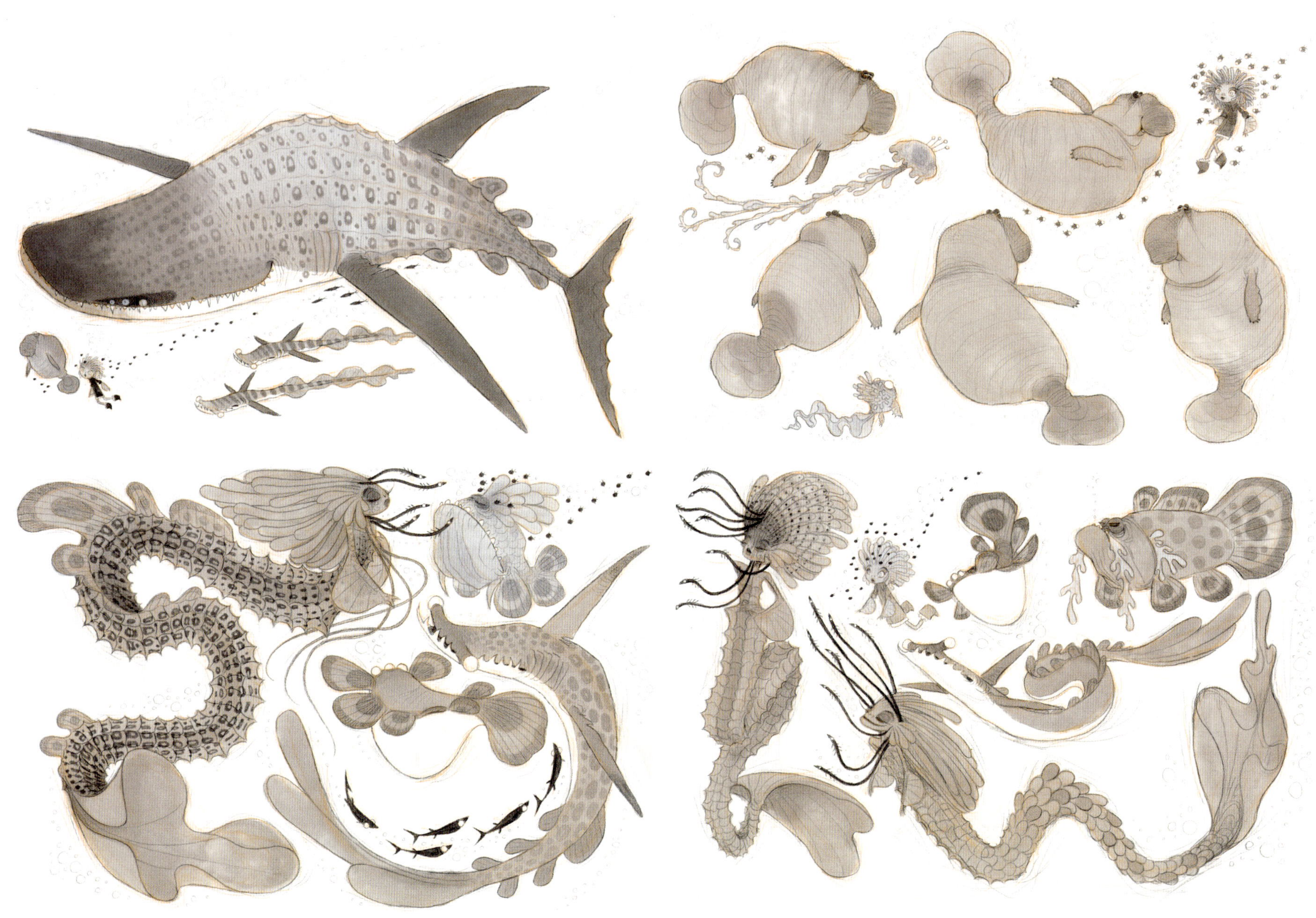

Above, opposite & overleaf: *Ruby Gillman: Teenage Kraken* (2019) character concepts • pp. 98–105: *The Wild Robot* (2024) character concepts

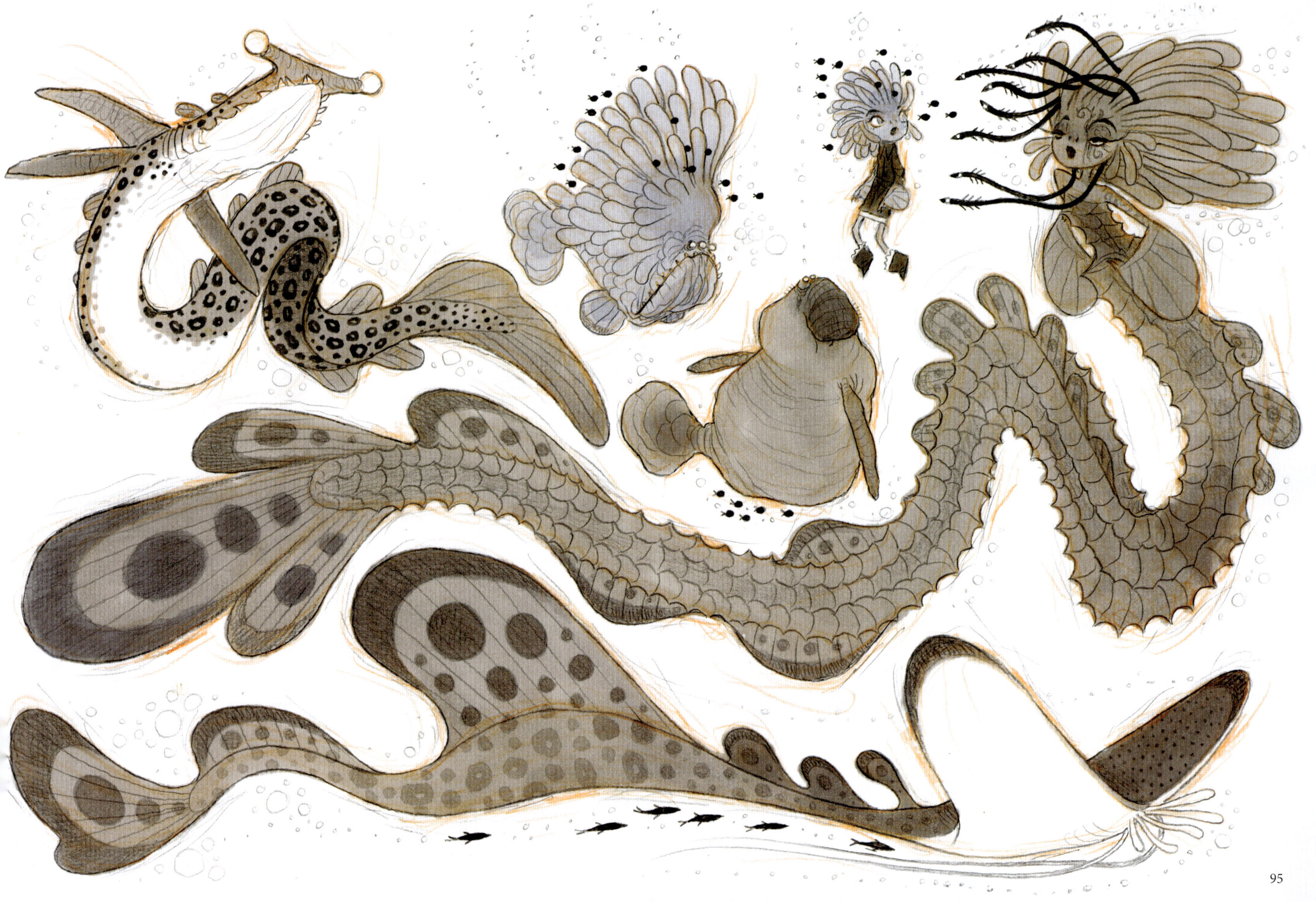

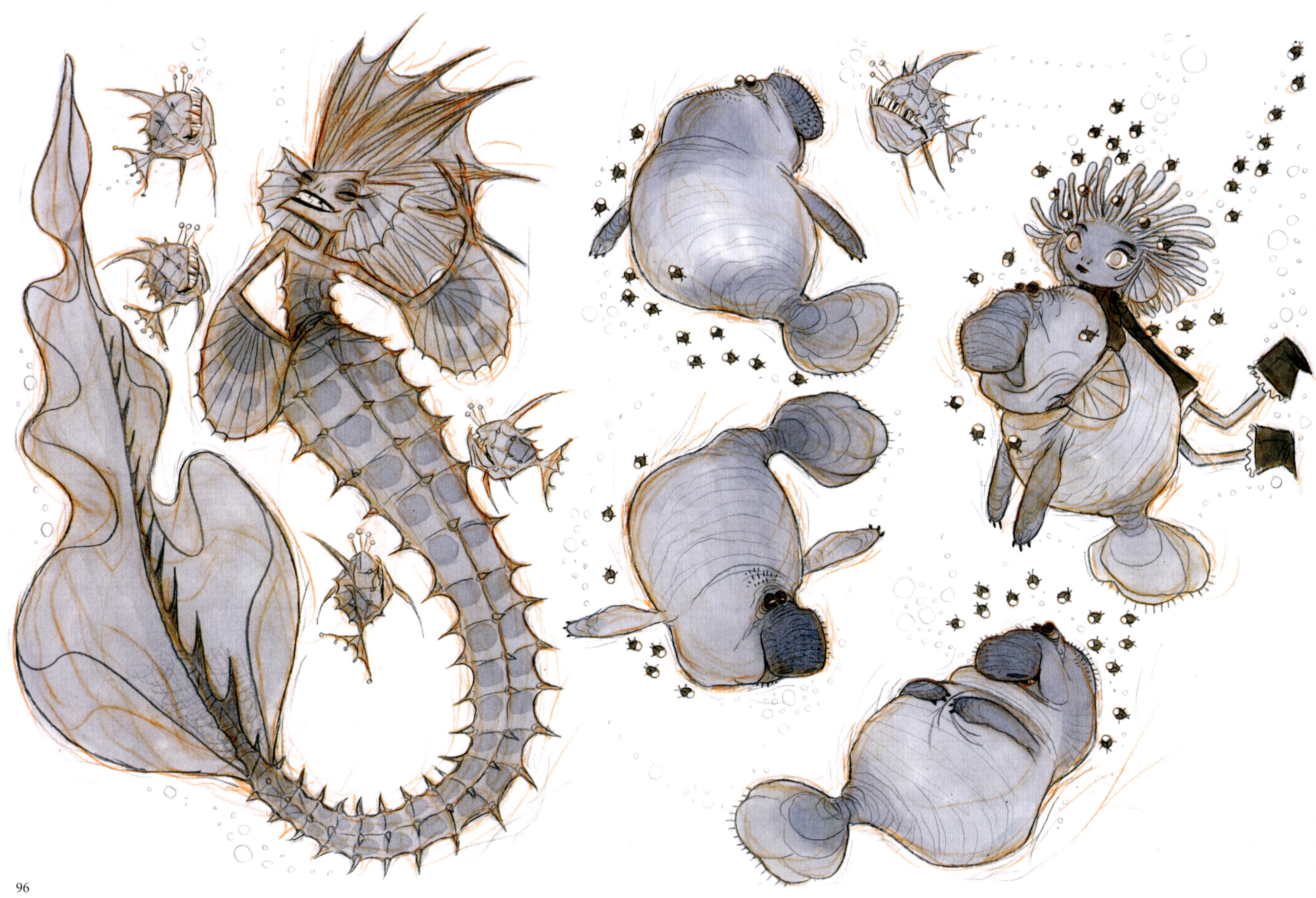

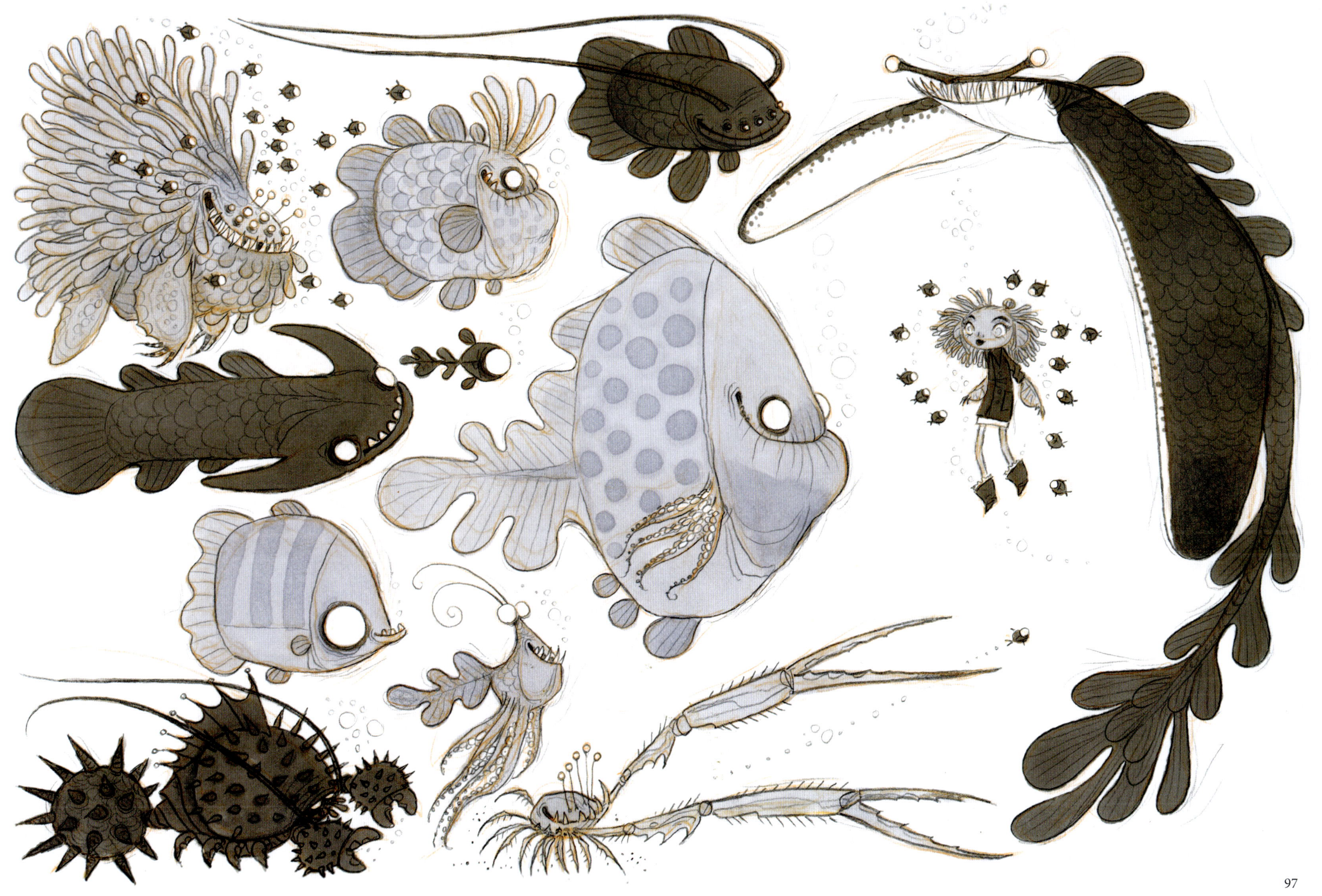

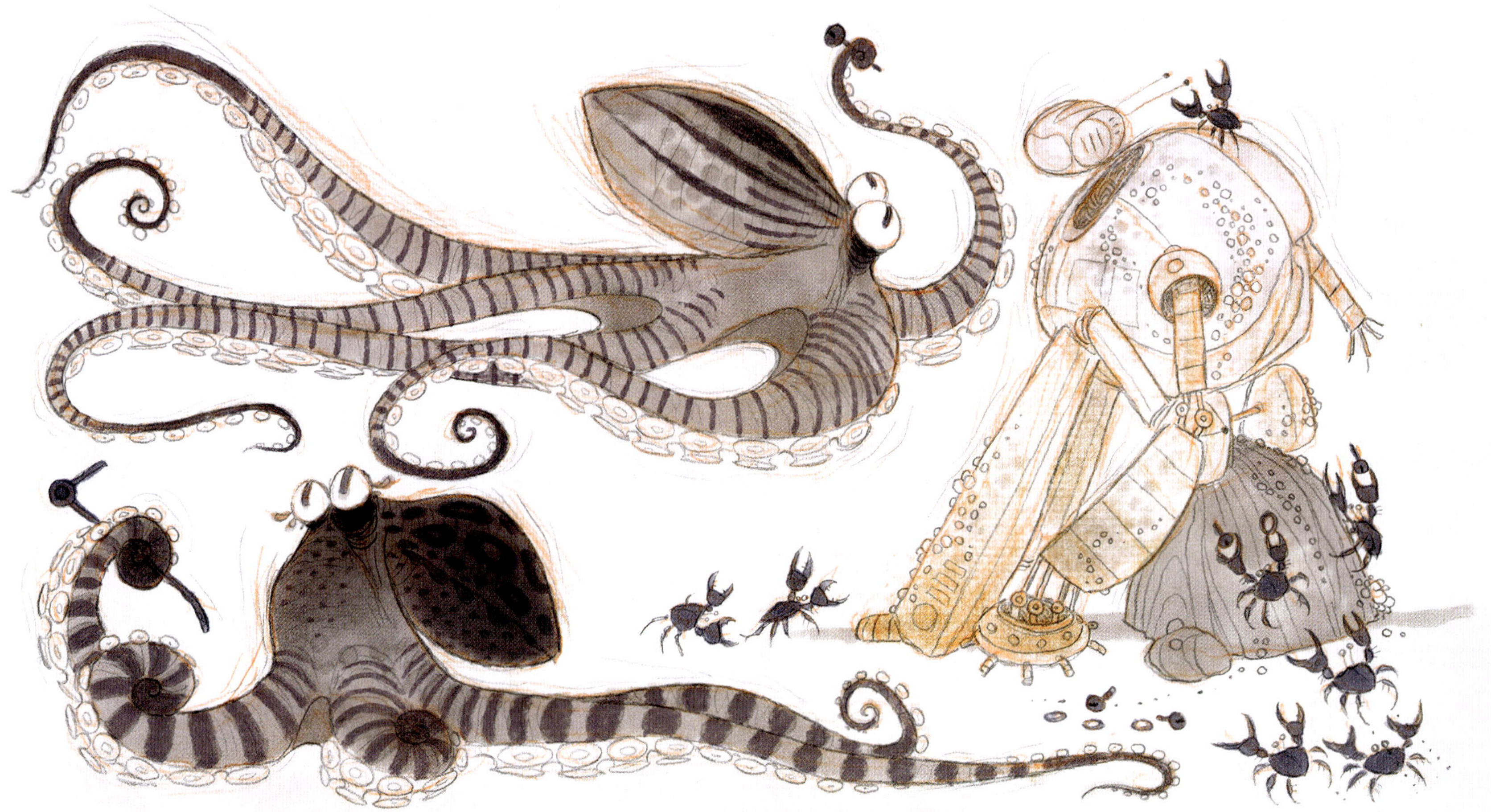

"If I were to describe Nico's work to someone, the first adjective I would use would be 'effortless.' You have to actually look at Nico's drawings directly to appreciate this description. Nico, I am happy to say, draws on paper. No stylus, no tablet. If you drop by Nico's room, you'll see stacks of paper all around. Stacks. Inches thick, page upon page, each page crowded with characters. I mean that quite literally. A page will be teeming with skunk designs, like some earthquake awoke a sleeping nest, rousting dozens of the critters who flooded out into the daylight, crowding together, filling every available inch of space. Gaps on the paper too small for, say, a skunk, dragon, or robot, will nonetheless be filled with little birds or bugs who alighted, seemingly out of curiosity. Nico's mind and pencil just cannot abide a blank spot, and will populate it with delightful, ever-inventive creatures. Before I begin to draw in the mornings, Nico's are among the drawings I seek out just to look at to remind myself why I love drawing in the first place. They remind me of the endless possibilities that are out there, and I think to myself, What would Nico do with this? How far could he take a single design or idea? *To look at his work is to remind yourself of how truly limitless a drawing can become and how a great drawing should feel: free, effortless, and joyful."*

—**Chris Sanders, director**

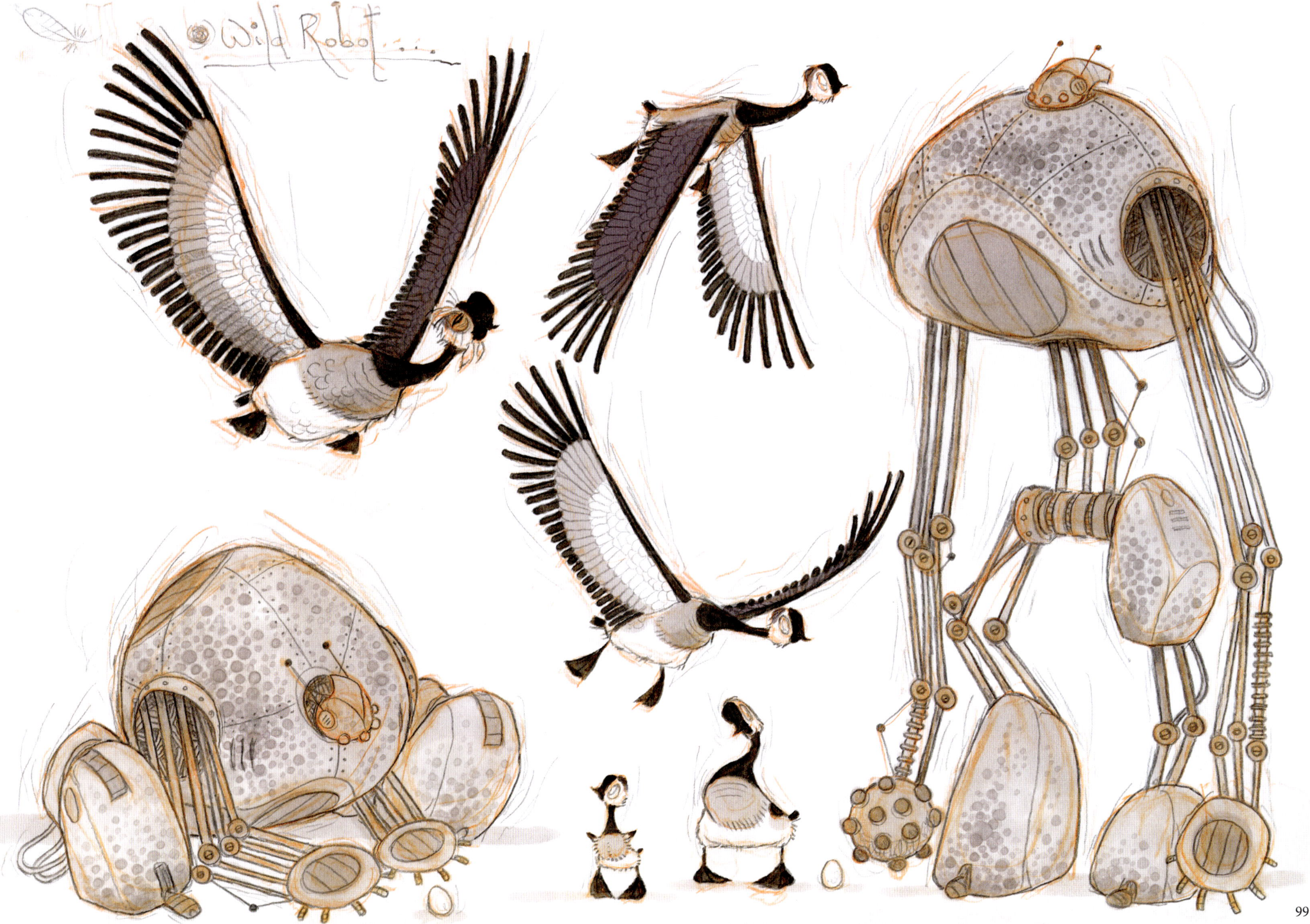
Wild Robot

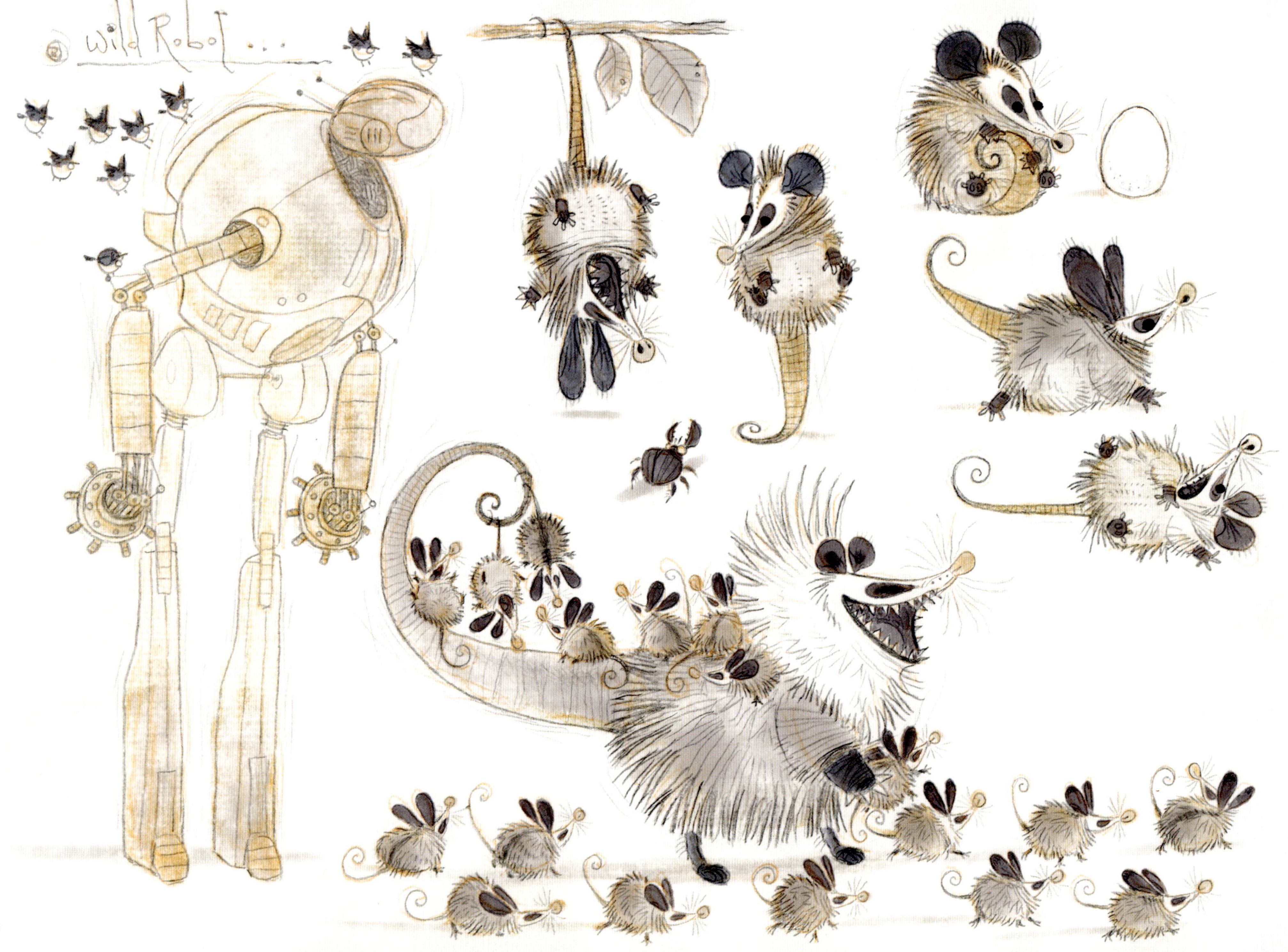
Wild Robot . . .

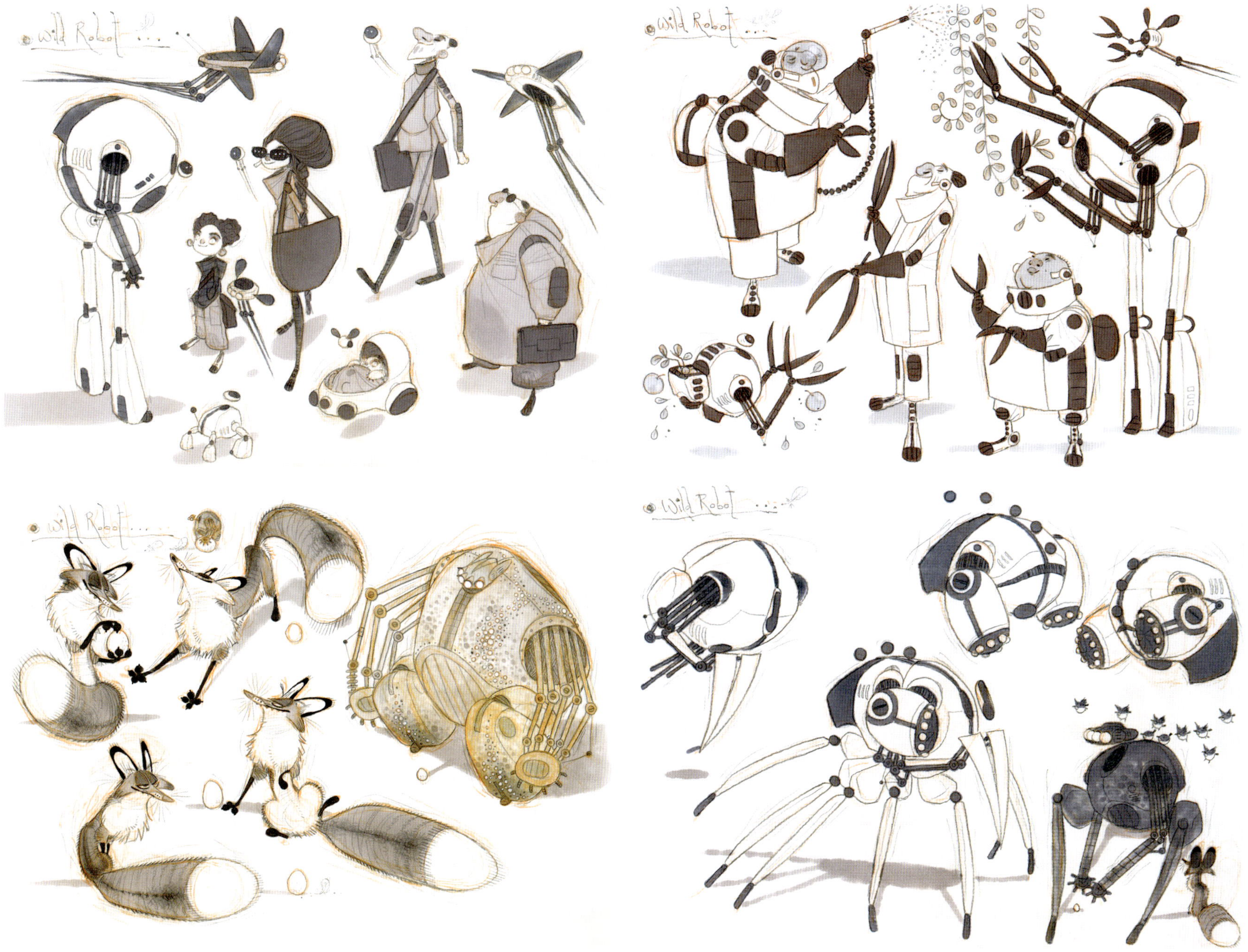
Wild Robot...
Wild Robot...
Wild Robot...
Wild Robot...

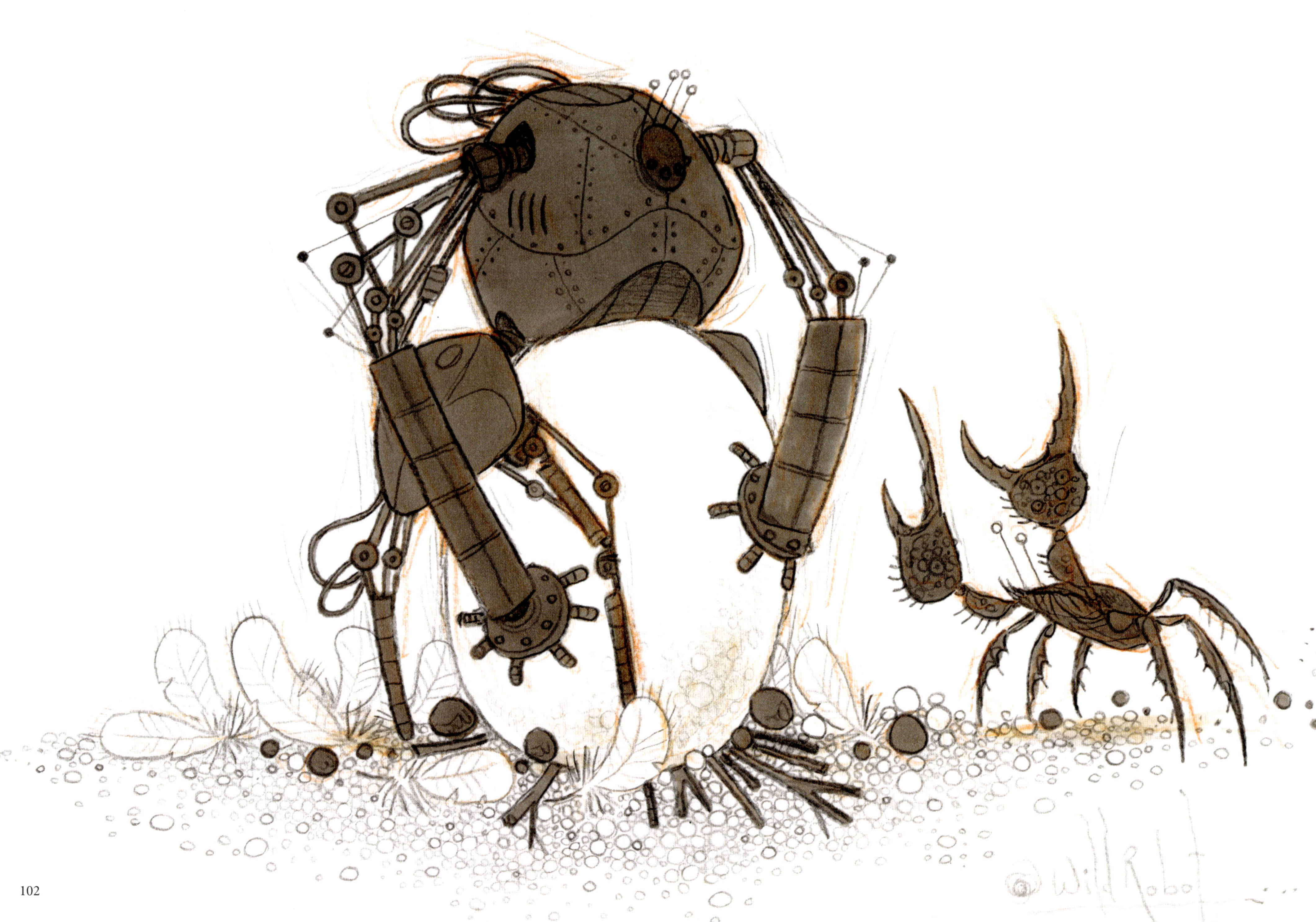

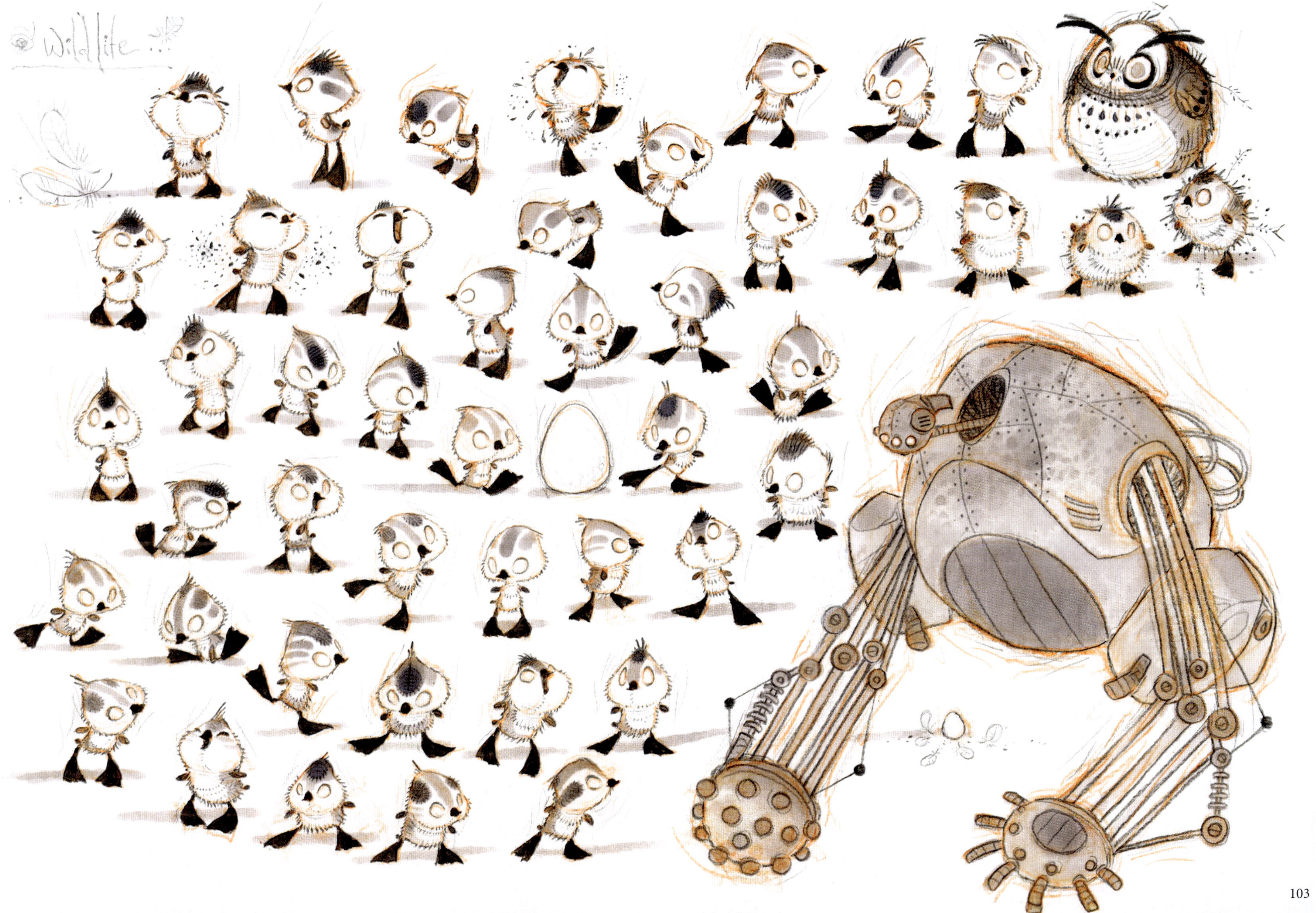
Wildlife

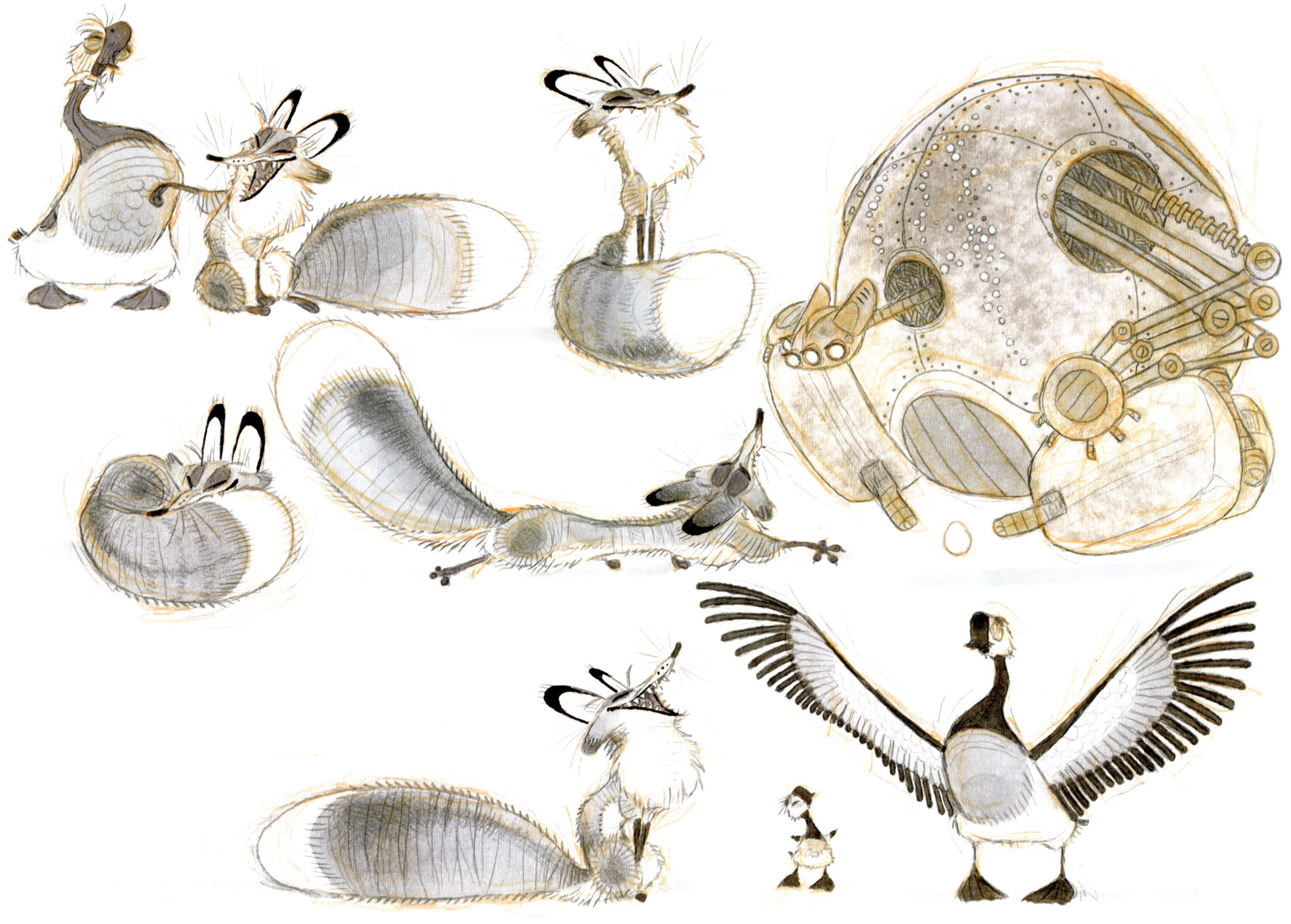

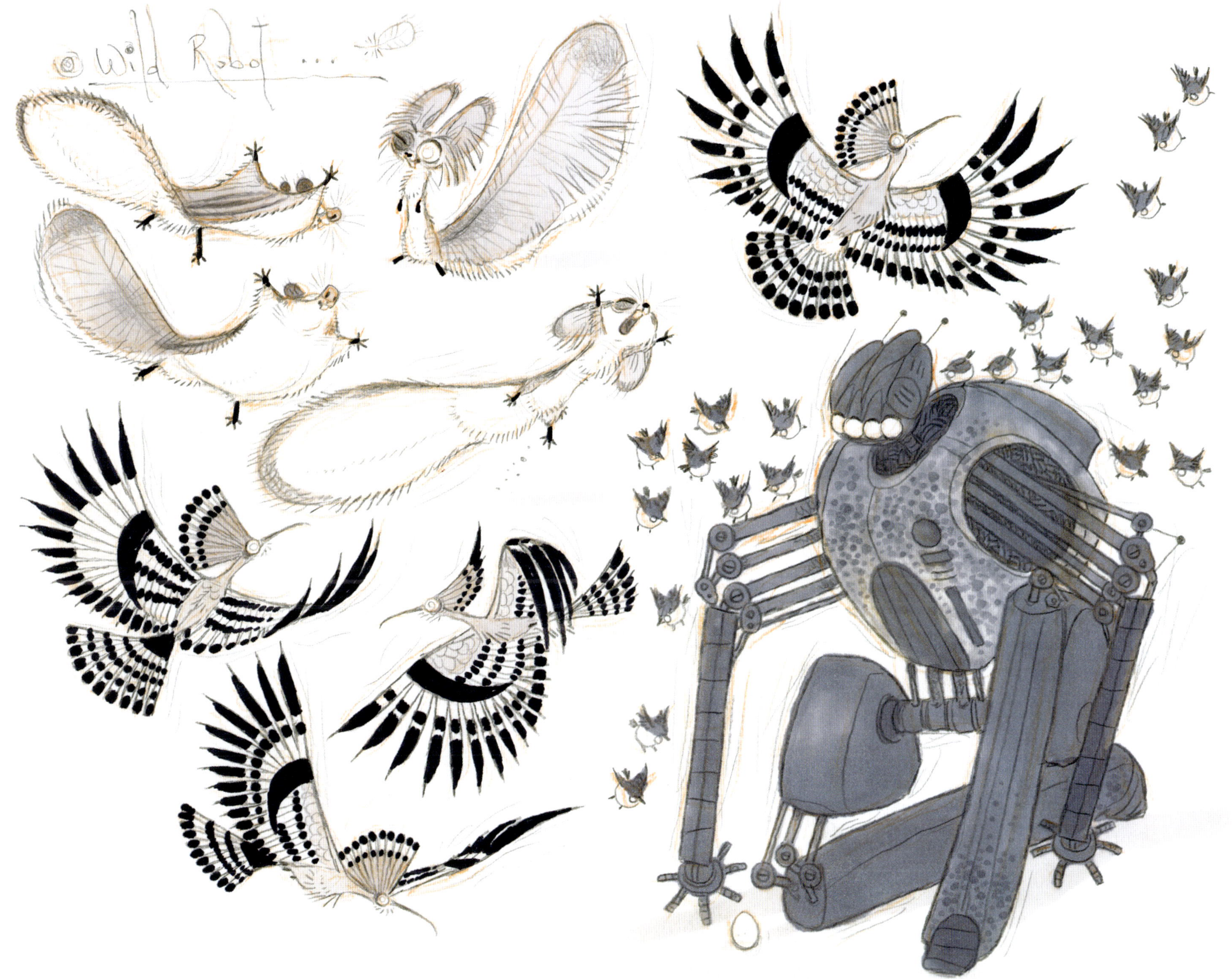
Wild Robot . . .

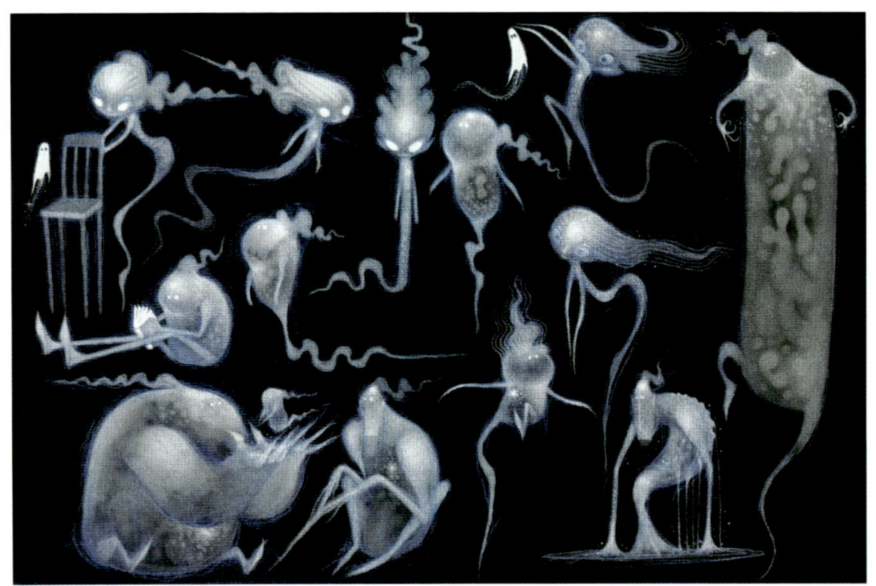

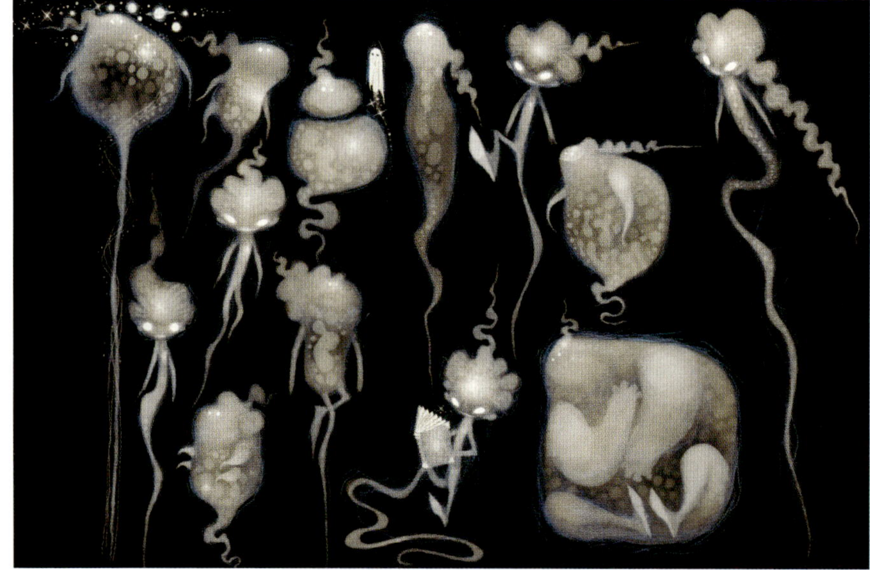

"When I think about Nico's work, I'm reminded of one of the central things many of us wrestle with as artists—namely, the idea of inhabiting a space that is not yet taken. In the more than thirty years I've known him, Nico has always simply inhabited Nico's space. Can you name his influences when looking at his work? Of course. Nothing comes from nothing. But you see one drawing by Nico and you will never be in doubt who the author is. This is a true gift. He shows us precisely how he sees the world, emphasizing what he and he alone is tickled by when observing nature. And here's another central point his creations never fail to show: Nature is the best artist of all, so best to observe her work directly and not to clutter your mind with how others interpret her. There's no separation between Nico as a person and his art, because showing us what he sees is his invitation into his heart. And what a heart! Much as many of us have tried, he remains inimitable."

—**Jakob Jensen, directing animator**

Above, opposite & overleaf: *Orion and the Dark* (2024) character concepts

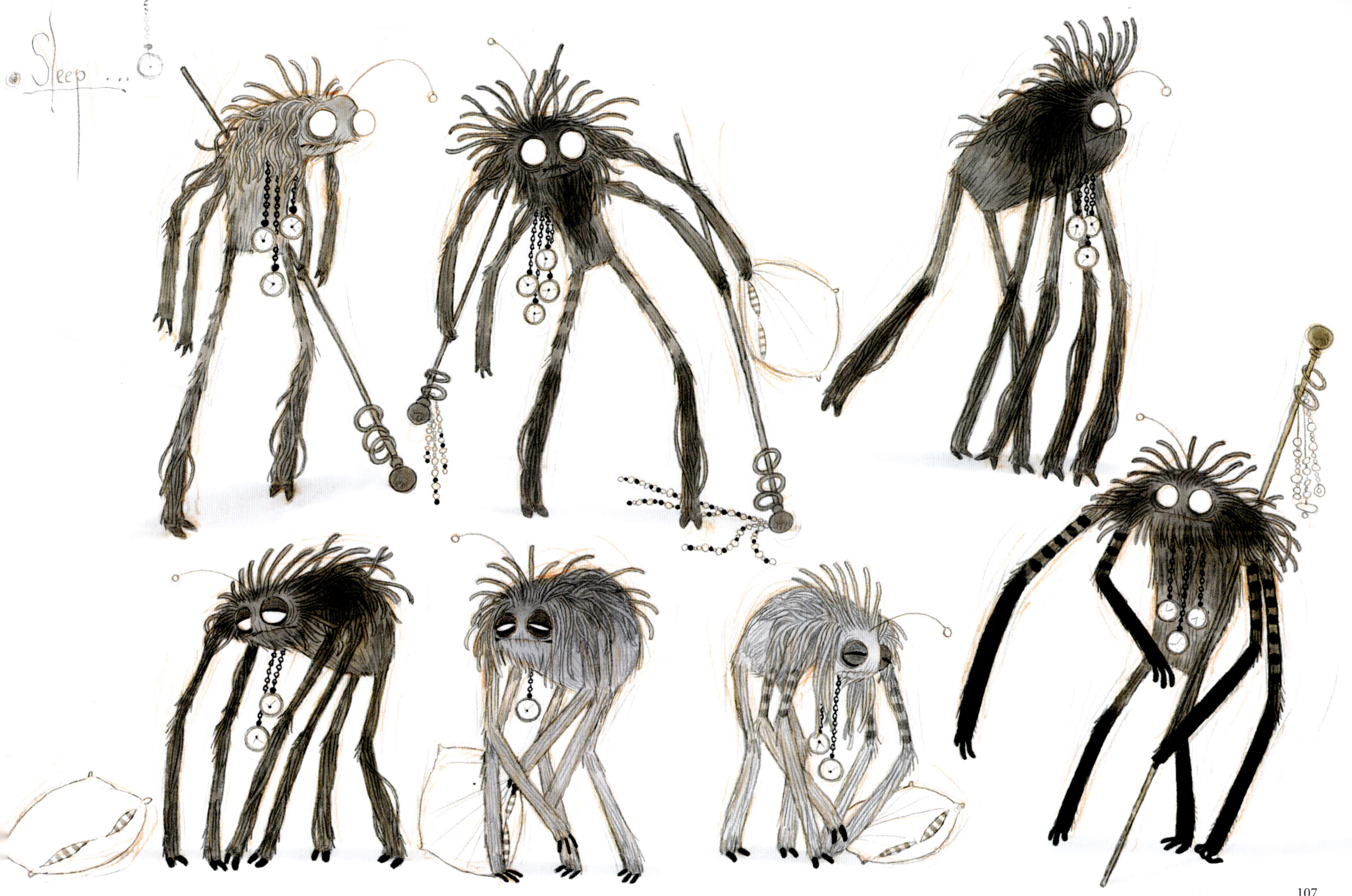
Sleep . . .

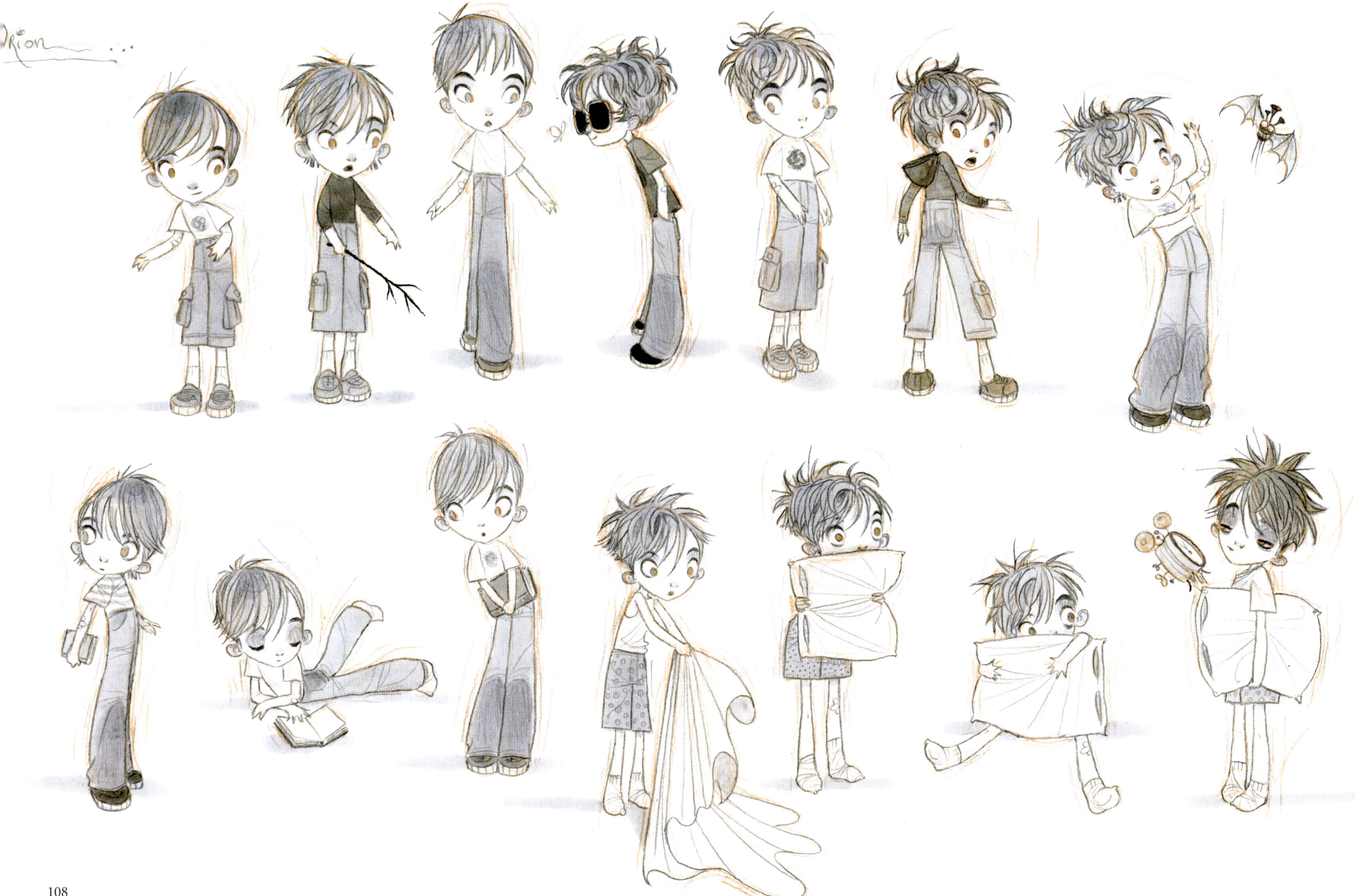
Orion ...

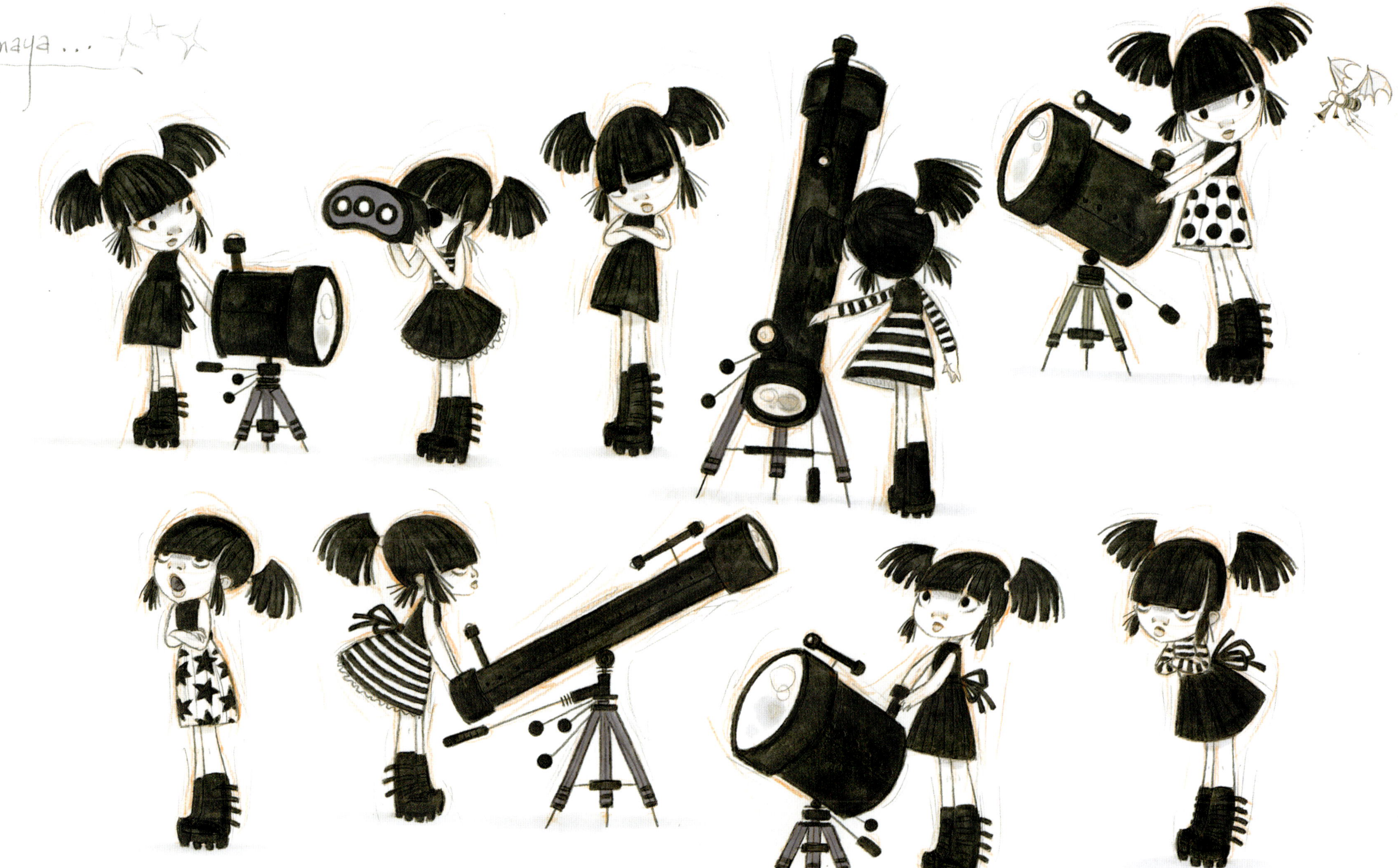
maya . . .

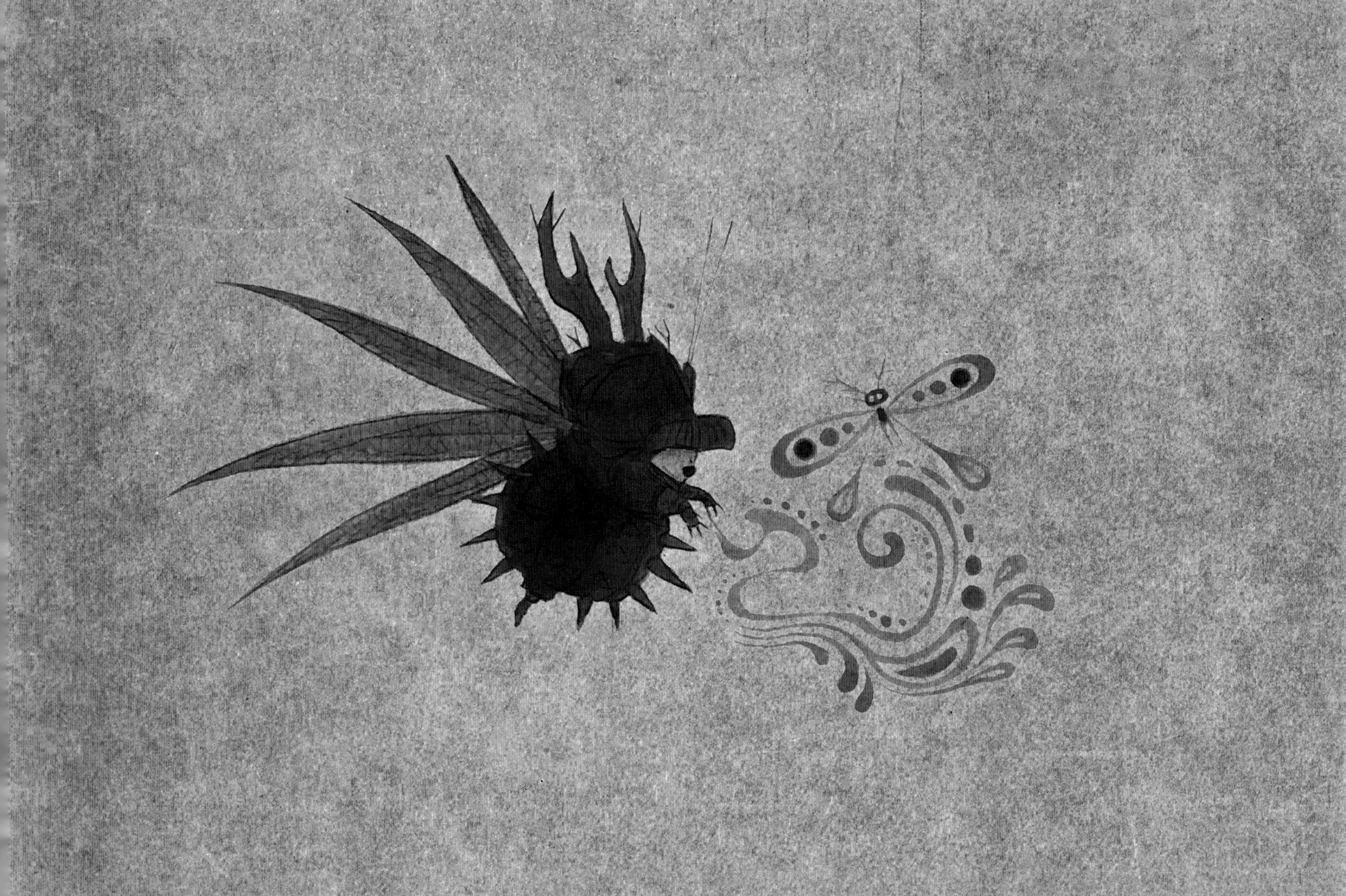

III

A Broader Drawing Board

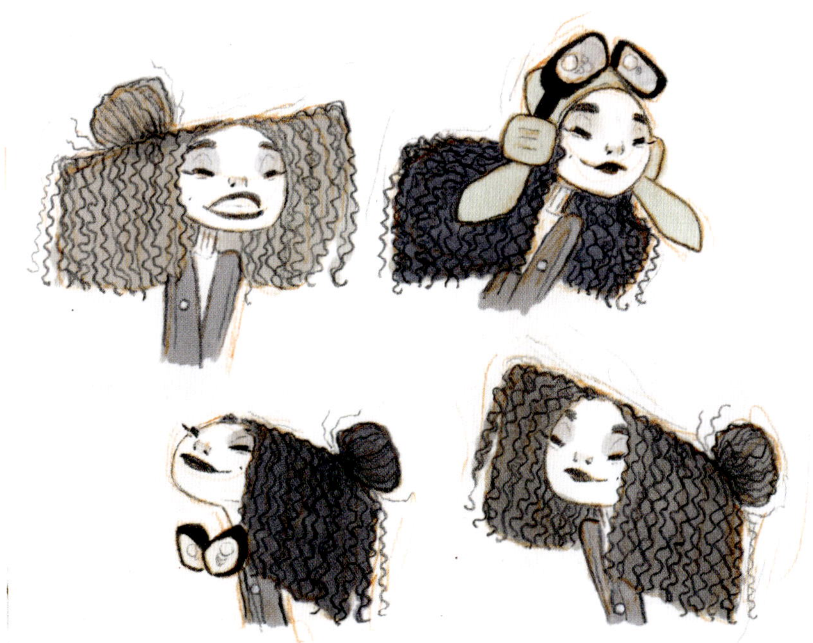

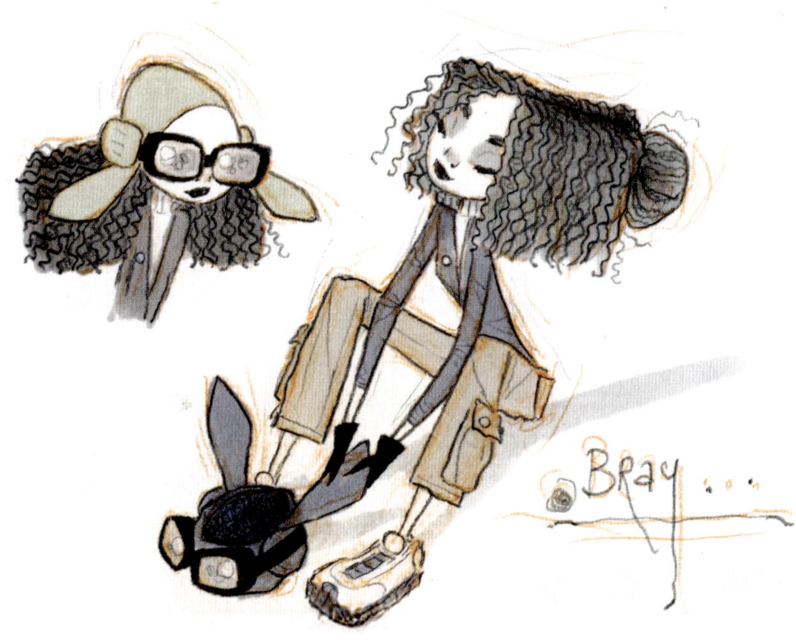

NICO HAS BRANCHED out widely in the animation realm, sharing his talents with Warner Bros. Pictures Animation, independent productions, and other creative entities.

"Nico's inspired designs have shaped countless beloved characters that are recognized around the world. Over the past two decades of working together, what stands out most about his impact is his unparalleled ability to breathe life and appeal into characters and worlds early in the creative process, helping define what makes each project unique. In animation, assembling the right team of artists is crucial—so finding someone with Nico's rare blend of versatility, artistic mastery, and ability to uncover a project's true essence is extraordinary. At Warner Bros. Pictures Animation, where we explore a wide array of animation styles, Nico's talents are invaluable—and somehow beyond his prolific contributions, his work is also something you just want to hang on your wall so you can be immersed in its fantastical beauty."

—**BILL DAMASCHKE, President, Warner Bros. Pictures Animation**

PRECEDING PAGES, ABOVE, OPPOSITE & PP. 114–131: Warner Bros. Pictures Animation character concepts

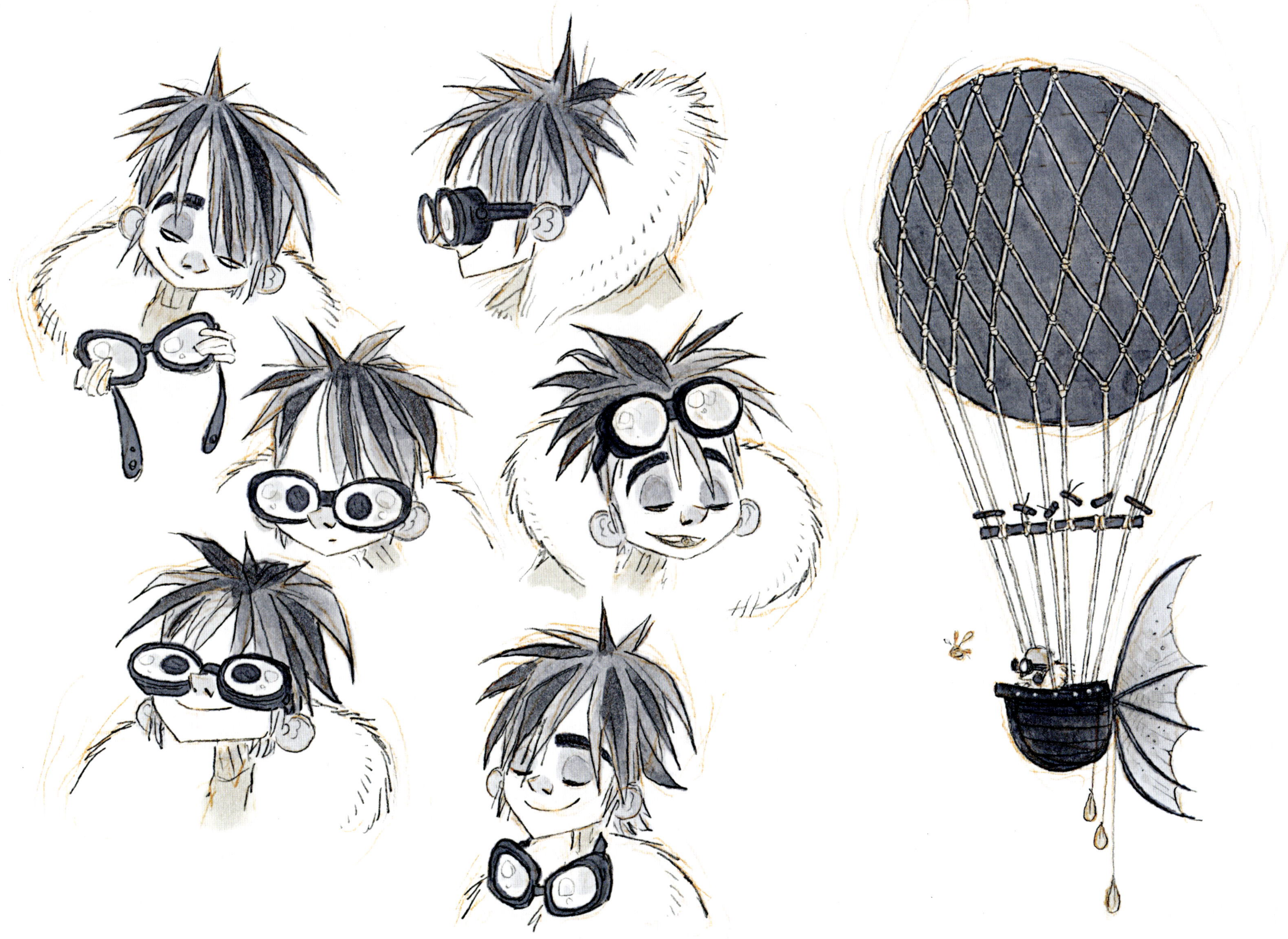

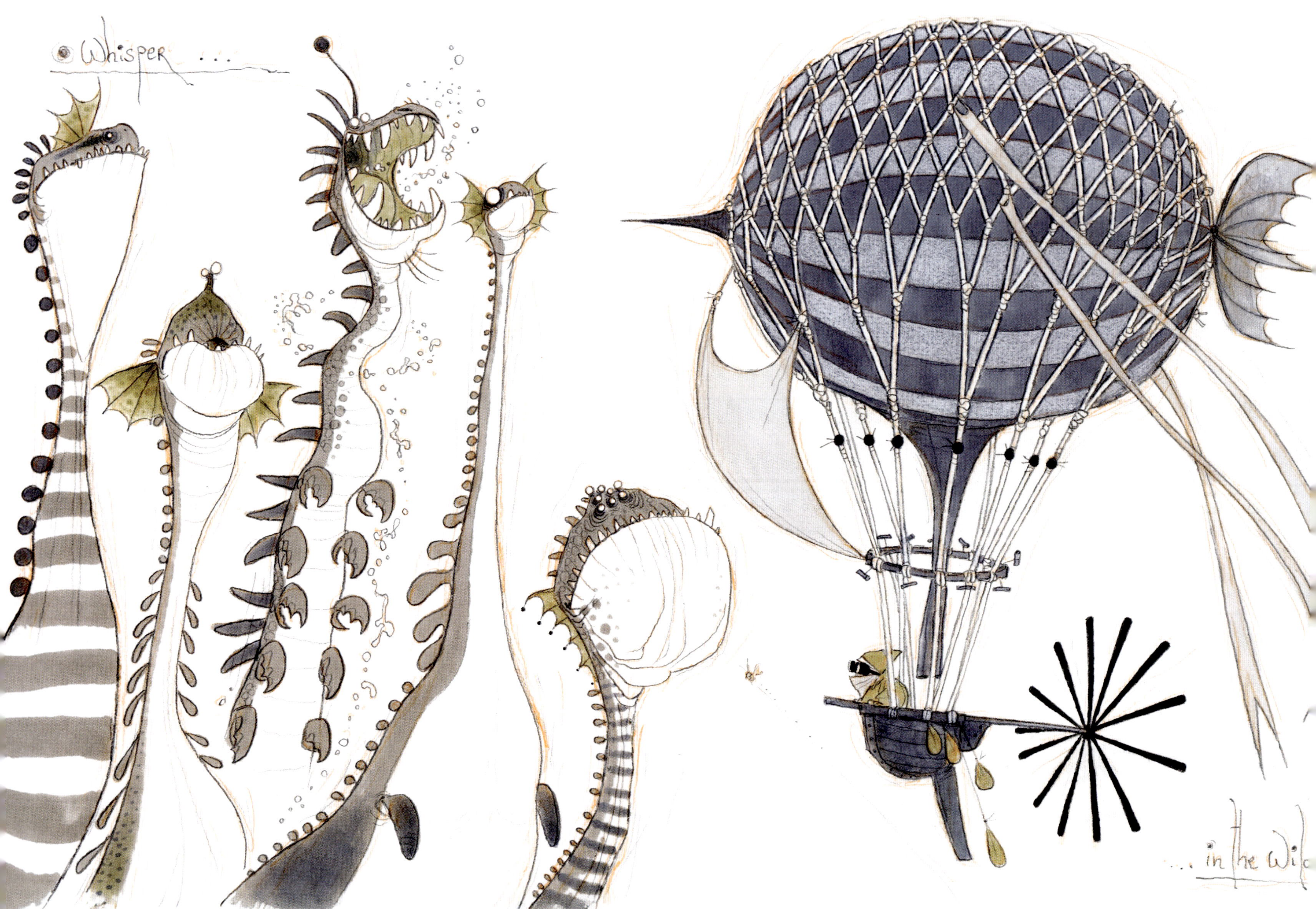
Whisper . . .
. . . in the

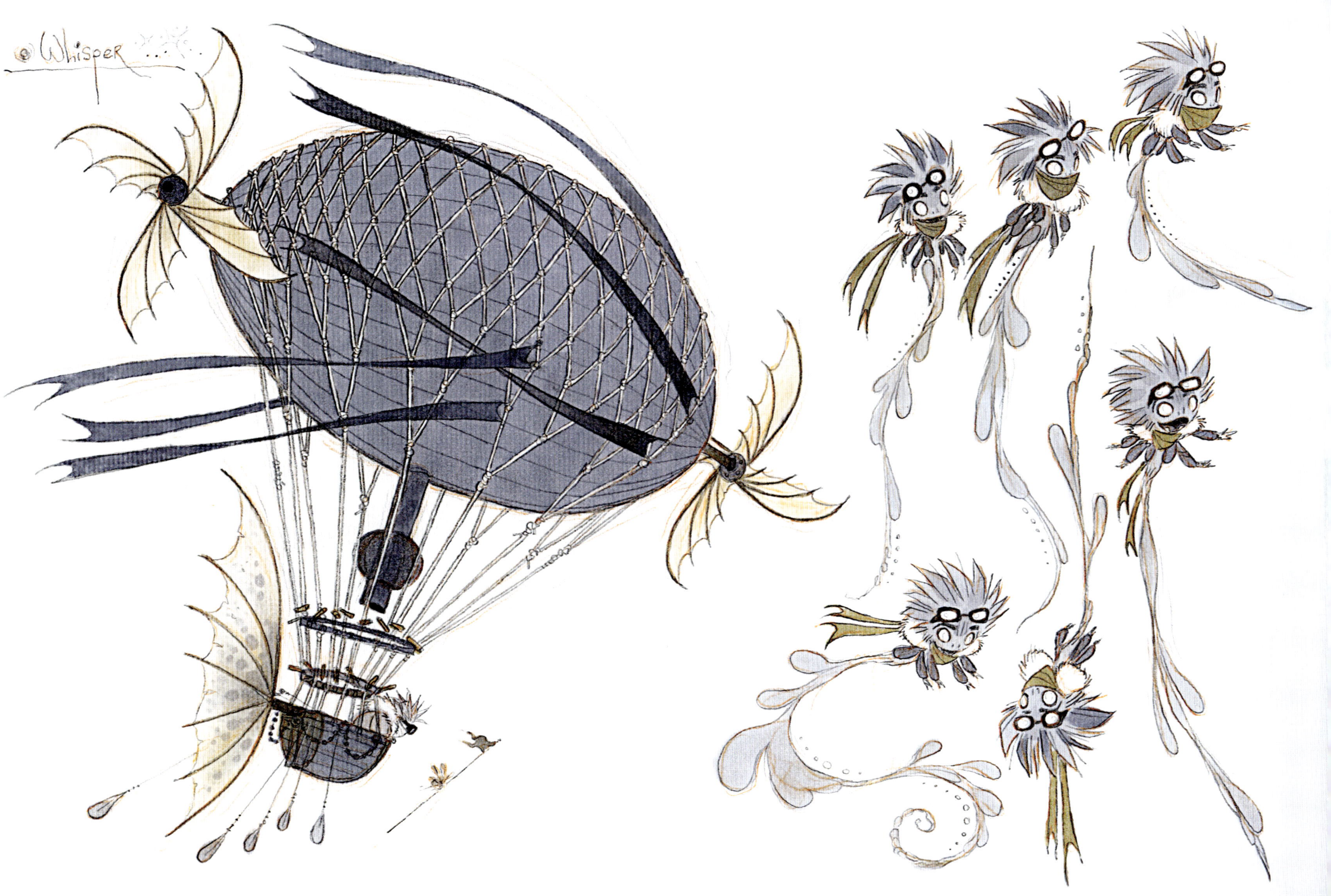
Whisper

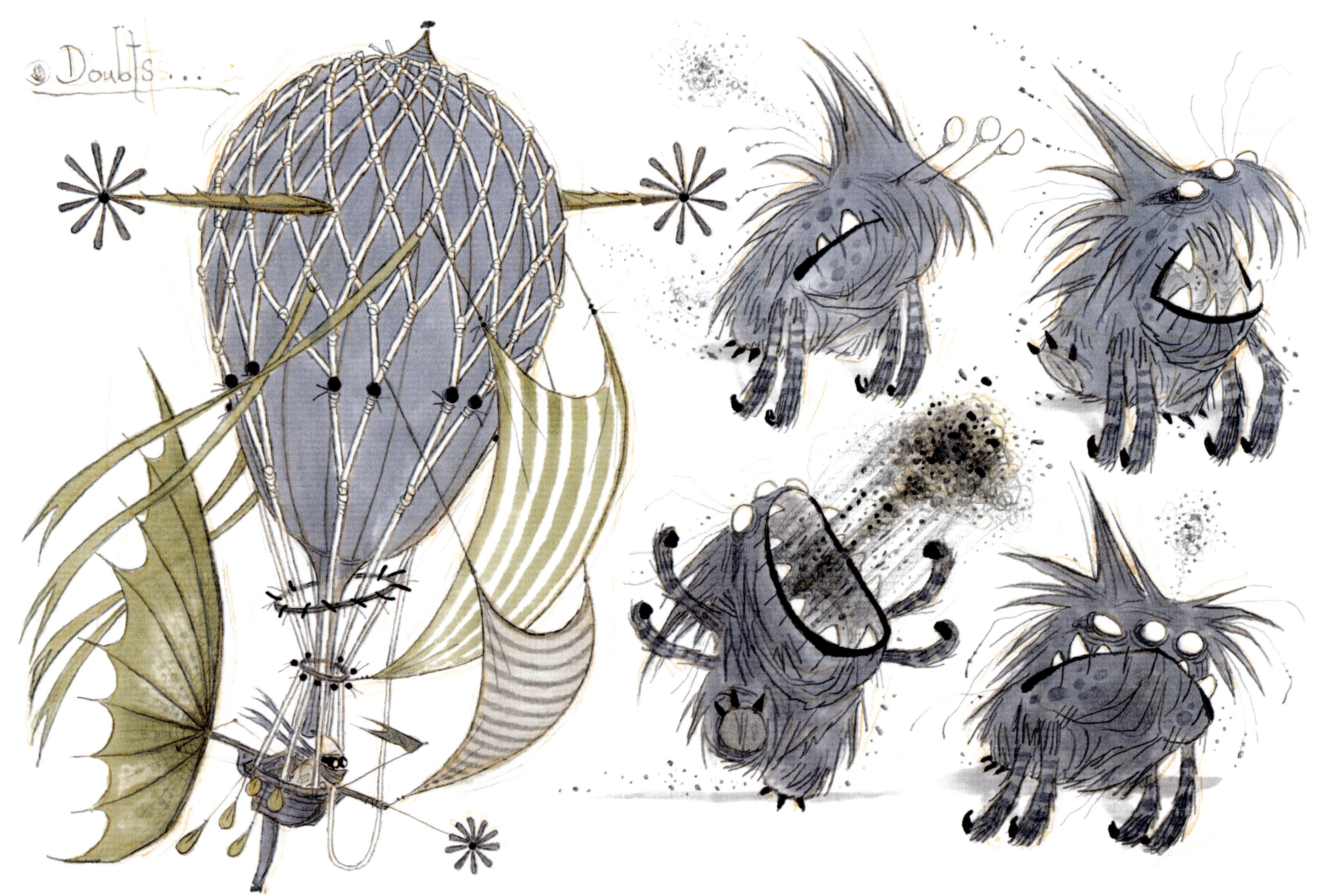
Doubts...

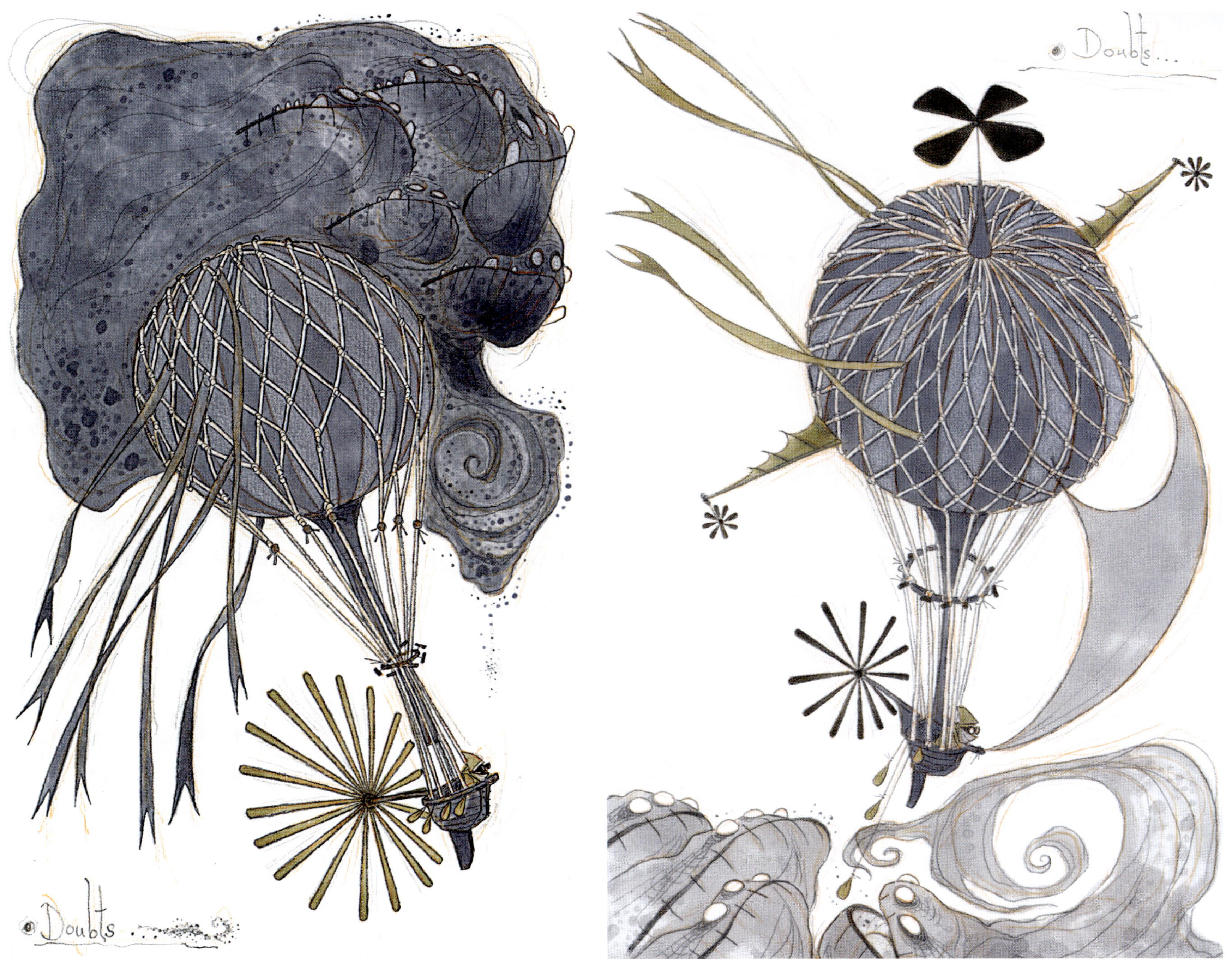
Doubts...
Doubts

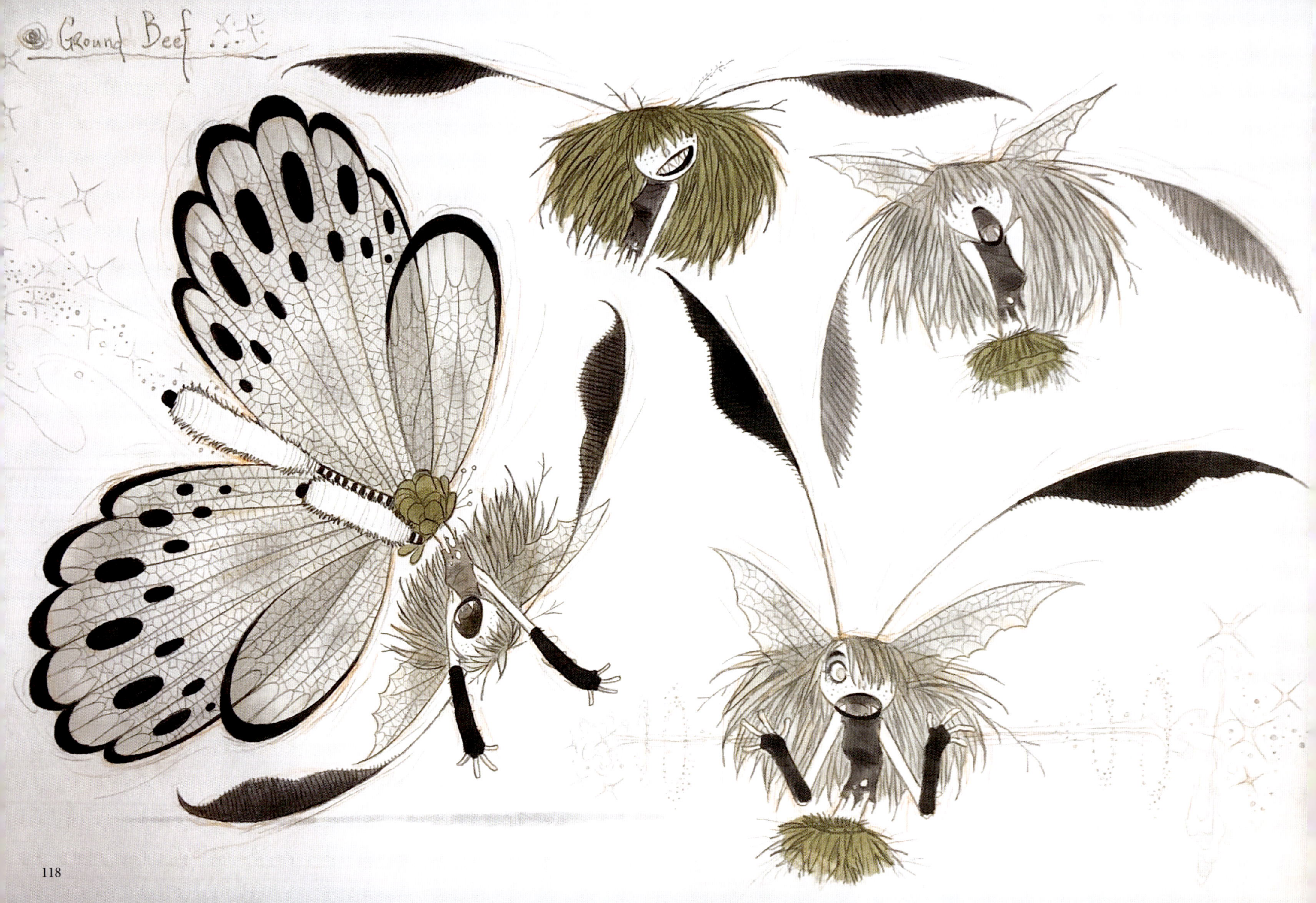
Ground Beef

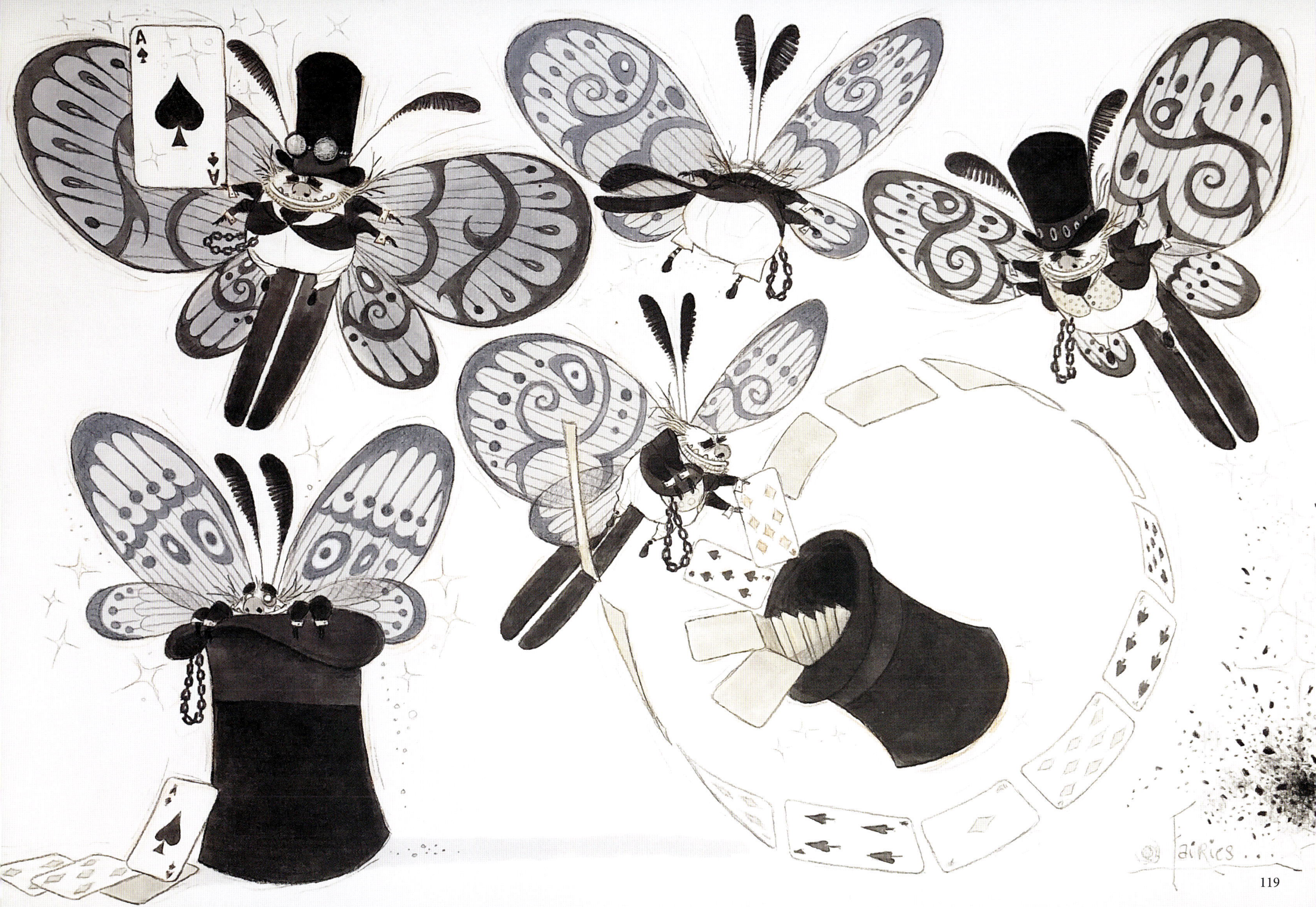

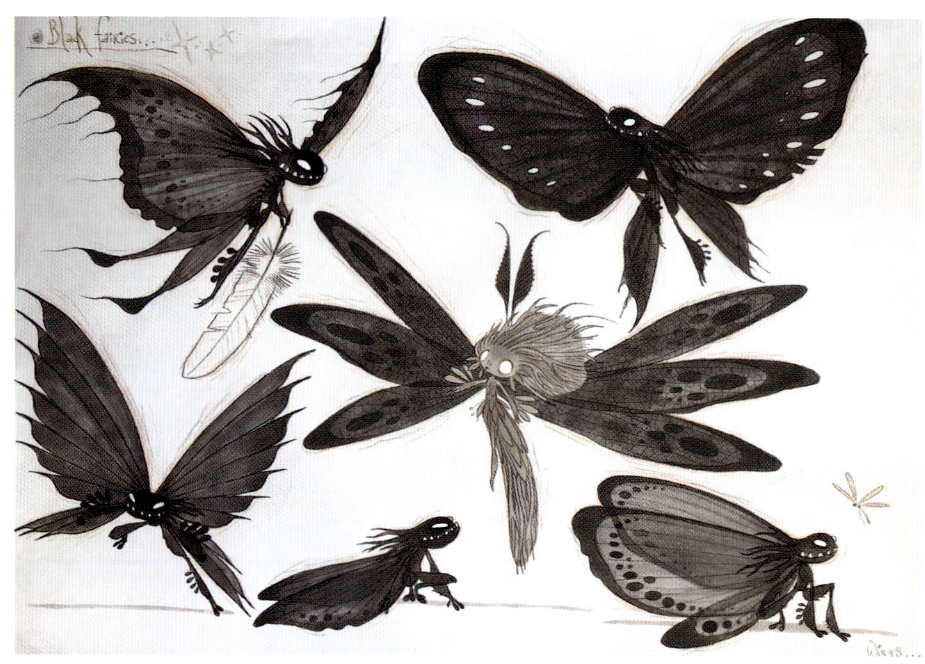
Black fairies...

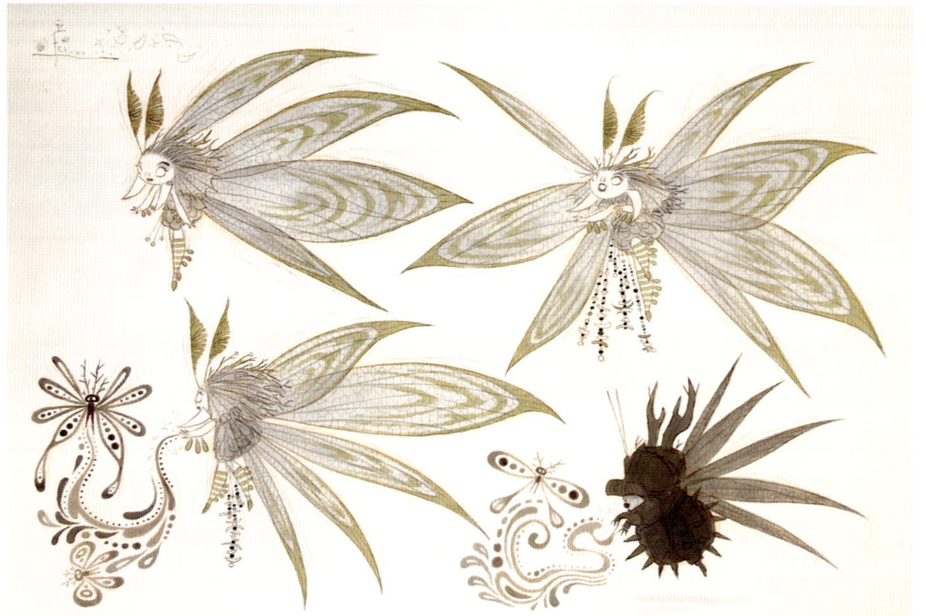

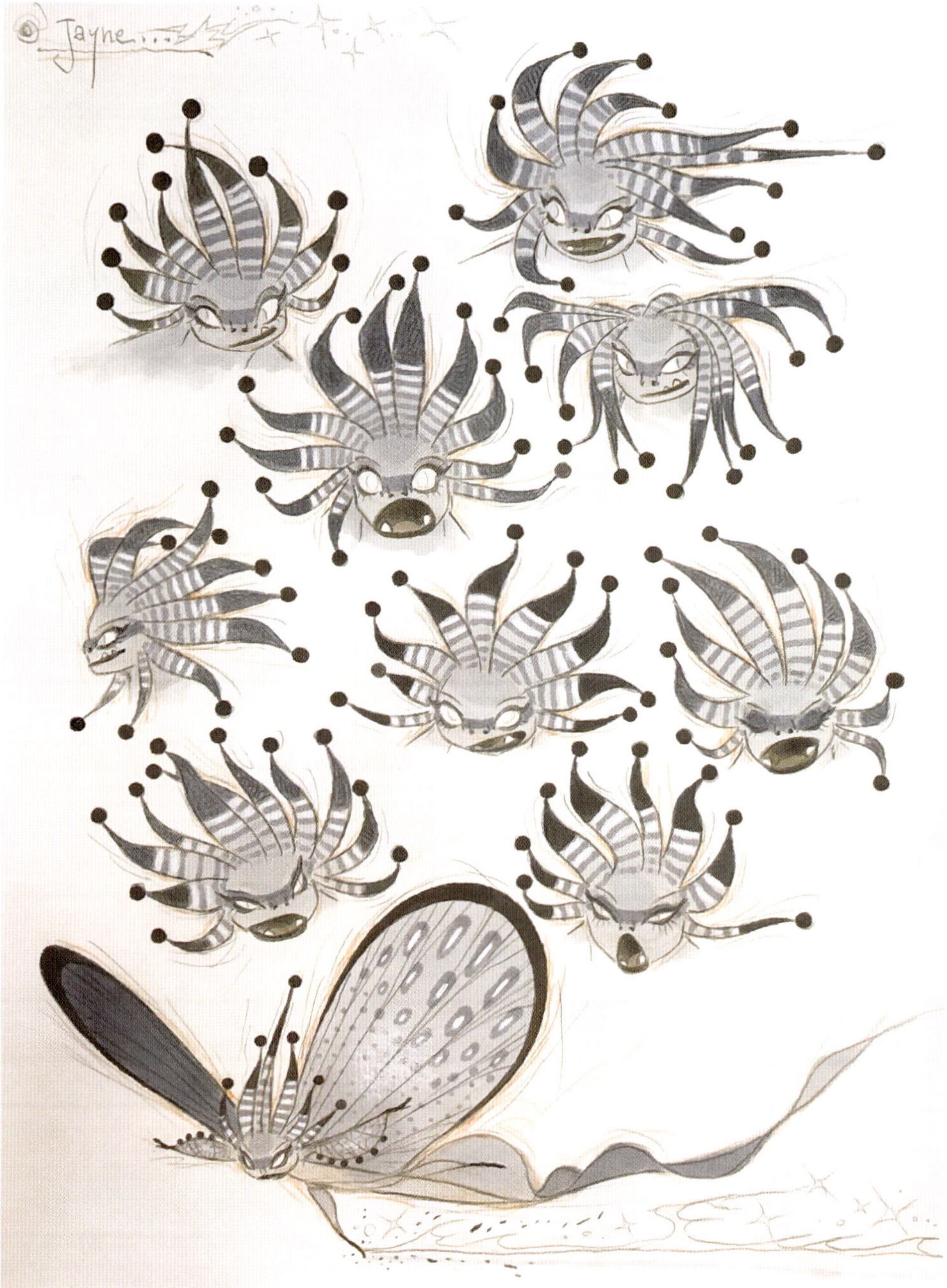

Jayne...

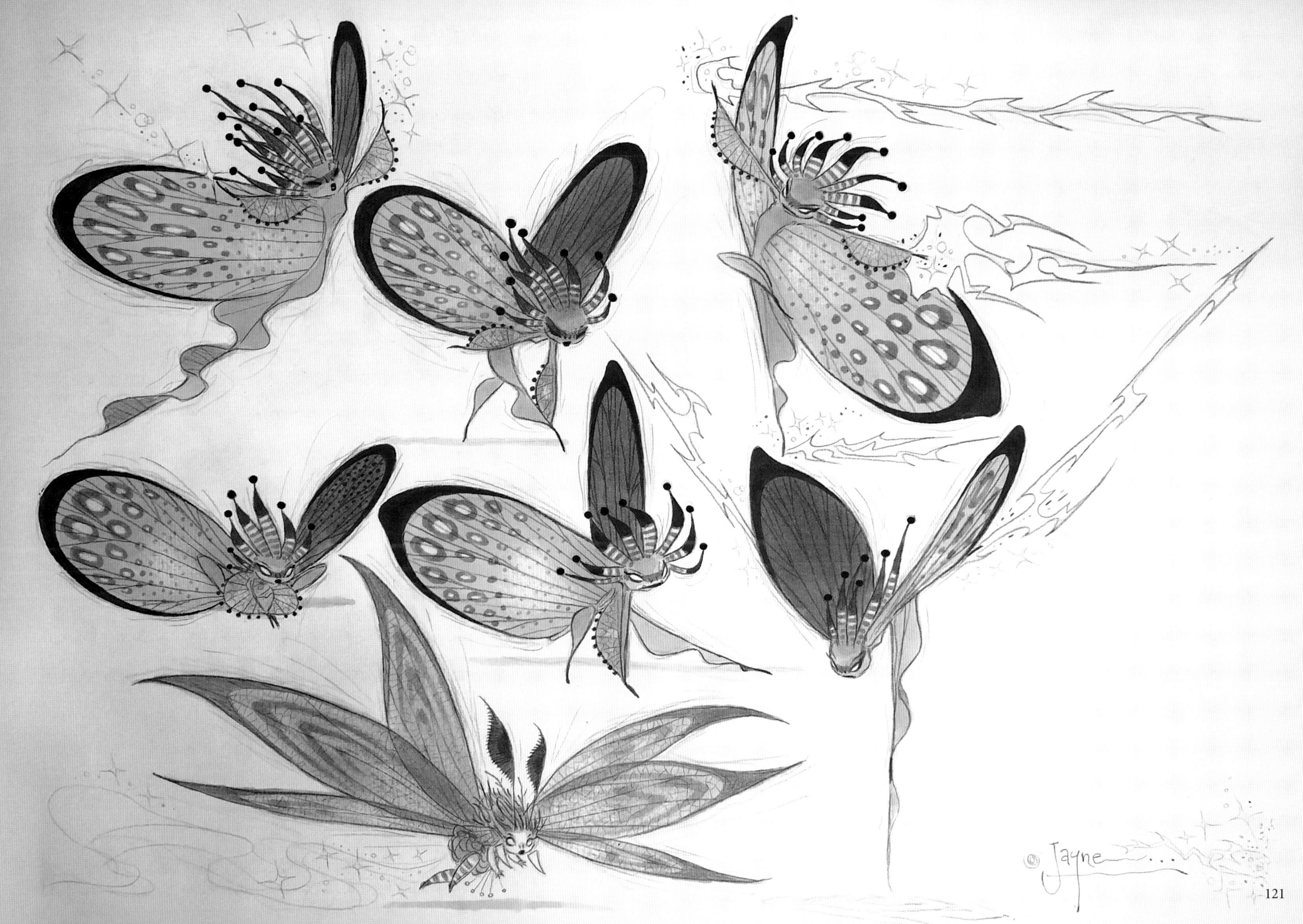
© Jayne

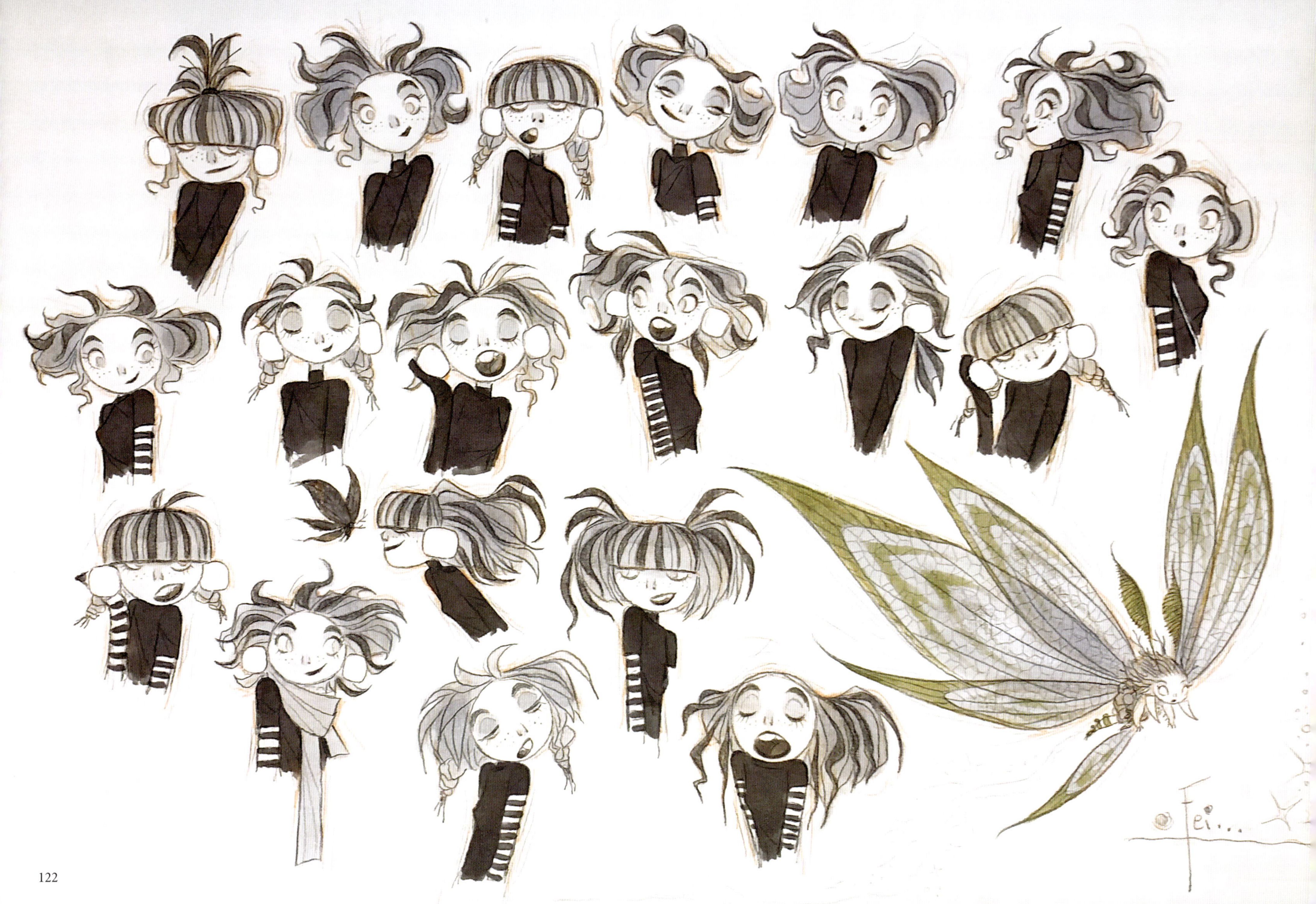
Fei...

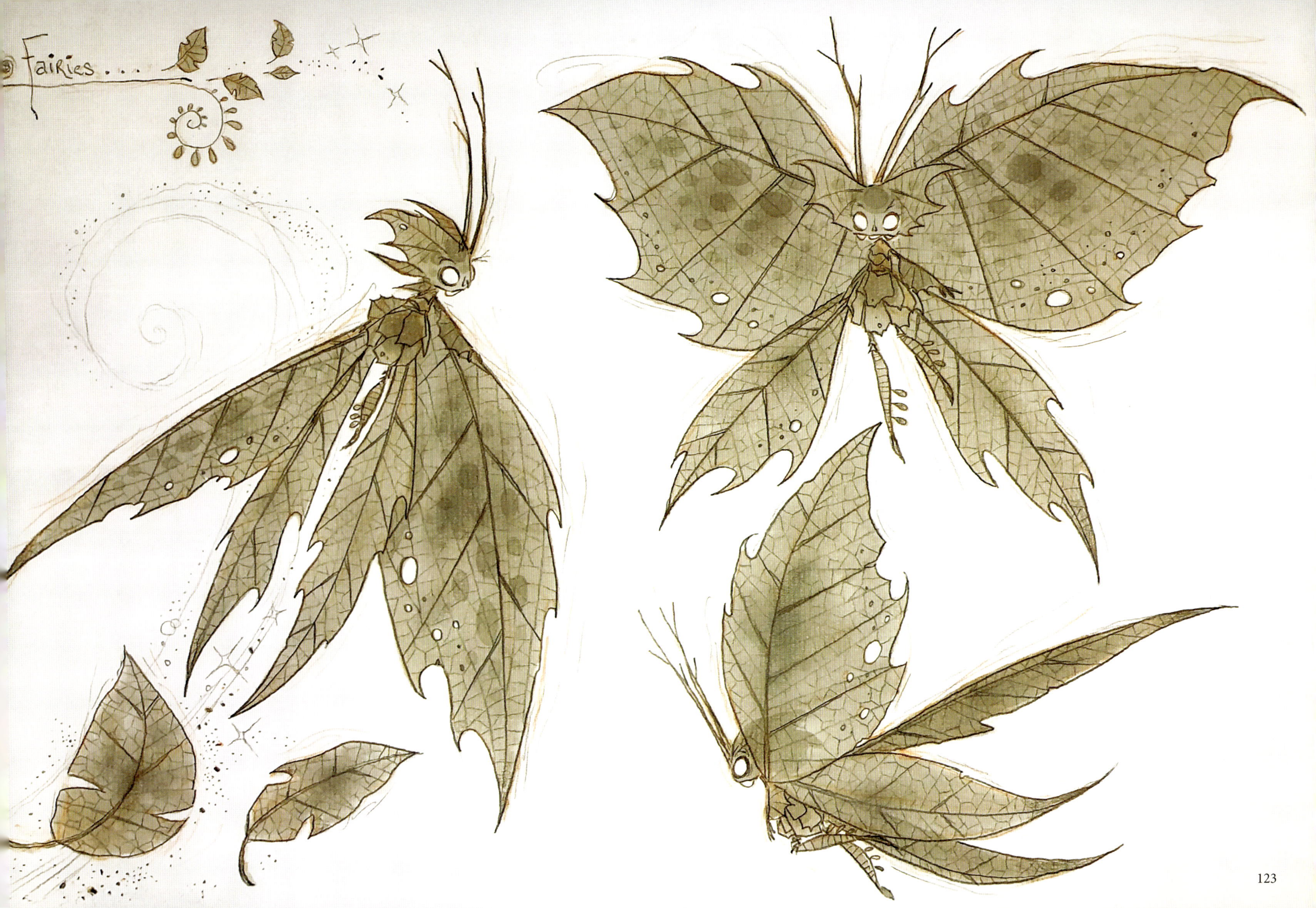
Fairies . . .

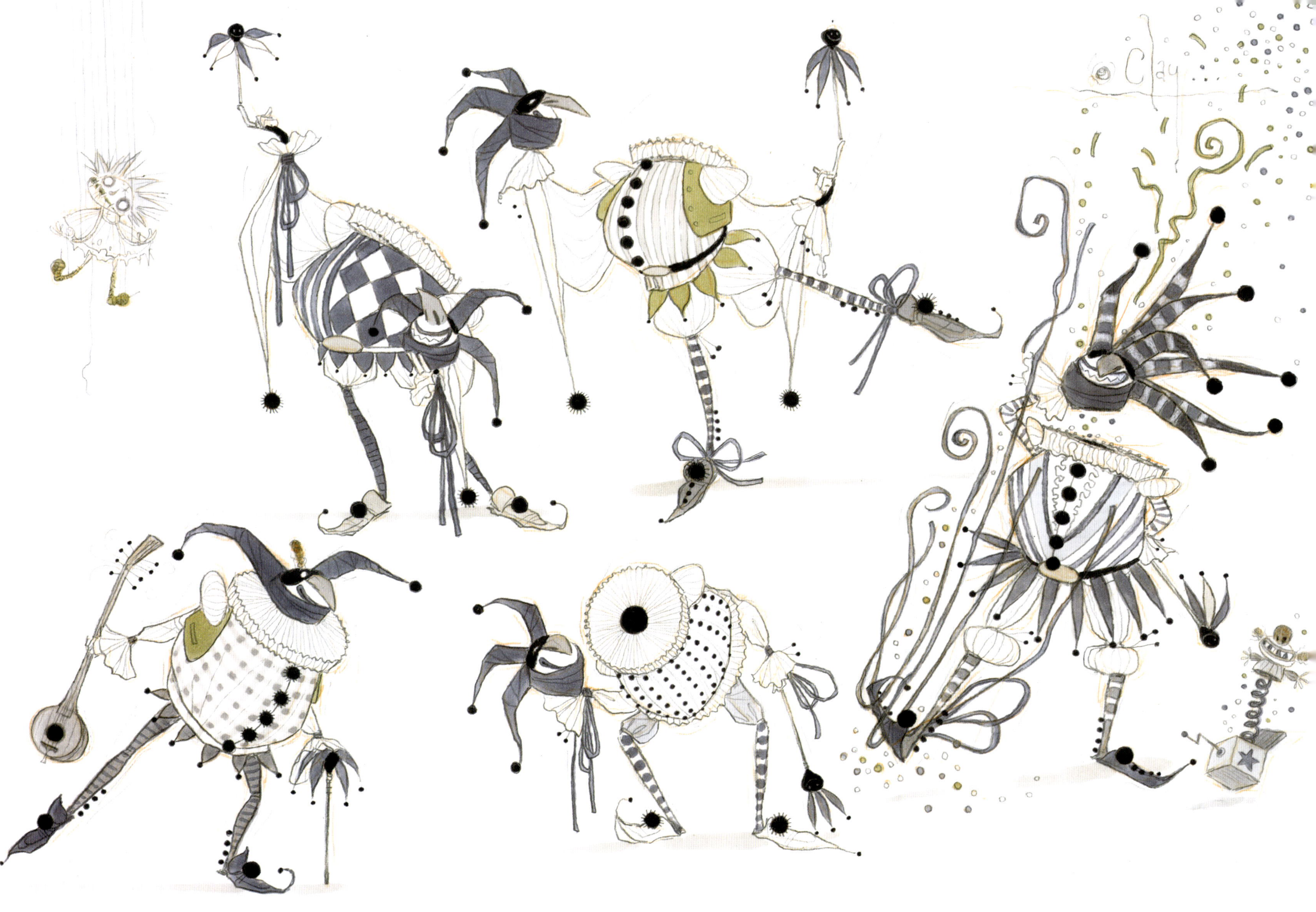
Clay

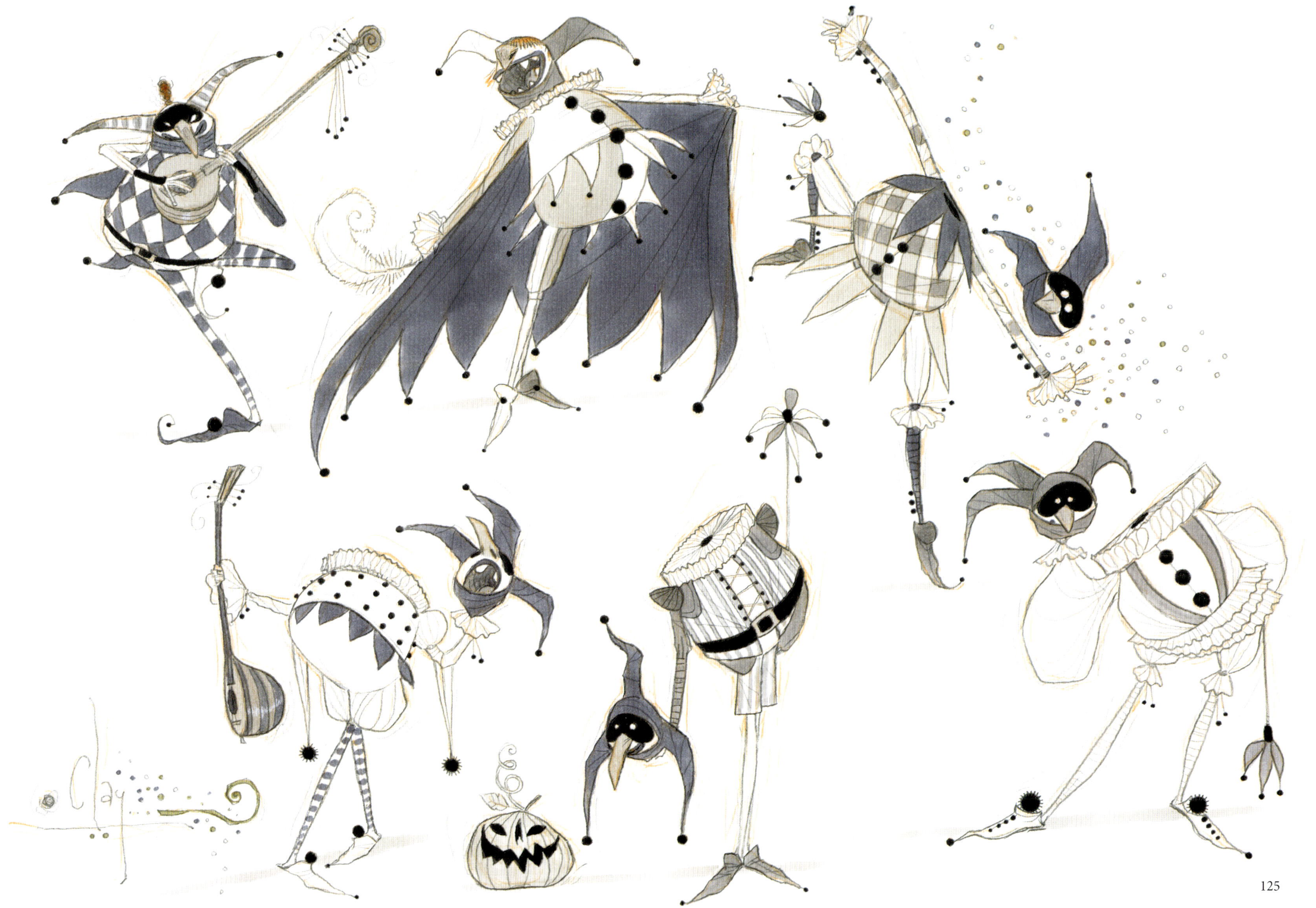
Clay

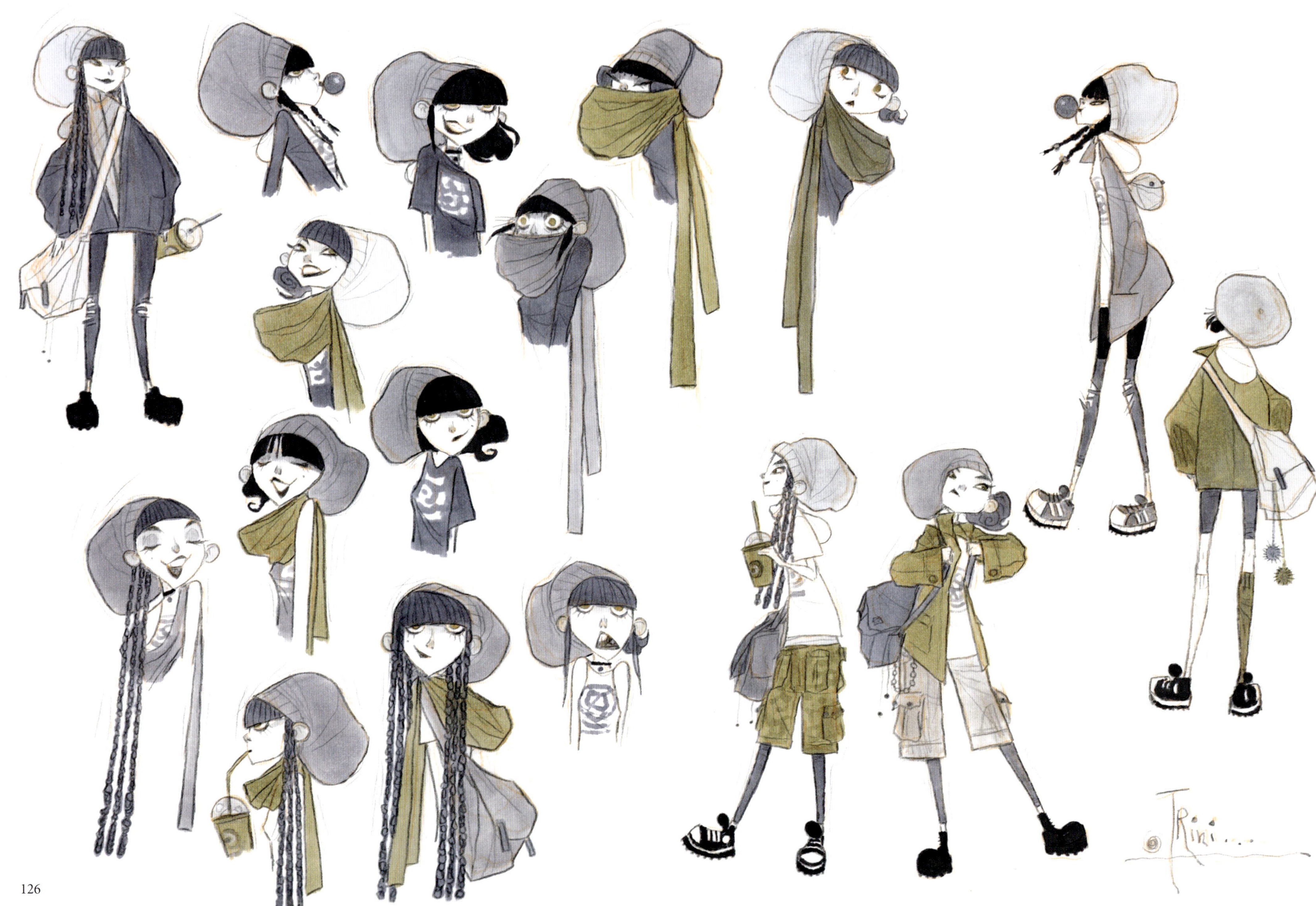

TRini....

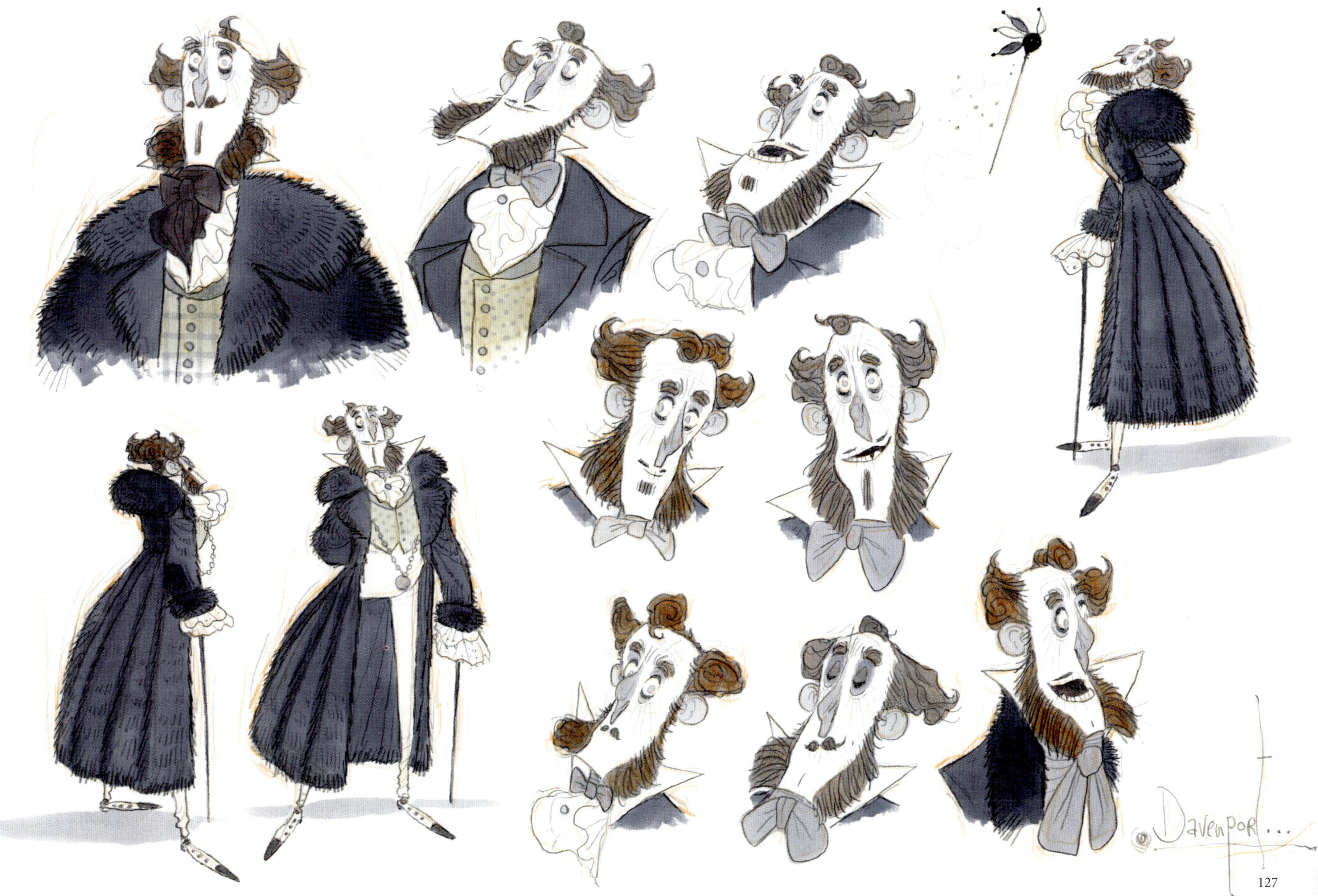
Davenport...

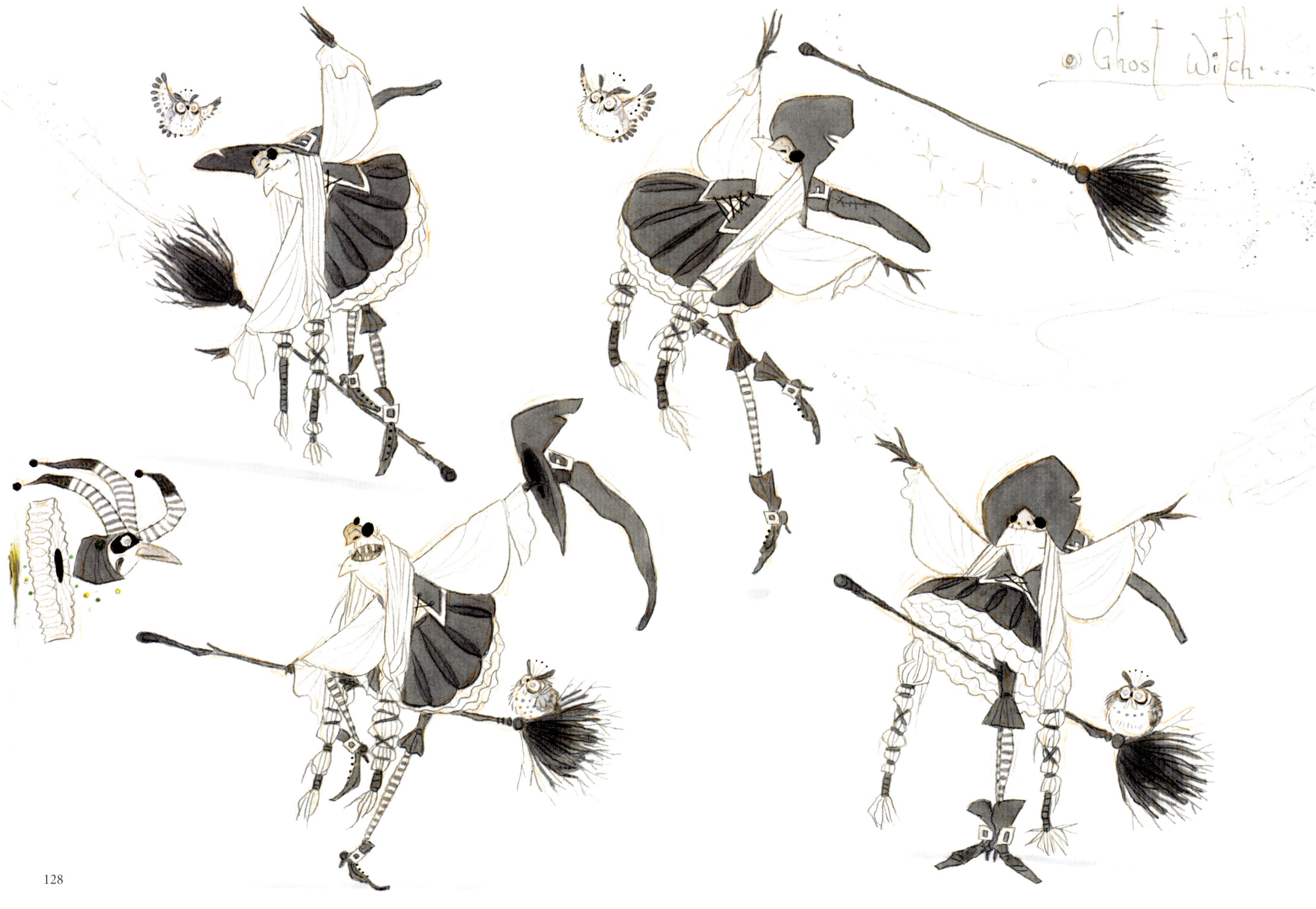
Ghost Witch...

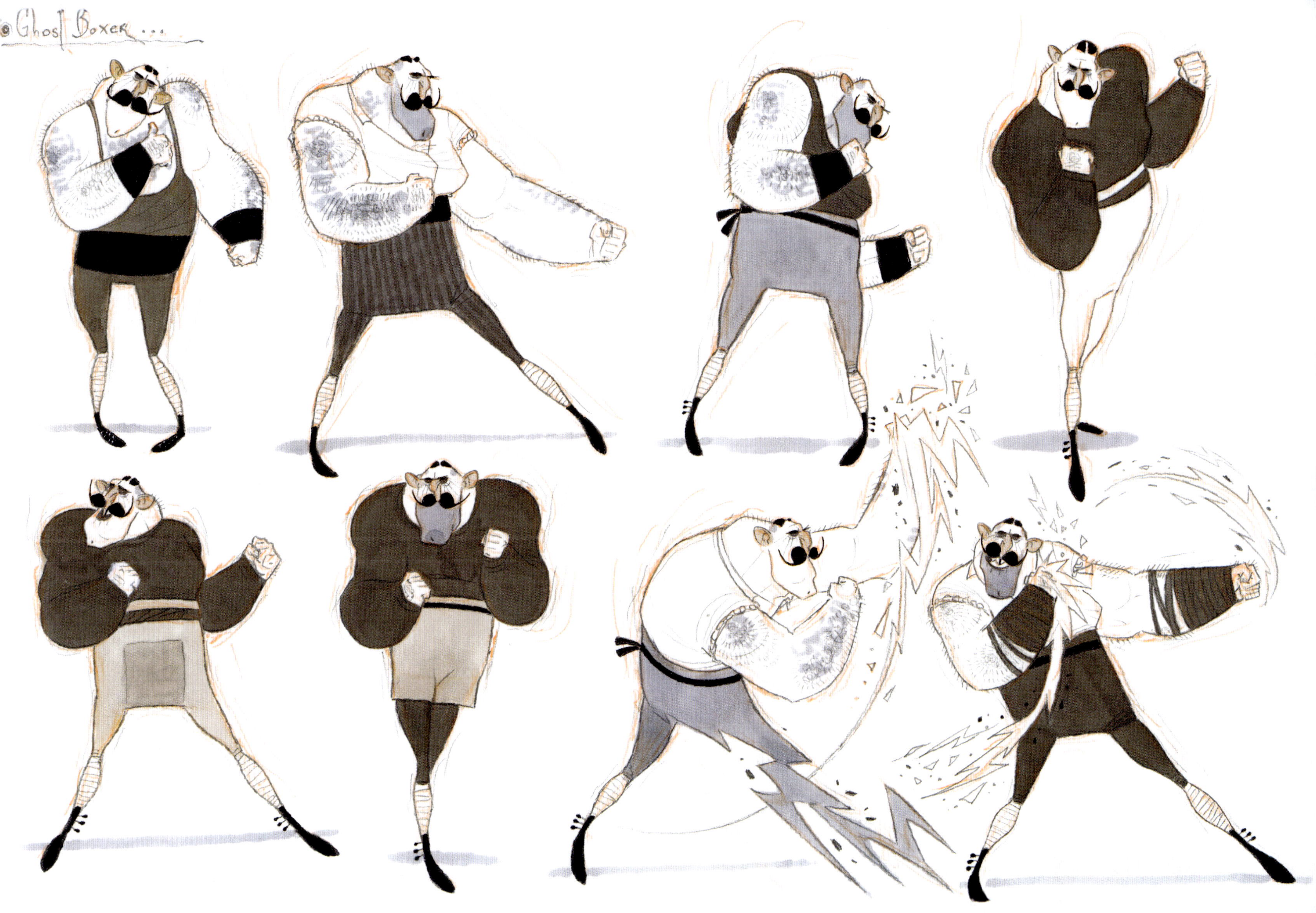

© Ghost Boxer ...

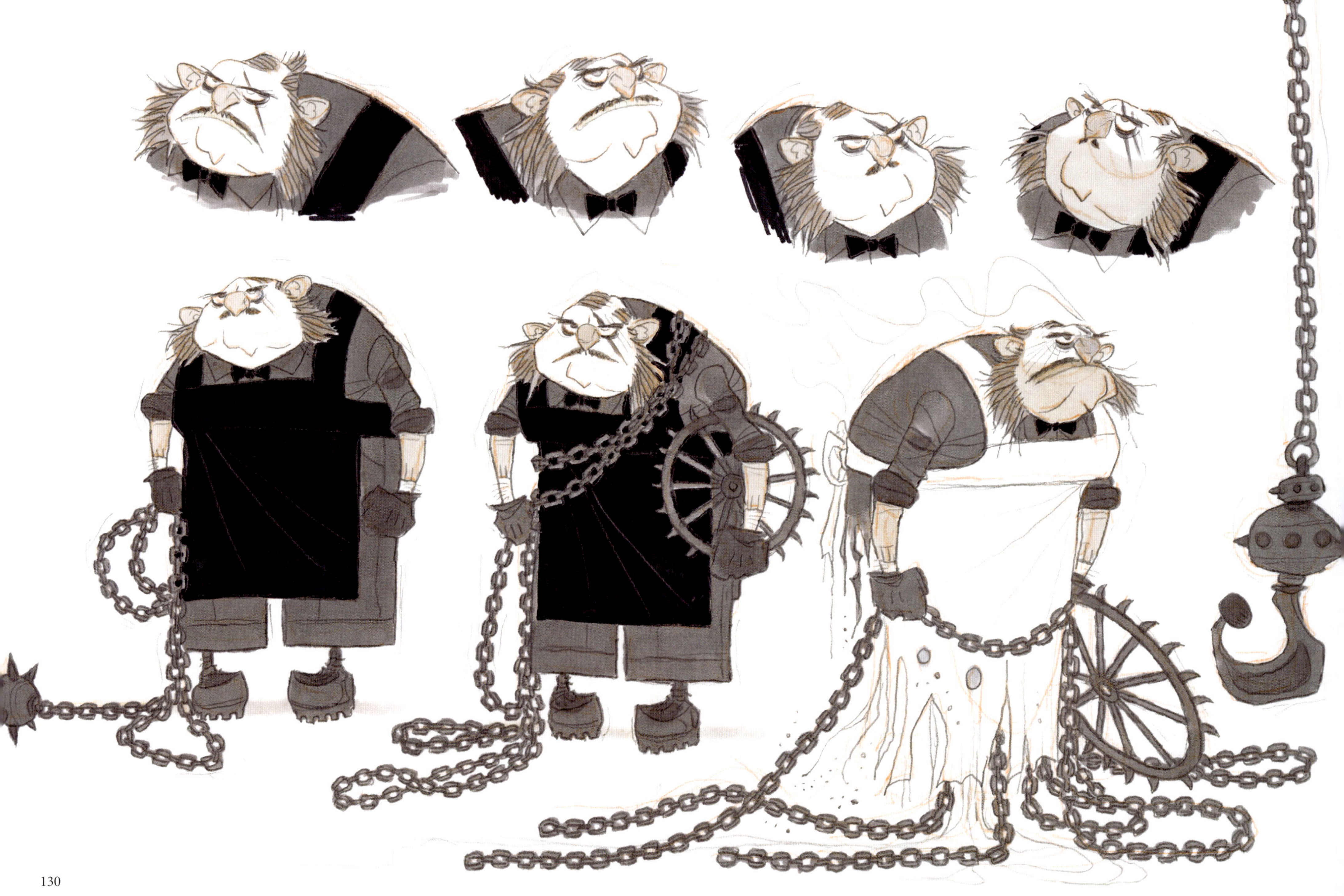

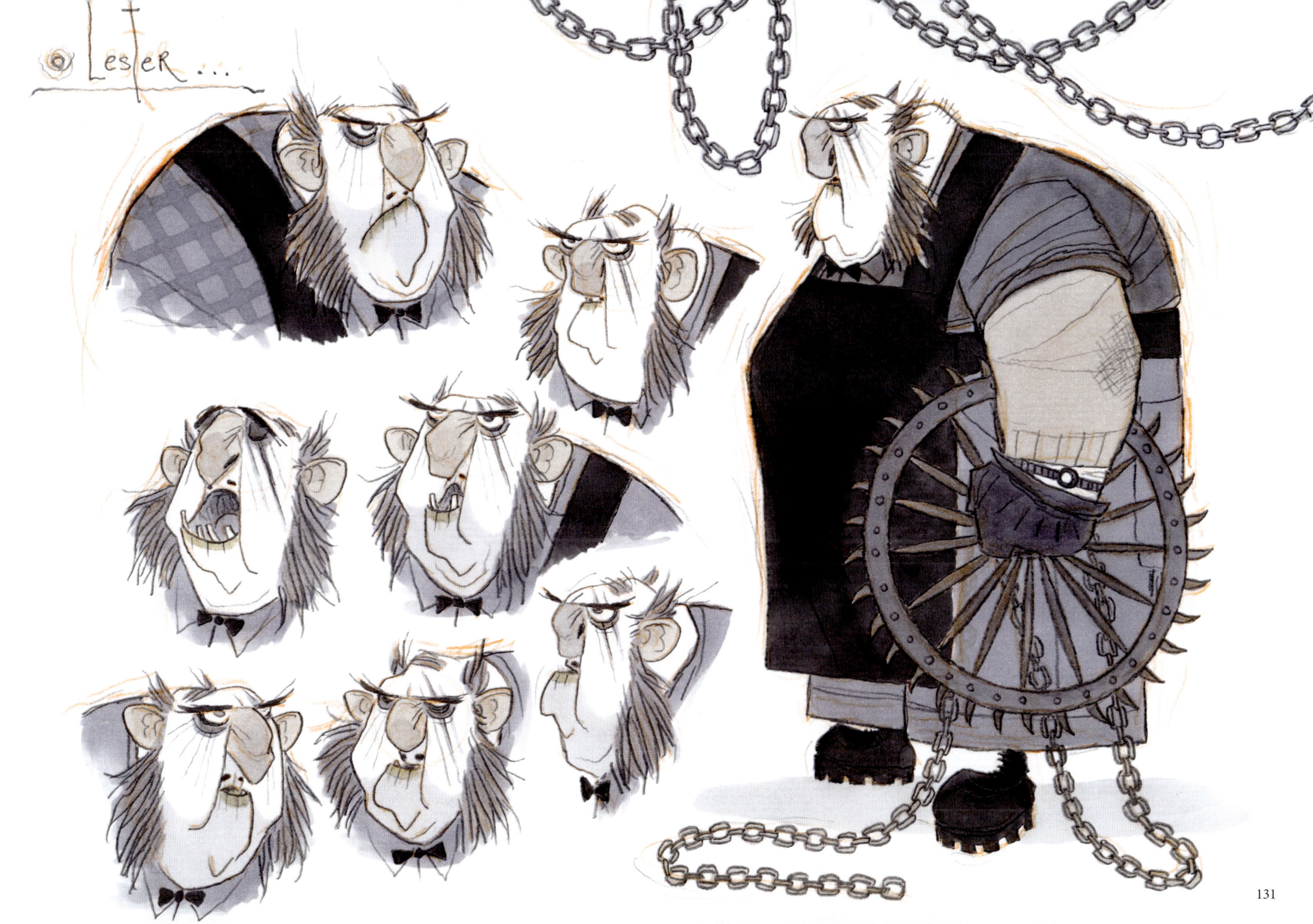
Lester ...

Visualizing Independent Vision

Amazingly, Nico has had time and space to help friends visualize their own projects along the way, his energy stretching itself across the paper to bring their imagination to animated reality. Somehow, he is continually and pleasantly surprised when fellow creators want to channel his creative talents into their projects, and perhaps it is this sense of wonder and humility that breathes unique existence into his characters beyond the obvious sharing of his natural skill set.

"Not only has Nico created some of the most iconic animated characters in film, but he also gave them a soul. Each of his drawings is a masterpiece, but those are not just pretty drawings. Unquestionably, they're immensely appealing and sophisticated, full of life, but they also demonstrate a great sense of humor, a childlike playfulness, and a genuine tenderness that would make anyone fall in love at first sight with those characters. Nico's designs for French Roast*'s characters were so original and unique that I felt obligated to stay as true as possible to his drawings in translating them to CG. The biggest challenge was to live up to Nico's genius."*

—Fabrice Joubert, director

Opposite & overleaf: *French Roast* (2008) character concepts

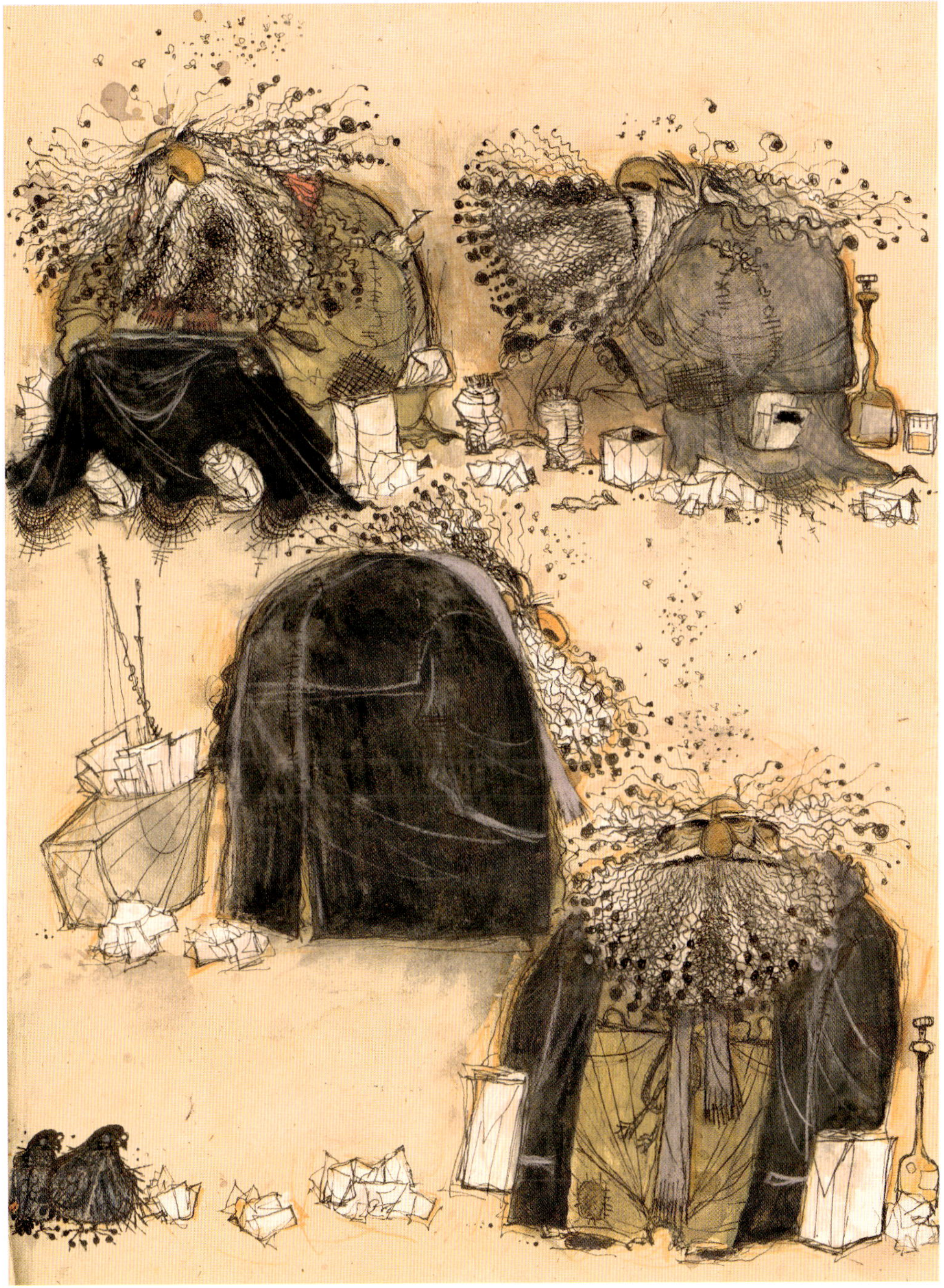

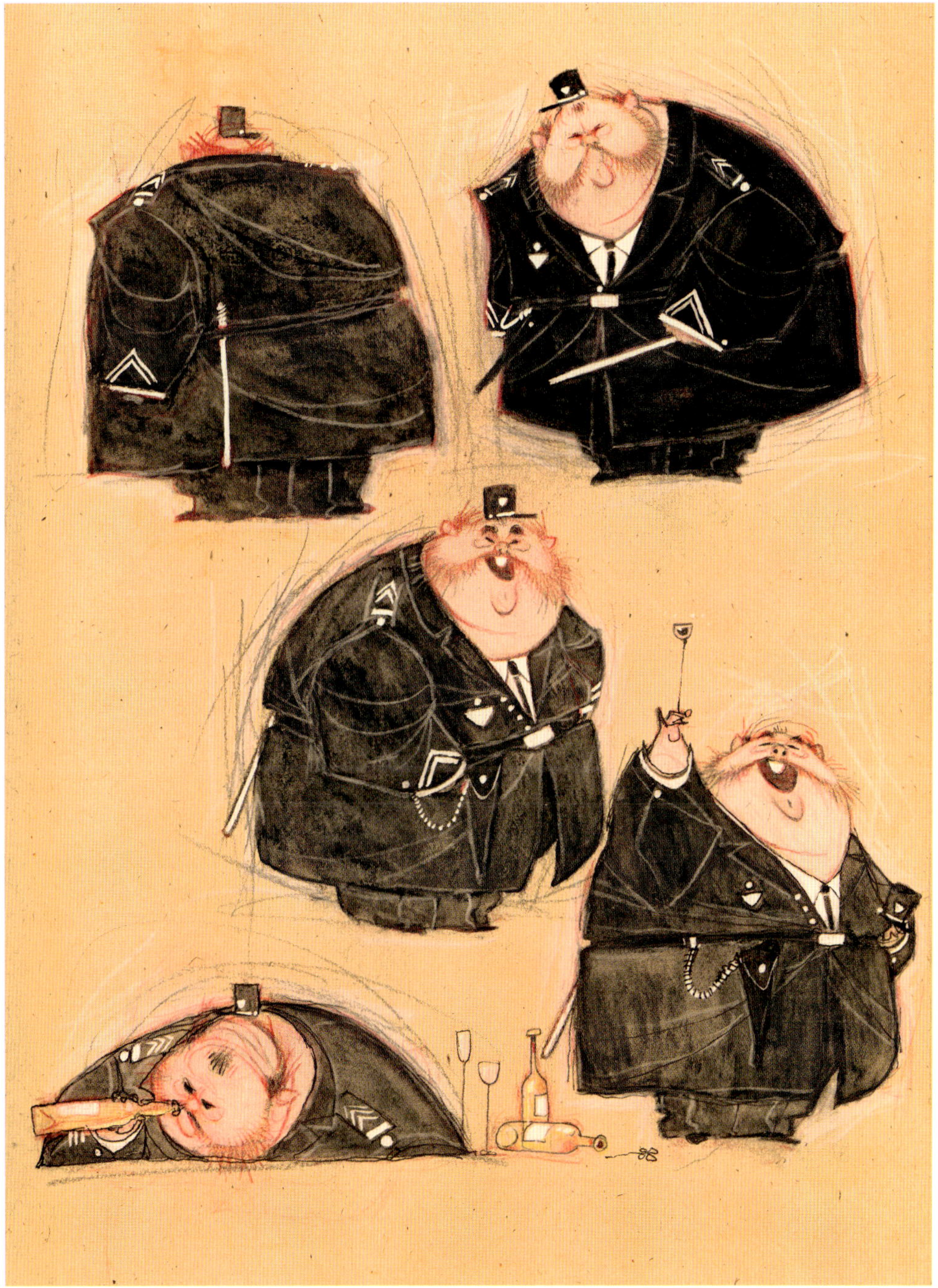

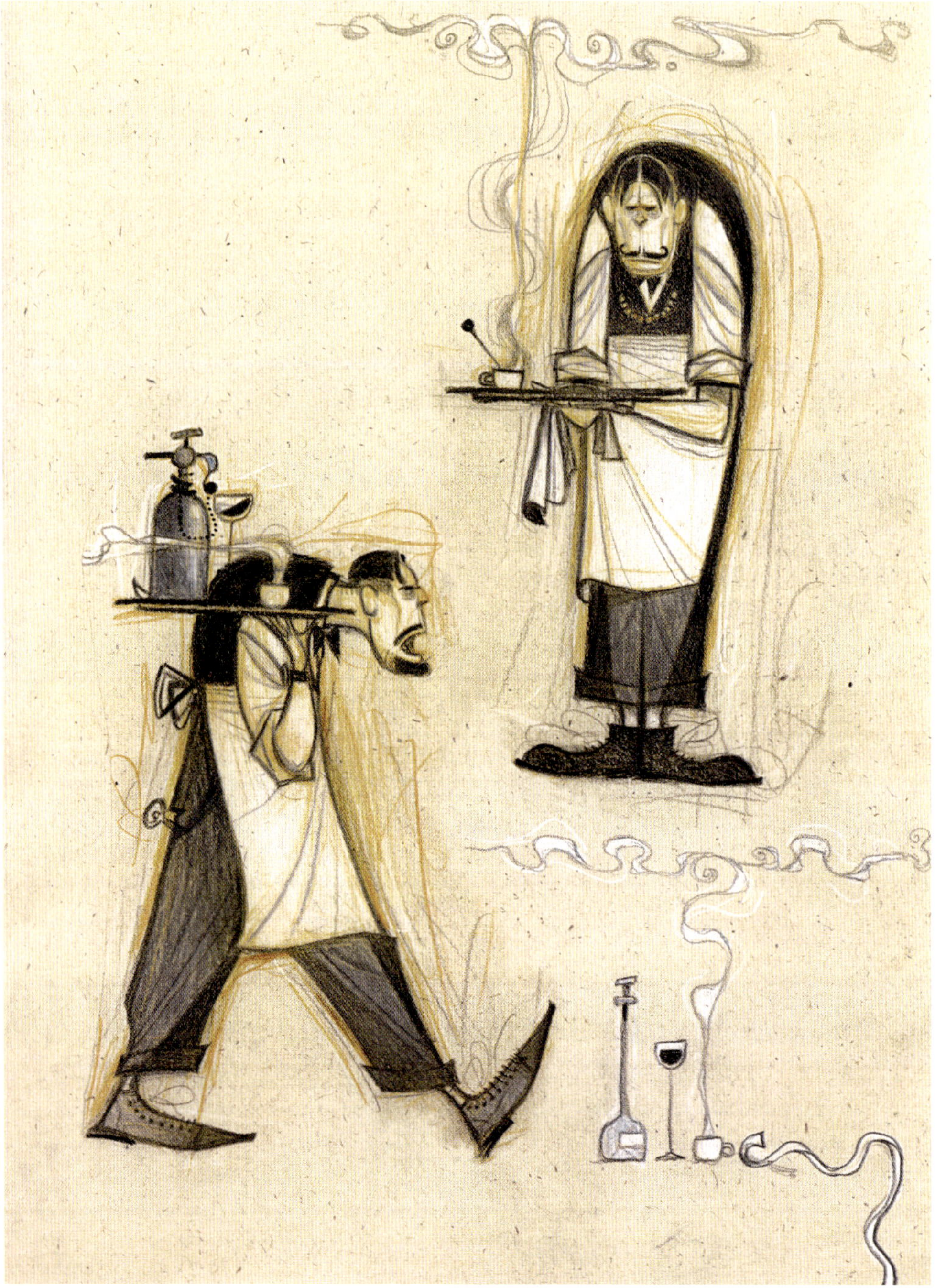

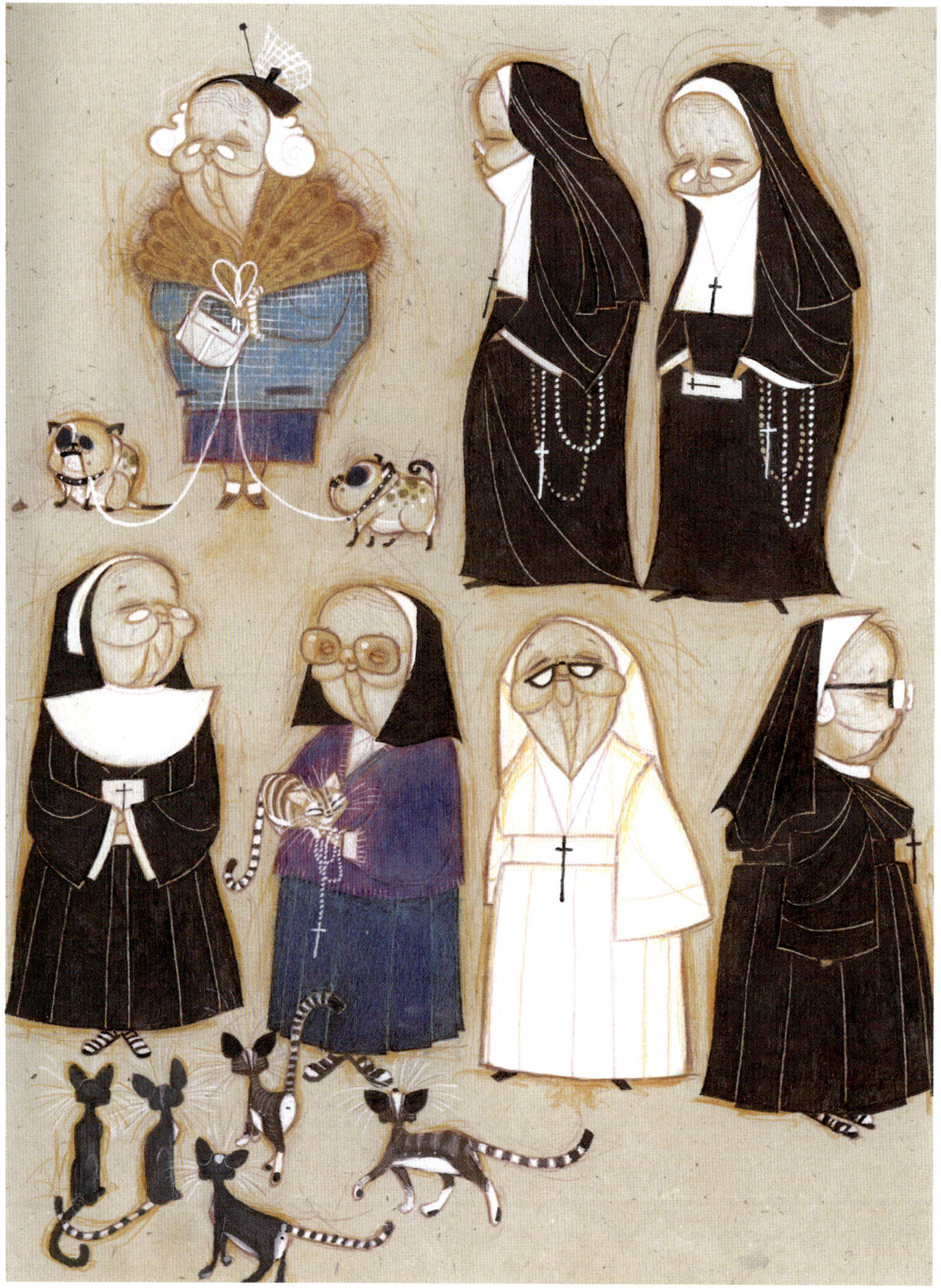

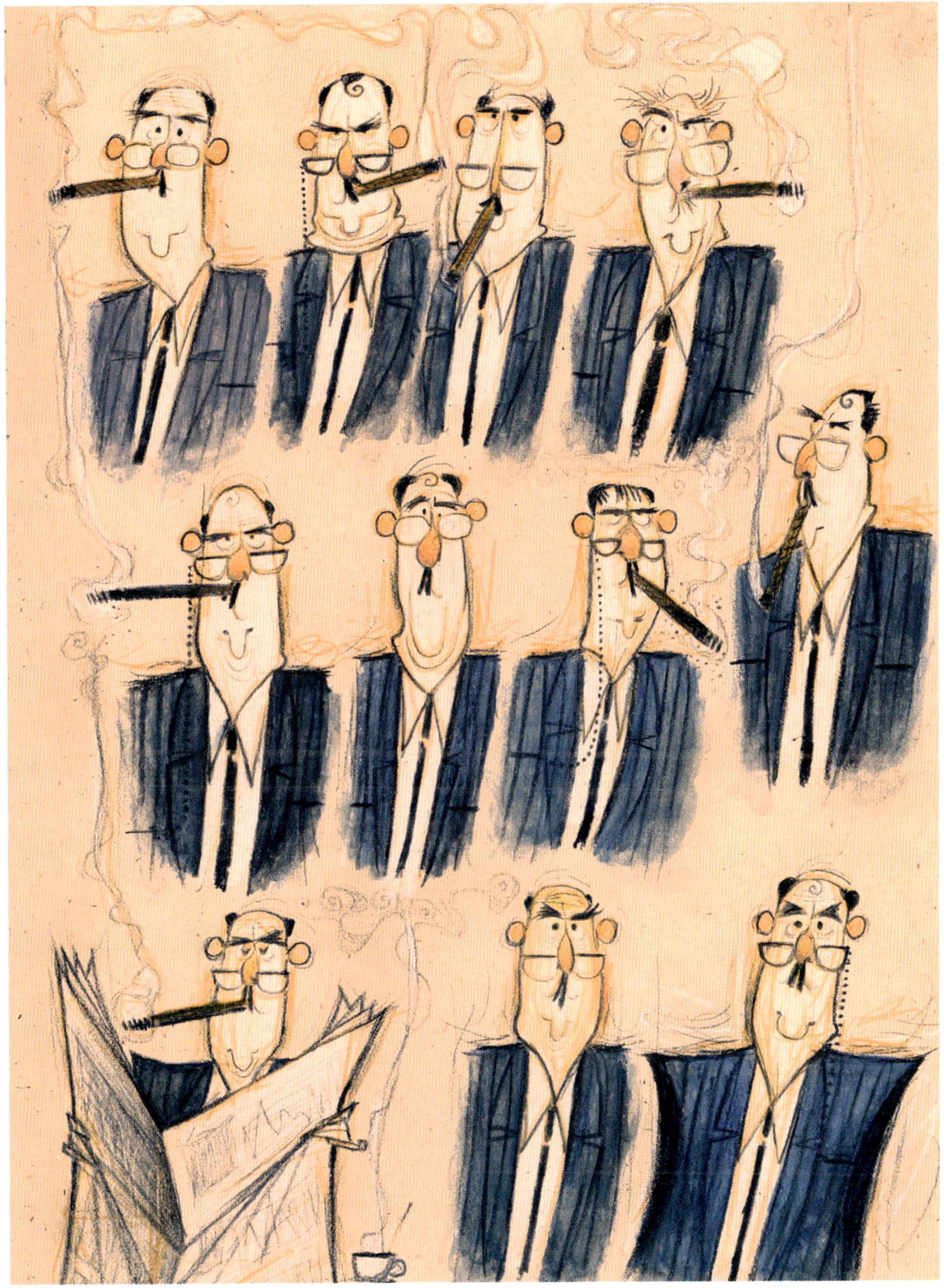

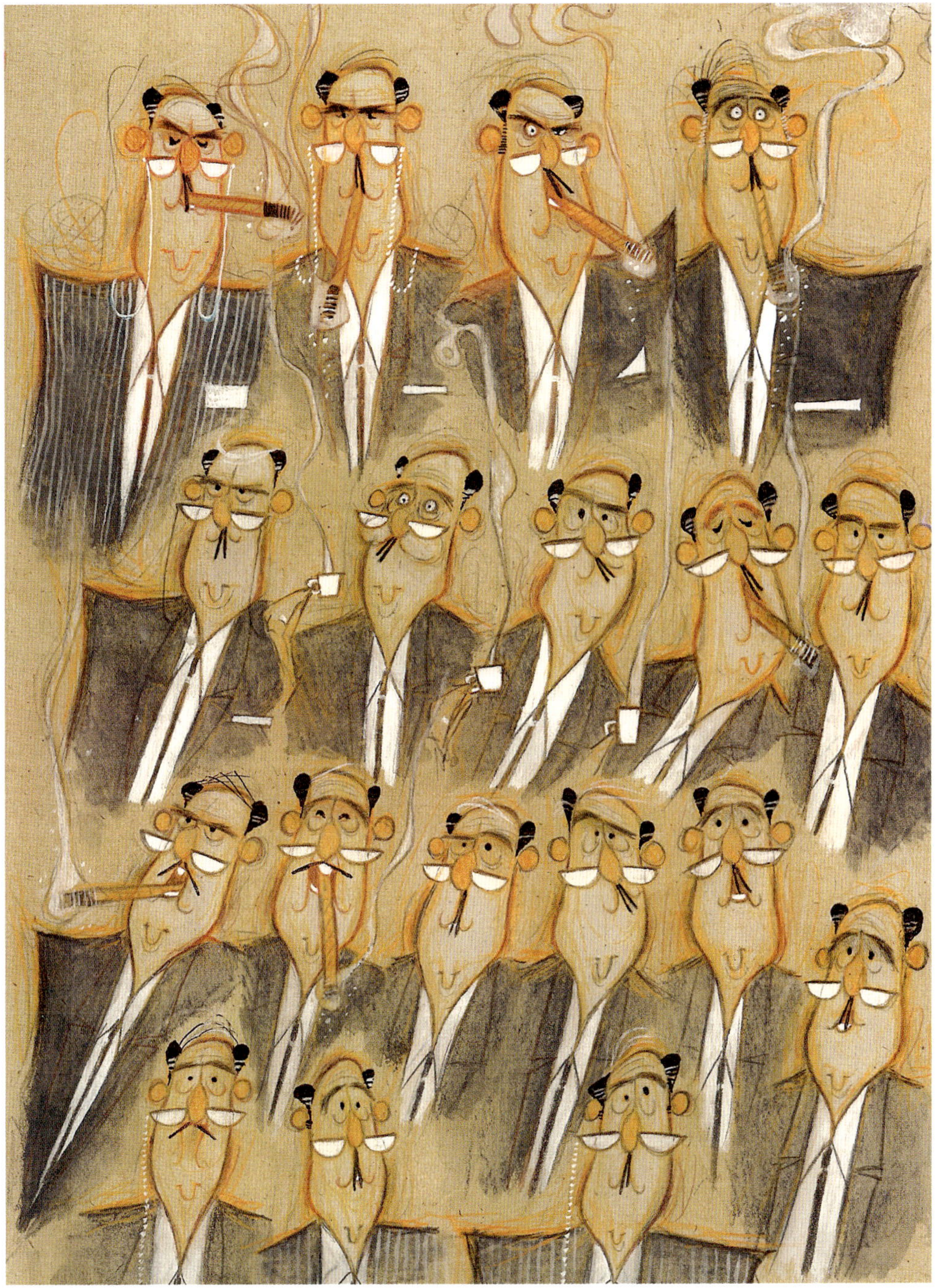

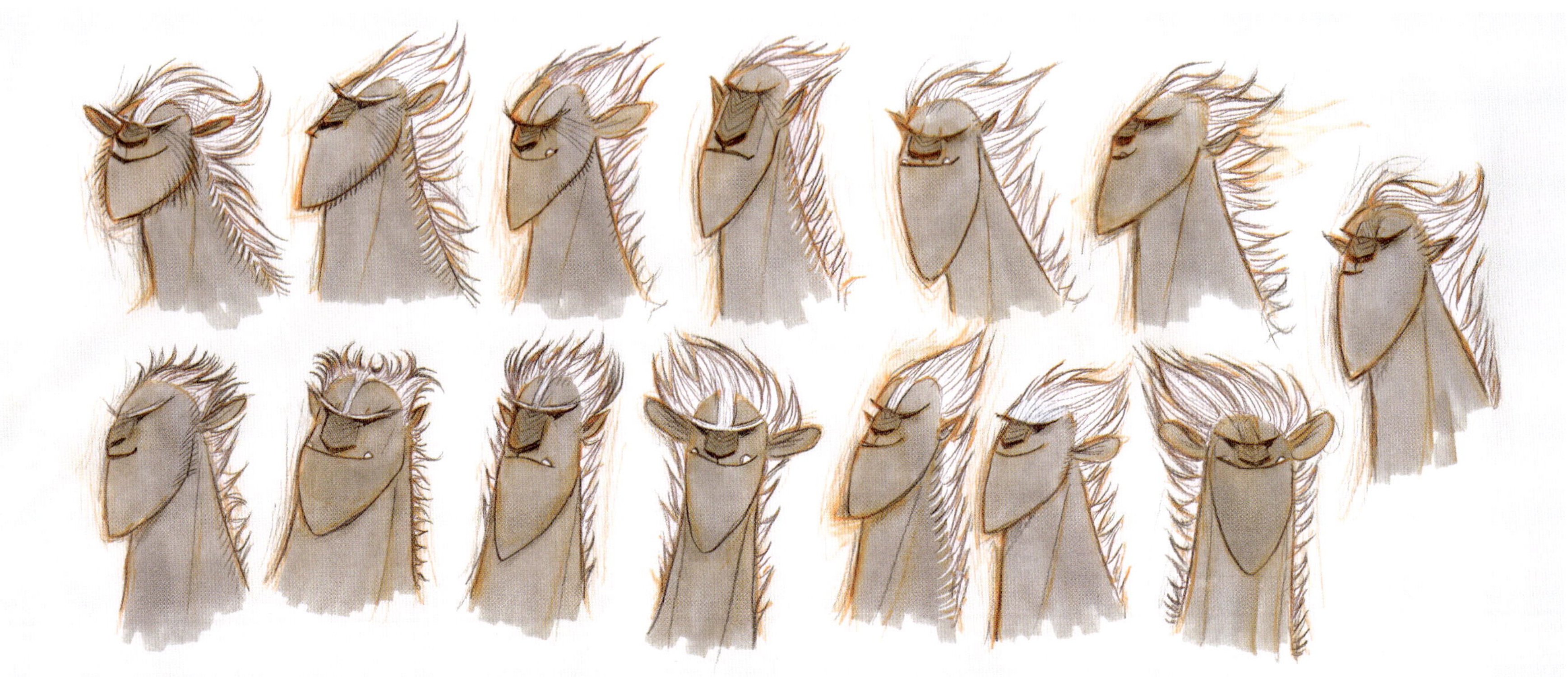

"When I was student at Gobelins film school, the admin office had a special drawer filled with sheets of cat drawings by Nicolas Marlet. We were captivated by the elegance and humor of those drawings. For us students, this drawer felt like a treasure chest of sacred relics. Years later, when I became an animator at DreamWorks, I finally had the chance to meet the master himself. It turned out that this ultimate master was an incredibly humble and kind person. What amazed me most was how Nico had preserved that childlike sense of wonder, seeing the world through a lens of poetry and humor. This essence is present in every drawing Nico creates. Just as an actor pours a piece of himself into each of his roles, Nico imbues his characters with his tenderness and his dreamlike artistic quality. In many ways, the character of Mune is Nicolas Marlet."

—**Alexandre Heboyan, director**

"Nico is like one of his drawings: sensitive and poetic. He seems to have fallen from the sky, or maybe from the moon, or even straight from a fairy tale. I had the great opportunity to collaborate with him on my first animated film. I can't draw, but I had this poetic character in my imagination. I described him to Nico with a few words. When I received Nico's first designs, I was blown away. As if Nico could read my mind, he nailed it right away. He brought Mune to life. Mune is the Guardian of the Moon. So is Nico. Wandering in the sky, among the stars. Chapeau bas, l'artiste, et bons baisers de la lune.*"*

—**Benoît Philippon, director**

Above, opposite & pp. 138–143: *Mune: Guardian of the Moon* (2014) character concepts

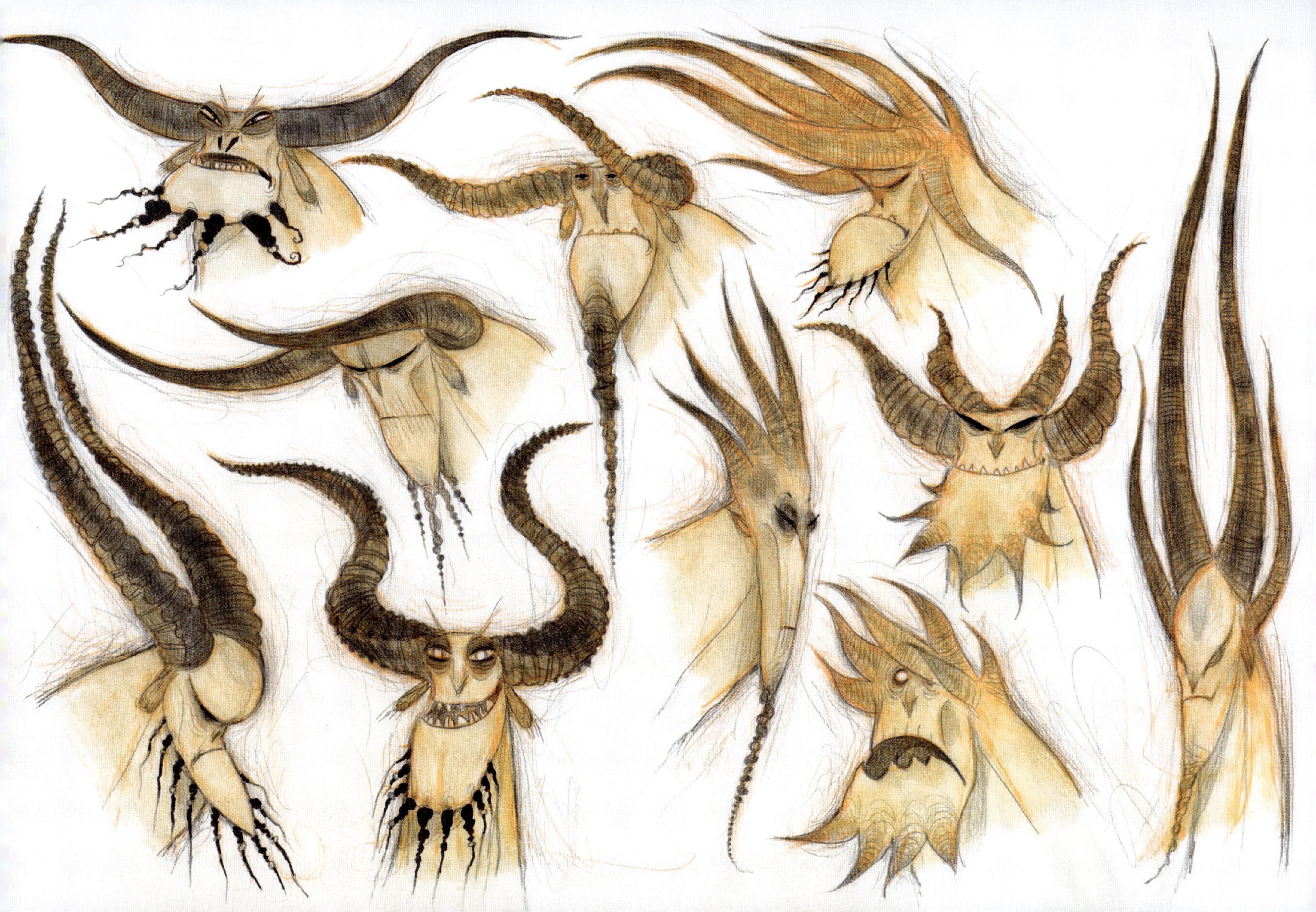

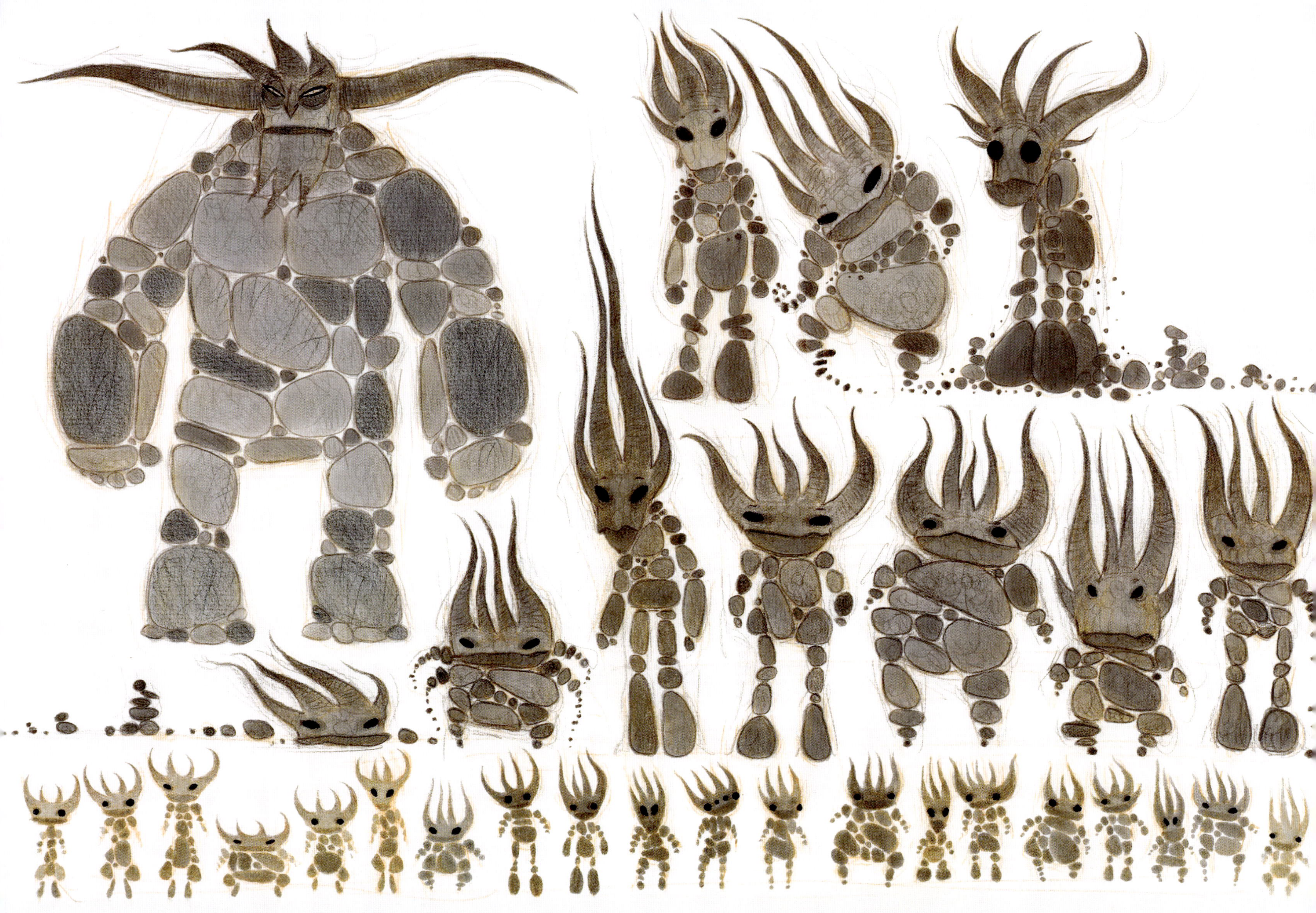

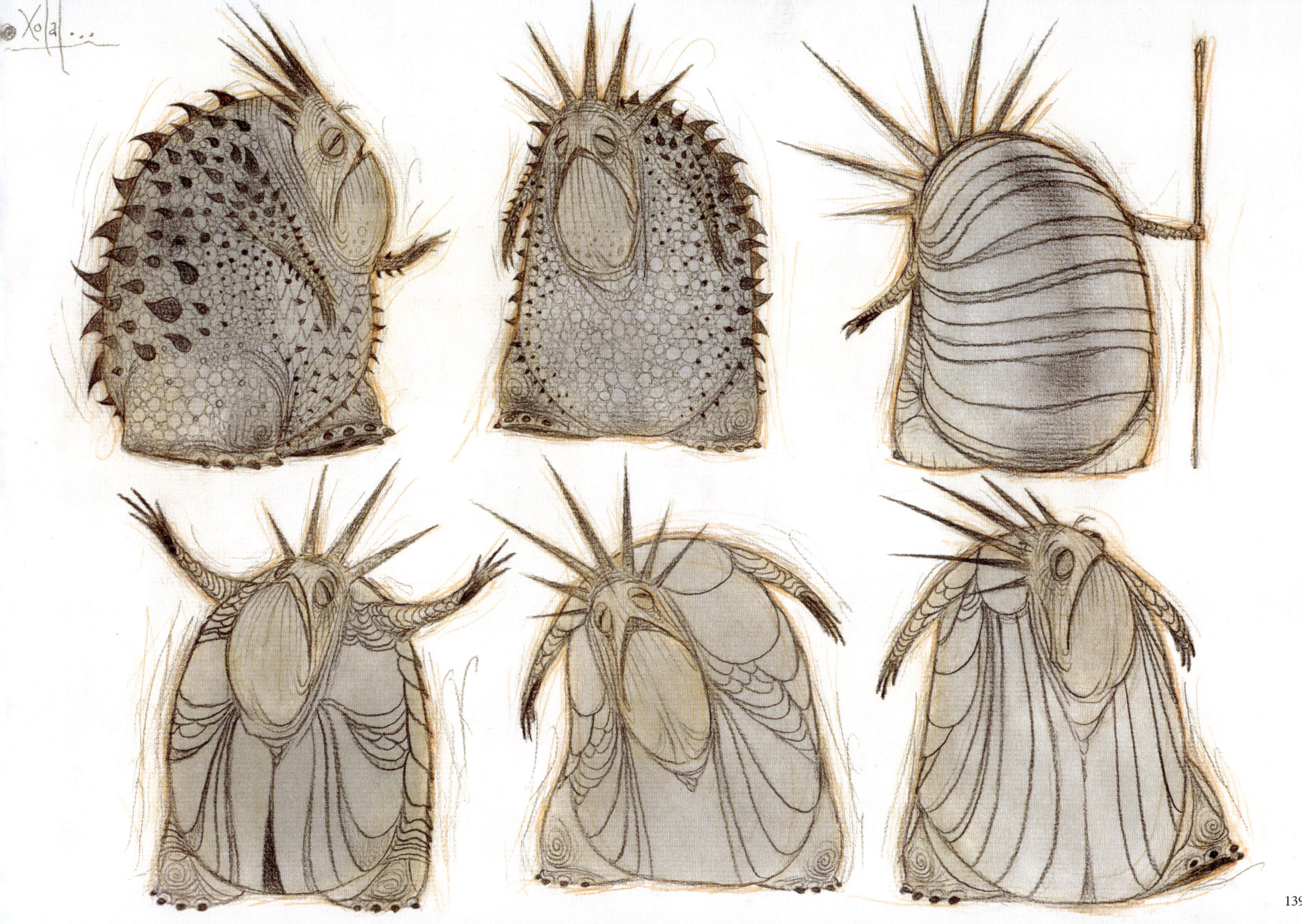
Xolal...

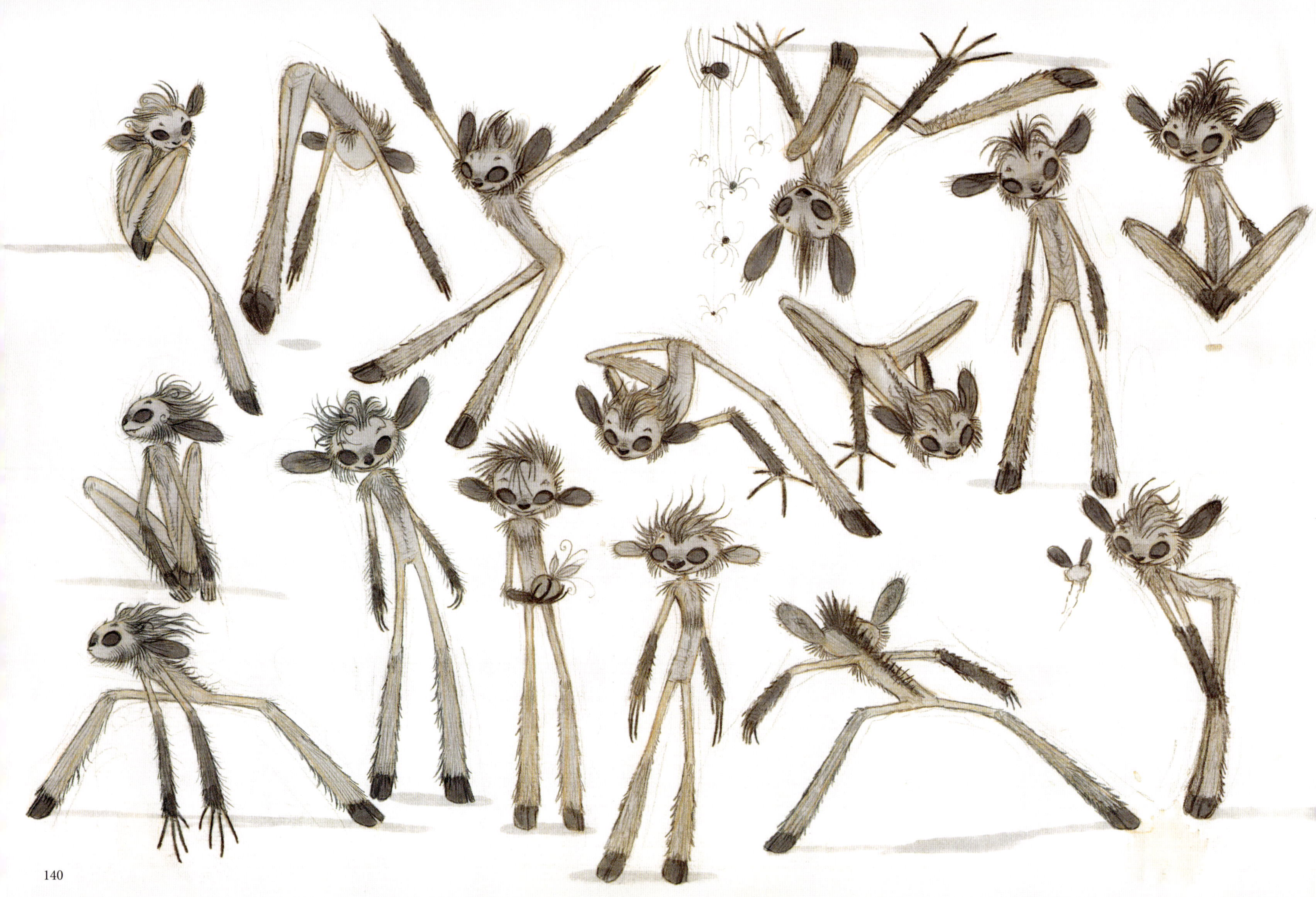

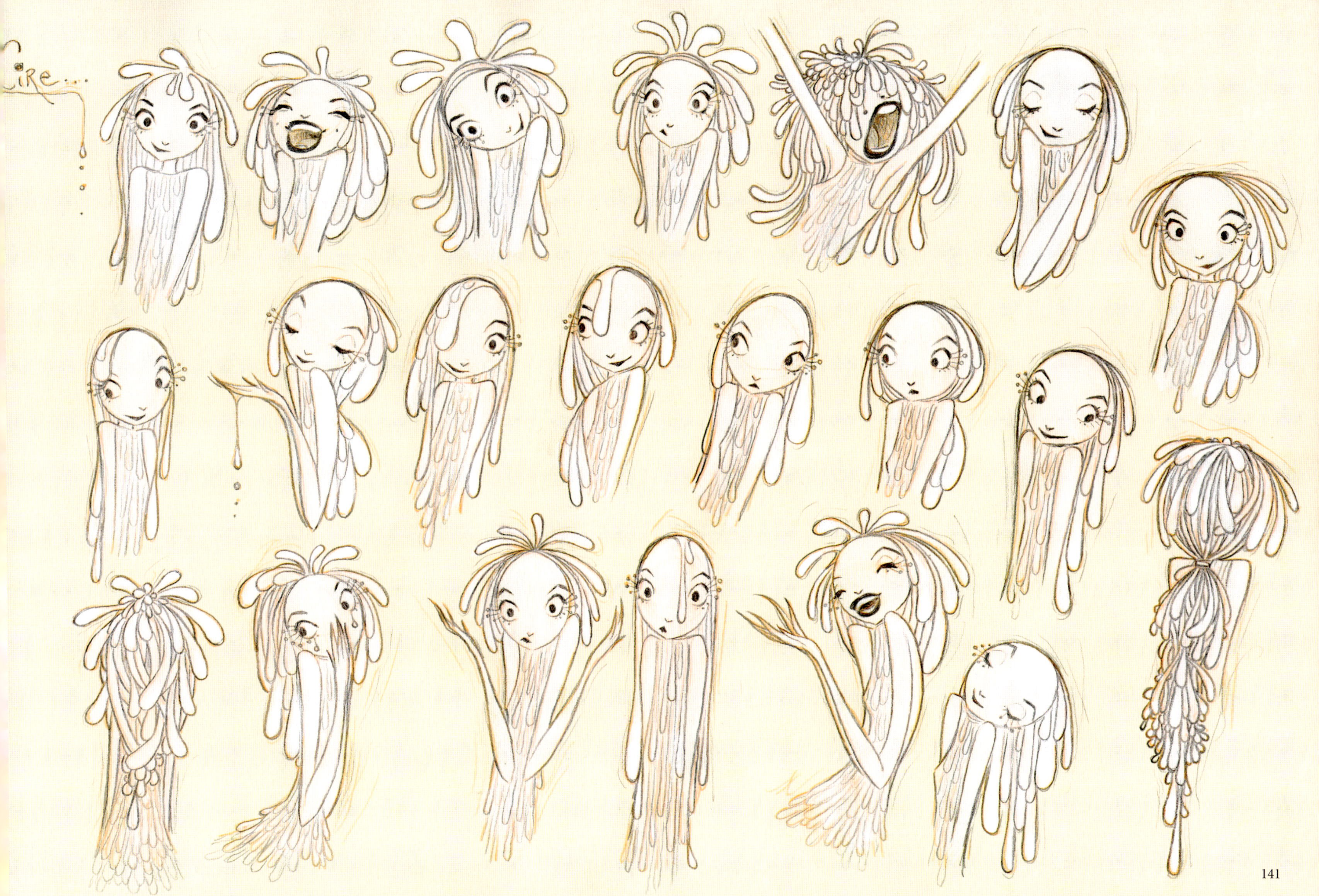
Cire....

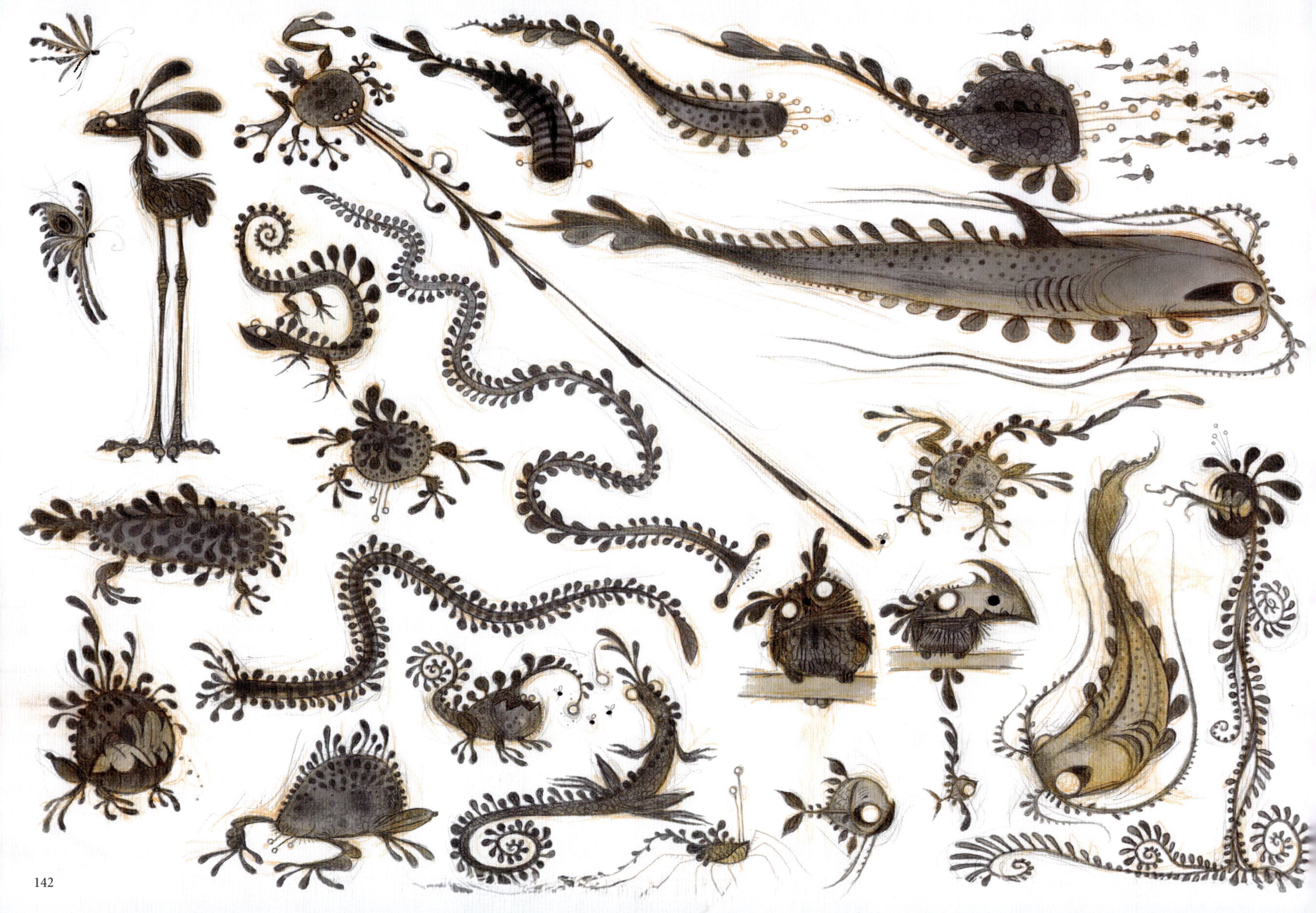

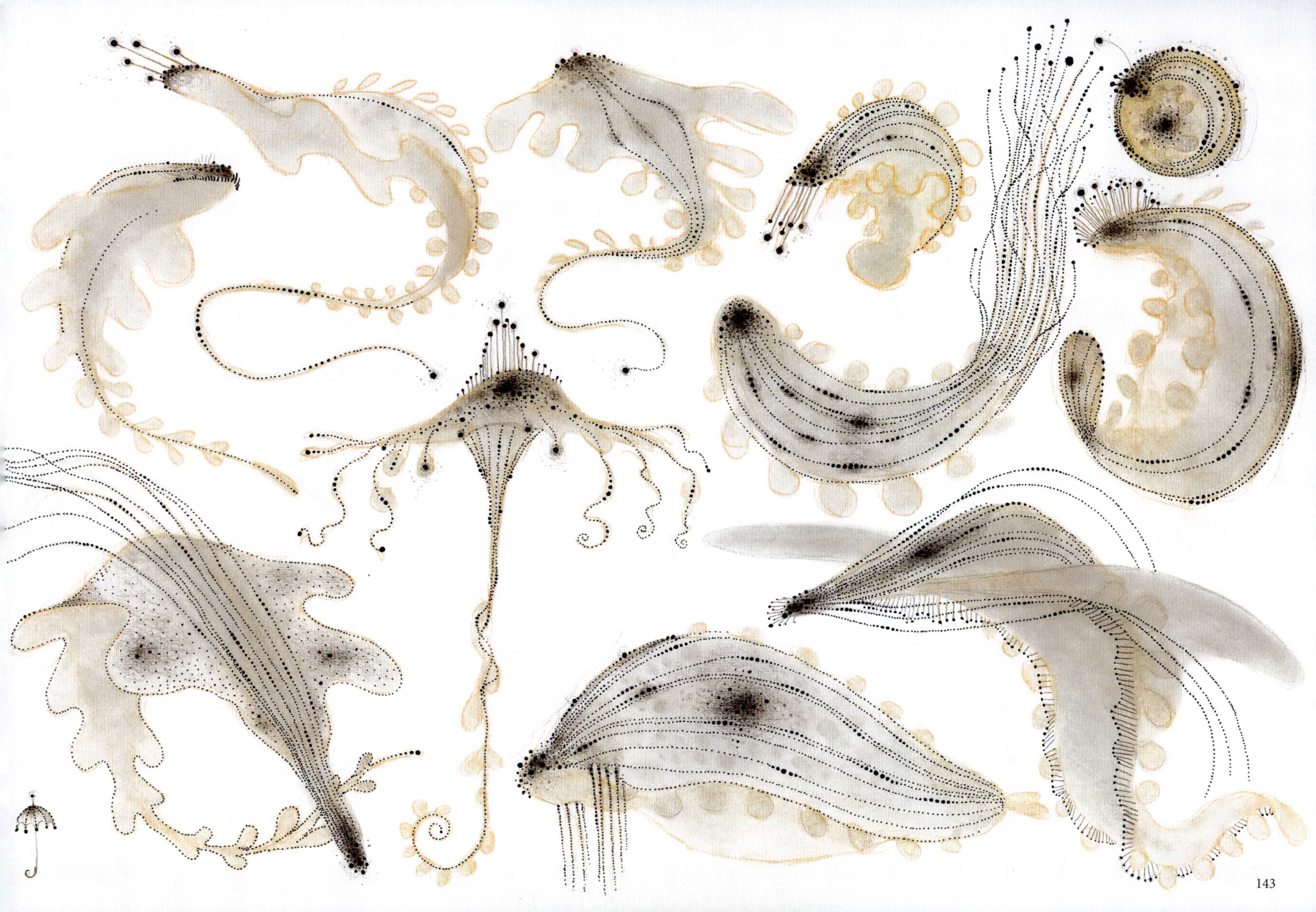

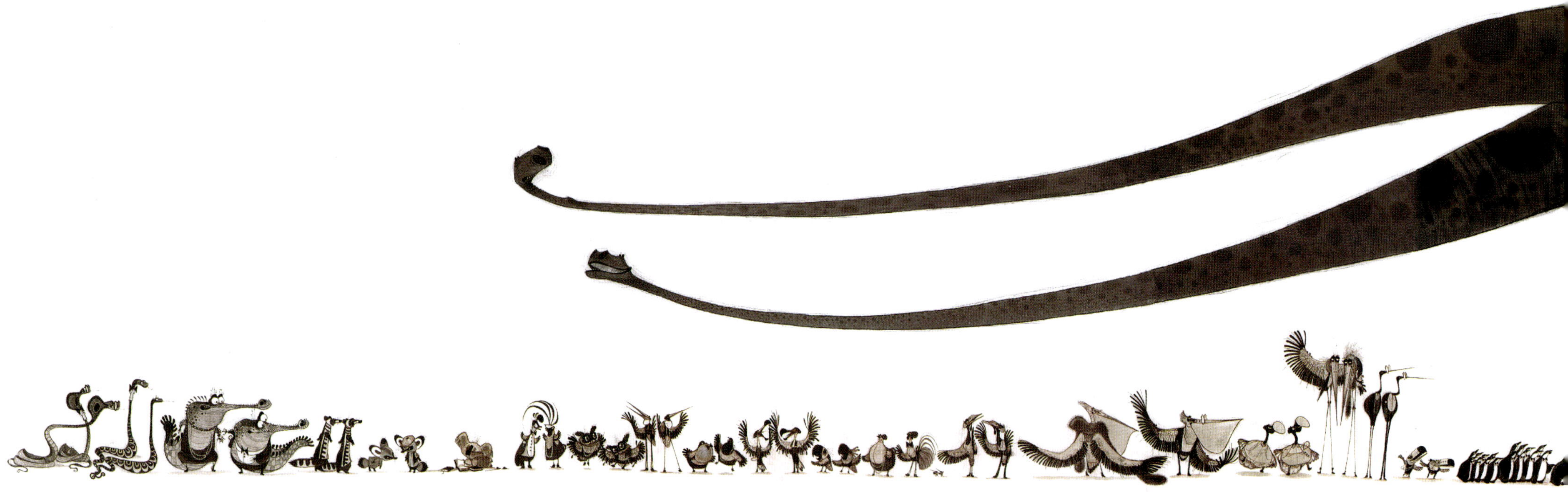

Unscreened & Unseen

So very much character art is created and never goes beyond the visual development stage, but such is the process in animation, and here is a peek into what could have been—or what someday may still find its way to the big screen. These are just a few of the countless pieces Nico has crafted that find their final resting place among the piles of paper on his desk or hidden away in the files of art that fill cabinet upon cabinet within the archives of various animation studios.

"I have been in awe of Nico Marlet's work for literally decades, and it still never ceases to amaze me. Nico presents his ideas for a character with not just two or three studies to a page but often with a dozen or more. The character remains consistent throughout, but each one has a subtle new idea attached—the pattern of fur, the knot on a garment, or the decorative flourish on a weapon. Every one of those drawings is a bounty of information, and I pity the director who has to choose one over the other."

—Peter de Sève, illustrator

Above, opposite & overleaf: DreamWorks Animation character concepts

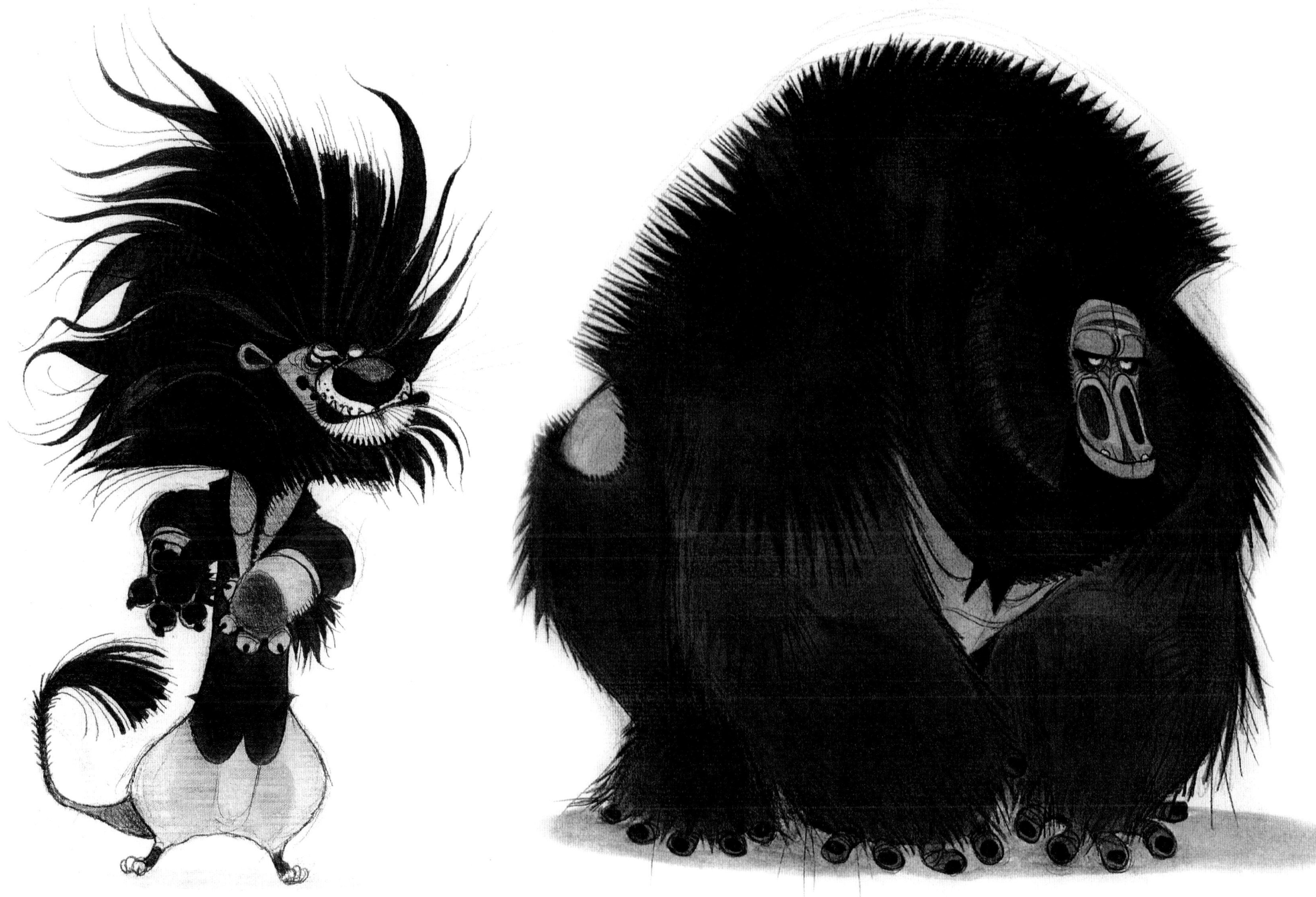

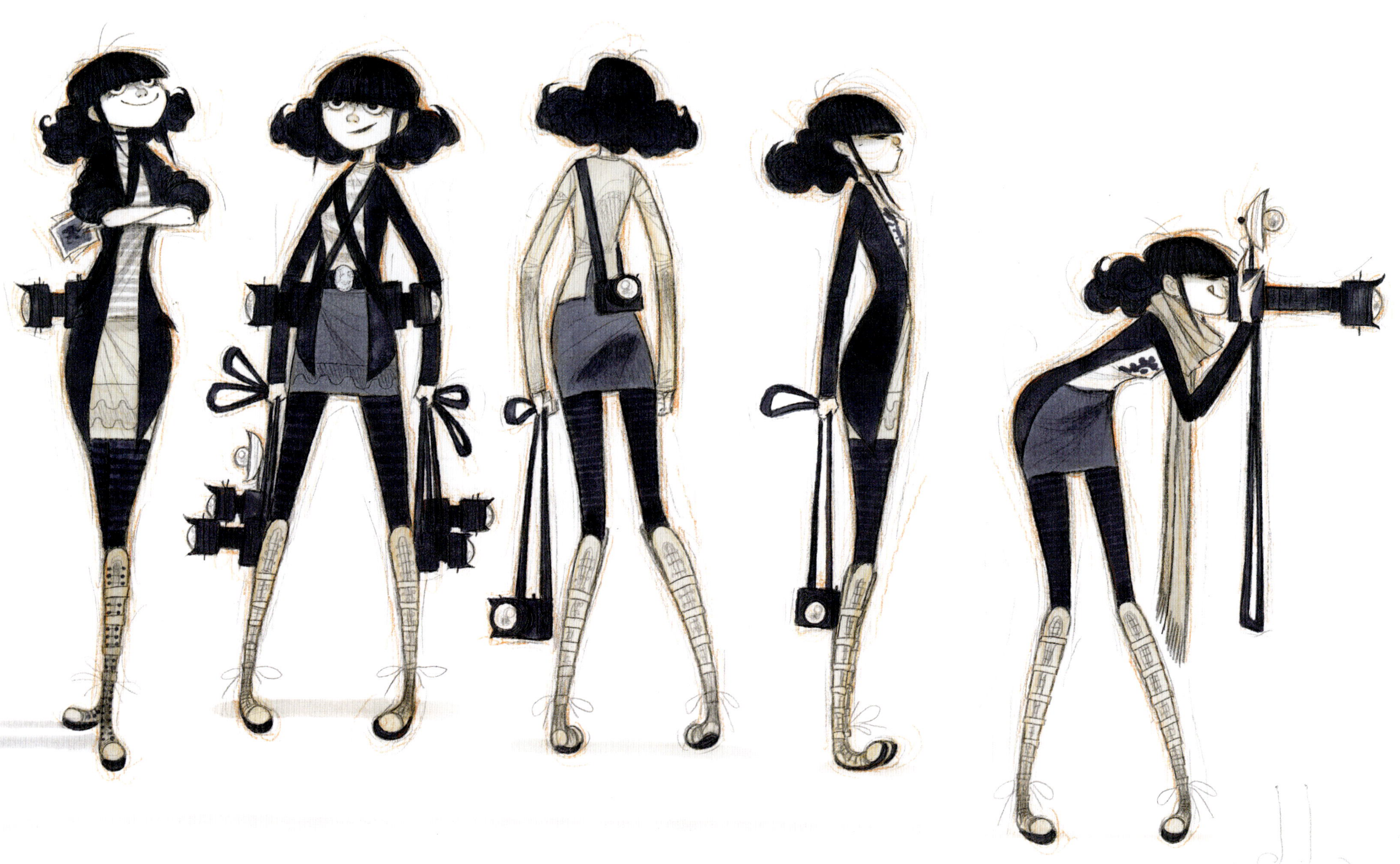
Shadow . . .

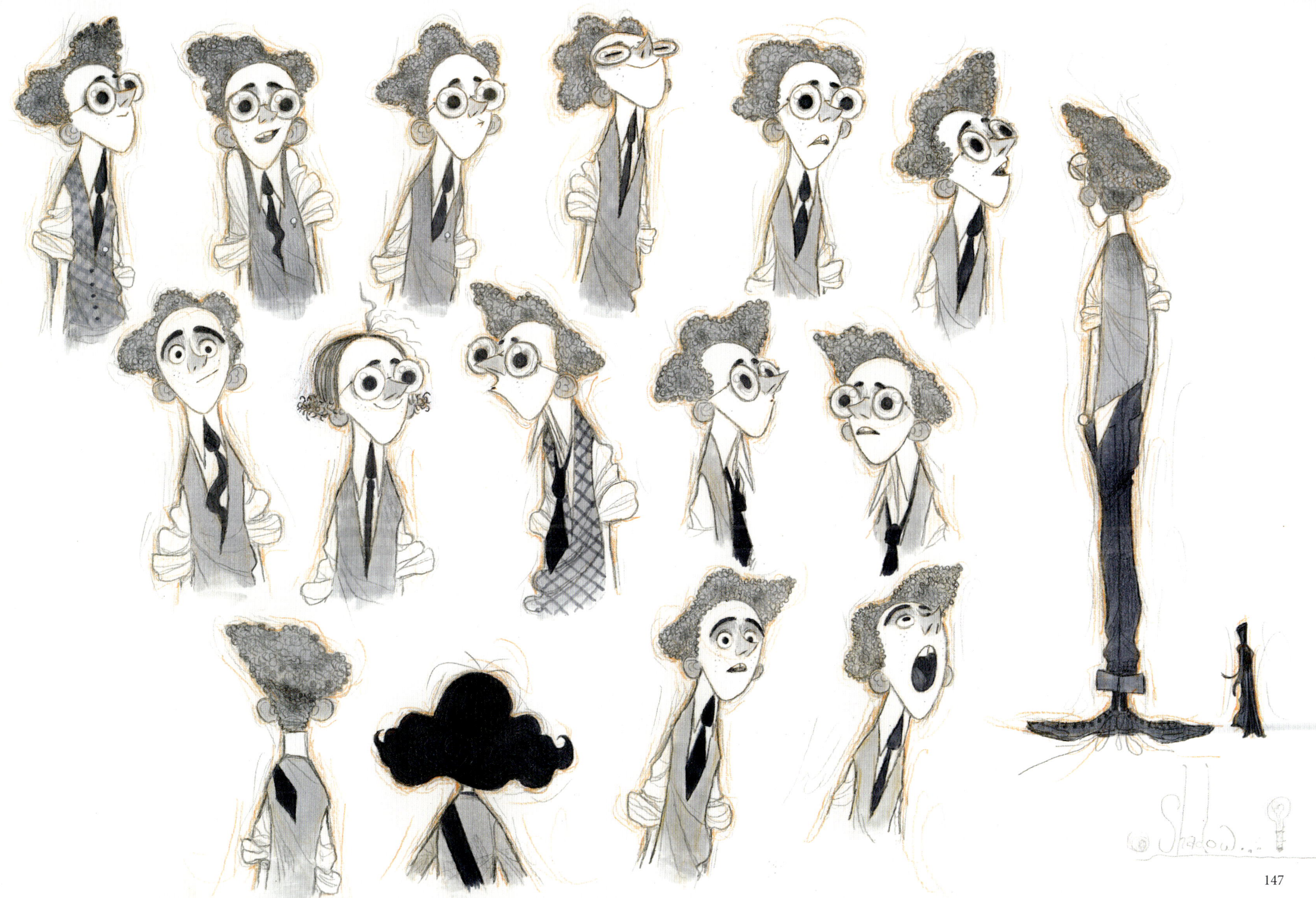
Shadow...

Flight, Fluff & Friends

Nico's love of animals and steampunk carry into his personal work. Every corner of his home is adorned with animal influence: drawings of his beloved Maltese and shih tzu pups, a magical miniature bronze collection worthy of its own zoo, a crocodile-enrobed mantlepiece, incredible flying machines, as well as his real-life pack of dogs, turtles, and koi. Woven among it all are plants and special relics that exude exquisite design details, all thoughtfully curated and cared for as a way to appreciate beauty in all forms.

The vibrant diversity of Nico's space and artistic practices stand as witness to his persona, manifesting his advice to other artists to realize "there's more than one way to express yourself. Try something else from time to time."

"With your beautiful soul, so touching in its accuracy and humanity, great Little Prince, Nicolas the First—what planet do you come from? Surely a neighbor of the one from which Franquin, Uderzo, Wendling, Kahl, and other benefactors of humanity descend. On your planet, you even tangled up flambéed dragons in salad, all as scintillating with beauty as with humor and friendship, while your pandas have the flexibility of karatekas. You sprinkle and perfume the pages of your notebooks with the fascinating beauty of the eternal feminine in the luminous wake of your pencil, dream creatures, slender, and undulating like seaweed, with forms so stretched that they become almost abstract and all the more sensual by the grace of your stylization.

"Your natural art of loving caricature doesn't distort the beauty of your subjects, nor does it condemn the ravages of time. Benevolent humor floats above the surface, just as love hovers over the beauty of youth. You naturally practice the law of all good drawing, knowing how to balance straight and curved lines. Thus, your drawing doesn't remain fixed and lends itself all the better to animation; it moves, dances, flies, and avenges us through this graceful alchemy between straight lines and curves—it swings!

"Another common point between love and humor: their freedom of disproportion or controlled exaggeration. The art of knowing how to measure one's excess, of daring, and measuring. Why not push the limits of proportion as long as harmony, beauty, and humor remain hand in hand in the end? Love exaggerates amusingly. And in graphically free love, anything goes if the resulting humor and beauty give it absolution."

—Jean Mulatier, illustrator

Opposite & pp. 150–159: Personal sketches illustrating friends, pets, holiday fun, and more

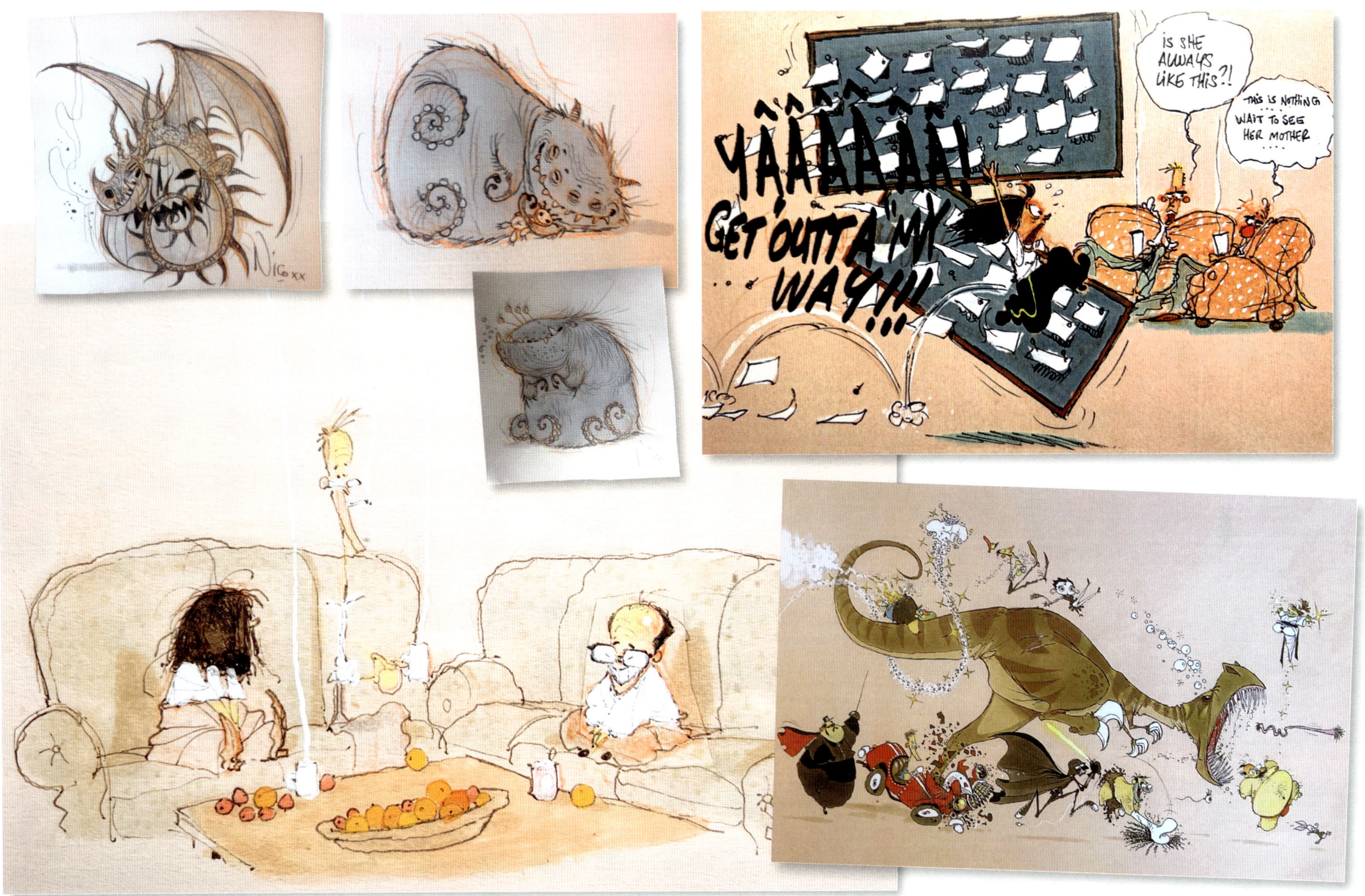

NICOXX
YÂÂÂÂÂÂÂ!
GET OUTTA' MY WAY!!!
IS SHE ALWAYS LIKE THIS?!
THIS IS NOTHING . . . WAIT TO SEE HER MOTHER . . .

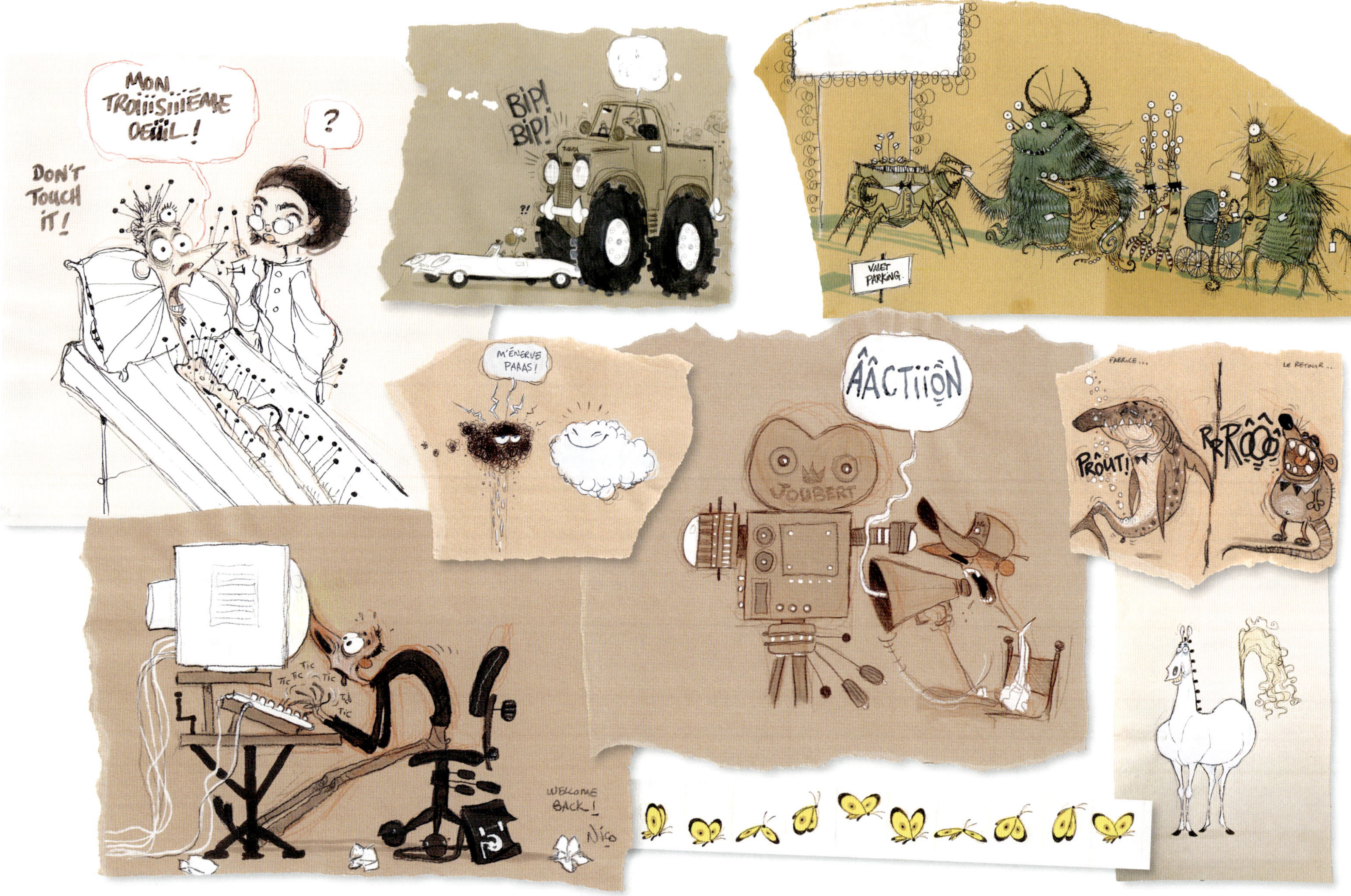
MON TROIIISIIIÈME OEIIIL !
?
DON'T TOUCH IT !
BIP! BIP!
VALET PARKING
M'ÉNERVE PAAAS !
ÂÂCTIIÔN
JOUBERT
FABRICE...
LE RETOUR...
PRÔUT !
RRRÔÔÔ
WELCOME BACK !
Nico

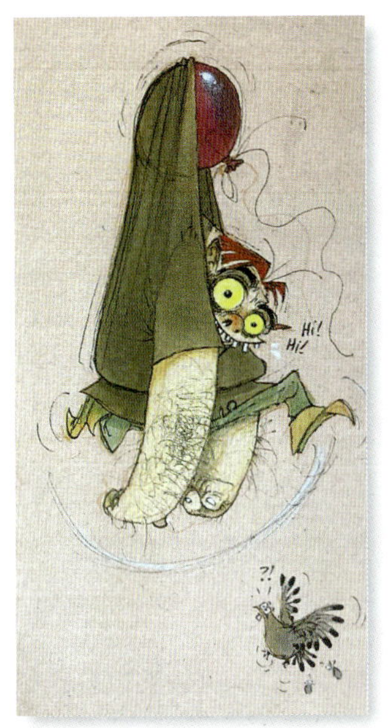
HI!
HI!

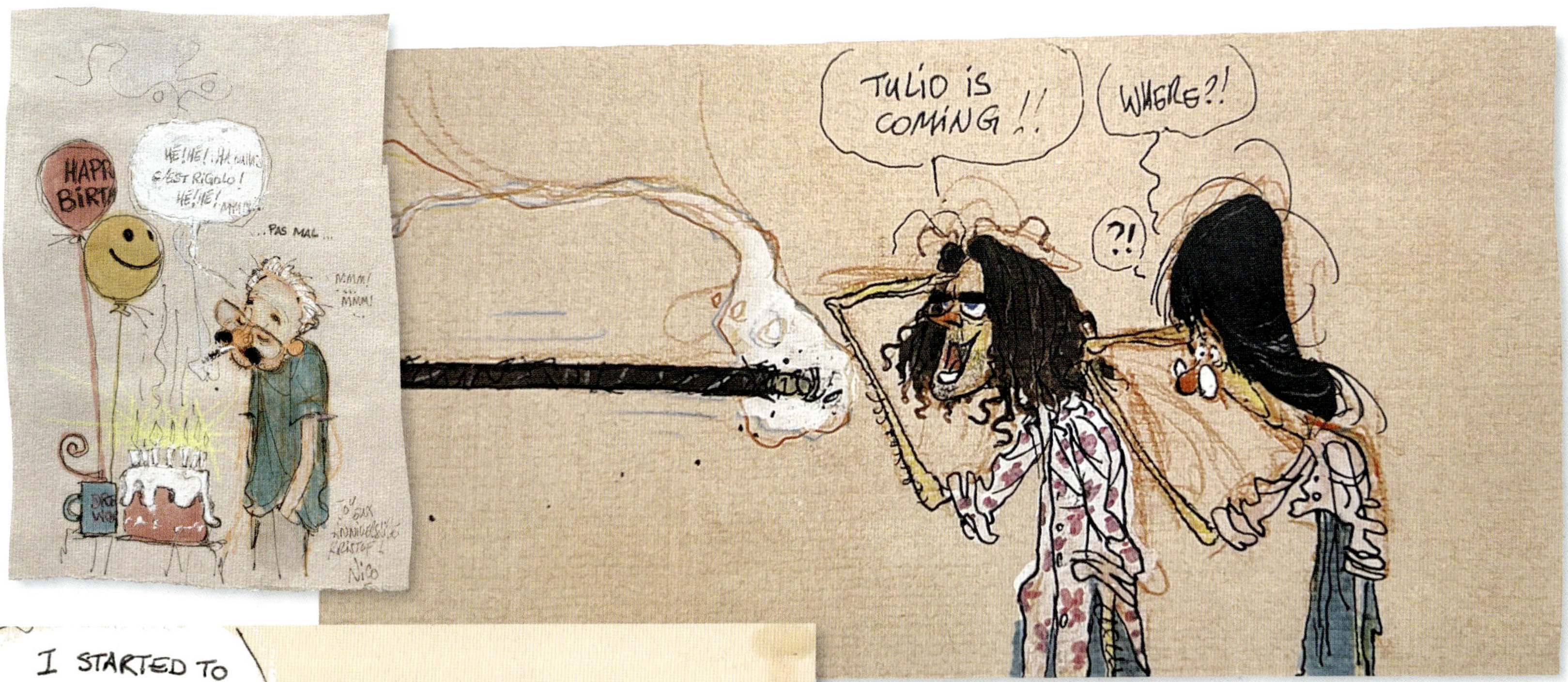
HAPP
BIRTH
HÉ!HÉ! ... C'EST RIGOLO!
HÉ!HÉ!
...PAS MAL...
MMM!
MMM!
NICO
TULIO IS COMING!!
WHERE?!
?!

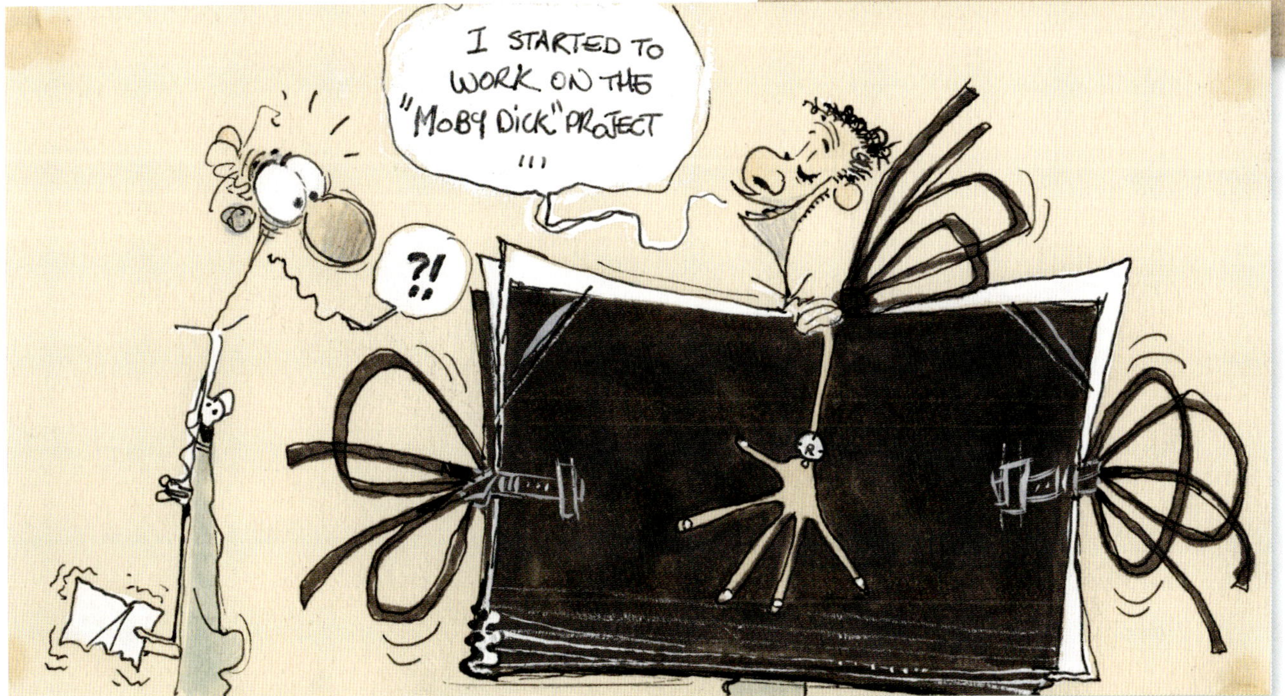
I STARTED TO WORK ON THE "MOBY DICK" PROJECT !!!
?!

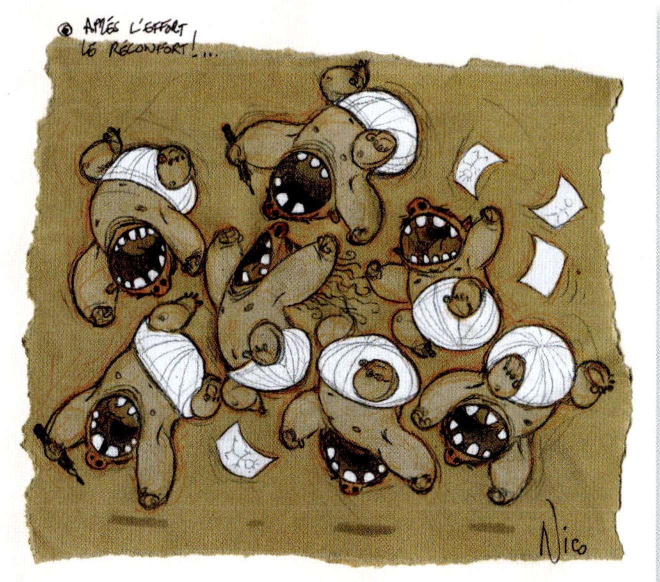
APRÈS L'EFFORT
LE RÉCONFORT!...
Nico

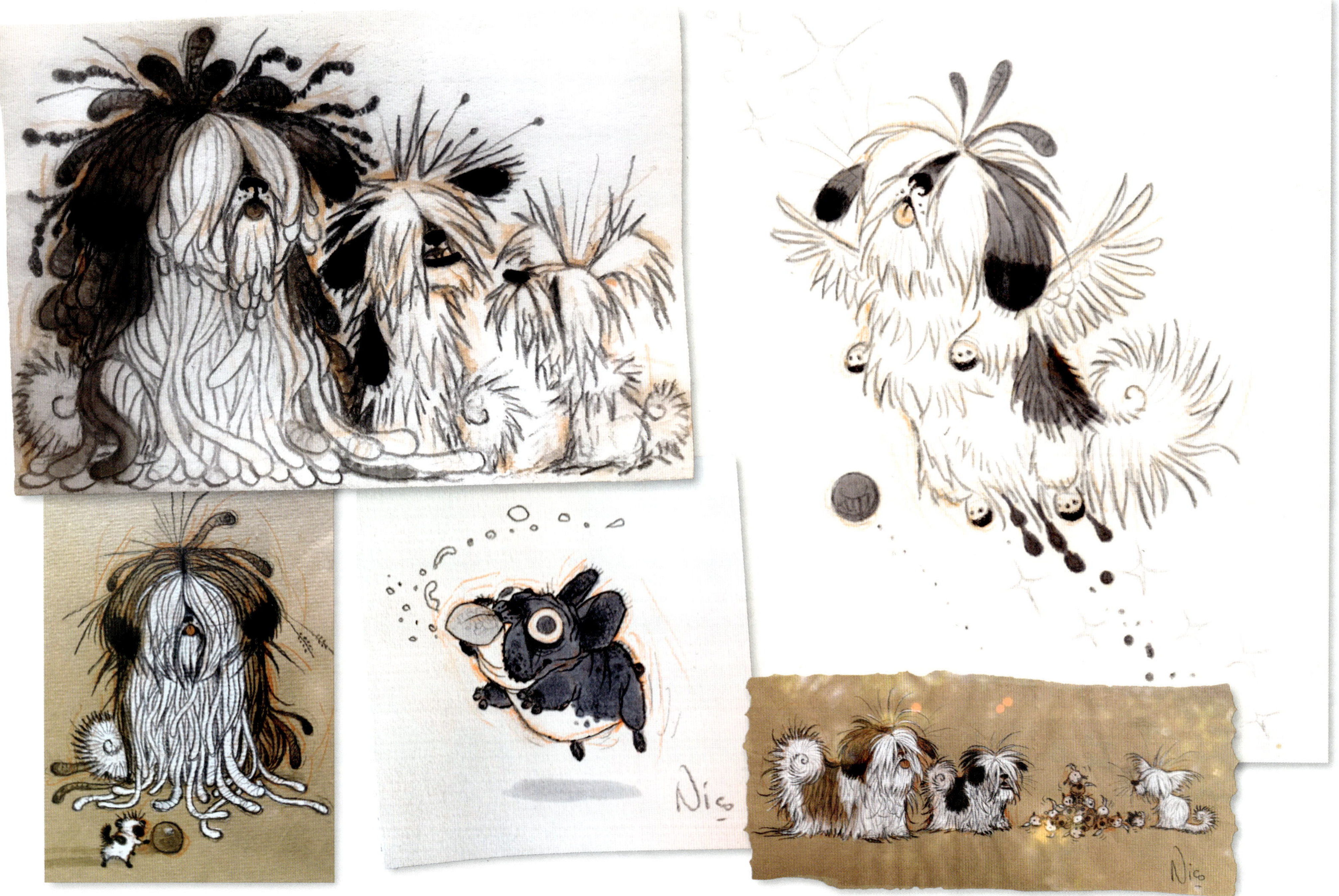

Nico
Nico

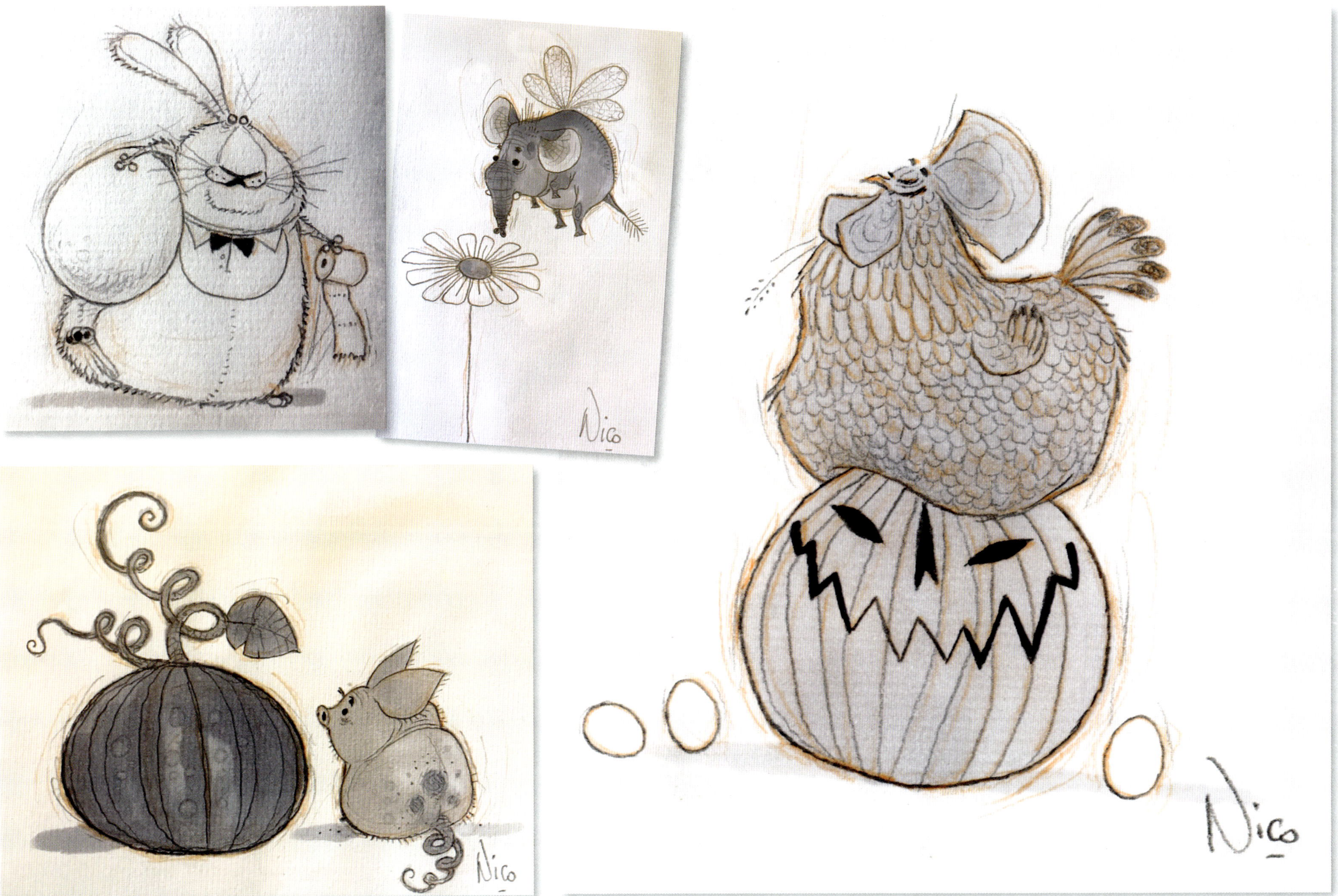
Nico
Nico
Nico

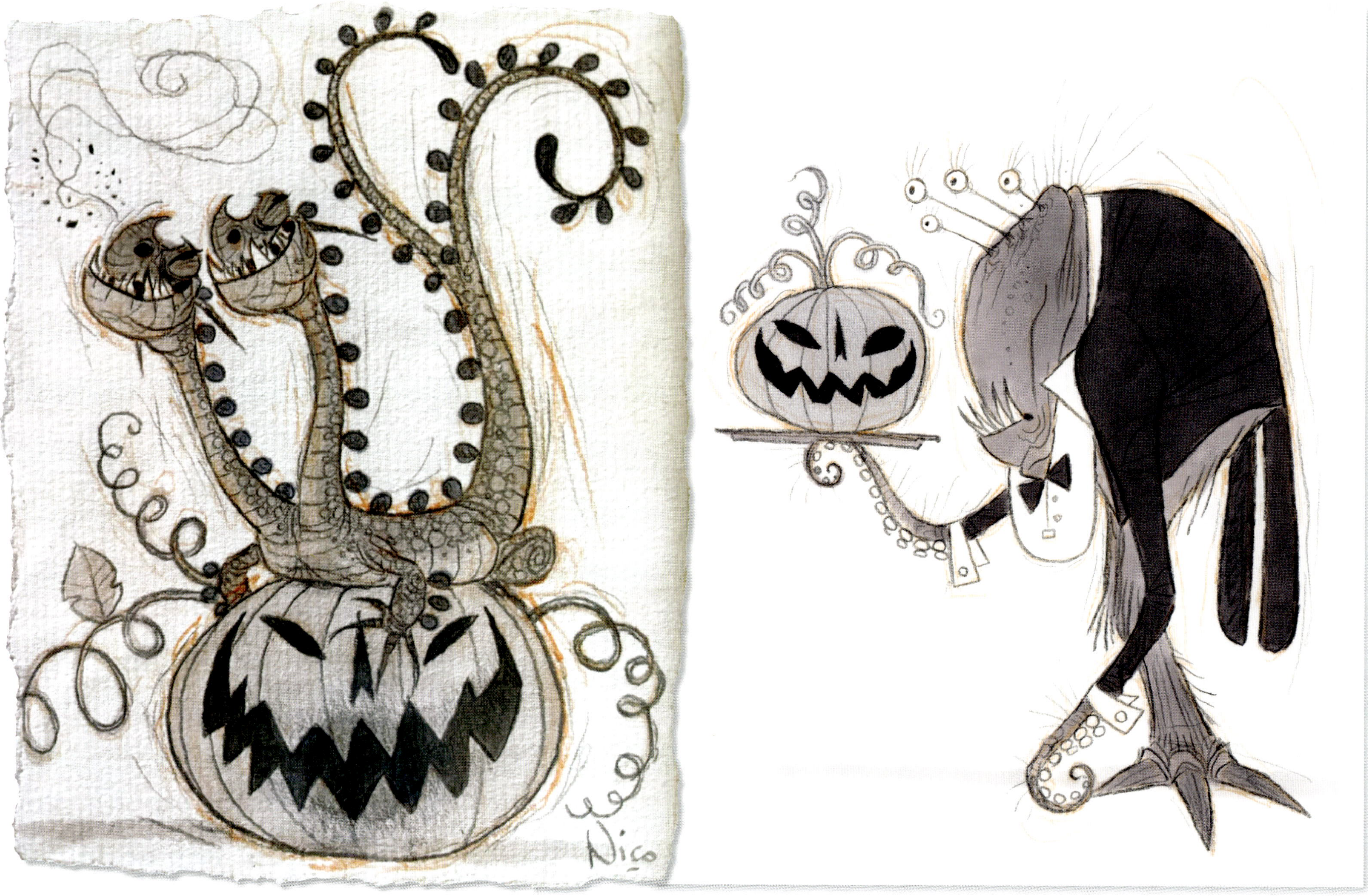
Nico

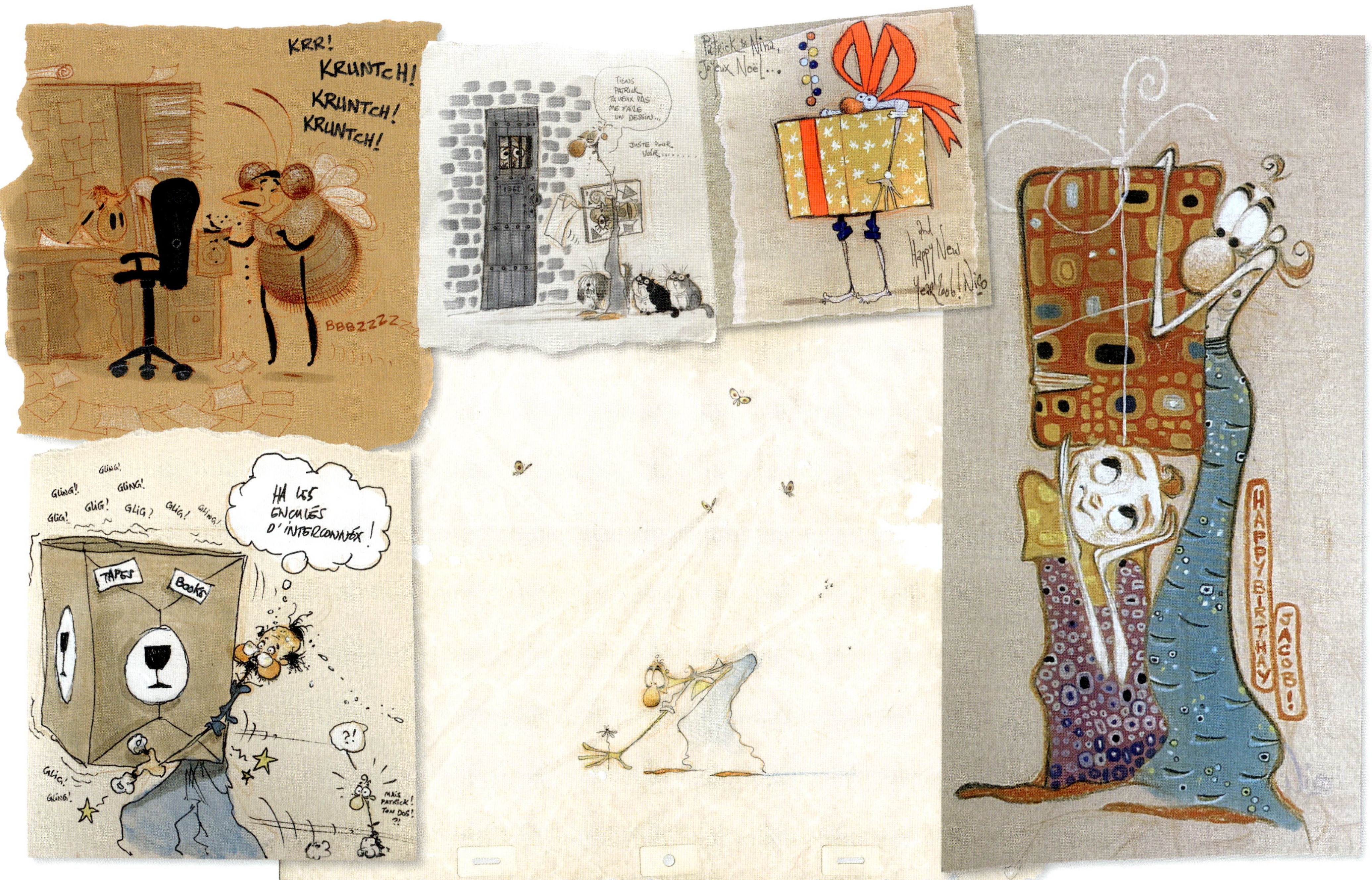
KRR!
KRUNTCH!
KRUNTCH!
KRUNTCH!
BBBZZZZ
TIENS PATRICK TU VEUX PAS ME FAIRE UN DESSIN...
JUSTE POUR VOIR.........
Patrick & Nina,
Joyeux Noël...
and Happy New Year 2006! Nico
HA LES ENCULÉS D'INTERCONNEX!
TAPES
BOOKS
?!
MAIS PATRICK! TON DOS! ?!
HAPPY BIRTHDAY JACOB!

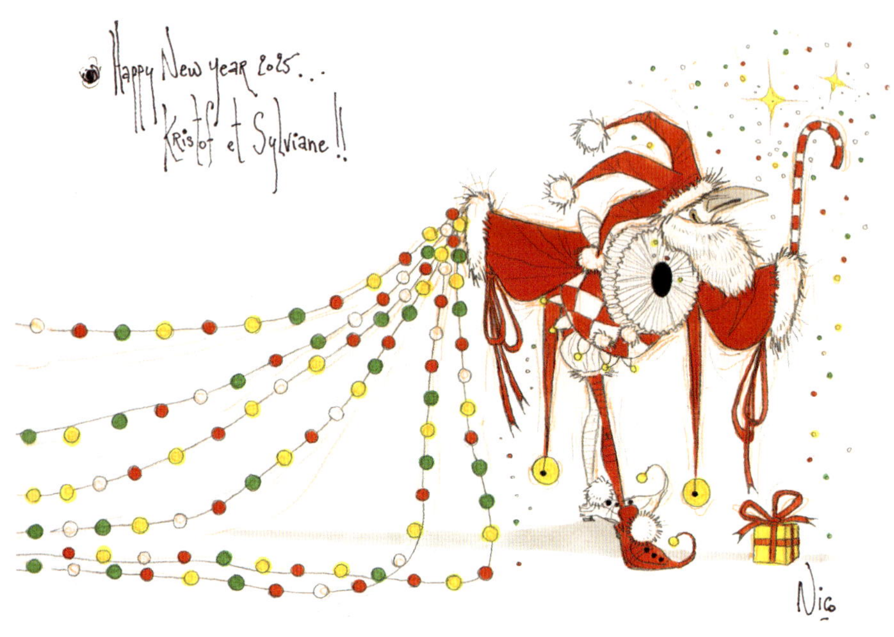
Happy New year 2025...
Kristof et Sylviane !!
Nico

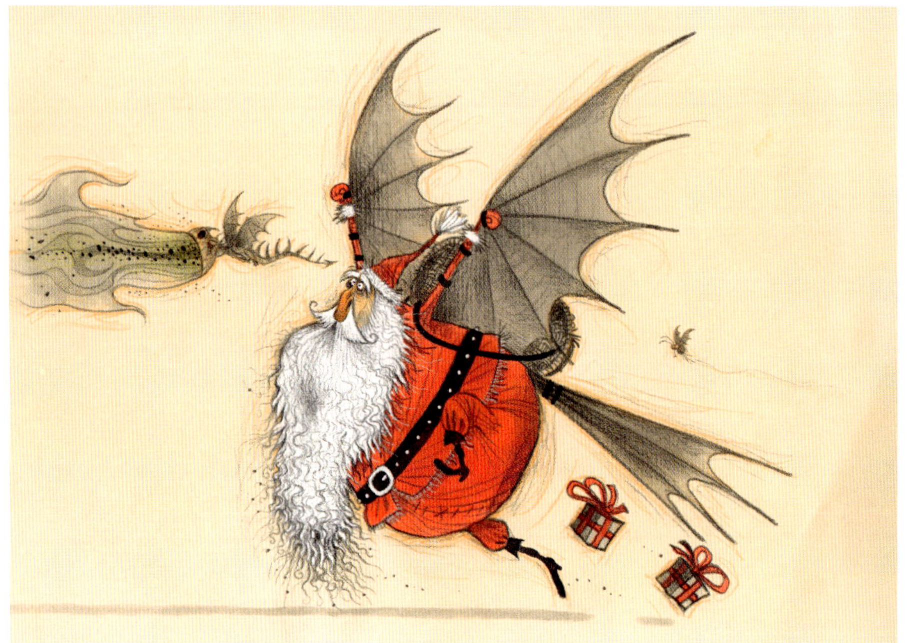

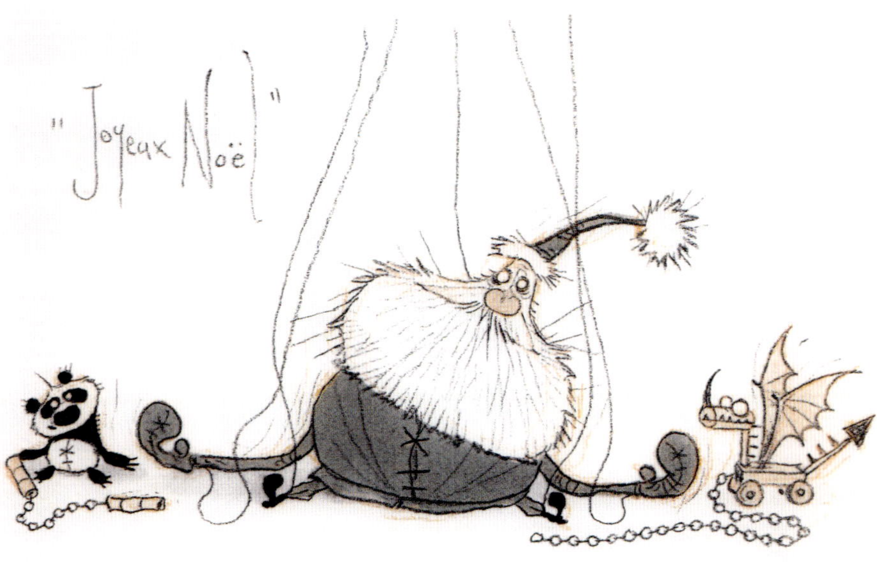
"Joyeux Noël"

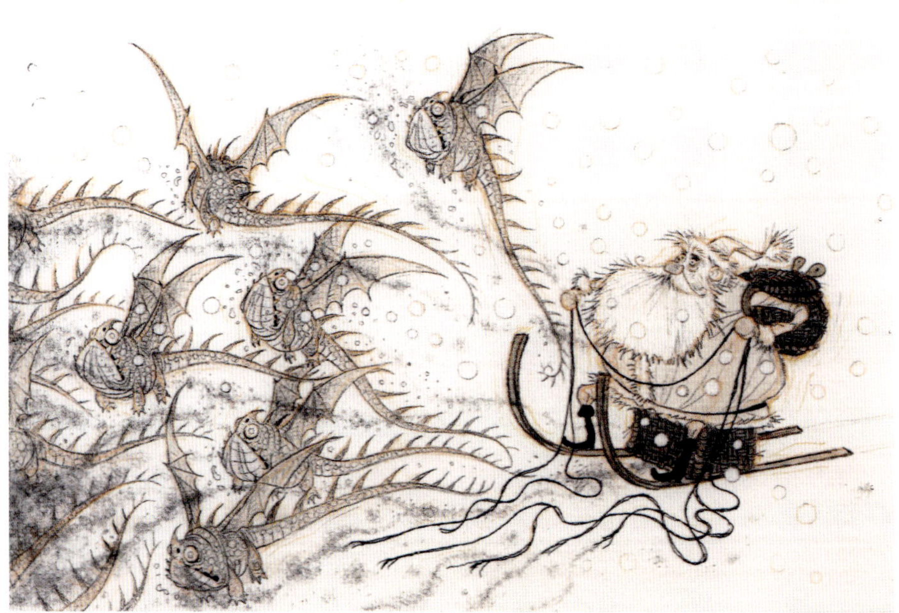

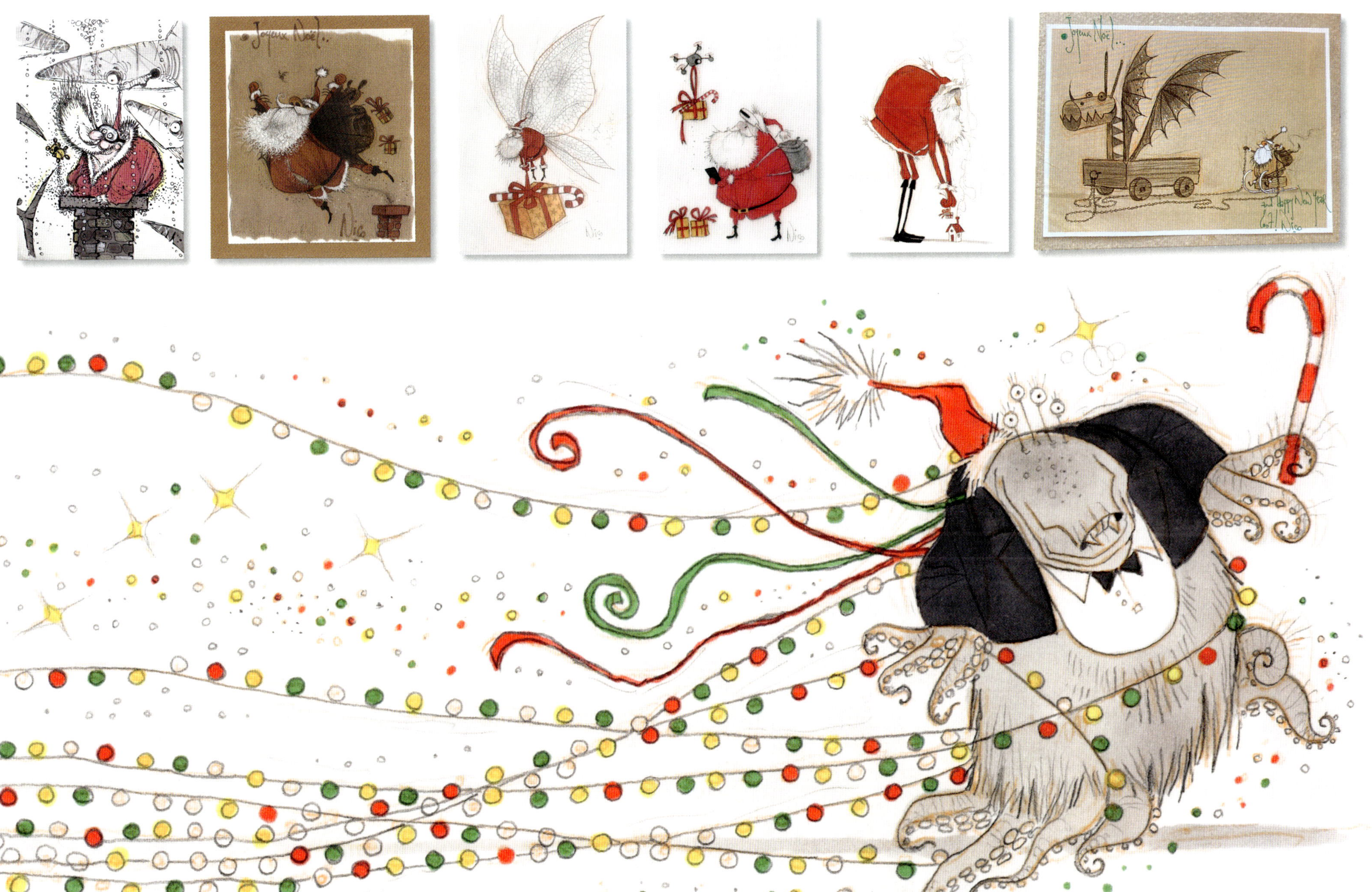
Joyeux Noël…
Nico
Joyeux Noël…
and Happy New Year
Nico

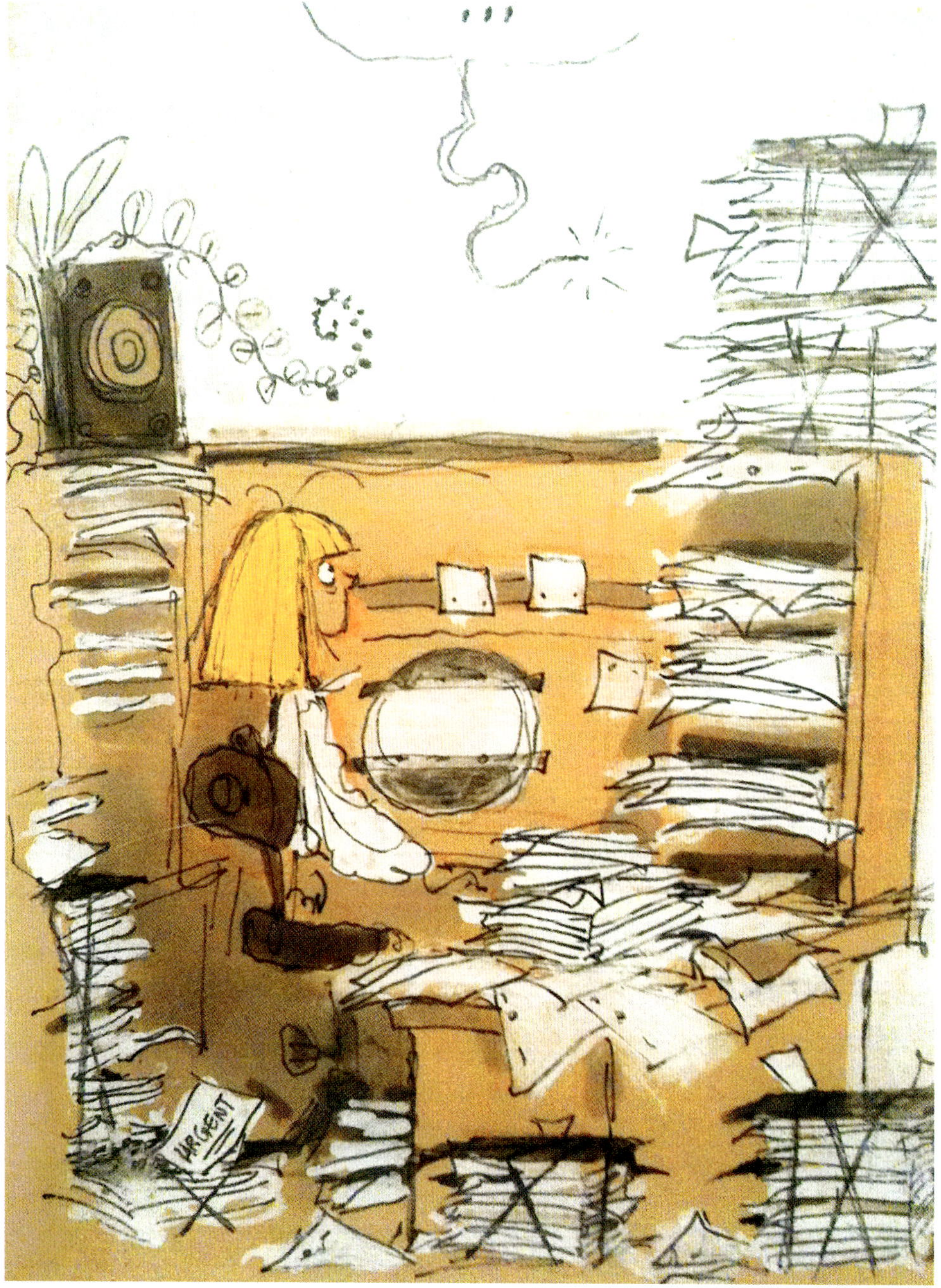

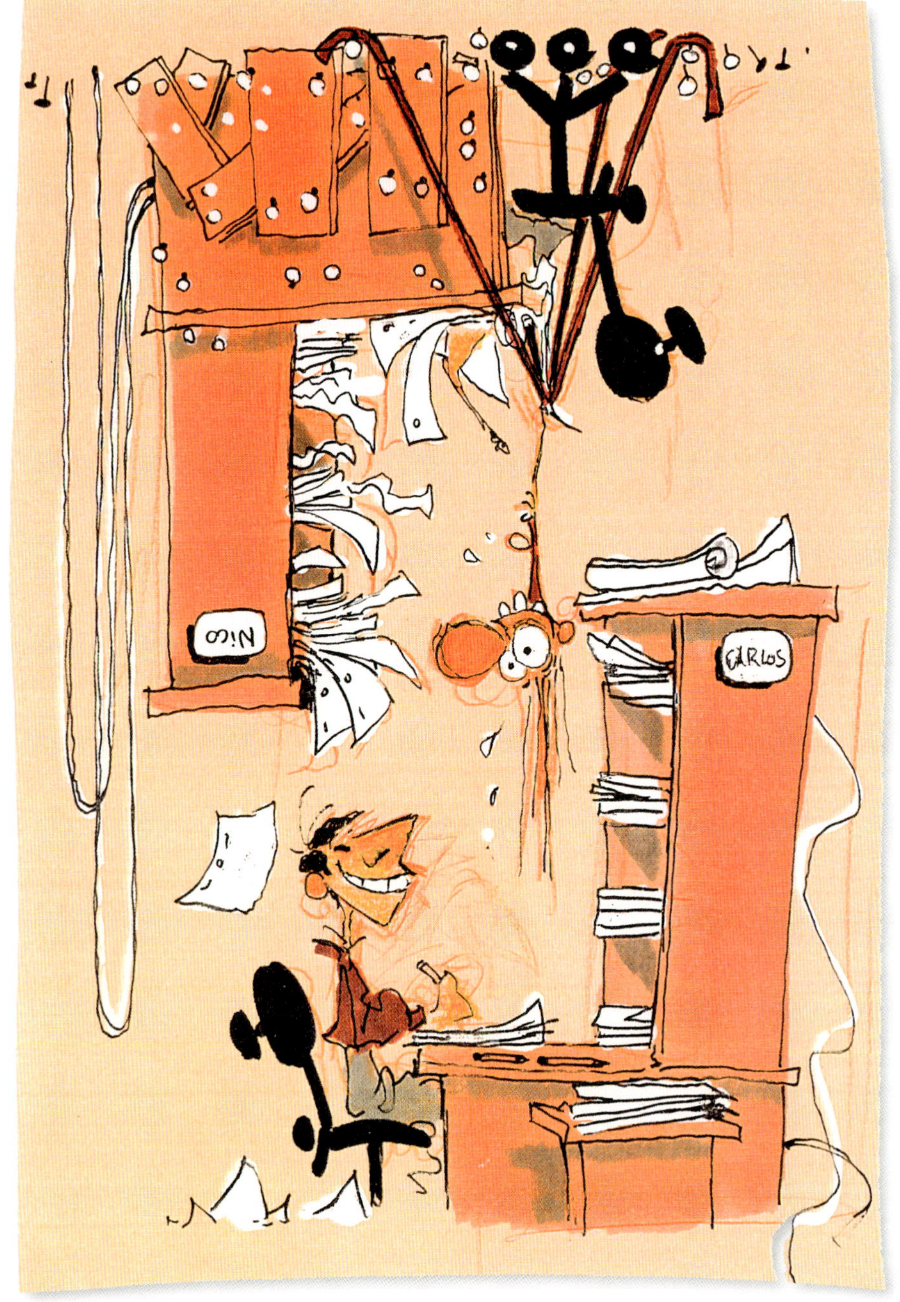
CARLOS

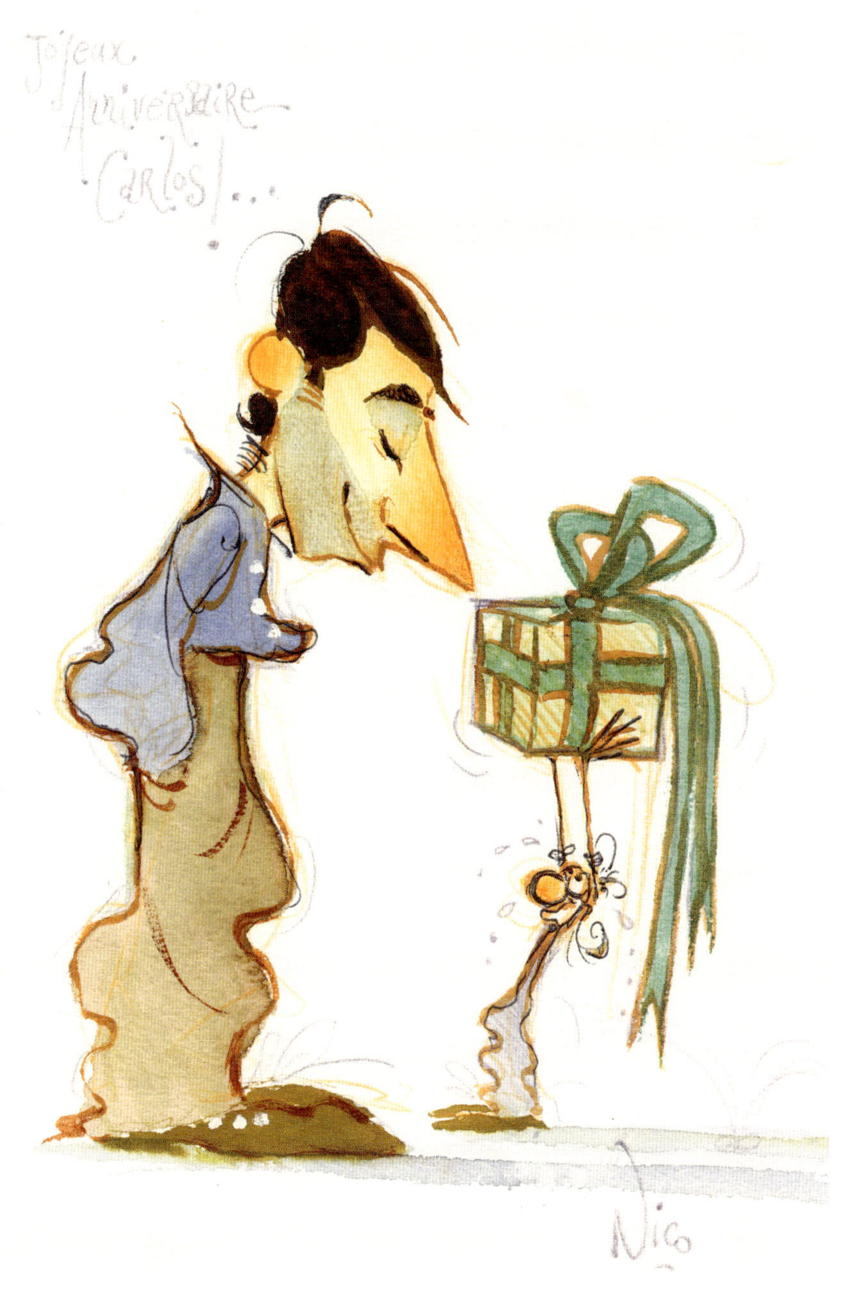
Joyeux
Anniversaire
Carlos!...
Nico

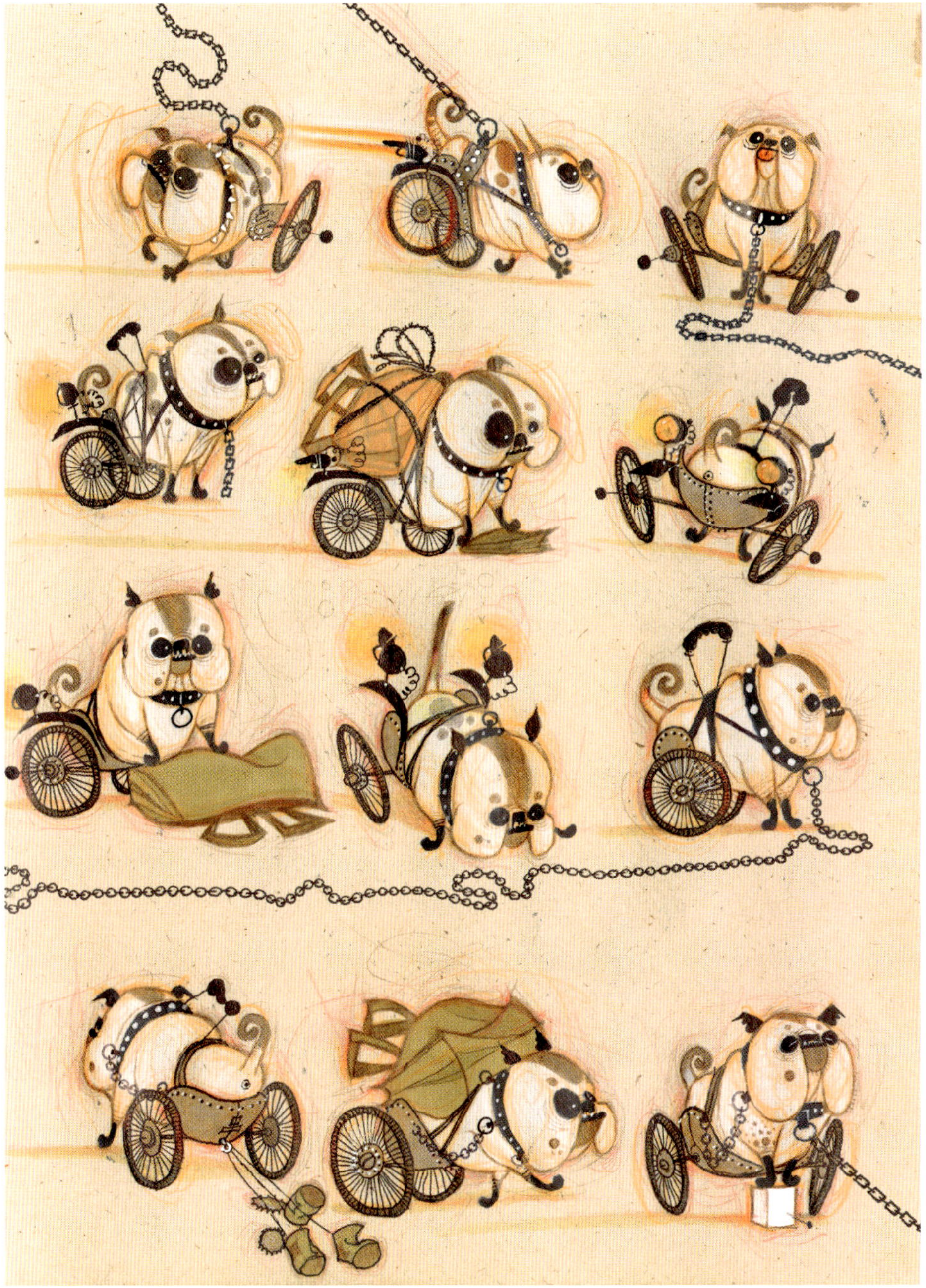

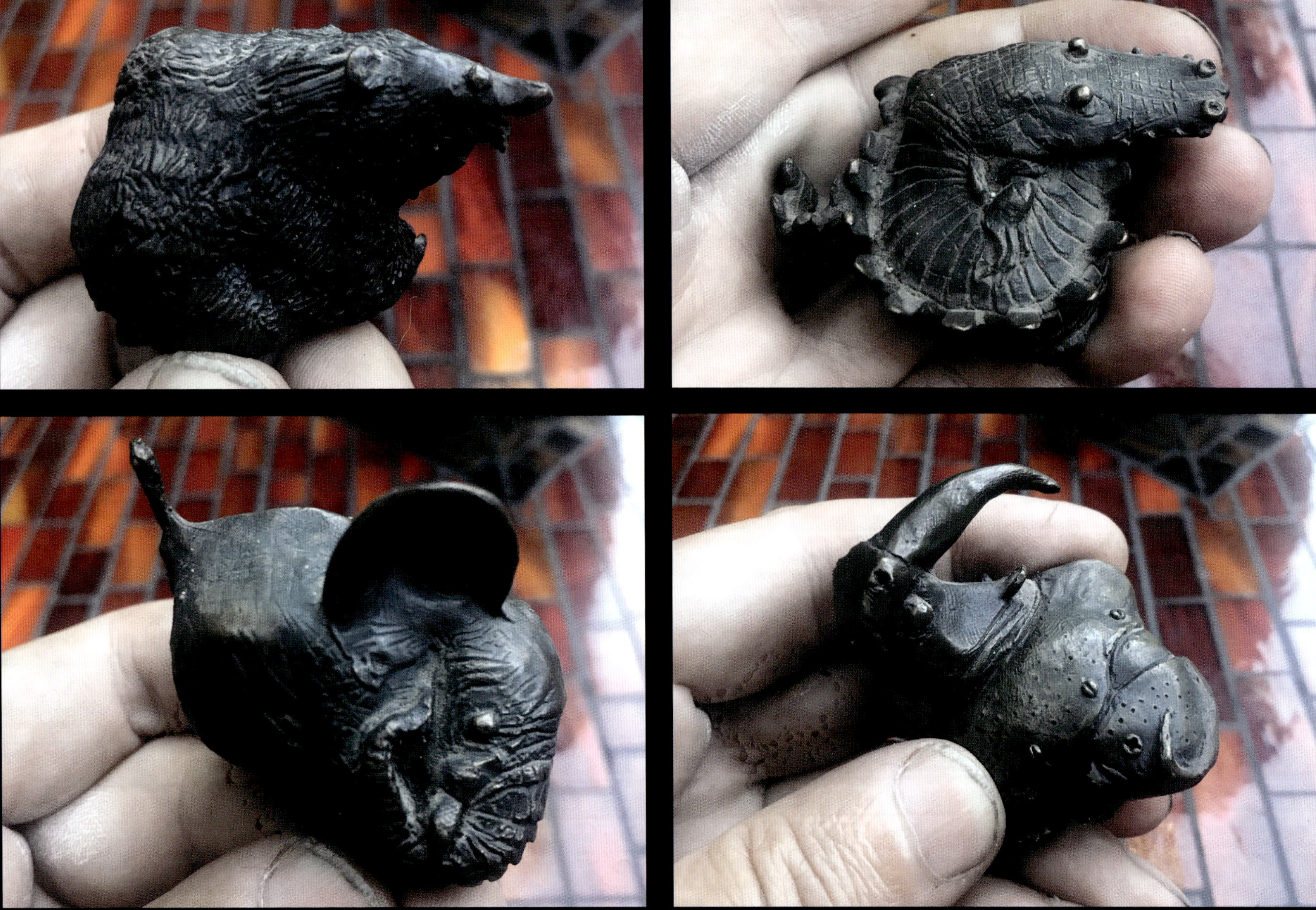

Above: Personal sculpts in bronze • Opposite: Maquettes for *How to Train Your Dragon*, *The Road to El Dorado*, and personal dragon sculpts • Overleaf: The artist at work in his sketchbook

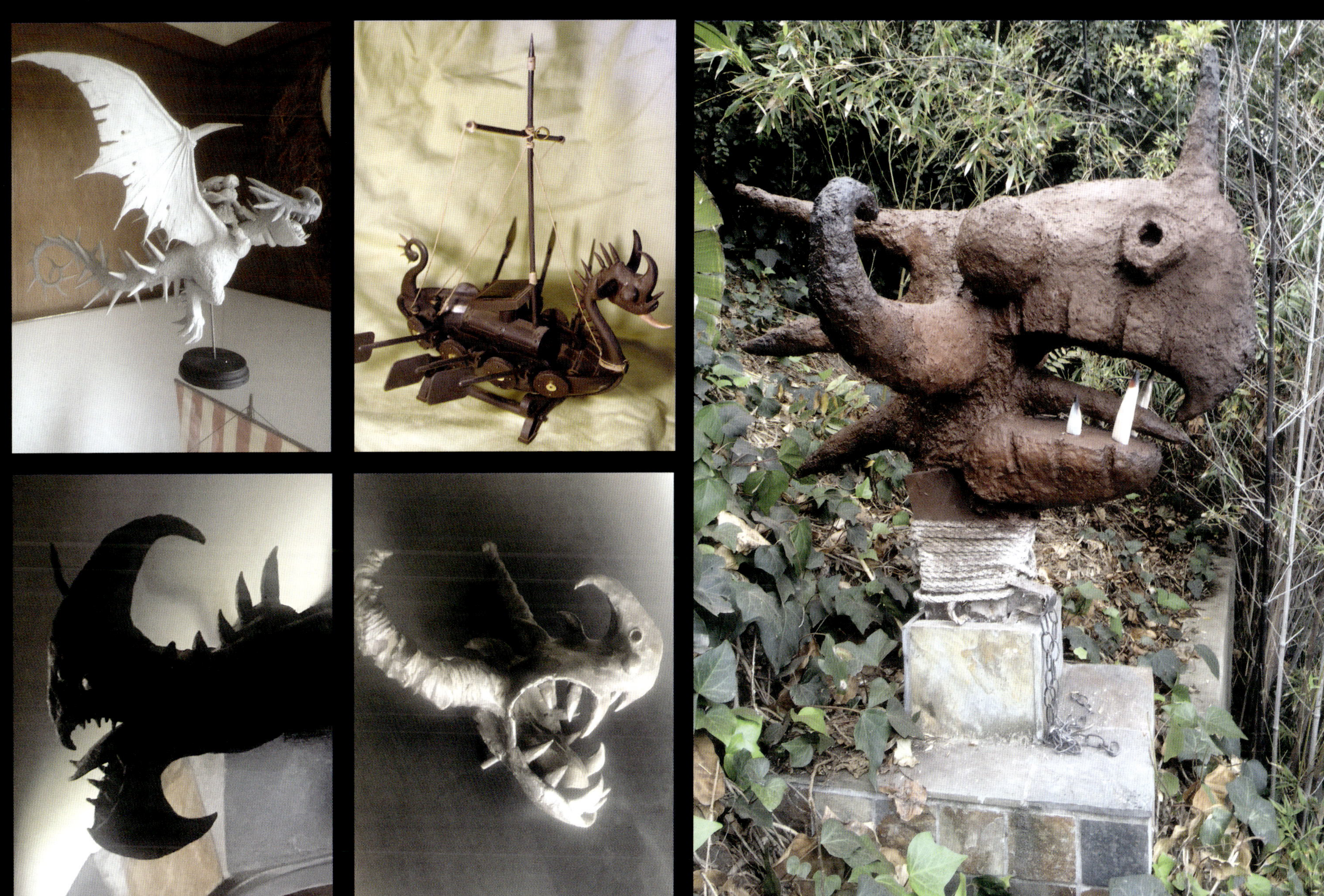

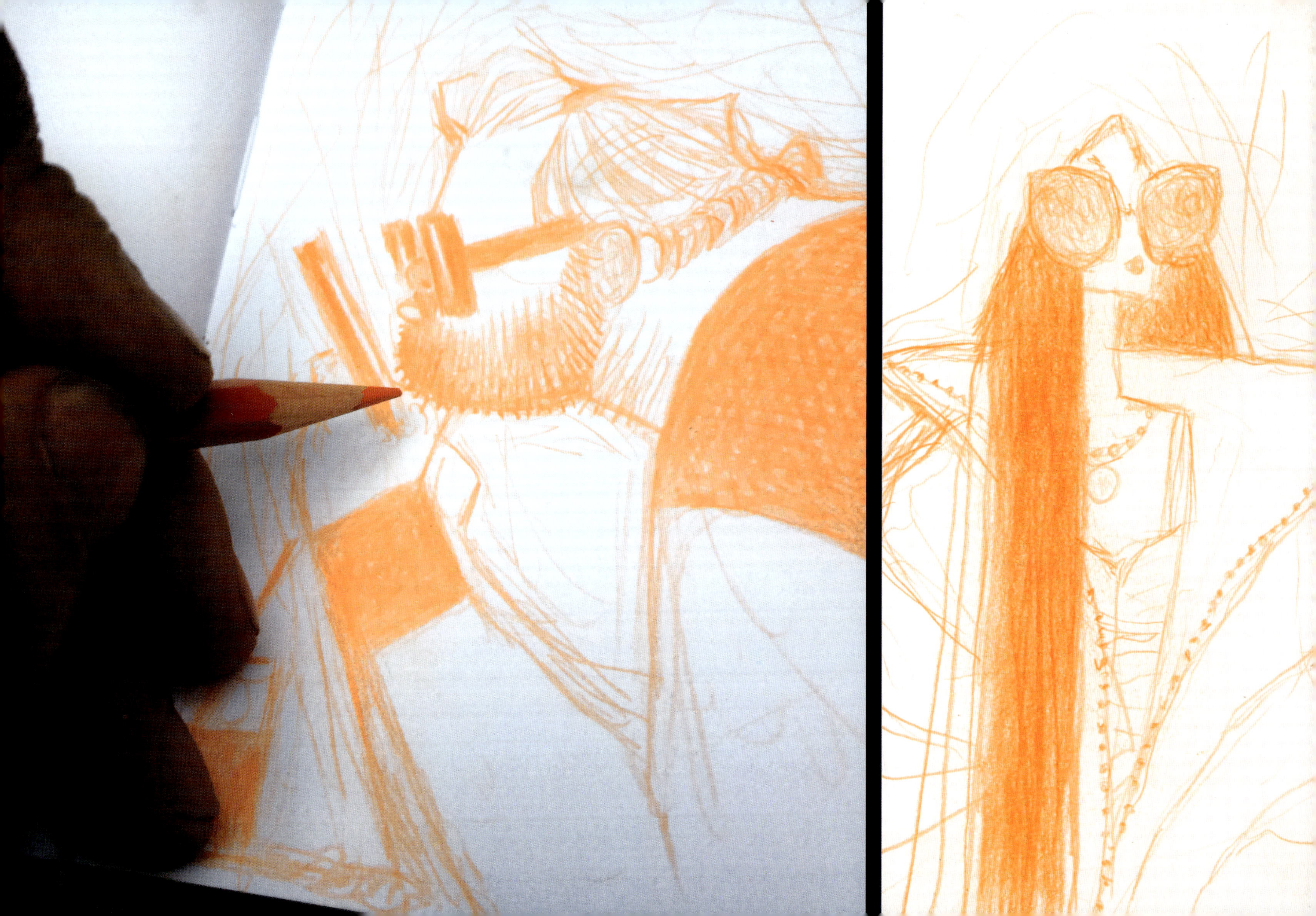

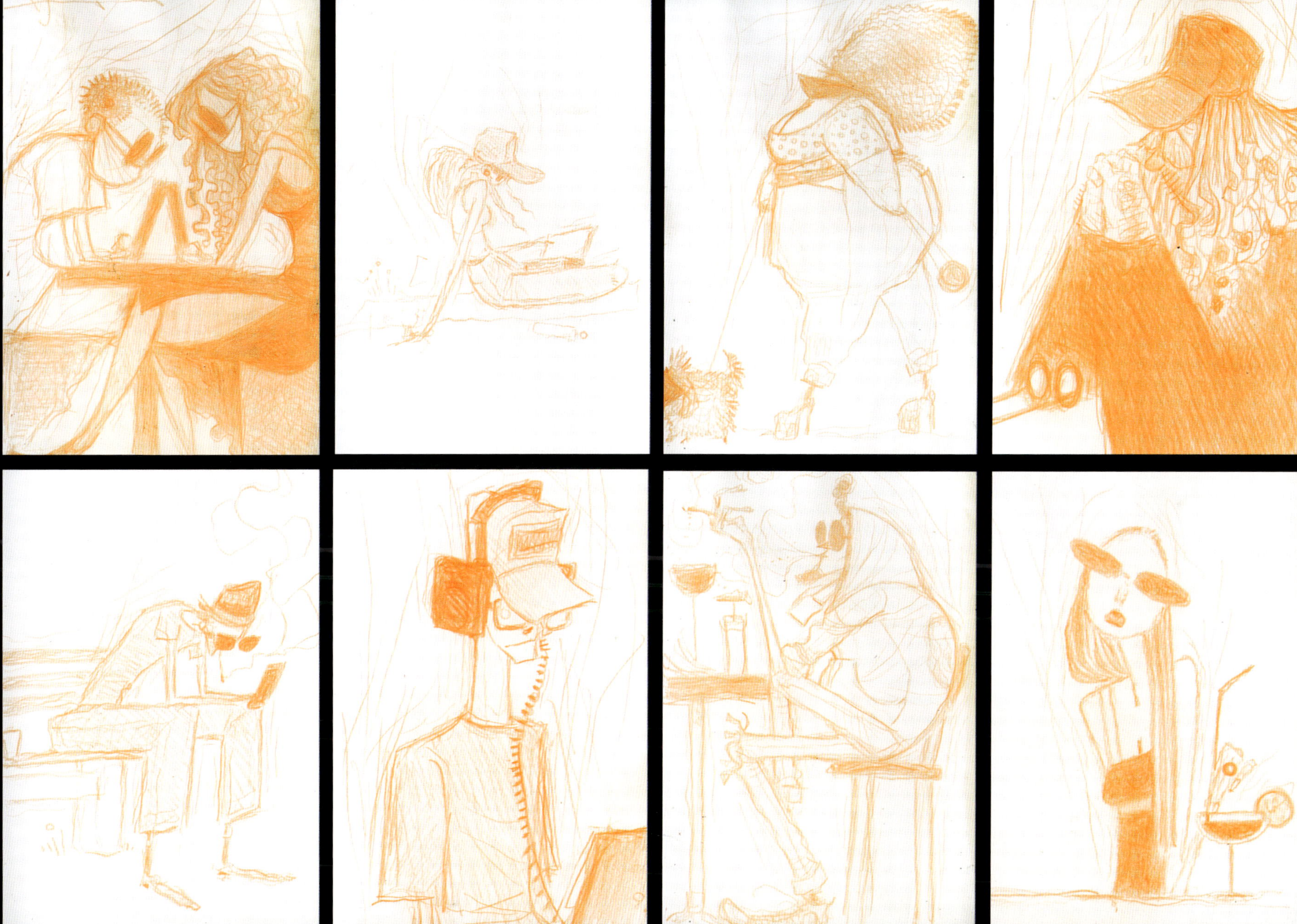

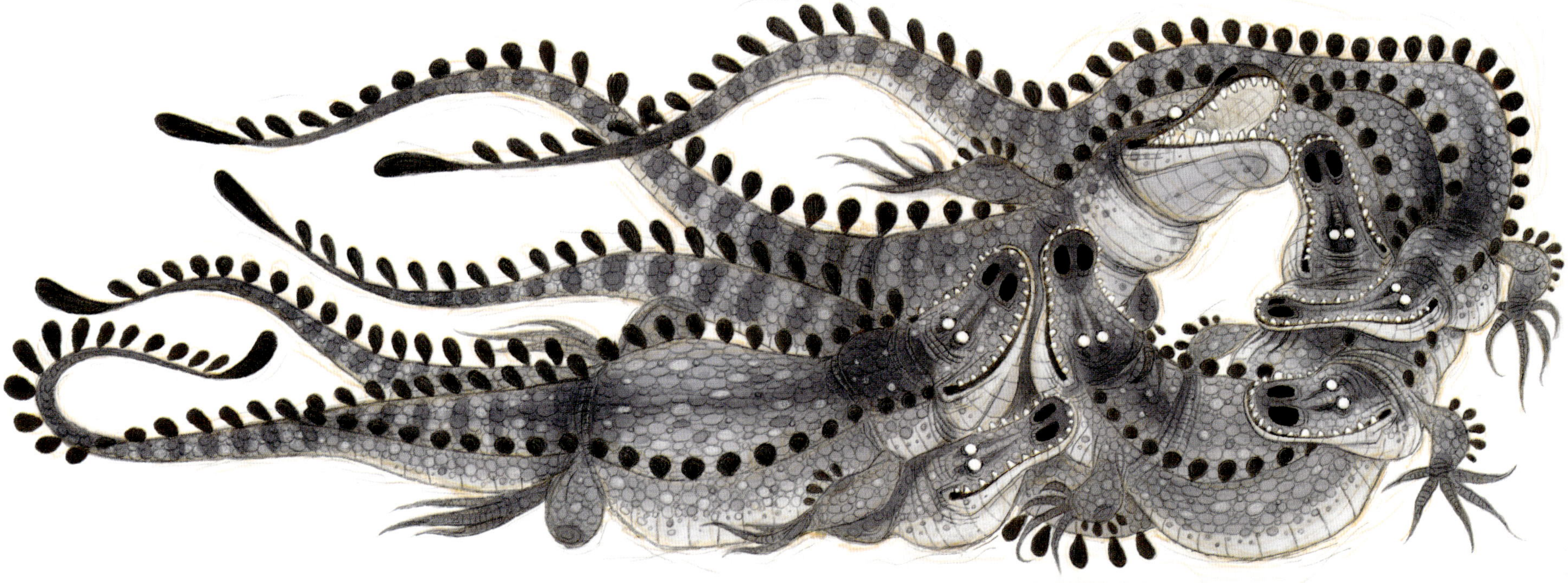

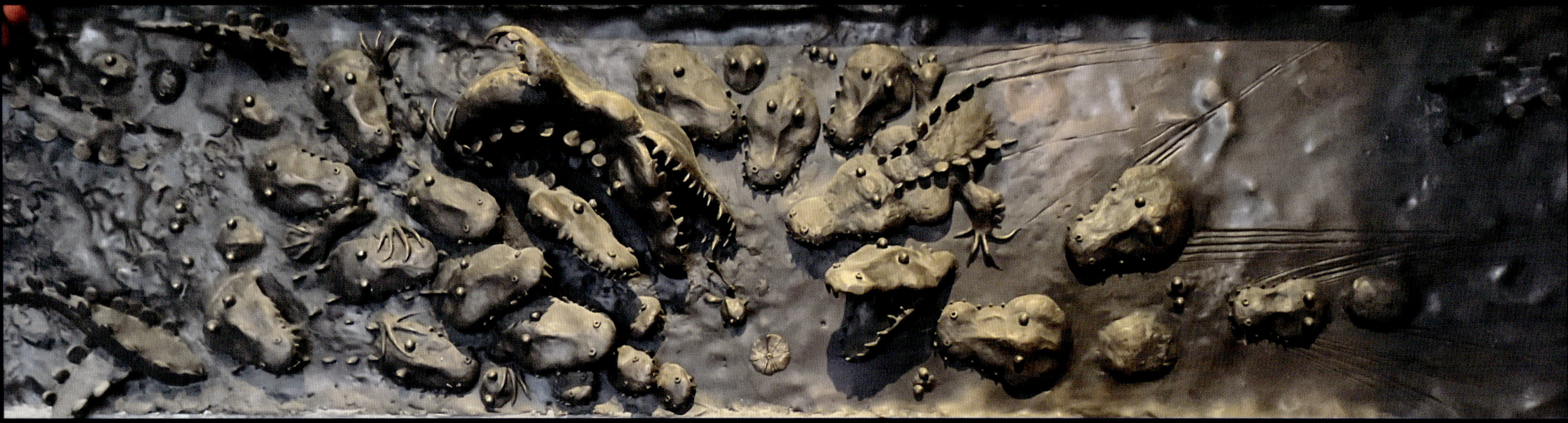

Above & Opposite: Progression of the bronze frieze that adorns Nico's mantle • Overleaf (left): Self-made sculpture and steampunk creations abound in Nico's home • Overleaf (right): *Dragon*-inspired sketching and Halloween buildout, designed by Nico and created in Eagle Rock (2008)

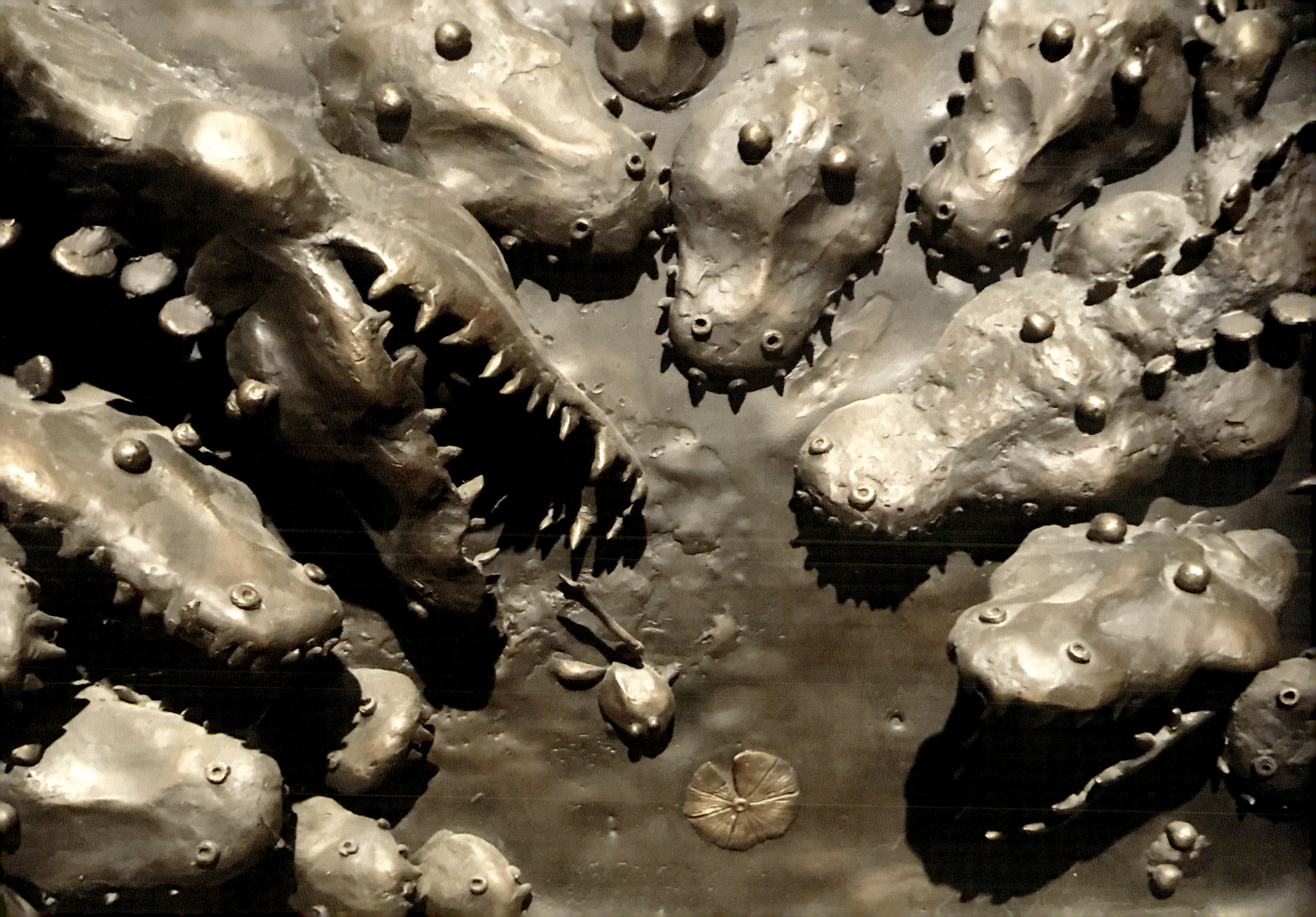

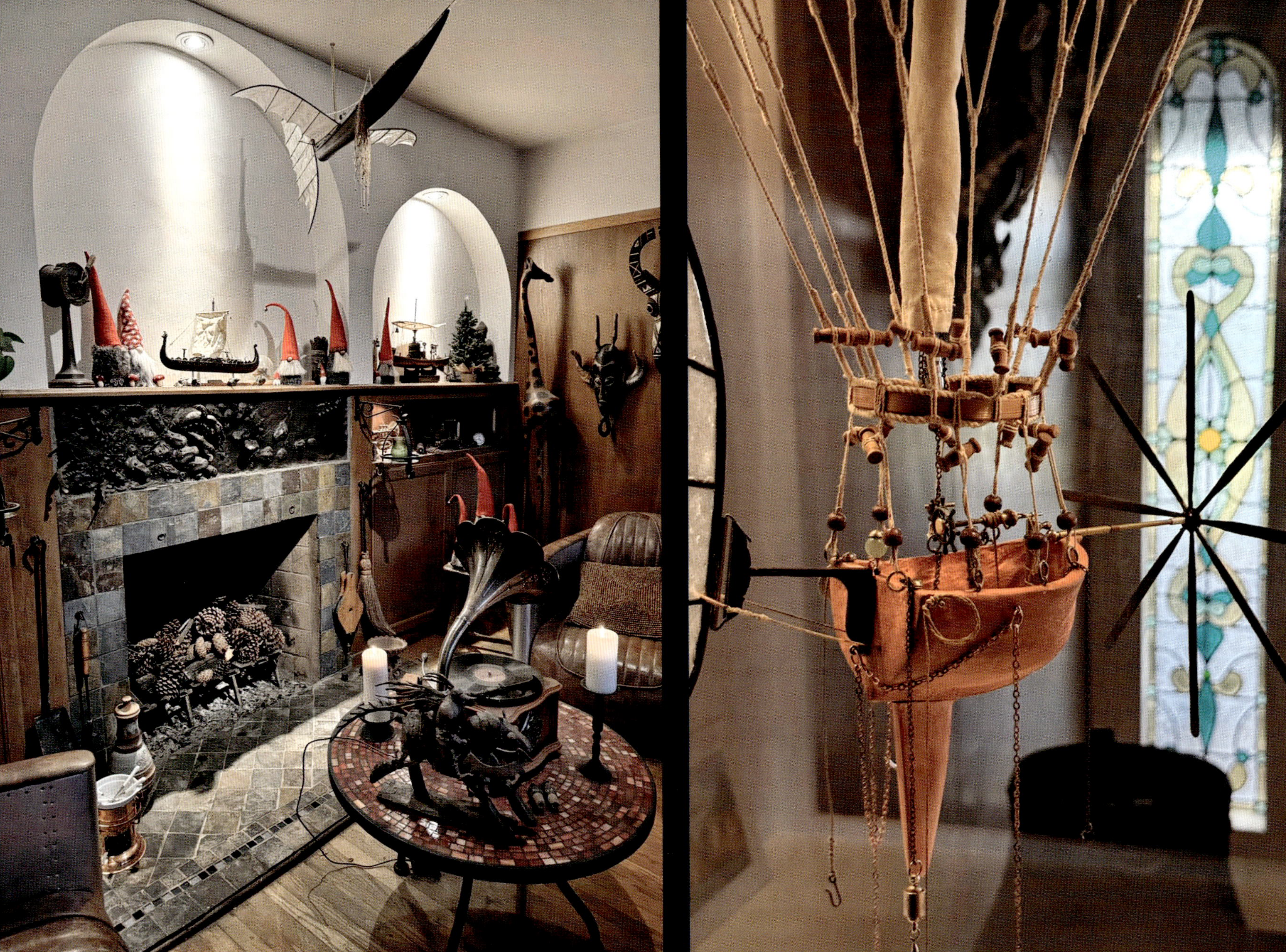

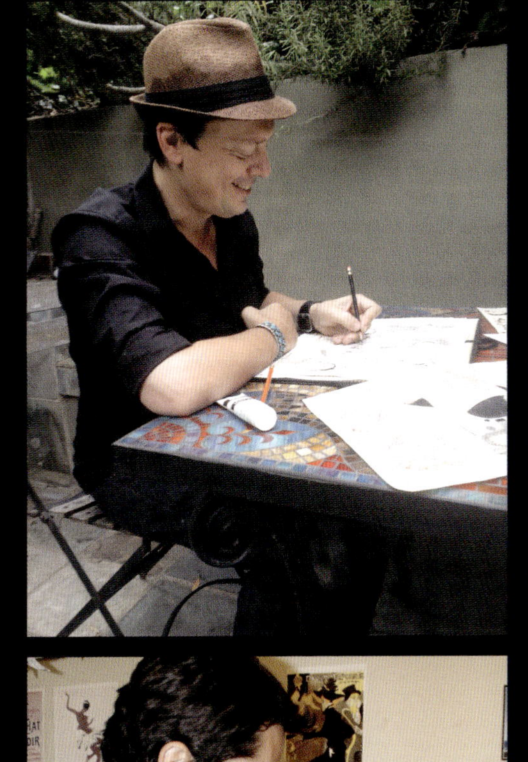
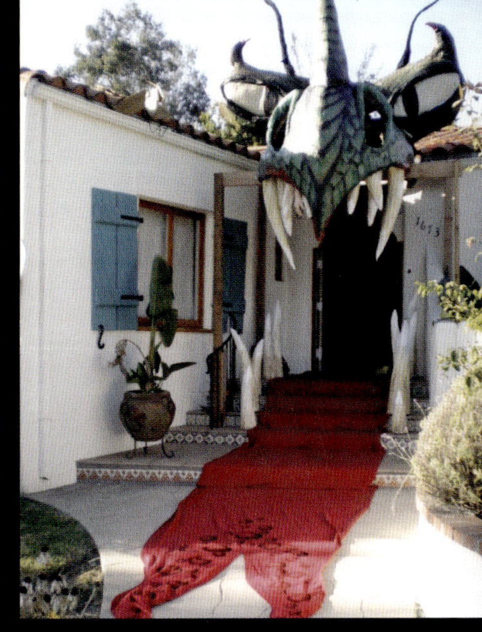
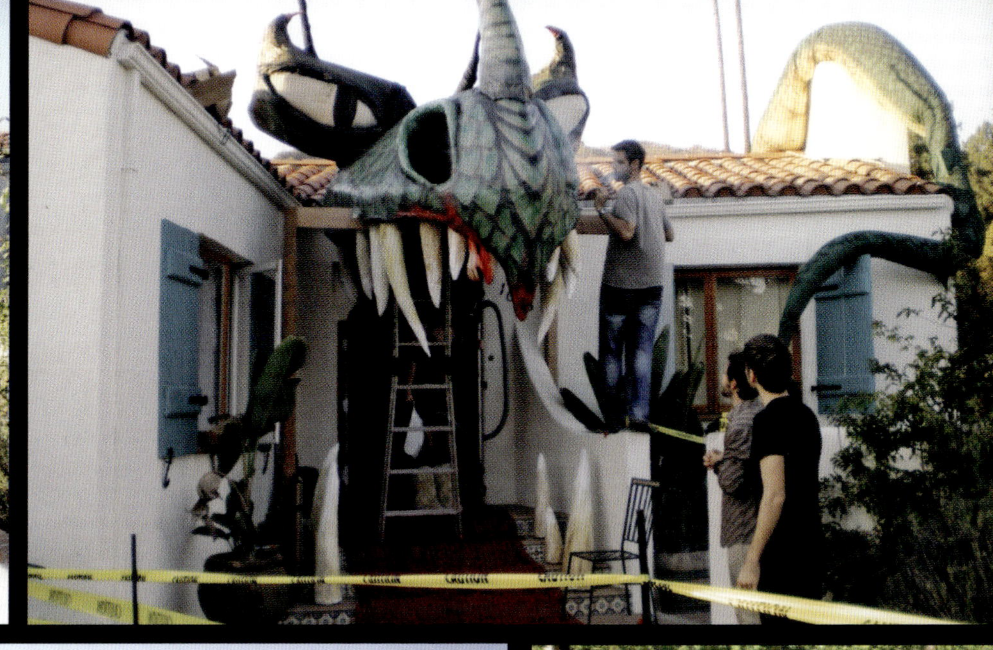
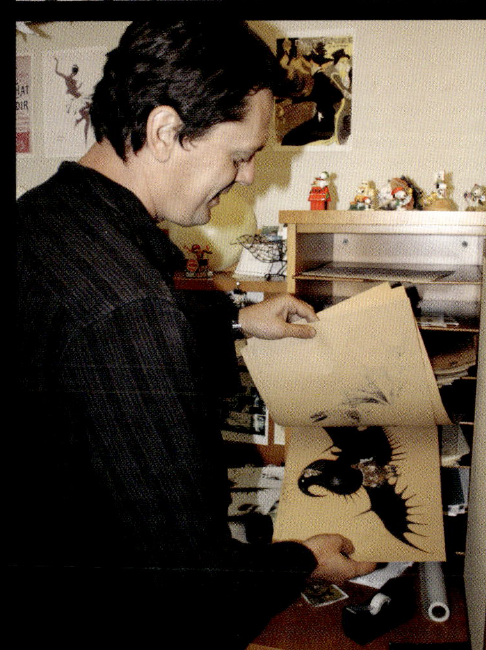
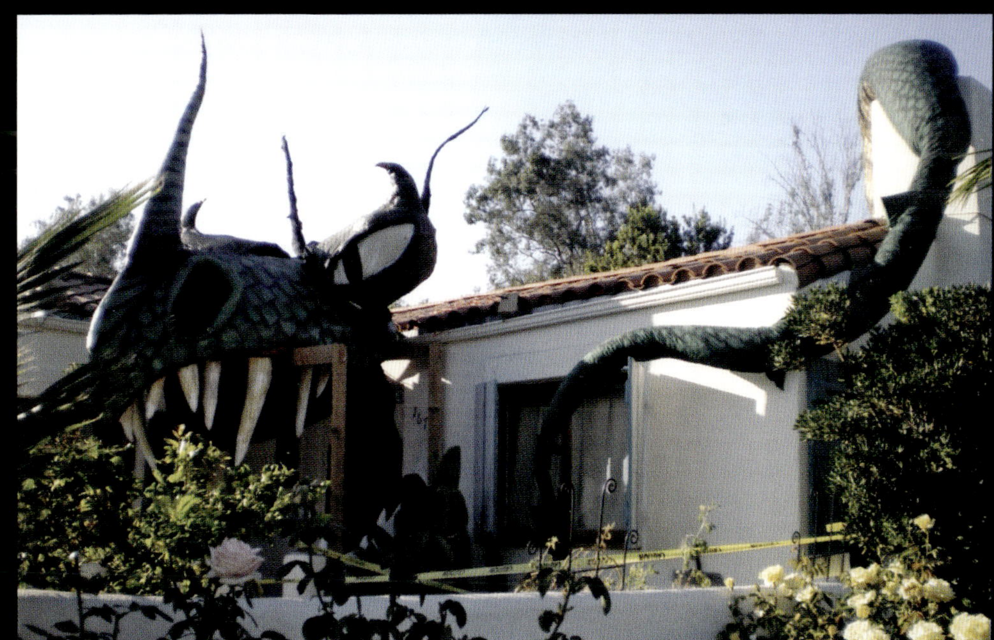
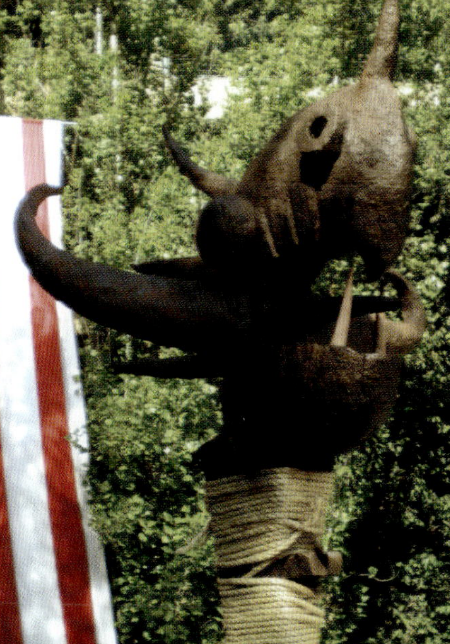

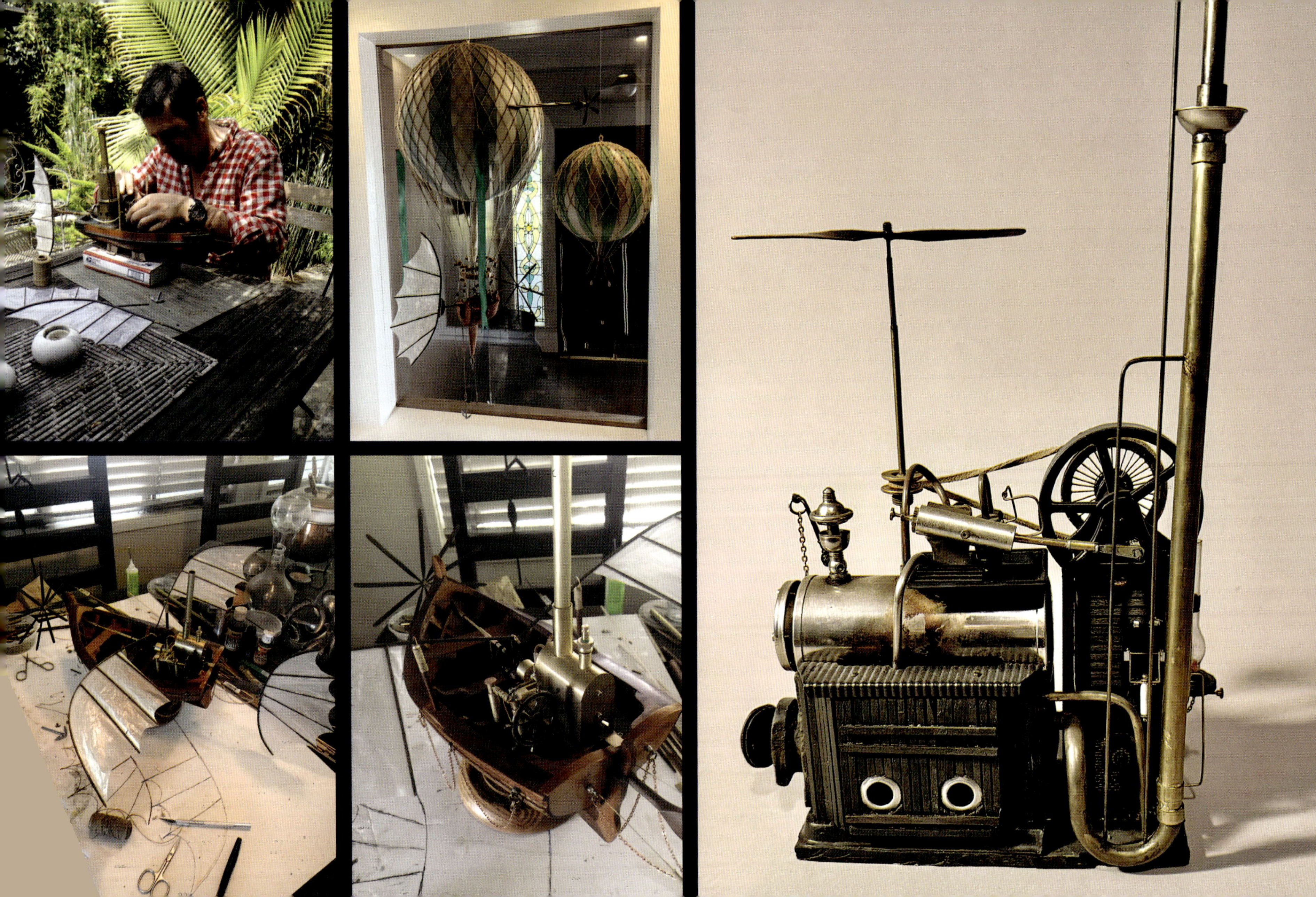

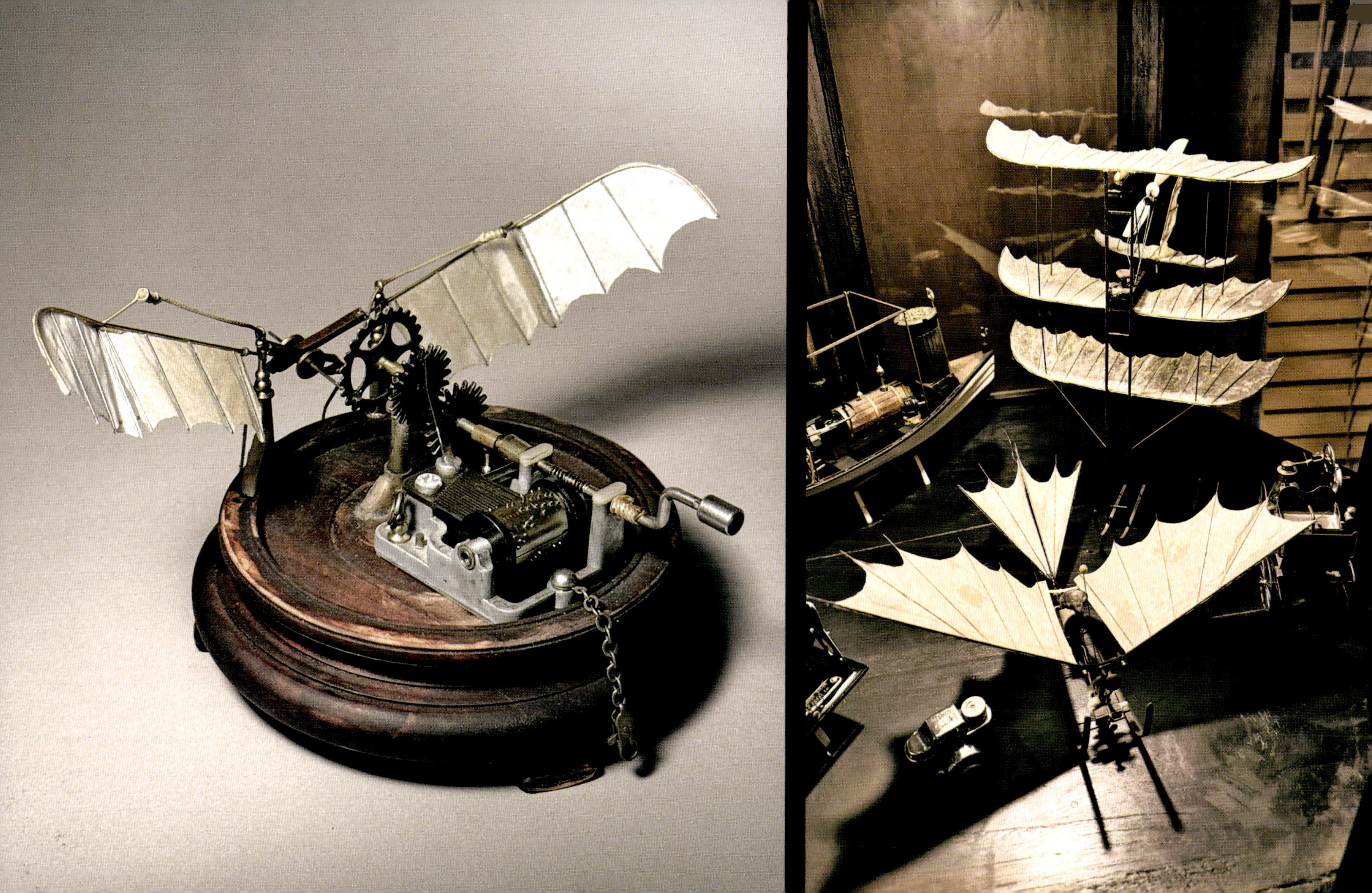

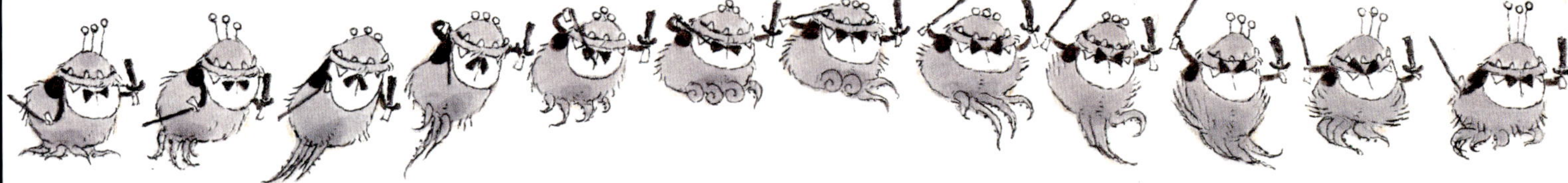

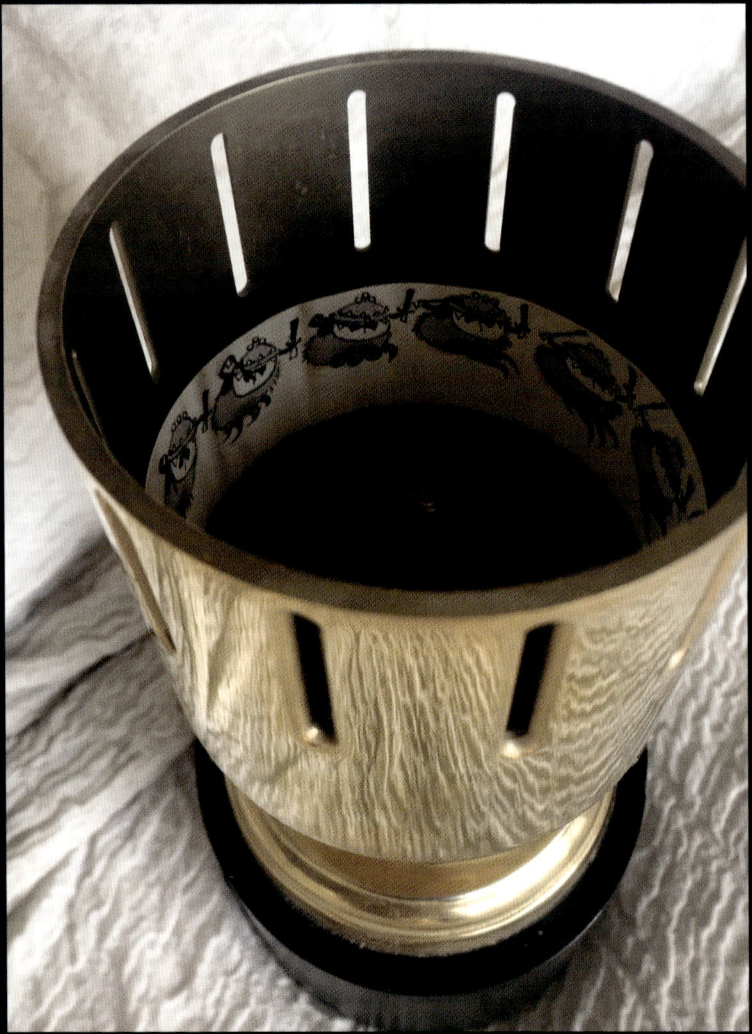

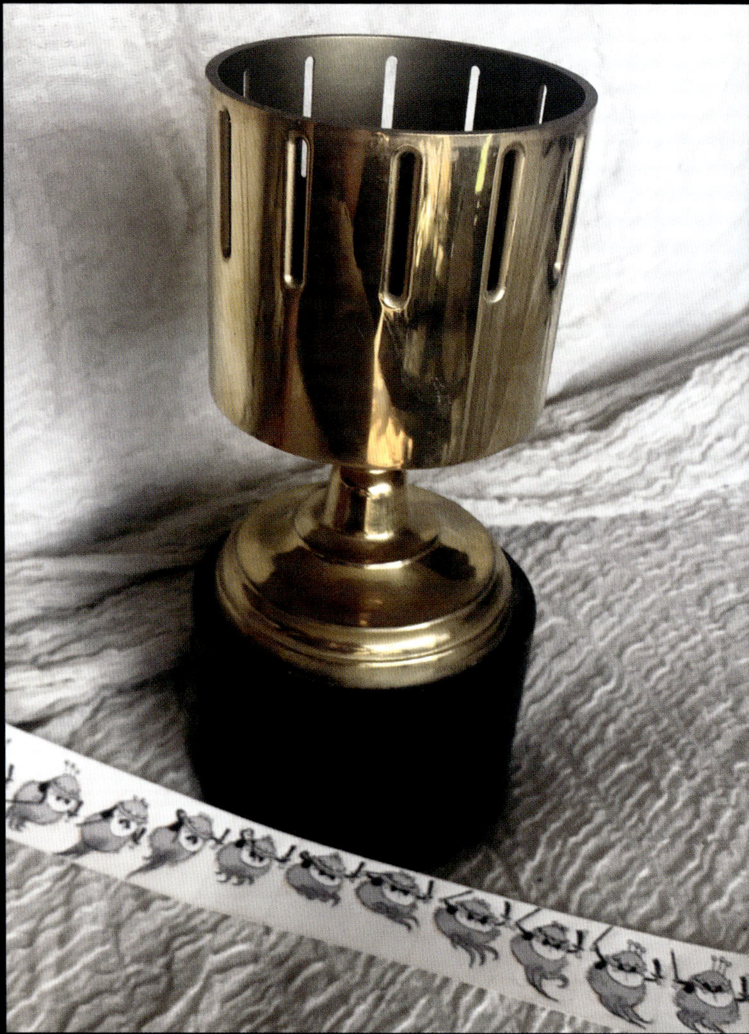

Preceding pages: Self-made steampunk and music box creations • Above: *Monsters, Inc.*–inspired illustration crafted by Nico to appear in zoetrope Winsor McCay Award for Pete Docter (2023) • Opposite: Sculpture of Nico's drawing crafted in bronze by Andrea Blasich

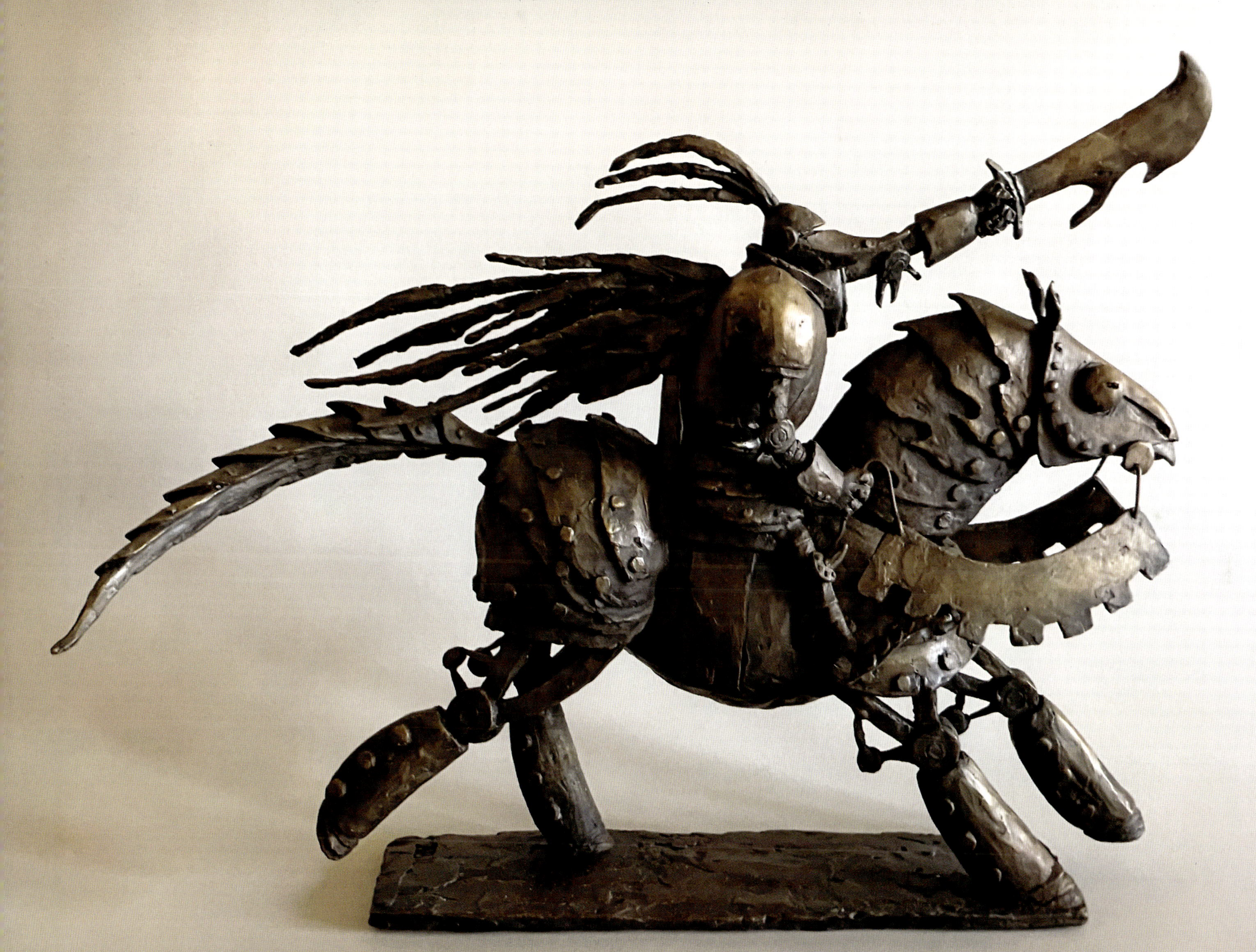

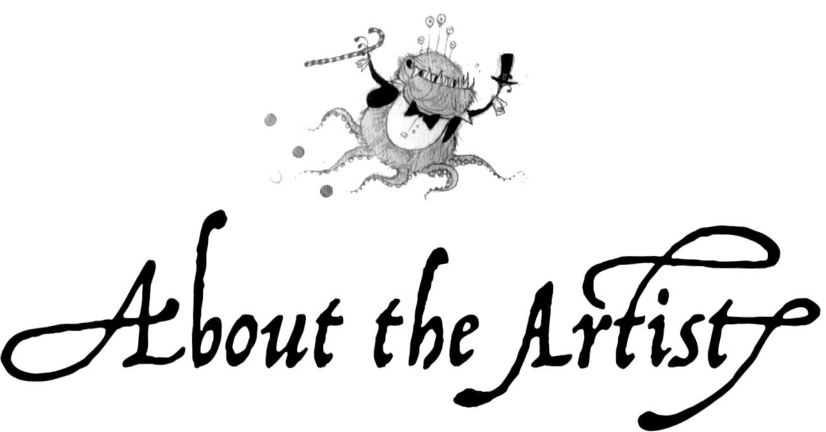

About the Artist

Nico doesn't talk much. And he especially hates to talk about himself, which led to great discussion about what to share within the pages of this book, as Kristof deftly expresses here:

> *There is one thing I have always wondered: Should we seek to know the personality and life of the artists in order to appreciate their work?*
>
> *Should we only admire the works, but refrain from trying to know their creators, so as not to risk being disappointed when we discover that they are—at best—just ordinary people?*
>
> *Can an artist's personality be discerned through their work?*
>
> *It's been a well-known fact for centuries that sensitivity is more valuable than technical mastery, but is the emotion an artwork arouses linked to the emotion the artist put into it or intended to put into it?*
>
> *Was Rodin less sensitive than Camille Claudel? Did Vasari confuse sensitivity and technical skill when he described the Mona Lisa in* The Lives of the Most Excellent Painters, Sculptors, and Architects? *Did Kandinsky really believe in "the spiritual in art"?*
>
> *Aren't we more moved by a Van Gogh or a Rembrandt than by a Paul Delaroche or a Barrias, precisely because of what we think we know about the lives and personalities of these artists?*
>
> *And yet, artists put so much of themselves into their work! Could they even do otherwise and still remain artists?*
>
> *Nico could have written what Léo Ferré, the famous French singer, once said:*
>
> "Il ne faut pas connaître les artistes. La vie d'artiste, c'est sur scène que ça se passe, la vie des artistes, c'est la vie privée, il y a eu des livres qui ont raconté ou qui racontent parfois des balivernes, parfois des vérités arrangées ou des vérités dérangées, c'est une autre histoire, leur histoire, quand ça n'apporte rien à la création artistique, laissons les chansons donner leur part de lumière . . . Et laissons dans l'ombre les histoires d'amour qui finissent mal en general . . ."
>
> *"We don't need to know artists. The life of an artist happens on stage; the life of artists is their private life. There are books that sometimes tell nonsense, sometimes arranged truths, or deranged truths; that's another story, their story. When it doesn't contribute anything to artistic creation, let's let the songs shed their light . . . And let's leave in the shadows the love stories that generally end badly . . ."*

The visuals in this book are all we need to know about Nico . . . but we felt it was our authorly duty to share a bit of biographical and geographical framework along the way for historical purposes.

Above: *Monsters, Inc.*–inspired illustration • Opposite: The artist's desk at DreamWorks Animation (2008–2023)

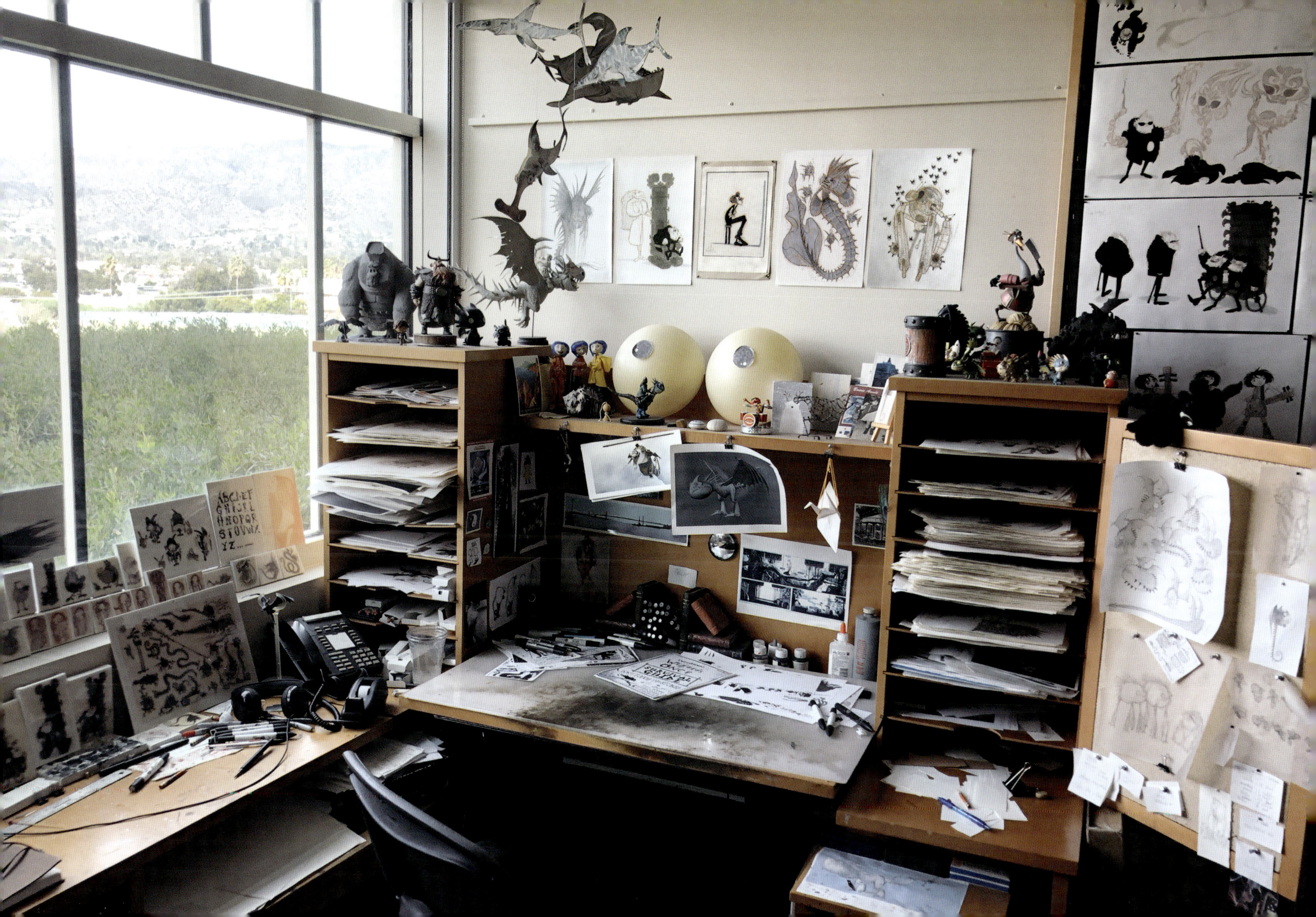

Contributors

Tracey Miller-Zarneke provided light narrative and a curated collection of reflections from notable industry colleagues about Nico Marlet. Tracey has drawn upon her firsthand experience in animation production by authoring eighteen books on the art of animation across seven studios, including DreamWorks' *How to Train Your Dragon* and the quartet of *Kung Fu Panda* films, which is how she first became enamored by Nico's drawings and charmed by the artist himself. Tracey has served as the technical editor on the second and third editions of the textbook *Producing Animation*, as editorial advisor on *Directing for Animation*, as author on the centenary update of *The Disney Book*, and as coauthor with Don Hahn of the historical tome *Before Ever After: The Lost Lectures of Walt Disney's Animation Studio*, among other published works. Tracey has also put her insider knowledge to work on documentary films about the animation industry, including *The Sweatbox* and *Waking Sleeping Beauty*, and into a variety of lectures about animation and its magical artists.

Kristof Serrand provided expertise on image inclusion and art direction, based on his intimate knowledge of Nico's work, style, and history.

After training at Gobelins and Beaux-Arts de Paris, Kristof began his animation career in the early 1980s, working alongside Jacques Rouxel, René Laloux, and Paul Grimault on the *Asterix* feature films at the Gaumont studios. In 1989, he moved to London to join Amblimation under the leadership of Steven Spielberg and then participated in the creation of DreamWorks Animation in 1995, where he worked as both supervisor and directing animator on more than twenty feature films. After twenty-five years in Los Angeles, Kristof returned to Paris in 2020 to work as animation supervisor and consultant for Netflix. He also served as a teacher in various schools, including Gobelins, and has personally contributed to the training, recruitment, and mentorship of many talented artists for more than thirty years—including Nico.

Opposite: Warner Bros. Pictures Animation character concept • Overleaf: *Balto* (1995) Character concept

Acknowledgments

Much gratitude goes out to the colleagues, friends, and fans of Nico whose positive energy and efforts made this collection possible, including Karina Kaidbey, Robbin Kelley, Jim Kennedy, Amy Krider, Dominique Louis, Cécile Marlet, Anna Preblud, Jerry Schmitz, Olivier Souillé/Galerie Daniel Maghen, and Dan Unser . . . with extra love being channeled to Margie Cohn, Pete Docter, Bill Damaschke, and Bonne Radford. Special thanks to Jack Black, Dean DeBlois, and all who provided their recollections and respect for Nico within the quotes shared in this book. The authors also offer their deepest appreciation for their publishing partners, including Connor Leonard, Aria Devlin, Peggy Garry, Krista Keplinger, Iain R. Morris, and also Chris Gruener.

Tracey is ever grateful for the beautiful friendship she had with Fumi Kitahara Otto, which was also the conduit for Tracey to enter the fabulous world of DreamWorks Animation and meet the incredible Nico Marlet in the first place. Tracey also offers her thanks to her talented, kind, and entertaining French partners in this creative endeavor.

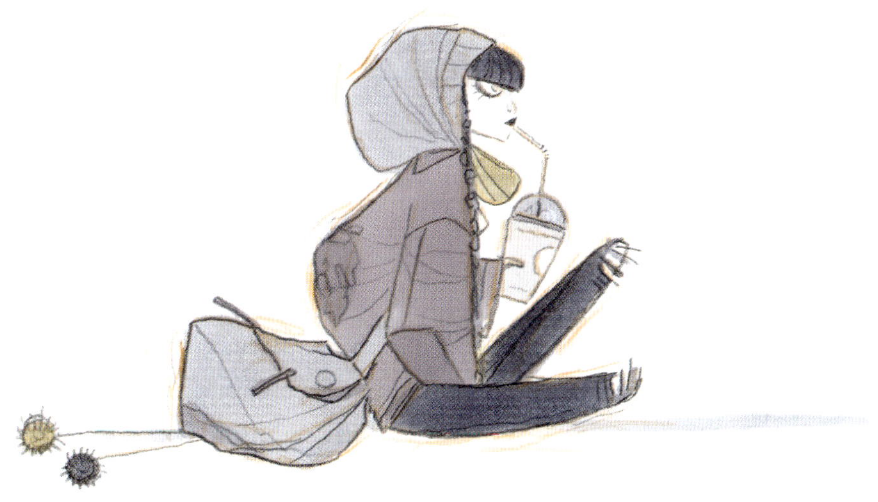

Colophon

Editor: *Aria Devlin*
Designer: *Iain R. Morris*
Design Manager: *Danny Maloney*
Managing Editor: *Krista Keplinger*
Production Manager: *Katie Gaffney*

A Library of Congress Control Number has been applied for.
ISBN: 978-1-4197-7935-0
eISBN: 979-8-88707-545-7

Published in 2026 by Abrams, an imprint of ABRAMS.

Printed and bound in China • 10 9 8 7 6 5 4 3 2 1

Abrams books are available at special discounts when purchased in quantity for premiums and promotions as well as fundraising or educational use. Special editions can also be created to specification. For details, contact sales@abramsbooks.com or the address below. Abrams® is a registered trademark of Harry N. Abrams, Inc.

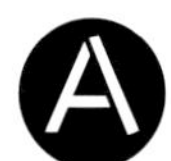

ABRAMS The Art of Books
195 Broadway, New York, NY 10007
abramsbooks.com

ABRAMS is represented in the UK and Europe by Abrams & Chronicle Books, 22-24 Ely Place, London EC1N 6TE and Média-Participations, 57 rue Gaston Tessier, 75166 Paris, France.

abramsandchronicle.co.uk and media-participations.com
info@abramsandchronicle.co.uk

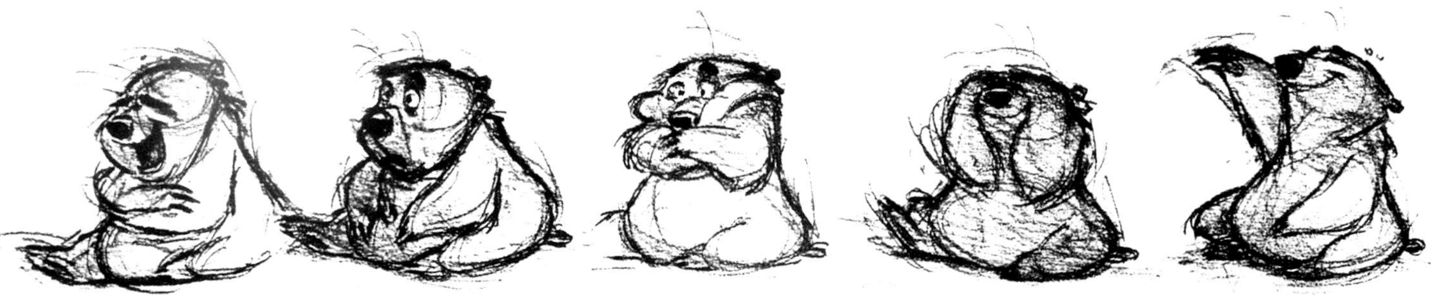